RED SOX
BY THE NUMBERS

RED SOX

BY THE NUMBERS

A Complete Team History of the
Boston Red Sox by Uniform Number

Bill Nowlin & Matthew Silverman

Foreword by **Joe Castiglione**

SPORTS
PUBLISHING

Sports Publishing books may be purchased in bulk at special discounts
for sales promotion, corporate gifts, fund-raising, or educational purposes.
Special editions can also be created to specifications. For details, contact
the Special Sales Department, Sports Publishing, 307 West 36th Street, 11th
Floor, New York, NY 10018 or sportspubbooks@skyhorsepublishing.com.

Sports Publishing® is a registered trademark of Skyhorse Publishing,
Inc.®, a Delaware corporation.

Visit our website at www.sportspubbooks.com.

10 9 8 7 6 5 4 3 2 1

Library of Congress Cataloging-in-Publication Data is available on file.

Cover design by Tom Lau
Cover photos: AP Images and Bill Nowlin (Pedroia)

Print ISBN: 978-1-61321-881-5
Ebook ISBN: 978-1-61321-889-1

Printed in the United States of America

Since childhood, #9 has always been my favorite. And, no, I don't mean Gordie Hinkle or Dusty Cooke. The number that means the most to me in recent years is 2004, but for other reasons.

— **B. N.**

In Storrs, Salem, Steamboat, San Francisco, or Scottsdale, Dave Bird is the most dedicated Sox fan on the planet.

— **M. S.**

Contents

FOREWORD

When I think of uniform numbers, it is the public-address announcers who first come to mind. Growing up in Connecticut, as I seldom admit, a Yankees fan (we learn from our mistakes), I learned my numbers from the "Voice of Yankee Stadium," the great Bob Sheppard, who always bellowed each number twice: "Now batting for the Yankees, number 7, the center fielder, Mickey Mantle . . . number 7."

Of course, as Little Leaguers, we all wanted to wear #7, though that created a lot of pressure to live up to the number. It was safer to be #14 like Moose Skowron, #10 like Tony Kubek, or in my case #12—worn by one of my first heroes, Gil McDougald. We quickly learned the numbers of the key players on the other teams as well: Al Kaline's #6, Bob Feller's #19, Willie Mays's #24, and Duke Snider's #4.

Now, as a professional broadcaster covering a major league team, numbers are not as critical for identifying players. Knowing the players personally and being with them every day, we recognize them by their swings, their body language, or physical characteristics, though certain numbers stand out: The parallels between numbers worn by great players from other franchises, like #5, worn by Baltimore's Brooks Robinson and Kansas City's George Brett, both third basemen, and especially those high numbers not normally associated with greatness like Tom Seaver's #41 and Roy Campanella's #39. Nowadays, many promising players are starting with high numbers and keeping them . . . like Jonathan Papelbon, #58. It used to be that young players were given high numbers and then changed to smaller digits once they became established, such as Clete Boyer, who went from #34 to #6, and Bobby Richardson, who went from #29 to #1.

The retirement of numbers has always been a source of great debate. While there are varying opinions on whose number should be hung from the rafters, I think the Red Sox have shown great restraint and have been much more judicious than most franchises . . . especially the Yankees and the Celtics, who lead the world in retired numbers. In fact, I have been privileged to have been at Fenway for the retirement of all those numbers that hang on the right-field facade. Though no one wore #9 after Ted Williams retired in 1960, his number was not officially retired until the mid-1980s, along with Joe Cronin's #4, followed by Bobby Doerr's #1. Carl Yastrzemski's #8 came later as did #27 for Carlton Fisk, #42 for Jackie Robinson, #6 for Johnny Pesky, and #14 for Jim Rice. I should hope many more will follow. My personal picks would be #45 for Pedro Martinez, the most spectacular pitcher in club history over his seven-year reign, and Roger Clemens's #21, despite what his current public perception is today. Mo Vaughn should get some recognition for #42, which of course has been retired by every club in honor of Mo's hero, Jackie Robinson.

When it comes to numbers, often overlooked is the foresight of the clubhouse men who make the final decisions on who is assigned what number. In recent years, Red Sox clubbie Joe Cochran has proven to be a great talent scout, assigning #5 to Nomar Garciaparra, #7 to Trot Nixon, and #15 to Dustin Pedroia. Tim Naehring, a personal favorite of Cochran, wore #11, and when Bill Mueller joined the club in 2003, Cochran gave the new third baseman #11 because he reminded him of Naehring. Mueller promptly won the batting title in his first season in Boston. Of course, it is puzzling how journeyman Chris Woodward was given #3. But Joe's track record is excellent.

Bill Nowlin and Matthew Silverman have done some wonderful research on uniform numbers and have found some amazing connections. You will find their work most entertaining and informative.

—**Joe Castiglione**

INTRODUCTION

An architect planning any residential or commercial construction or renovation in Hong Kong is mindful of the concept of *feng shui*—meaning good livelihood and fortune—when approaching design. Some pay large sums for feng shui consultants to advise them. We'd love to report that assigning uniform numbers to Boston Red Sox ballplayers is given as careful consideration, but lying leads to bad feng shui. That's not to say there is no thought involved, and some players do in fact have strong preferences. Some players, both in the early days of numbers and now, are superstitious and very much prefer one number over another; others could hardly care less. The authors of *Red Sox by the Numbers* do not fall into the latter group.

This book tells the history of the Red Sox through their uniform numbers. There is a method to our nonlinear madness. Essentially, we take every Red Sox player, coach, and manager since 1931 (when numbers were first doled out), divide them into chapters based on uniform number, and then provide commentary on the person, the team, the time, the size of his mud chops . . . the idea of the book is to have a little fun and learn something about your team you never knew. Or forgot.

We're there with you, lamenting or basking in Game Six, glancing at the clock the moment before Keith Foulke pitches to Edgar Renteria, smiling when 71-year-old Ted Williams pulls a hat from his jacket and doffs it to the Fenway throng, and misting up when he does it again at 80 during the 1999 All-Star Game. These aren't just numbers on the back of someone's shirt, they represent a bond that complete strangers passing each other in faded "B" hats on the street can simultaneously share—even in Phoenix. People move, but they bring their Sox with them.

Because ballplayers can be superstitious—and some might dare say fickle—an alphabetical index in the back of the book puts together all the numerical moves by individuals over a career, whether it's Garry Roggenburk wearing four numbers in three years in the 1960s, or Carl Yastrzemski donning a single number longer than any player in Red Sox history. To cover all the bases, there is a section dedicated to the unresolved Sox number questions. *Red Sox by the Numbers* begins each chapter with a chronological list of every player to wear the uniform number, singling out those with the longest tenure. Keep in mind, the years next to each name refer only to the years he wore that given number. Multiple Red Sox have worn different numbers during the same year; they are listed in order worn. Notes are included for brief switches or circumstances when players wore the same uniform number *the same day*. Also included is a total of how many times each number has been issued. Though that can be determined more than one way, we define this such that when Paul Byrd was issued #36 in 2008 and again in 2009, despite Brad Penny having worn it in between, we count #36 as having only been issued once to Byrd. Similarly, coach Dave Magadan was issued #29 on two occasions in that same span, but we only count it as one issuance.

Each chapter contains a sidebar: an observation on something pertaining to the team, number, uniform, or perhaps a telling photo related to a Red Sox number. And if things aren't esoteric enough, we test your brain with an "MOP"—Most Obscure Player—in each chapter. The heart of the book, however, lies in the discussion of selected Sox who have worn each number. If we wrote a sentence about everyone who's donned a Red Sox uniform number, this book would be bigger than . . . we could say the Green Monster, but Red Sox fans are a bright lot, so we'll just say it might be too heavy to put in your bag and bring with you on the T. Feel free to read on the go, but make sure first pitch finds you in your bleacher seat, in front of your TV, or within earshot of Joe Castiglione, who so kindly penned the foreword. If Joe likes a Red Sox book, there's something to it.

One final thing. We might occasionally be flippant in an assessment of a player, manager, or event, but we're covering a lot of ground here and trying to have fun as we recall the numbers before us. Our respect for each man's talents on the baseball diamond has never been in question. We would gladly give our right arms—because they weren't strong enough to get us between the lines—to stand on the Fenway grass in mid-game and feel that ever-so-slight tug of a big league number on our backs.

Joe Cochran: Sox Number Man

"I don't go soliciting number changes."—Joe Cochran

Joe Cochran is the man who hands out uniform numbers to the Red Sox. He's the clubhouse and equipment manager for the team, and has been working for the Red Sox since he started on the grounds crew in 1984. Joe moved inside in 1990, working in the visiting clubhouse. He made the move to the home clubhouse in September 1991. He matched numbers to Red Sox players for a long times, from then until 2012 when Tom McLaughlin took over the responsibility. "There's a lot of history here. It's fun to be a part of it," Joe says.

With assistant equipment manager Edward "Pookie" Jackson, Joe works almost around the clock throughout the season. "I run the day-to-day operation of the clubhouse and, going on the road, handle the transportation of the equipment. There's spring training, road games, bats, balls, uniforms. If they do well, we work an extra few weeks, which is no problem.

"I travel with the team. In each city, there's a visiting crew of batboys and clubhouse assistants and a head guy that runs the visiting clubhouse. Sometimes we don't see much daylight. We're in the bowels.

"We have a crew of six people, including myself on this side, and a crew of five guys on the other side. It's pretty similar, pretty much like that in every other park. You have two kids in uniform on the field during the games, and then guys doing the laundry, getting the meal ready for after the game."

The schedule usually begins at about [JASON] start. It often ends after midnight. "It's a monotonous routine, but it's automatic, day-in and day-out," he says.

"I work closely with the traveling secretary. Jack McCormick does a great job. We have a truck waiting that he has lined up in each city. We unload the baseball equipment first, put the luggage in the back, go on to the hotel, and then on to the stadium. There's a crew waiting for us to take care of what we need.

"We do the laundry after the game. There's a laundry room in the grounds crew area. We go down there and use those machines. There's a lot of laundry in the course of a day. Plenty of laundry. We do about three big loads every game. You'd be amazed how much the guys go through. From dress time on the board to the time the game starts, forty guys. They'll change to eat; they'll change to lift. Not necessarily the uniforms, but everything underneath they'll change. We do the laundry ourselves. We used to bring them out to air, hang them out in the left field corner, but we don't do that anymore.

"We do all the players' stuff. During the game, I'm in the clubhouse most of the time. I'll catch an inning, just to get out. There's a lot going on up there, kids doing a lot of laundry. There's only about two or three innings of down time, and then it picks up. We've got a ten-minute window before it gets crowded, really quickly.

"We have a tailor that we send out to when uniforms get torn [see Chapter 13]. You can have five pairs of new pants in a locker, but you have a lot of superstition in this game and a lot of [players]—the majority of them—they'd sew them up until they actually fall off their body. We have a guy over in Somerville that we send out to. Neil DeTeso of Riddell. He sends a guy. They pick it up. They bring it back the next morning. Or, if we have to, in a pinch, we'll run it over. It's convenient." DeTeso handles all the shirts and pants; the rest of the laundry is done at the ballpark.

The uniform numbers, that's another story. One might think that's where the romance of the game kicks in. And there's no denying that the numbers do add that sense of history more than the laundry per se. Majestic is the official uniform provider for Major League Baseball and before spring training, the company will sew on all the numbers for Joe and Pookie. But players come and go, sometimes on very short notice. They have to be ready for almost anything.

The reality of it is prosaic. The numbers are not stored in a beveled etched-glass case reserved for hallowed objects. "We have them in like pizza boxes," Joe explains. "We have the alphabet. We have Latino apostrophes and what not, those small letters for like Irish, Tom McLaughlin with a small 'c.' We've got a numbering and a lettering kit." The numbers and letters are no longer raised wool, but are flat and thin, and can be sewn on quickly and easily. They look more like iron-on numbers than the older style numbers that went on the flannel uniforms, but almost all of today's uniform numbers are made of "tackle twill," most commonly Poly-Pro Twill manufactured by Webster Fabric of Chesterfield, Missouri. Webster supplies all of the twill to Major League Baseball, the National Basketball Association, the National Football League, and the National Hockey League. The numbers themselves are actually heat-pressed onto the fabric. Red Sox clubhouse man Pookie Jackson says that all of the Red Sox numbers are supplied by VF Imagewear, part of the same company that owns Majestic.

And a couple of thin, flat, pizza-style boxes don't add much bulk on the road. "We travel with all the blanks, extra decorations, lettering, and numbering, and if we make a trade for someone or someone gets called up and we don't already have a shirt made up for him, there's someone in each city that takes care of the numbers for us." Someone like Neil DeTeso of Riddell. They work through the visiting clubhouse manager in each city they visit.

"They have seamstresses lined up in every city; there's a Neil in every town." Joe will supply the blanks, a spell-out form for the incoming player's name, and if he's new, assign him a number. "I carry a lot of stuff with me. Numbers and unis are just one component. Everything goes through the visiting clubhouse manager. What I have to do, is I go to the ballpark, pull out the shirt, size them up, get all the decorations and numbering and letterin . . . . Give that to the visiting clubhouse manager and he takes care of it."

It's Joe who makes the decision who gets what numbers, working from a list of available numbers. "We'll figure it out. Veteran guys, we'll call them, try to line them up. [Mark] Kotsay last season, it worked out. I was in New York, called him up, and number 11 was available. It was a perfect lateral move. You get a guy like Eric Gagne: [Curt] Schilling wore 38 so the guy will flip it over—83. Some guys will start fresh, too. David Ortiz in honor of Kirby Puckett. He wanted 34. I remember talking with him about that. 'Kirby wore this number.' Guys will do that. They'll take a number of their idol growing up."

Though fading, there remains a bit of a preference for lower numbers. Players called up from the minors often wind up with higher numbers since lower ones tend to be taken or retired, as is the case of #1, #4, #6, #8, #9, #14, #27, and #42. We asked Cochran, "When you are assigning a number to a player, is it something you consider has a historic significance, maybe even take a little pride? 'I'm giving this number to this guy.'"

After a long pause, Joe answered, "I don't know about that. On a personal level, number 11, when we came aboard—Pookie and I and Tommy [McLaughlin]—Tim Naehring wore that. Actually, Naehring was 65 and had a pretty good camp. He was on base and I believe—I don't know who we were playing but some veteran player, I don't remember who he was—said, 'You're having a pretty good camp.' And Naehring gave me a look and pointed to his number: 'Am I going to make this team?' Lo and behold, that was the year he ended up the starting shortstop with us wearing number 11 after camp broke. If you make the team, like [George] Kottaras this year . . . it's an accomplishment to make a big league team for a young kid out of camp."

Most rookies just find the uniform in their locker, number assigned. But seniority counts and Joe will try to find a suitable number for established players. The veterans do get preference, without a doubt. Some have strong feelings. Some could not care less. A rookie rarely gets a choice, though someone like a Nomar Garciaparra who seems destined for stardom may get a little extra consideration. "When they come up, we'll tell them, 'Don't worry about the number on the back of your shirt when you come up; it's the front of the shirt which counts.' In due time, when things work out, there might be a number available where the guy's still in Pawtucket and there's a chance he might come up again, we'll hold it for him. It's almost like you talk with some people, number lingo is its own language."

Though Jim Rice wasn't elected to the Hall of Fame until 2009, no one had worn #14 since he retired in 1989. Has Joe ever had a situation where a player really wanted a given number and he had to steer them away from that? "No. I just think that with the history here . . . Fenway with the Red Sox . . . guys know. They know their baseball. You're not going to see too many people come in here and ask for a Jim Rice. He hasn't been in uniform for some time. But they know. They know who wore 14. You go back ten years even, guys know." One suspects that not all players are that familiar with Red Sox numerology, and that from time to time there may be a little guidance offered.

Number 21? No one's worn it since Roger Clemens left for greener pastures, and as recently as 2007, the Sox were putting on a full-court press to try to get Clemens back to complete his career with the Red Sox. When the Clemens saga took a sour turn, did the number become tainted? Cochran is diplomatic, but matter-of-fact. "We'll cross that bridge when it comes. No one's asked for it since he's left. The history . . . first guy to wear it . . . a pitcher? Like I said, these players know the history of the Red Sox."

Edward "Pookie" Jackson, co-guardian of the numbers at Fenway and right-hand man to Red Sox equipment manager Joe Cochran.

Saying No to the Future

The continuity of the Red Sox uniforms goes back to the earliest days of the twentieth century. Historians on the subject such as Marc Okkonen and Mike Cesarano point out that the team was wearing a red sock on the uniform as early as 1908, when the club adopted "Red Sox" after the Boston Braves abandoned the look due to imagined safety concerns (believing the red dye from the socks seeping into spike wounds could prove lethal). By the last year of the twentieth century, no one in club history had ever died from such a malady—but the entire team could possibly die of embarrassment.

In 1999, the real estate firm Century 21 developed a promotion with Major League Baseball coined "Turn Ahead the Clock." Previous "Turn Back the Clock" games, where teams wore replicas of old-time threads—notably for interleague games between the Sox and the relocated Braves—had proved popular. This new promotion had teams wear what someone imagined baseball uniforms might look like in 2021; a year when taste, apparently, will have been scientifically eradicated.

For the September 18, 1999, game at Fenway against the Detroit Tigers, another old-time American League club whose uniforms had largely stood the test of time, both teams were supposed to wear futuristic uniforms. Some players were heard to grumble about wearing what was in effect an advertisement for a real estate company. Others, no doubt, feared looking as foolish as some of the other clubs who'd donned the uniforms over the summer. (The Mercury Mets were a particularly memorable uniform abomination.) When the Tigers and Red Sox took the field, not a futuristic uniform was to be found. According to sources, the uniforms "failed to show up" on time. Funny, the same thing happened to eight other teams.

#1: The Silent Captain

Bobby Doerr wore #1 for 13 years and saw it retired in 1988, two years after he was inducted into the National Baseball Hall of Fame. Ted Williams called Doerr "The Silent Captain" and that name is better remembered than any statement from the second baseman himself. Doerr let his play talk for him. Ted both talked and hit enough for everyone else.

On the subject of Williams, it should be noted that Doerr wore #9 before Ted did. Bobby wore that number as a 19-year-old rookie when he first broke in with Boston in 1937. Come 1938, Doerr silently switched to #1. His 223 career home runs rank eighth all-time for Sox sluggers—perhaps the quietest 223 homers ever. The total gives him more Red Sox home runs than a lot of big names in Boston baseball: Jimmie Foxx, Rico Petrocelli, Nomar Garciaparra, Jackie Jensen, Tony Conigliaro, Jason Varitek, Carlton Fisk, George Scott, and Reggie Smith, and is almost twice as many as Trot Nixon, Frank Malzone, Mike Greenwell, and Fred Lynn. But when you think of Sox sluggers, Doerr is not usually high on the list. His career line (.288 average, .362 OBP, .461 SLG) assured that pitchers did not take him for granted. In Doerr's only World Series, his .409 average against the Cardinals in 1946 was the best of any Sox regular.

Doerr, who was born the final year of World War I, was given the middle name of Pershing in honor of the army's commanding general in 1918. So it seemed fitting he left to join the army for what turned out to be the final year of World War II after leading the American League in slugging and just missing the 1944 batting title at .325, the highest mark of his career. When he came back, he placed third in the '46 MVP voting—his pal Ted won it with Detroit's two-time MVP Hal Newhouser second. Doerr knocked in 100 runs six times in all and had one last great season in 1950, leading the league in triples, knocking in a career-high 120 runs, and matching his pre-war best with 27 homers.

This premier digit has always been popular—before, after, and even during Doerr's career. Both **Ben Steiner** and then **Ty LaForest** snuck in and wore #1 during 1945 with Doerr in the service. Almost as soon as Bobby retired in 1951, **Fred Hatfield** snagged the number. Hatfield was traded to the Tigers in a massive deal in June 1952 that brought Boston **George Kell**. As a Tiger, Kell beat out Ted Williams for the 1949 batting title by one hit, preventing Ted from achieving an unprecedented third Triple Crown. Kell didn't disappoint in Boston, hitting .305 over three seasons. Kell and Doerr wore #1 in Boston less than a year apart, and would follow one another into the Hall of Fame three decades later (Kell in 1983 and Doerr in '86).

"Impossible Dream" third baseman **Joe Foy** wore #1 as the Red Sox took the 1967 pennant; his name would be reviled by Mets fans for the "Impossible Trade" that resulted in Amos Otis going to the Kansas City Royals for the troubled Foy in 1970. A number of yeoman infielders have worn the number, including **Grady Hatton**, **Billy Consolo**, **Don Buddin**, **Eddie Bressoud**, and all the way up to **Chico Walker**, the last player to wear the first number. Consolo had asked for the number because of his admiration for fellow second baseman Bobby Doerr. **John Mc-Namara** wore it for three seasons as a manager before it was retired for Doerr; he switched to #2 for his closing months as skipper.

The most beloved man since Doerr to don #1 was **Bernie Carbo**. He was wearing #1 when he hit the game-tying homer in the bottom of the eighth during Game Six of the 1975 World Series. No one grabbed

#1 when he was sent to Milwaukee the following summer, so it was his to take again a few months later when the Sox sent the yet-to-blossom Cecil Cooper to the Brewers to get back Bernie and Boomer (George Scott).

Billy Conigiliaro was one of three players to wear #1 in 1969. **Joe Azcue** of Cienfuegos, Cuba, came over from Cleveland in mid-April, hit .216 in 19 games, and then was traded to the Angels for **Tom Satriano**, who fit in Azcue's #1 jersey (Satriano weighed 185 pounds, Azcue 190). Billy C. and Satriano also wore #4 that year. That's a lot of swapping, but in the year that brought the world Woodstock, the moon landing, and the Miracle Mets, maybe a pair of Sox were just trying to keep themselves entertained on a third-place team that never got within double-digits of the Orioles after June.

The first Mexican-born ballplayer in the major leagues was Baldomero Melo Almada Quiros—otherwise known as **Mel Almada**. Almada and Chile Gomez of the Phillies were the only two Mexicans to play in the majors until the 1940s. Born in Huatabampo, Sonora, and descended from a long line of Castillian royalty, Almada's father was the Mexican consul in Los Angeles (and his brother Luis was also a pretty good Pacific Coast League player). In five seasons for the Red Sox, the left-handed-hitting outfielder batted .272 and drove in 102 runs. Mel's best season was 1935, when he played in 151 games and hit .290. In mid-1937 he was traded with brothers Wes and Rick Ferrell to the Washington Senators.

The entire continent is represented at #1. During the final year of World War II, Edmunston, New Brunswick, native Biron Joseph "Ty" LaForest joined the Red Sox. In 204 at-bats, he hit .250 with a couple of home runs. He died just after turning 30 years of age in 1947. He had caught pneumonia and collapsed on the field following the third day of spring training. LaForest never recovered and died in early May.

Rabbit Warstler was actually the first Red Sox batter to wear a number in a major league game, though at the time he wore #4. He switched to #2 in '32 and a year later graduated to #1, which he would have been wearing in the first game of '31 if he had any sense of history. **Bill Sweeney** had the number instead. The first baseman has the distinction as the first #1 in Sox lore, batting third in the inaugural game with numbers in 1931. Sweeney hit .295 in his second of two seasons with the club, though he managed just one homer in 528 plate appearances. Still, you'd think that might be good enough to stick with the Sox of that era. He played another 11 seasons of minor league ball, batting .321 and awaiting the call that never came.

Urbane Pickering, who went through four numbers in two years in Boston, made #1 the first number in Red Sox history to have more than one wearer. He was called up on April 18, 1931, to fill in for Sweeney, who was in bed with a fever. With no other uniforms available, he slid on Sweeney's #1 for the game at Yankee Stadium. He got his own uniform soon enough, taking #34 after Sweeney's fever broke.

MOST OBSCURE RED SOX PLAYER TO WEAR #1—Ed Gallagher was the only pitcher to ever wear #1, and he may hold the distinction as the worst player on the worst Red Sox team of all time. A Dorchester native and Boston College man, "Lefty" must have either known the best places to go after games or the '32 Red Sox were that desperate for pitching; with a 43–111 ballclub, there may be some truth on both sides of that argument. The southpaw debuted in July and appeared in just nine games over the course of the year—with three starts and three losses. His 12.55 ERA nearly doubled the next-worst mark of anyone on the team with at least 20 innings pitched. That's saying something given Boston's bloated and brutal 5.02 team ERA.

Day One

Let's start at the beginning. There's always been some question about when exactly the Red Sox first put numbers on the uniform. All agree it happened in 1931, but did it start Opening Day?

Research for this book definitively reveals that the Red Sox wore numbers before the '31 season even officially started. During the preseason City Series against the Boston Braves on April 11–12, there is a reference to them wearing numbers and the sports-page cartoons in the *Boston Post* depict them wearing numerals both on their home (April 12 issue) and road (April 13 issue) uniforms. The *Boston Herald* game account on April 12, referring to the first game in the series, ended with this brief paragraph: "The Sox are numbered, big and generously, and the fans liked the innovation." The following day's *Herald* discussed Bill Sweeney wearing #1, and opined, "Bill Sweeney is No. 1 among the Red Sox, probably because he's got the best of names for a ball player."

The notion that numbers matched position in the batting order was never true with the Red Sox, nor was it true for field position. The Opening Day lineup of April 14, 1931:

SS Rabbit Warstler   #4
LF Russ Scarritt   #12
1B Bill Sweeney   #1
RF Earl Webb   #15
3B Jack Rothrock   #3
2B Bobby Reeves   #2
CF Tom Oliver   #14
C Charlie Berry   #9
P Wilcy Moore   #31

The numbered Sox took it on the chin in their first game, falling at Yankee Stadium, 6–3, in front of 70,000. Victimizing them were two former Red Sox sent to New York before numbers were ever stitched on their Hall of Fame backs: Babe Ruth, #3, who clubbed a homer in the game, and winning pitcher Red Ruffing, #18, traded by the Sox the previous May. It was the first game as Yankees skipper for Joe McCarthy, also Cooperstown bound, who would end his career as manager of the Red Sox.

#2: Rem Dawg

Jerry Remy, the pride of Somerset, Massachusetts, is second to none. He wore #2 longer than any other player in Red Sox history. That alone would make him the most famous wearer of that number, but his nightly pulpit in the broadcast booth as the de facto voice of Red Sox Nation—or at least NESN—makes him seem every bit as important as many of the greats who played alongside him, even though "Rem Dawg" didn't hit a home run in his final six seasons in Boston. While his 98 steals in seven seasons in Boston are fewer than he had in three years with Anaheim, he was more inclined to stay where he was with the stacked lineup behind him. Remy was indeed fast with his feet—as well as with his mouth.

Rem Dawg's place as the favorite #2 seems secure, but his place as the longest running man in that uniform was threatened. Bench coach **Brad Mills**, Terry Francona's #2 man, made a bid with five seasons in that number until he was hired to manage the Houston Astros in October 2009. It would be six years if he hadn't surrendered it for a season to **Willie Harris**, who batted 100 points lower (that would be .156) than he had the previous year as a sparkplug off the bench for the world champion White Sox. He even had a hit in his only time up in the ugly Sox-on-Sox 2005 ALDS. Yet while wearing Sox Red in '06, he accumulated just seven hits over four months before he was rightfully demoted to Pawtucket.

Number two at #2 is another second baseman: **Doug Griffin**. He played in 614 games (to Remy's 710) from 1971–77, including one at-bat—a line out as a pinch hitter—in Game Five of the 1975 World Series. Denny Doyle was acquired from the Angels in June of '75 and hit for a .310 average after the deal, locking him in to play every postseason inning. Griffin had come to the Red Sox from the Angels in the Tony C. swap in 1971, starting a Boston-to-Anaheim circle that brought the Red Sox three second basemen over a 14-season span in Griffin, Doyle, and Remy. An Angelic second coming.

The first to wear #2 was a second baseman, but he was no Angel and no Superman, for that matter. **Bobby Reeves**—not to be confused with original TV Superman George Reeves or Christopher Reeve on the big screen—appeared in just 34 games and hit a paltry .167 in 1931. Nicknamed "Gunner," Reeves must have had a good arm. Perhaps that was why manager Shano Collins let him pitch a game—and not just to a couple of batters. Reeves threw the final 7 1/3 innings on September 7. There wasn't a lot to lose; the Sox were 44 games out of first place at the time and it was the second game of a doubleheader. They'd lost the first game (as one might expect, given the 44-game deficit), and three pitchers had combined to allow 12 runs to the Senators by the second inning of the nightcap. So Shano handed Gunner the ball—and let him keep it. He faced 29 batters, walked one, and allowed only six hits. The final score was 15–1.

Next in line to wear #2 was Boston native **Andy Spognardi**. Andrea Ettore Spognardi played 17 games to close out the 1932 season, batting .294 (10-for-34, with one double and one RBI). Not bad, but the BC man chose a career in medicine, serving as a doctor in the area for many years. He died in Dedham on the first day of 2000.

A man constantly surrounded by doctors (in a positive way), **Mike Andrews** was the favorite of the now-graying generation inspired by the "Impossible Dream" team, the Sox club that seemingly came from nowhere (a half-game out of last place in a ten-team league) to win the 1967 pennant. Andrews was a key cog at second base during the season, and hit .308 during the '67 World Series. Over five years, he batted .268 for the Red Sox and represented them in the 1969 All-Star Game. Since 1979, until his retirement at the end of 2009, he was executive director of the Jimmy Fund, raising money to facilitate great inroads in the fight against cancer in children. Mike recalled that, at least for a while, there was a practice of having the second baseman wear #2. "When I arrived for spring training in '67, number 2 had already been assigned to me; back then as a rookie you didn't start requesting numbers," he explained. "I don't know if it had been somewhat of a tradition that number 2 went to second basemen but I know that Griffin and Remy wore it after me. Didn't [Chuck] Schilling wear it before me?" He did, indeed.

Chuck Schilling, no relation to Curt, spent his entire five seasons in the majors with the Red Sox wearing #2. A second baseman, too, he came to the plate more often than any player in the majors as a rookie in 1961. His 167 hits and 78 walks in 738 trips to the plate produced a .340 on-base percentage, but he was never so selective or indispensible again. **Eddie Kasko** followed in the tradition, playing second base and third for the '66 Sox.

The 1930s were not a great decade for the Red Sox, but you can at least say they didn't tear families asunder. The Red Sox traded both **Rick Ferrell** (a catcher, who wore #2) and his brother Wes (a pitcher, who wore #12) on June 11, 1937. The Brothers Ferrell, along with Mel Almada, went to Washington in exchange for Ben Chapman and Bobo Newsom. Manager Joe Cronin's feelings about Wes were clear in his comment on the battery of brothers: "Funny, the difference between those two brothers. I sure hated to lose Rick—good ballplayer, hard worker, easy to get along with." Though some would argue that Wes was the more talented sibling—and he certainly had more power, out-homering his backstop brother, 38–28—Rick wound up in the Hall of Fame, the only Red Sox #2 in Cooperstown. And the cap on his plaque bears a "B," even though his five years in Boston were the shortest stay in his 18-year career.

After the Ferrell trade, Chapman slipped on Almada's #1 and Bobo took Wes's #12—though not his spot in the Cronin doghouse. Rick's #2

17

went unworn until 1938, when it was taken by another catcher, **Gene Desautels**. He hit .291 his first year and then started hitting more like a backup catcher.

Two managers wore #2, and both had surnames starting with "Mc": **Marty McManus**, way back in 1933 as a player–manager for a seventh-place club, and **John McNamara** in 1988. In the latter's case, he'd actually worn #1 since taking the helm in 1985, but when Bobby Doerr's number was retired on May 21, 1988, McNamara began wearing #2—until he was relieved of his Red Sox uniform altogether at the All-Star break.

More colorful but not necessarily coherent personalities in #2 were **Jimmy Piersall** and **Carl Everett**. Both had observers scratching their heads, albeit for different reasons.

Piersall, a schoolboy star from Waterbury, Connecticut, had a nervous breakdown in 1952 . . . while wearing #2. Based on what we've seen from the film about the incident, *Fear Strikes Out*—with unathletic Anthony Perkins as Piersall—we believe it had more to do with his hard-driving father (played by Karl Malden) than his choice of number. In any event, Piersall switched to #37 when he returned.

Everett was on edge without much pushing from anyone else. A tremendously talented athlete, he came from Houston in the Everett-for-Everett deal (Carl for Adam) following the 1999 season. Everett batted .300 as the everyday center fielder in 2000 and his 48 home runs over two seasons in Boston represented the most he hit for any club during his career. The problem, you see, was that there were many stops along the way because Everett's mouth and temper always had clubs looking to move him for the sake of harmony and sanity. His most memorable incident was bumping umpire Ron Kulpa at Fenway during a nationally televised tantrum that earned him a 10-game suspension—and really, he deserved a longer sentence. Among his many outspoken beliefs, Everett scoffed at the existence of dinosaurs because they weren't in the Bible. Dan Shaughnessy *of* the *Boston Globe* thus dubbed him "Jurassic Carl."

Jacoby Ellsbury could have had a longer run with the Red Sox, but he chose to test the waters of free agency and was rewarded by the

New York Yankees with an offer no one could refuse, and which the Red Sox considered far beyond their perception of his projected future value. As of the close of the 2015 season, it looks like the Red Sox were right. Shortstop Xander Bogaerts snapped up #2 as soon as it became available and in his sophomore season in 2015 ranked second in the American League in batting average. He looks to have a bright future ahead of him.

MOST OBSCURE RED SOX PLAYER TO WEAR #2—Al Evans was a backup catcher on a 1951 club that ran a lot of catchers through the roster: Les Moss, Buddy Rosar, Aaron Robinson, Matt Batts, Mike Guerra, Sammy White, and Evans. Our man Al was one of three (with White and Guerra) who were error-free, but then again White only appeared in four games. Al caught in 10 and pinch-hit in two others. Not that he was hot with the bat—he mustered just a .125 average (3-for-24), including a double. He did walk four times, drive in two runs, and score once. Al wasn't without experience. He'd played 11 seasons for the Washington Senators before being claimed off waivers over the winter. On August 15, with Lou Boudreau's hand broken and Doerr's sacroiliac ailing, the Sox sent Evans down to Louisville and retrieved infielder Mel Hoderlein.

Just Missed

The 1930 Red Sox were a pretty anonymous group, losing 102 times and finishing 50 games behind the world champion Philadelphia Athletics. Beginning in 1931, scorecards told the story at Fenway Park and throughout the American League. Previously, Boston megaphone man Walter E. "Stonewall" Jackson had been the only way many fans knew the identity of a new player entering the game. Jackson had worked off and on since 1903 and he kept his job. Many of the pre-numbered Sox did not.

The 1930 Sox finished in last place, as had the 1929 Red Sox before them. And the four Sox teams before them. (The 1924 Sox missed last place by a half a game in the standings, ruining what would have been an unbroken streak dating back to 1922.)

Hod Lisenbee, who appear in 41 games for the numbered Sox in 1931, started the final game for the no-number Sox in 1930. Second baseman Bill Regan, catcher Johnnie Heving, and pinch hitter Jim Galvin were retired without a peep and without a number in the ninth. The opposing pitcher for the Yankees? It was Babe Ruth, pitching at Fenway.

For Ruth, it was the first time he'd pitched since October 1, 1921. After nine full seasons of rest—well, he had won eight home run titles in the meantime, including the '30 crown—Ruth returned to the mound where he'd first broken into major league ball as a pitcher for the 1914 Red Sox. He threw a complete game and won, 9–3, scattering 11 hits. Ruth would pitch once more—at the end of the 1933 season—and toss another complete-game victory over the Red Sox, giving him a lifetime pitching record of 94–46 and a 2.28 ERA. And we might as well mention that in his career the Babe allowed 10 home runs and hit 714.

The last pitcher to appear for the Red Sox without wearing a number was Jack Russell, who took over for Lisenbee. Members of the 1930 Red Sox who never played in a number-bearing jersey for Boston were: "Whispering Bill" Barrett, Bill Bayne, Frank Bushey, Joe Cicero, Ced Durst, Frank Mulroney, Bill Narleski, Red Ruffing, Ben Shields, Charlie Small, and Phil Todt. Most of the names are forgettable, save for Ruffing, who was traded in the prime of his career in May 1930 from Boston to the Yankees for Durst (plus $50,000). Durst called it quits after the '30 season. Ruffing went from back-to-back 20-loss seasons in Boston to a 15–5 record in New York and eventually to the Hall of Fame.

#3: The Beast

Jimmie Foxx wore #3 for the Sox from 1936 through 1942, one of 11 members of the Hall of Fame to wear #3. The imposing Foxx—known as "The Beast"—was already one of the biggest stars of his day when Tom Yawkey wrote a big check to acquire him from Connie Mack's Philadelphia Athletics. Foxx did not disappoint. He gave the Sox 222 home runs and hit for a .320 average over his seven seasons. His 1938 season was indeed beast-like: his .349 average, .462 OBP, and .704 slugging each led the league, as did his 175 RBIs, which remain the most in club history. His 50 home runs was the club standard for 68 seasons—until David Ortiz topped it in 2006—and Foxx was the first Red Sox player named MVP (though Tris Speaker won the 1912 Chalmers Award, a short-lived forerunner of the MVP).

"Double X" was far from the only slugger to wear #3. There was a stretch from 1946 through 1957 when the numeral was worn consecutively by **Rudy York**, **Jake Jones**, **Walt Dropo**, **Dick Gernert**, and **Norm Zauchin**. Each of the quintet made their mark with the home run, though not always consistently. York had a couple of big home runs in the 1946 World Series. Jones—an ace fighter pilot credited with shooting down seven

Jimmie Foxx

Japanese planes in World War II—hit most of his roundtrippers in a concentrated burst after the Red Sox acquired him in a mid-June 1947 trade from the White Sox (a deal that sent York to Chicago). After donning York's #3, Jones homered in each game of a double-header the day he turned up, the second of those a walkoff grand slam in the bottom of the ninth. He hit 13 of his 16 Red Sox homers that year at Fenway, more than even Ted Williams. Though Dropo pounded out 34 homers and drove in a league-leading 144 runs as the AL's Rookie of the Year in 1950, he never reached those levels in subsequent seasons. Gernert hit 19 home runs his first year, 21 his second, but was also unable to maintain the pace. Zauchin was another of those big right-handed power hitters. He banged out 27 homers in 1955, his first (and only) full year. His 105 strikeouts led the league—he never even had 100 at-bats in any of his two subsequent seasons in Boston.

Pete Runnels was no power hitter, but he did win the American League batting title in 1960 (.320) and 1962 (.326) despite only hitting 29 homers in five full seasons with the Red Sox. **Jack Rothrock**, the first player to wear #3, was one of those rare ballplayers who played at least one game at every position, though the one game he pitched and the one game he caught were both in 1928, before the Sox—or any other team—wore numbers.

Two big disappointments with #3 on their backs were **Grady Little** and **Edgar Renteria**, though for different reasons. Manager Little, because he favored instinct over statistics (despite an apparent direct order to follow the stats) and left Pedro Martinez in long past the prescribed pitch-count limit in the infamous Game Seven of the 2003 ALCS, which the Yankees rallied from three runs down to win. Renteria, who, as a Cardinal, became part of the never-gets-old Red Sox highlight reel by making the last out of the exhilarating 2004 World Series, took a four-year, $40 million contract to come to Boston the next year. The Red Sox dumped the underperforming shortstop after one season. **Mike Lansing**, another middle infielder with a pretty big contract, turned out to be a pretty big bust, too—he hit a combined .234 for the 2000 and 2001 seasons. Second baseman **Mark Loretta** (2006) was one of those single-season Sox the club has begun to feature. He played 155 games, hit a solid .278, and only made four errors all year long—his fielding percentage of .994 eclipsed Bobby Doerr's team record set in 1948.

All in all, there are a lot of infielders who've worn the number in the last several decades, ranging from popular players like **Dalton Jones** of the Impossible Dream team of 1967 and **Jody Reed** of the late '80s and early '90s, to less-remembered players like **Dick McAuliffe**, **Steve Dillard**, and **Jack Brohamer**, who started at third base in the one-game playoff in 1978 (when outfielder Dwight Evans, suffering from vertigo, began the game on the bench). There's even our favorite friend-seeking service proprietor, **Buddy Hunter**. The single-digit numbers were, likely due to tradition, considered an infielder's number. Second baseman **Jeff "Frito" Frye** missed all of 1998 due to injury, but the Sox held his number for his return.

David Wells wore #3 in 2005, as well as #16. The aforementioned Renteria *also* wore #3 and #16 in 2005. Why the switcheroo? The former Yankee Wells started the season wearing #3, his tribute to another great Red Sox pitcher: Babe Ruth (though, admittedly, Ruth only wore #3 while with the Yankees since he had been numberless with Boston). Renteria had worn #3 with the Cardinals through the 2004 campaign, but he began his time in Boston as #16. When they took the field on May 29, they'd swapped numbers: Renteria, wearing #3, had the only four-hit game in his short Sox stint; Wells, wearing #16, won the game, allowing two runs on six hits in 8 1/3 innings at Yankee Stadium. Renteria had paid Wells—"a lot," he said. Wells explained transaction #3: "He wanted to do a swap. I wrote down a number, and that was it. I took a number I had years ago." The #16 may have been a tribute to the Yanks' "Chairman of the Board" Whitey Ford.

As good a definition of a key backup player as there could be, catcher **David Ross** was an integral part of the 2013 World Champion Red Sox.

MOST OBSCURE RED SOX PLAYER TO WEAR #3—Tommy Matchick, who batted .071 in '70, was tempting, but a very recent member of the Red Sox merits the nod: **Joe Thurston**. Joe played on the 2008 Red Sox, but he didn't play much. He never made an error during his four games in left field, though he only had five chances. His first game for Boston was on April 17, filling in defensively for Manny Ramirez in the ninth against the Yankees. Inserted for offense in a blowout win the next day, he grounded out to close out the eighth. After Manny was ejected in the second inning on the April 20, he took over, grounded out twice, and got hit by a pitch. Dustin Pedroia pinch-hit for him the last time up, and tied the game with a double. In his last game for Boston, April 21, he played the whole game, got up to bat five times, struck out the first time up, and popped out to the infield the next four times. He got a much better gig as a semi-regular infielder for the Cardinals in 2009.

It's All Relative

Is there a gene that influences the choice of uniform numbers? Most players don't actually select the numbers they wear and any choice they have is inevitably limited by the retired numbers and those worn by others on the team when they first arrive. Perhaps Pedro and Ramon Martinez both preferred #5, but Nomar had it when Pedro first arrived and, of course, once Ramon turned up he and his brother couldn't wear the same number at the same time.

Because of this numbers theme, our count of Sox relatives forces us to exclude pitching brothers Ed and Tom Hughes (1900s), fly-shagging freres Roy and Cleo Carlyle (1920s), and the Gaston brother battery of righty Milt and backstop Alex, who were on the same Sox squad in 1929. All these brother combinations played before the days of numerals on jerseys. (Though Milt Gaston hung around after his older brother departed and went 2–13 wearing #19 for the 1931 Sox.) This list only deals with blood kin, but honorable mention goes to Rick Miller—a #3 for part of his Sox tenure—for marrying teammate Carlton Fisk's sister.

The fraternal fraternity is listed in order of appearance with the Red Sox—by family member and by number—along with fathers, cousins, uncles, and grandfathers. There is an asterisk if they were on the Sox the same season, which had to make Mom happy—but she couldn't have liked that no son took his father's old number. And if anything in the chart below is wrong, my brother did it.

BROTHERS	Numbers	Years with Sox
*Rick Ferrell	#9, #7, #2	1933–37
*Wes Ferrell	#12	1934–37
Roy Johnson	#18, #3, #4, #3	1932–35
Bob Johnson	#8	1944–45
Ed Sadowski	#8	1960
Bob Sadowski	#21	1966
*Tony Conigliaro	#25	1964–67, 1969–70,
*Billy Conigliaro	#4, #1, #40	1975
		1969–71
Marty Barrett	#17	1982–90
Tommy Barrett	#33	1992
*Pedro Martinez	#45	1998–2004
*Ramon Martinez	#48	1999–2000
FATHER/SON		
Ed Connolly Sr.	#10	1929–32
Ed Connolly Jr.	#29	1964
Walt Ripley	#18	1935
Allen Ripley	#28	1978–79

BROTHERS	Numbers	Years with Sox
Dolph Camilli	#28	1945
Doug Camilli	#34	1970–73 (coach)
George Susce	#36, #29, #43	1950–54 (coach)
George D. Susce	#41, #27	1955–58
Haywood Sullivan	#44, #16, #30	1955, 1957, 1959–60
Marc Sullivan	#15	1982, 1984–87
Dick Ellsworth	#36	1968–69
Steve Ellsworth	#28	1988
GRANDFATHER/GRANDSON		
Shano Collins	#32, #21	1921–25 (player);
Bob Gallagher	#44	1931–32 (manager)
		1972
Sam Dente	17	1947
Rick Porcello	22	2015
UNCLE/NEPHEW		
Dom Dallessandro	#16	1937
Dick Gernert	#14, #3, #41, #25	1952–59
Matt Batts	#5, #14	1947–51
Danny Heep	#29	1989–90
Ramon Aviles	11	1977
Mike Aviles	3	2011–12
Ernie Riles	12	1993
Willie Harris	2	2006
Terry Shumpert	2	1995
Mookie Betts	50	2014–15
COUSINS		
*Mike Cubbage	#39, #22	2002–03 (coach)
*Chris Haney	#56	2002
*Anastacio Martinez	#67	2004
*Sandy Martinez	#58	2004
*Dale Sveum	#41	2004–05 (coach)
*John Olerud	#19	2005

As we can see, the numbers most frequently worn from among these family members are #2, #3, and #28, each number having been worn by three players.

#4: Cronin

Number of times this number was issued: 22

Longest tenure by any given player: 12 seasons, Joe Cronin

Joe Cronin was a star shortstop who'd hit .304 over seven seasons for the Washington Senators, until his uncle-in-law, Clark Griffith, sold him to Tom Yawkey and the Red Sox for $250,000 in time for the 1935 season. He took a vacation from #4 for one year in 1936, wearing #6 and suffering his worst year with the team. **Eric McNair** wore it that one year and swapped digits with the skipper before the '37 season. Cronin spent the next decade in #4, batting an even .300 overall in his 11 seasons as player–manager with the Red Sox. He served two seasons as a non-playing manager, then became the club's general manager, and later was president of the American League. Joe was elected to the Hall of Fame—as a player—in 1956.

Another Red Sox player–manager was **Lou Boudreau**, who served as such for four games in 1952, but he spent the rest of his tenure affixed to the bench from 1952 through 1954. Neither his play for Boston in 1951 (a .267 average under Red Sox manager Steve O'Neill) nor his work as Red Sox manager (229–232) was all that outstanding. His better years were behind him in Cleveland. He was inducted into the Hall of Fame in 1970, as a player.

When **Sam Mele** broke in with Boston in 1947 and hit .302 in his rookie year, he was wearing #14. Dropping 10 digits didn't help at the plate; in 1948 he batted .233 and only saw about half as much action. After 10 games and a .196 average in 1949, he was sent out of town (traded to Washington, with Mickey Harris, for Walt Masterson). Mark Armour, author of *Joe Cronin: A Life in Baseball*, offers a story behind Mele's taking #4. Cronin wanted Joe McCarthy to take #4 in 1948 (when McCarthy succeeded Cronin as manager). McCarthy declined—he did not wear any number—and Cronin decided it should be worn by a position player. He offered it to Mele, who took it, hit .232, and then the GM had him take #27 . . . with the Senators.

Jim Gosger's name cropped up again in April 2009, after Kevin Youkilis hit an extra-inning walkoff home run against the Yankees. Researchers found the last time it had been done during the regular season was June 4, 1966, in the 16th inning, off New York's Dooley Womack. The batter was, of course, Mr. Gosger, wearing #4. It may have boosted him as trade bait; nine days later, he was on his way to the Kansas City A's. Nine different Red Sox wore #4 in the 1960s, starting with **Lu Clinton** and running all the way to **Tom Satriano**, who took it into the next decade.

Speedster **Tommy Harper**'s name has cropped up frequently in recent years as Jacoby Ellsbury threatened—and then passed in 2009—Harper's 1973 team record of 54 stolen bases. Harper, the first man to bat for both the Seattle Pilots and Milwaukee Brewers, also had two stints as coach of the Sox. He still lives in the Boston area, and has enjoyed watching Ellsbury, offering him what advice he can.

"Golden Boy" **Jackie Jensen** led the league in runs batted in three times: 1955 (116), 1958 (122), and 1959 (112), but his fear of flying saw him quit after '59. He gave it the old college try again in '61. Unfortunately for Jensen, the league had expanded to include West Coast play by this time—thanks to the Angels—and that was just too much for him to stomach.

Carney Lansford, a Californian initially drafted by the Angels, and who later returned to Northern California for 10 years with Oakland, had the biggest year of his career in the first of his two seasons with the Red Sox. He batted .336 in 1981 to become the first right-handed hitter to win the AL batting title since Alex Johnson in 1970 and the first Sox hitter to claim it since Carl Yastrzemski in '68.

Lansford was part of the return from the Angels—along with Mark Clear and Rick Miller—for Rick Burleson and **Butch Hobson**. Clell Lavern Hobson Jr., a wishbone-running quarterback for Bear Bryant at Alabama, chose baseball as a profession and was handed #51 for his two games with the '75 Sox. He took #4 the next year and took the third base job from Rico Petrocelli.

Hobson added sock to the Sox at the bottom of the order, but the only time he led the league in an offensive category was in 1977, when he struck out 162 times—paradoxically, it's the only year he finished in the top 25 in MVP voting (he ranked 23rd). His 43 errors in 1978, a horrific .899 fielding percentage, marked the first time since 1916 that a regular player's defensive average registered below .900 for a season. As Red Sox manager for 439 games (the team won 47.2 percent of them) in 1992–94, Butch wore #17. By that time, Cronin's #4 had been retired.

MOST OBSCURE RED SOX PLAYER TO WEAR #4—You can't get more obscure than **Bill Schlesinger**. He'd been with the ballclub out of 1965 spring training, but for the May 4 game against the Angels—at Dodger Stadium, no less—Schlesinger was so not expecting the call to pinch-hit that his bats had been left in the clubhouse. "The first thing I did," Schlesinger remembered, "there's three steps going up out of the dugout. Well, I tripped there and I fell on the third step and skinned up my knee. So now it's time for me to go up and hit because the guy just made the second out. I'm walking up to the plate with this donut and I keep pounding that bat on the ground, trying to get that donut to come off, and it wouldn't come off. I'm getting closer and closer to home plate and this umpire's looking at me and he says, 'Come on, come on! It's five to nothing here and I've got a dinner date one hour from now.' He says, 'Do you need help with that donut, getting it offa that bat?' I said, 'Yeah, kinda.' So the umpire takes the bat and gets the donut off the bat." When Schlesinger finally stepped into the box, he hit a ball off home plate that jumped high in the air but was pulled down by catcher Buck Rodgers and thrown to first to get Schlesinger by a half a step. Three days later, he was with Kansas City's farm club in Lewiston, Idaho. He never played in the big leagues again.

Like Father, Like Daughter

While there have been 10 brother combinations on the Red Sox and six father-son combos, there has obviously never been a father-daughter combination. But Gina Satriano came the closest.

Her father, Tom Satriano, was an Angel for the first nine seasons of that club's existence, coming to Boston for Joe Azcue at the '69 trading deadline. "Satch" spent the rest of that year plus 1970 with the Red Sox, hitting .189 and then .236 while wearing #4 in his final major league stop. Daughter Gina also played pro ball, but it was her mother, Sherry, who put in the hours and challenged Little League under Title IX to get her onto the diamond. The first girl in California to play Little League—surviving not just the boys but many threats off the field—wound up playing for the Colorado Silver Bullets. She pitched 29 times in 1994–95 and wore #42 for the professional women's baseball team coached by Hall of Famer Phil Niekro. She even played in Fenway Park, losing to the Boston Park League team. She found other work, as a deputy district attorney in Los Angeles.

#5: Nomah

Because he wore it for nine recent seasons with the Red Sox, shortstop **Nomar Garciaparra** is fixed in the minds of most Sox fans when you mention #5. He certainly made people forget **Scott Fletcher** pretty darn quick.

Tens of thousands of #5 T-shirts were sold for the popular Garciaparra, who burst on the scene as the 1997 Rookie of the Year, stroking 209 base

Nomar Garciaparra

hits, batting .306, setting an AL rookie record with a 30-game hitting streak, and becoming the first Sox frosh since Walt Dropo in 1950 to collect 30 homers. Young "Nomah" had a winning smile and played with the sort of positive energy that won him legions of admirers. It didn't hurt that he won the AL batting title in back-to-back seasons, 1999 and 2000. In fact, his batting average increased every one of his first five years in the league, including marks of .323, .357, and .372 from 1998–2000. One wondered just how high he could fly. He missed most of the 2001 season, though he recovered to hit .310 in 2002. But things started to turn sour. He was uncomfortable in the public eye, and the media began to brand him as surly. When general manager Theo Epstein dealt Nomar at the trading deadline in 2004, it seemed to reenergize the eventual world champion Red Sox. Cause and effect? It's impossible to know; there are far too many factors involved, including luck. But one did wonder how long it would be until another player was given #5. That question was answered in 2009 when **Rocco Baldelli** donned #5—a number the Woonsocket, Rhode Island, native had worn in Tampa Bay.

The older folks among us may recall **Vern Stephens**, another very good shortstop. Stephens appeared in eight All-Star Games and led the American League three times in runs batted in, driving in 159 for Boston in 1949 (tied with teammate Ted Williams) and 144 in 1950 (tied with teammate Walt Dropo). He'd led the league once before all by himself, in 1944 for the St. Louis Browns, three RBIs ahead of Boston's "Indian Bob" Johnson—one of the reasons the Sox traded for Stephens after the '47 campaign.

Even before Stephens was **Jim "Rawhide" Tabor**, a third baseman wearing the number for his position. Tabor was an Alabaman with great potential as a slugger but with a penchant for drink and a problem with self-discipline. He drove in 101 runs in 1941 and 95 in 1939. The only thing he ever led the league in was in getting caught stealing bases. He never did seem to give up, though he was rubbed out 54 times in 123 career attempts. Tabor batted .273 over seven seasons with the Red Sox.

Brady Anderson wanted to wear #9, but it wasn't available in Boston. No Kid-ding. "That was always what I wore growing up, because of Ted Williams," he told us. "I either wore his or when I couldn't get number 9, I tried to wear number 6 because of Stan Musial." The closest available numbers in Boston in 1988 were four digits off the mark:

#5 and #13. He opted to go down and avoid 13. Anderson hit .230 in the 41 games he appeared in during his rookie year. Then he and Curt Schilling were traded to the Orioles for Mike Boddicker, who served the Sox well. In the four seasons before 1996 and the four seasons after, he averaged 17.6 homers, but in 1996 he hit 50. There's always been suspicion about juice in that sudden boost.

Never to be confused with any slugger was shortstop **Spike Owen**, who hit eight homers in three seasons in Boston. Spike was his given name, as if he were a bulldog. He came over to the Red Sox in a pennant-winning year, 1986, but he only hit .183 in 42 games. Owen tore up the ALCS, though, hitting .429, and played a solid World Series against the Mets, batting .300.

Denny Doyle won a place in the hearts of that generation's Sox fans when he came to Boston in trade in mid-June of 1975 and hit .310 for the rest of the season, mostly playing second base and playing it solidly. During his 22-game hitting streak that summer, *Sports Illustrated* asked if Joe DiMaggio's 56-game streak might be in jeopardy. "I doubt if DiMaggio would be too worried if he came down to the batting cage and saw this little guy in there choking up on the bat," Doyle replied.

Five years after his Big Red Machine stamped out both Doyle's and New England's dreams of Game Seven glory in the '75 World Series, **Tony Perez** came to Boston as a first baseman and designated hitter. He drove in 105 runs in 1980—his seventh and final 100-plus season—but averaged just 35 RBIs in each of the next two seasons. His selection to the Hall of Fame in 2000 rested on the damage he'd done to NL pitchers for the Reds, though the three homers he hit off the Red Sox in the '75 Series—two off Reggie Cleveland in Game Five and a titanic shot off a Bill Lee floater in the deciding game—might have garnered a few HOF votes.

Polar opposites in matters of race wore #5 in the middle years of the 20th century. **Mike "Pinky" Higgins** wore it in his first stint as third baseman for Boston in the 1930s and then as manager for most of eight seasons (given his alcoholism, he didn't manage the full year in either 1959 or 1960). Higgins was an unabashed racist, and almost certainly a big part of the reason the Red Sox were the last major league ballclub to integrate. Overcoming racism to play big league ball was Greenville, Mississippi's **George Scott**—"The Boomer"—known for his flowery language (a home run was a "tater") and dress (he wore a helmet in the field for protection from unruly fans and a necklace made of "second basemen's teeth").

Signed by the Red Sox, he spent his first six seasons with Boston, five with the Brewers, and parts of three more back with the Sox (he wore #15 in 1977–78). Boomer's Milwaukee seasons were the better ones on offense, as he won the home run and RBI titles in 1975—when he might otherwise have helped Boston in the World Series. He also batted .283 as a Brewer compared to the .257 he hit for the Red Sox. His defensive work earned him eight Gold Gloves (his first three for the Sox) and he did pole 154 taters for Boston. With the middle name of Charles, he could have gone by George C. Scott, and then Boomer might have rumbled up the aisle to receive the 1970 Oscar for *Patton* famously declined by the actor that shared his name.

Two less dramatic first baseman wore #5 in the 1970s: **Danny Cater** and **Bob Watson**. Cater—the piddly return for Sparky Lyle—came with promise but wound up being the punchline for a ridiculously one-sided deal with the Yankees. Watson, a star with the Astros and later the first African American GM, was acquired by the Red Sox in 1979. He played just 84 games for Boston, but on September 15 he became the first player in history to hit for the cycle in each league. Watson signed as a free agent with the Yankees that November, replacing George Scott, who'd finished the '79 season in the Bronx in his last major league stop. A week after Watson signed in New York, Tony Perez replaced him in Boston, completing the #5 circle. These days, Watson doles out MLB's suspensions for ballplayers who stray from the straight and narrow.

When the Red Sox engineered the unloading of somewhere around a quarter-billion dollars' worth of contractual obligations in a deal that sent Carl Crawford, Adrian Gonzalez, and Josh Beckett to the Los Angeles Dodgers, there was a fourth player when went from Boston to L.A.—that was **Nick Punto**. Certain wags still refer to the deal as the "Nick Punto" deal. His portion of the obligation was about $1.5 million.

The barroom rumor of the Sox and Yankees swapping Ted Williams for Joe DiMaggio wore off like a hangover. Can you imagine Teddy Ballgame in #5? Imagine this . . . and that's a "B" on his cap in a very early 1939 photograph of uncertain provenance turned up by James Kaklamanos.

Next to pick up number 5 was Jonny Gomes, who seems to have something of a knack for landing on postseason-bound teams—Cincinnati, Tampa Bay, Oakland, and (for 12 games at the end of the 2015 season) the Kansas City Royals. He was a real clubhouse presence and a significant part of the 2013 World Championship Red Sox.

MOST OBSCURE RED SOX PLAYER TO WEAR #5—Buddy Hunter singled, doubled, drove in the go-ahead run, and scored twice in one inning on July 8, 1973, as part of a nine-run top of the 10th against the White Sox. It was the most runs ever scored by the Sox in an extra-inning frame and—no surprise—the Red Sox won, 11–2. He played every other year between 1971 and 1975, with a declining number of at-bats each season: 9, 7, and 1. His lone contribution to the 1975 pennant-winners was a June 1 groundout that set his career average in stone at .294, a mark that looks good in the encyclopedia. A Tom Kelly bunt flustered the second baseman in the bottom of the eighth and a Twins run scored. The Sox held on to win as Hunter snared a liner in the ninth, his final play in a major league game. Hunter got a $250 share of the Red Sox World Series money in 1975, though it was less than the batboy received.

#6: The Pesky Pole

Johnny Pesky told us how he came to get #6: "When I first came to the Red Sox, I had 16, but Cronin wanted infielders to have single numbers. Tabor was 5, I was 6, Bobby was 1, and Foxx was 3," he said, referring to Sox on the bases Jimmie Foxx, Bobby Doerr, and Jim Ta-

Johnny Pesky

bor. It was a number Pesky wore through his terrific rookie season, when he led the league in base hits with 205 and came in third in MVP balloting (Ted Williams won the Triple Crown that year, but—astonishingly—placed second behind New York's Joe Gordon, who led the league in just two categories: striking out and grounding into double plays.) Had there been a Rookie of the Year award before 1947, Pesky would clearly have won it.

After three years in the navy during World War II, Johnny came back and led the league in hits in both 1946 and 1947 as well. Losing those three seasons to war may well have cost him a berth in the Hall of Fame, though he's in the Red Sox Hall of Fame and had his number retired in 2008. And don't forget his pole in right field. Pesky wore a few other numbers as well: #22 as manager in 1963–64, #35 as coach in 1975–80 and a brief reprise for a few days as manager in 1980, and #66 as a coach in 1992, 1995, and 1996. But it's as #6 he will always be remembered.

Pesky remains an irrepressible admirer of Ted Williams, and back in his younger days sometimes did handstands to display his jersey number upside-down while crowing, "Hey, look at me! I'm Ted Williams!"

Johnny never stood much on the privileges of position. When he was asked to take over as manager of the 1990 Pawtucket Red Sox, he was 70 years old and already a legend. He could have insisted on his traditional #6—but when he learned that a Pawsox player was wearing the number, he replied, "The player who has it, keeps it. It won't matter what's on the back, as long as Red Sox is on the front." He wore #19, and the *Providence Journal*'s Joe McDonald reports that he'd also spend mornings folding laundry with clubby Chris Parent—just as he'd done as a kid in Oregon for his hometown Portland Beavers. When he was told his number was being retired before a game in September 2008, Pesky's response was typical Pesky: "When I heard about it last night, I was told that the bosses wanted to see me and I thought I'd done something [wrong]."

Before Pesky, #6 had been worn every season since 1931, although **Eric McNair** had been the only man to wear it for more than one season. His .156 average in 1938 made sure he wouldn't see a third season in Boston. A pair of #6s with more staying power was **Rico Petrocelli** and **Bill Buckner**.

Buckner started with #16 when he first arrived, in 1984, dropped 10 digits and wore #6 from 1985–87, and wore #22 during his 1990 reprise (he'd worn that number as a Dodger and Cub). Buckner's 102 RBIs in

1986 were second only to Jim Rice for the Sox and earned him the honor to wear #6 in that year's World Series. Unfortunately, when it came time to close out Game Six, #11 Dave Stapleton was on the bench, rather than filling in for late-inning defensive purposes. But the Sox would never had made it to the Series in the first place without Buckner. That moment marred a remarkable October and a great career.

Rico wore #6 for two Series: 1967 and 1975. He was top dog in a 1968 infield that's one of the lowest uniform number totals ever for an infield quartet: Petrocelli (#6), George Scott (#5), Mike Andrews (#2), and Joe Foy (#1). That adds up to 12. Playing at a time when a dozen homers would have been big-time power for a middle infielder, Rico socked 40 in 1969. Forty years later it's still the most homers in a single season for a Red Sox shortstop. All told, Petrocelli hit nine grand slams and, since he never played for another team, every one of his 210 home runs benefitted the Red Sox, placing him 10th all-time among Boston batters.

It remains one of the great tragedies of Red Sox baseball that another player who similarly hit all of his homers for the Sox (11 of them) died as a result of a pulmonary embolism early in his second Sox season. **Harry Agganis** had begun a promising career in 1954, but became ill and died early in the 1955 season. Agganis wore #33 for the Boston University football team to honor his hero, Sammy Baugh. He'd been offered a $100,000 bonus to play football for the Cleveland Browns, but Agganis felt more strongly about playing baseball for his hometown team and reportedly settled for half that amount with the Sox. The Agganis Arena sports complex at BU honors Harry today.

Odell Hale spent just two months in Boston in 1941, but he remains part of one of the great anecdotes in Fenway Park history. On September 7, 1935, Hale was playing third base for Cleveland and the Red Sox had two men on and nobody out. Joe Cronin's screaming line drive hit off Hale's forehead, deflected into the shortstop's glove to start a 5–6–4–3 triple play.

Two-time former AL batting champ **Mickey Vernon** wore the number during the two years he played first for the Red Sox, 1956 and

1957. His .310 average in '56, and his past record, earned him a spot on that year's All-Star team. When his average plunged in '57, the Red Sox placed him on waivers over the winter. The Tribe took him and he hit 52 points higher. Vernon's Cleveland teammate **Vic Wertz** came over in the Jimmy Piersall deal after the '58 season. Famous for hitting the longest out in World Series history (the legendary ball caught by Willie Mays in the 1954 Series), Wertz hit the ball pretty far at Fenway during his three-year Sox stead. The first baseman hit .282 with 19 HRs and 103 RBIs in 1960 and finished 14th in the MVP voting. (Ted Williams, in his final season, finished one spot ahead of Wertz.)

One of the last men to wear #6 won over Boston fans with his love of the game: catcher **Tony Pena**. It certainly wasn't his .234 average over four years that endeared him to Sox fans; it was his hustle, smarts, and catching prowess. Fellow backstops **Rick Cerone** (1988–89) and **Damon Berryhill** (1994) sandwiched Tony's tenure.

Boston clubhouse manager Joe Cochran may have gone too far in trying to accommodate a veteran. No one had worn #6 since 1995 infielder **Chris Donnels** (1995) (.253 AVG/.317 OBP/.385 SLG in 91 at-bats). One might think the number had been informally retired, but when **Gary Gaetti** signed as a free agent in early April 2000, he wasn't able to have his habitual #8 and took #6 instead. The number couldn't have helped him. He had 10 at-bats and failed to get a hit. It's not good when a designated hitter can't hit, and Gaetti's major league career ground to a halt just 10 days after signing. To be fair, he did drive in one run with a sacrifice fly in his final game. It was game 2,507 of his career and RBI 1,341.

MOST OBSCURE RED SOX PLAYER TO WEAR #6—Johnny Welch, the second Sox player to wear it after **Hal Rhyne**, spent a full five seasons with the Red Sox, and still never distinguished himself in the eyes of history. He pitched for Boston from 1932 through 1936, and even won 13 games in 1934, second only to Wes Ferrell's 14. But he also lost 15 and had a 4.49 ERA. He was 33–40 for the five fairly forgettable Sox teams. He was waived to the Pirates in mid-1936, fell ill a couple of years later, and died at age 33.

Who, What, Wear, When?

Players were not married to uniform numbers early on and experimented freely from the first year they were sewed on Red Sox uniforms in 1931. To get an idea of how quickly players discarded numbers, no one who was the first to don a given Sox number kept it for longer than two years until 1974. This list features the year each number was worn for the first time. When more than one player wore a number in a given season, all players are listed. When a coach or manager is the first to wear the number, the first player to wear it—along with the year that happened—is included.

Uni	Player	First Worn
#1	Bill Sweeney	1931
#2	Bobby Reeves	1931
#3	Jack Rothrock	1931
#4	Rabbit Warstler	1931
#5	Otto Miller	1931
#6	Hal Rhyne	1931
#7	Ollie Marquardt	1931
	Bill Marshall	1931
#8	Pat Creeden	1931
	Urbane Pickering	1931
#9	Charlie Berry	1931
#10	Muddy Ruel	1931
	Marv Olsen	1931
#11	Ed Connolly Sr.	1931
#12	Tom Winsett	1931
	Russ Scarritt	1931
#13	Bob Fothergill	1933
#14	Tom Oliver	1931
#15	Earl Webb	1931
#16	Howie Storie	1931
	Gene Rye	1931
	Johnny Lucas	1931
#17	Al Van Camp	1931
#18	Danny MacFayden	1932
	Roy Johnson	1932
#19	Howie Storie	1931
	Milt Gaston	1931

Uni	Player	First Worn
#20	Milt Gaston	1931
#21	Danny MacFayden	1931
#22	Jack Russell	1931
#23	George Stumpf	1931
	Ed Morris	1931
#24	Hod Lisenbee	1931
#25	Ed Durham	1931
#26	Bob Weiland	1932
#27	Bill McWilliams	1931
	Jim Brilheart	1931
#28	Bob Kline	1931
	Marty McManus	1931
#29	Walter Murphy	1931
#30	Jud McLaughlin	1931
#31	Wilcy Moore	1931
#32	Shano Collins	1931 (manager)
	Rudy Hulswitt	1932 (coach)
	Al Schacht	1936 (coach)
	Tommy Thomas	1937
	Stew Bowers	1937
#33	Rudy Hulswitt	1931 (coach)
	Mike Meola	1933
#34	Urbane Pickering	1931
#35	Joe Gonzales	1937
#36	Pinky Higgins	1946
#37	Paul Campbell	1941

Uni	Player	First Worn	Uni	Player	First Worn
#38	Ed McGah	1946	#61	Jin Ho Cho	1998
#39	Eddie Pellagrini	1946	#62	Marino Santana	1999
#40	Bill McKechnie	1952 (coach)	#63	Paxton Crawford	2000
	Buster Mills	1954 (coach)	#64	Dustin Pedroia	2006
	Russ Kemmerer	1955	#65	Carlos Valdez	1998
#41	Earle Combs	1952 (coach)	#66	Joe Cascarella	1935
	Del Baker	1953 (coach)	#67	Eddie Riley	2001 (coach)
	George D. Susce	1955		Anastacio Martinez	2004
	Dick Gernert	1955	#68	Devern Hansack	2006
#42	Andy Gilbert	1942	#70	Kyle Weiland	2011
#43	George Susce	1952 (coach)	#71	Nate Spears	2011–12
	Frank Malzone	1955	#72	Xander Bogaerts	2013
#44	Ben Steiner	1946	#73	Bryce Brentz	2014
#45	Paul Schreiber	1952 (coach)	#76	Jose Iglesias	2011
	Dick Pole	1973	#77	Josh Bard	2006
#46	Paul Campbell	1946	#79	Justin Thomas	2012
#47	Billy MacLeod	1962	#81	Lou Lucier	1943
#48	Vic Correll	1972	#82	Johnny Lazor	1943
#49	Pete Smith	1962	#83	Eric Gagne	2007
#50	Andy Merchant	1975	#84	J. T. Snow	2006
#51	Bob Guindon	1964	#85	Don Kalkstein	2006 (psychology coach)
#52	Jody Reed	1987			
#53	Sammy Stewart	1986	#86	Brian Abraham	2013–14 (bullpen catcher)
#54	Roger LaFrancois	1982			
#55	Bob Veale	1972	#87	Mike Brenly	2015 (bullpen catcher)
#56	Zach Crouch	1988			
#57	Nate Minchey	1993	#88	Jason LaRocque	2005 (bullpen catcher)
#58	Jeff McNeely	1993			
#59	Daryl Irvine	1990	#91	Alfredo Aceves	2011–12
#60	Dana LeVangie	1997 (coach)	#94	Dalier Hinojosa	2015
	Hanley Ramirez	2005			

#7: Reggie, Rooster, Trot, Dom, and Dr. Strangeglove

The man they called "The Little Professor"—**Dominic DiMaggio**—is one of those borderline Hall of Famers, better than several others already in the Hall, but still never quite making the cut. He came up a few years after his celebrated brother, Joe, and some didn't take him as seriously because he wore eyeglasses at a time that few ballplayers did. He compiled a .298 lifetime average, played in seven All-Star Games, and led the league in runs scored in 1950 and 1951, but his career came to a sudden halt just three games into the 1953 season. Dominic was considered as good a center fielder as there was. Had he been playing center field at the end of Game Seven of the 1946 World Series (he was removed after pulling a hamstring trying to leg a double into a triple), Leon Culberson wouldn't have taken his place and been just the tiniest bit slow retrieving the ball during Enos Slaughter's "Mad Dash," perhaps changing the whole World Series outcome. A split second's difference in 1946 and a generation or two (or three) might not have been scarred for life waiting 86 years between championships.

"Who's better than his brother Joe? Dom-in-ic Di-Mag-gio." Dom DiMaggio was the first president of the BoSox Club, and was even part of a group that tried to buy the Red Sox in the mid-1970s. His 34-game consecutive hitting streak in 1949 remains the longest in Red Sox history. When he died in 2009 at age 92, the game lost a man who went out of his way to do the right thing both on the field and off it.

Ranking second to Dom D. in #7 tenure was **Trot Nixon**, a 1993 first-round draft pick who took six seasons before he landed a full-time job in the majors in 1999. He never quite drove in 100 runs (his high was 94 in 2002), he never hit as many as 30 homers (28 in '03), but he was a hard-playing right fielder whose grittiness served as the model for the so-called "Dirt Dogs." His best year was 2003, when the team as a whole set a number of offensive records; Trot hit .306, drove in 87 runs, and had career highs with .376 on-base and .578 slugging percentages. Harder to quantify was his ability to come through at key moments, often against the Yankees. Trot was a .283 lifetime hitter in the postseason, including a .429 average *against* the Sox in the 2007 ALCS.

"The Rooster"—**Rick Burleson**—was a scrappy player like Trot Nixon, but at shortstop. Fiery might be a better word. Bill Lee once said of Burleson, "Some guys didn't like to lose, but Rick got angry if the score was even tied." Joe Garagiola, though, believed him even-tempered: "He comes to the ballpark mad and he stays that way." Fifth overall pick in the 1970 draft, his .284 average made him the Red Sox rookie of the year in 1974. He hit .292 against Cincinnati in the '75 World

Series (and .444 in the ALCS to end Oakland's three-year world championship reign). When it came to contract negotiations, the Rooster might have rubbed Haywood Sullivan the wrong way. Despite four All-Star Games and a Gold Glove, plus

Dom DiMaggio

strong fan support, he was traded to the Angels after the 1980 season. Injuries prevented him playing like he had in his seven seasons in Boston.

After six games in '66 when he got his feet wet, **Reggie Smith** effectively kicked off his 17 seasons of major league ball playing for the Red Sox in the magical year, 1967. He was a switch-hitter with power and speed, and a real asset in center field. His father had played in the Negro American League. When Reggie first came through the system, he had such a good arm that manager Billy Herman wanted him to pitch, but Dick Williams was manager in '67 and he wanted to install the rookie in center field. A bad back prevented Mike Andrews from starting the season, though, and come Opening Day, there was Reggie Smith playing second base. Versatility could have been his middle name: on August 20, he became the first player in franchise history to homer from both sides of the plate in a game (he still holds the club record by doing it four times). Smith's breakout year was 1969, when he hit .309. It had only been only a few years since the Red Sox had integrated and racism made his stay in Boston less than enjoyable. He was often overshadowed by the "other Reggie," but Reggie Smith was a seven-time All-Star (two trips for Boston) who thrived as one of the game's more feared sluggers in his prime—unfortunately most of that period occurred after the Red Sox traded him to St. Louis with Ken Tatum for Rick Wise and Bernie Carbo in 1973.

We wouldn't want to forget **Dick Stuart** and he wouldn't want us to. He turned up in Boston for Johnny Pesky's managerial debut in 1963, leading the American League with 118 RBIs. His 42 home runs ranked not just second in the AL to Harmon Killebrew's 45, but only Jimmie Foxx (50 in 1938) and Ted Williams (43 in 1949) had hit more in a season for the Sox at the time. The next year he drove in 114 runs, and was gone, and so was Pesky. Stuart was a decade too early for the DH and "Dr. Strangeglove" (or "Old Stonefingers," if you prefer) was a perfect candidate for any "hitting only" detail. His adventures in fielding resulted in a staggering 53 errors over just two years in Boston.

Two successive #7 Sox wound up in the Hall of Fame: **Rick Ferrell** (1934–35) and **Heinie Manush** (1936). Ferrell, the catching end of a brother duo, also wore #9 and, #33, and was discussed at #2. Heinie did most of his Manushing elsewhere, though he batted .281 at age 34 and was released by the sixth-place Sox. The next year Heinie hit .333 in Brooklyn. He later managed in the Red Sox farm system.

The Sox ran through a string of single-season #7s from 1989 through 1995. **Nick Esasky**'s 108 RBIs in 1989 (the only year he played for Boston), which were 42 more than his next-highest total of the eight seasons he played—he can thank Pete Rose's prolonged pursuit of the all-time hit record for squandering his youthful power on Cincinnati's bench. Esasky's career ended abruptly due to vertigo shortly after he signed with the Braves. Clown turned commentator **Steve Lyons** played for the Red Sox three different times. In 1991, his only season as a Sox #7, "Psycho" played all four infield positions, all three outfield positions, and even served as closer for a day in a 14–1 defeat at the hands of the Twins, throwing shutout ball in the top of the ninth.

Lyons wasn't the only #7 to pitch. In 1944, with the team depleted like all others due to war, backup shortstop **Eddie Lake** pitched not once, not twice, but on six separate occasions. Standing 5- feet, 7-inches, Lake's line as a pitcher was 19 1/3 IP, 20 hits, two HRs, 11 BB, seven K, and a respectable 4.19 ERA. The league ERA was 3.40. The following year he hit .279—by far his best season at the plate—and walked so often (106 times) that he led the league in on-base percentage (.412). Off that season, Lake was shrewdly traded for Tiger slugger Rudy York.

Like Lyons and Lake, **J. D. Drew** was nearly called on to pitch—only it was in the All-Star Game. Terry Francona had run dry of pitchers in the 15th inning of the 2008 contest, but the AL finally broke the deadlock and everyone was so relieved Drew didn't have to pitch that he was named the game's MVP (though it might have also had to do with his game-tying home run in the seventh). That 2008 was the first All-Star appearance of his ballyhooed and well-compensated career speaks to how often he's been injured or hasn't met expectations. He went on the disabled list with a back problem a month after the All-Star Game. Drew returned in late September and had his second solid postseason for the Sox. He had a productive 2009 as well and had Boston's lone homer during their quick ALDS exit.

Joe Vosmik hit .320 in his rookie year and drove in 117 runs. Sadly, it was for the Indians. Acquired by Boston in time for the 1938 season, Vosmik batted .324, drove in 86 runs, led the league in hits with 201, and scored 121 runs. The next year Ted Williams turned up on the scene, and had a spectacular season. With Dom DiMaggio ready to step in and play center field in 1940, the Red Sox did something they didn't always do: they made the right move at the right time, concluding that their Bohemian outfielder was perhaps in decline, and certainly expendable, so Vosmik was sold to the Dodgers.

There should always be a special spot for locals who played for the Red Sox such as Dorchester's **Bill Marshall.** Born on Valentine's Day in 1911, he made the Red Sox when he was 20 years old—briefly—appearing in just one game (June 20, 1931). He never got an at-bat. Inserted as a pinch runner, he experienced a thrill many of us never will—crossing the plate in a major league game. The run tied the game in the ninth, 4–4, in Detroit, but the Tigers won it in the bottom of the inning. Unfortunately, that's all Marshall ever got to do with the Red Sox. Three years later, he collected eight plate appearances for Cincinnati and got a base hit. Playing second base, he made one error in eight chances. That was his career.

MOST OBSCURE RED SOX PLAYER TO WEAR # 7—You want more obscure than Bill Marshall? Try **Steve Rodriguez**. It was hard to even figure out who he was in the minors. In 1995 he played with four other Pawsox with the same surname: Carlos, Frank, Tony, and Victor—all four unrelated Rodriguezes played in the majors at some point. Steve debuted on April 30 that year in Boston—ironically during Frankie Rodriguez's first major league start, a 17–11 loss to the White Sox. The shortstop reached on an error his first time up but died on first base. In Steve's only fielding chance that game, he made an error. He batted eight times with the Red Sox, collecting one single, one walk, one steal, and a fielding percentage of .667. You'd have to ask the Tigers why they took him after he was placed on waivers. He hit .194 for Detroit in his final 31 at-bats in the majors.

Plain as the Name on Your Back

One seems souvenir jerseys on the backs of some Sox fans—Williams 9, for instance. There was never any such jersey in The Kid's day. The Red Sox have never worn home uniforms with their names on the back. They first made the leap into putting names on the back of their road jerseys in 1990. The announcement was made on January 5 that year that Red Sox road uniforms would henceforth bear names over the numeral on the back of the jersey. This innovation was reportedly pushed through by general manager Lou Gorman. A Red Sox fan was quoted as grumbling, "If you don't know who the player is without a name, you don't deserve to be a Red Sox fan."

#8: YAZ

No one besides **Carl Yastrzemski** wore #8 after 1961. Likewise, no one has hit for the Triple Crown since he did it in 1967. His 44 homers, 121 RBIs, and .326 average were monster—or at least Green Monster—numbers for that pitching-dominated era.

Carl Yastrzemski

That was the year of Yaz, finishing with a flourish with as clutch an end of the year as any player has ever had. "Yaz hit 44 homers that year, and 43 of them meant something big for the team," George Scott said of the season. "It seemed like every time we needed a big play, the man stepped up and got it done."

Yastrzemski had 23 hits in his final 44 at-bats, driving in 16, and scoring 14. He hit 10 homers in his final 100 at-bats, including 10 hits in his last 13 at-bats. In the last two games of '67 against the Twins, with the Sox needing to win both games to help avert a tie for the pennant,

Yaz went 7-for-8 and drove in six runs. And then he hit .400 with three homers in the World Series. He followed that with another batting title in '68, though his .301 is the lowest ever for a batting champ and is further illustration of the Grand Canyon–esque disparity between thrower and swinger in the "Year of the Pitcher."

Come 1975, Yaz and the Sox made the postseason again. This time he hit .445 in the ALCS and .310 in the World Series. Yaz played 3,308 regular season games for the Red Sox, was named to 18 All-Star squads, and was inducted into the Baseball Hall of Fame in 1989, the same year his number was retired at Fenway. Teammate and philosopher Bill Lee once observed that when Yaz lay on his side, his back bore the symbol for infinity.

Eight players donned #8 in the first five years the Sox wore uniform numbers, and then the Doc arrived. **Doc Cramer** (1936–40) had the second-longest tenure in #8 next to Yaz, hit .302 over his five years, and had a career ERA of 4.50—thanks to pitching four innings in a 1938 game. Cramer made the All-Star team four straight seasons, including a start in right field in the 1939 game. He accumulated an even 3,400 plate appearances while with the Red Sox and hit a grand total of one home run. It came in 1940, the year he led the league with an even 200 hits. One of them was his May 21 homer. You've heard of a "mistake pitch"—this must have been a mistake hit. He didn't whiff often, with just 99 Ks in those five seasons.

Lou Finney hit .301, one point less than Cramer, during his time with the Red Sox, interrupted when he spent 1943 and 1944 farming for the war effort in Alabama. His number was already taken when he first came back, by **Bob Johnson**, but Finney reclaimed it in 1945 after, once more, farming in the first part of the season. As for "Indian Bob" Johnson, his 1944 and 1945 seasons were the last two of his 13 years in the majors. Still, his .431 on-base percentage at age 38 led the majors in '44. He hit for a .324 average that year. Bob's brother Roy, also part-Cherokee, played with the Sox a decade earlier, finishing his major league career with a nearly identical .298 average to Bob's .296. (Roy hit .313 over three-plus years in Boston, wearing #18, #3, and #4.)

Boston's primary catcher in the postwar, pennant-winning year 1946 (and the early part of '47) was **Hal Wagner**, who hit just .230 in the regular season and an unfortunate .000 in the World Series in 13 at-bats.

But, then again, he didn't make an error in the Series so there's that to be said for him. And there's something to be said for **Al Simmons**, the Hall of Fame RBI-machine of the 1920s and 1930s, who batted .300 and knocked in 100 runs in 12 of his first 13 seasons in the majors. Out of the game in 1942, the depleted World War II club brought back "Bucketfoot Al" in '43, but he hit like a 41-year-old with his foot caught in a bucket for the Sox. He batted just .203, drove in 12 in 133 at-bats, and hit the last of his 307 career home runs.

MOST OBSCURE RED SOX PLAYER TO WEAR #8—Red Kellett got up nine times in nine games and struck out in five of those 1934 at-bats. He never quite managed to get a hit, but he did walk once for a career .100 on-base percentage. He was versatile in the field, though, appearing in four games at shortstop, two at second base, and one at third. He had 15 chances and made two errors. Boy, was his face red.

When the Numbers Go Up

Over the last quarter century, the Red Sox have retired #1, #4, #6, #8, #9, #14, #27, and #45 (with #42 retired throughout professional baseball for Jackie Robinson in 1997). What follows are details of the days these numbers were officially retired by the Red Sox.

#4 Joe Cronin and #9 Ted Williams: May 29, 1984

Although newspaper accounts the day after Ted Williams's last game reported that Teddy Ballgame's number had been retired in 1960, his #9 was retired beyond a shadow of a doubt on this day along with the #4 of his first manager, Joe Cronin.

But the game that followed the proceedings did not count. Minnesota held a 5–0 lead after four innings before rain washed the game away. The Twins only had themselves to blame for the loss of a win. Because of the pregame ceremony for Cronin and Williams, the Twins cable station booked its programming based on a projected 8:30 P.M. start. The festivities concluded before 8 P.M., but the game was delayed until Twins TV was ready. Had they used that extra half-hour to play, they would very likely have finished five innings before the drenching rains.

#1 Bobby Doerr: May 21, 1988

There were no worries about the game counting or the Red Sox losing—Bruce Hurst earned an 8–4 win over the Angels on a Saturday afternoon—but the manager lost something. John McNamara, who had worn #1 since taking over the Red Sox in 1985, surrendered #1 to posterity and Bobby Doerr. He took #2 and took it on the chin when he was relieved of his Red Sox uniform at the All-Star break and replaced by Joe Morgan.

#8 Carl Yastrzemski: August 6, 1989

Carl Yastrzemski joined Ted Williams, Joe Cronin, and Bobby Doerr as the fourth man so honored. Yaz's number gave the right field facade configuration of 9, 4, 1, 8—which fatalists and conspirators later interpreted as 9–4–18, the eve of Boston's last victorious World Series in September 1918. The numbers were later rearranged in numerical order (some say mistakenly) when the facade was repainted.

After the Sunday afternoon ceremony, Roger Clemens started and got the first out against Cleveland, but he was removed after two singles and a walk loaded the bases. Dennis Lamp relieved and all three Indians crossed home plate. "The Rocket" was all right and so were the Red Sox, who scored six times, and Rob Murphy got the win in relief.

#27 Carlton Fisk: September 4, 2000

Carlton Fisk's #27 was the fifth number of a former Red Sox player to be retired (and the first double-digit number so honored, for those keeping score). The Labor Day afternoon game saw Carl Everett drive in his 100th run, becoming just the sixth switch-hitter in major league history to drive in 100 runs in both leagues. Pedro Martinez topped Seattle and former Sox southpaw Jamie Moyer, 5–1.

#6 Johnny Pesky: September 28, 2008

Originally scheduled for a Friday night, the Johnny Pesky ceremony was moved to Sunday, the final day of the 2008 season. The opponent was the Yankees, but in a surprising—and in no way disturbing—development, the Red Sox had locked up a postseason berth and the Yankees were out of the playoffs for the first time since before the 1994 strike. The Yankees scored twice in the ninth to tie the game, but Jonathan Van Every knocked in the winning run in the 10th inning.

#14 Jim Rice: July 28, 2009

Like former Red Sox teammates Carl Yastrzemski and Carlton Fisk, Jim Rice was honored in Boston the same year he was elected to the Hall of Fame in Cooperstown. The Red Sox hosted Oakland on a Tuesday night, and it looked like the club's record on days it retired a number would remain perfect, but the A's rallied with three in the ninth and won in the 11th inning.

#45 Pedro Martinez: July 28, 2015

Continuing the Yaz, Fisk, and Rice practice, Pedro Martinez was also honored in Boston the same year he was elected to the Hall of Fame in Cooperstown. Fenway Park was sold out, but the score was disastrous—a 14–1 defeat at the hands of the powerful Toronto Blue Jays. The nine-run sixth inning broke the back of the Bosox. Jays winning pitcher was R. A. Dickey, Cy Young Award winner (for the Mets) in 2012. The Red Sox finished in last place for the second year in a row, but fans still basked in the afterglow of the 2013 World Championship season.

#9: "The Greatest Hitter Who Ever Lived"

Ted Williams

Barring a handful of aberrations, no player has consistently worn #9 since 1939 when "The Kid" broke in with a rookie season like no other: the 145 runs batted in by young **Ted Williams** has never been matched. We could fill a book of nothing but superlatives about Mr. Williams—and already have. He's widely considered the greatest Red Sox player of all time—and you won't get an argument about that here. He was an All-Star 19 times in 19 seasons of play, the only American Leaguer to win the Triple Crown twice (and he wasn't voted MVP either time, though he won a couple of those trophies, too). He hit a club-record 521 homers, and probably would have hit around 700 if he'd not devoted three years to service in World War II and two more (as a Marine Corps fighter pilot serving alongside John Glenn) in the Korean War. He is, of course, the last man to hit .400.

One would have thought the Sox might have held the uniform number for a player who had entered military service, especially a player who in just four years, had been the rookie of the year before there was such an award, hit .406, and won the Triple Crown. No one did wear #9 in 1943, but catcher **Johnny Peacock** wore #9 in 1944 . . . until he was traded on June 11. **Lou Finney** donned #9 for part of the season. (Uniform numbers expert Mark Stang has a scorecard from the September 4, 1944, game in Washington showing Finney with the number. Stang discounts the rumor that Hal Wagner briefly wore #9 that year because upon closer inspection, the poorly printed Athletics scorecard in question really showed him with #19.)

For a portion of one 1955 game, pitcher **Frank Sullivan** wore #9 . . . at the same time as Williams was wearing it in left field. Evidence points to August 28, a blistering hot day in Kansas City. "I had to change shirts every inning," Sullivan wrote, "and wound up the game in one of Ted Williams's uniforms."

Merv Shea, **Gordie Hinkle**, and even Hall of Famer **Rick Ferrell** wore #9 for a spell in the 1930s. Just a dozen Red Sox, however briefly, ever wore #9 in a game, from **Charlie Berry** in 1931 to **Ben Chapman**, the year before Ted came up. And **Bobby Doerr** the year before that (he was better suited as a #1). Chapman only played 1 1/2 of his 15 seasons with Boston—the second part of 1937 and then all of 1938. In his one full year, he hit .340 and drove in 80 runs. Not the kind of production you'd think to dump, but the Sox had every bit of faith in Ted Williams, so the Sox packed off Chapman to the Indians for Denny Galehouse and Tom Irwin.

Shea? He was a catcher who hit .143 in 16 games during 1933. The Sox were much better off with Rick Ferrell, who played the rest of the season in the #9 uni. Hinkle? He was a catcher, too, and his only year in the majors was 1934, backing up Ferrell, who had switched to #7 (and later #2). Hinkle got into 27 games and hit .173.

Charlie Berry was also a catcher—makes one wonder how an outfielder ever wound up with it—and worked without a number from 1928 through 1930. When the Sox handed out numbers in '31, he was the first assigned #9, batting .283 and driving in 49 runs. He was traded to the White Sox in 1932 as part of a five-player trade that saw **Smead Jolley** come to Boston—and put on the #9 shirt.

Smead Jolley. Now there's a name. You don't see too many kids named Smead any more. He also went by "Guinea" and "Smudge." The outfielder (he caught five games, too) wore #9 his first year, and #4 his second. His .309 average in '32 was higher than his team's winning percentage: Boston won less than 28 percent of its games. Smead's 99 RBIs led the Sox, and so did his 18 homers. Dale Alexander, however, led the Sox and AL in hitting at .367.

Since this chapter mentions everyone else who wore #9, it would be rude to ignore **Dusty Cooke**. He spent more time than anyone not named Ted wearing #9. Coming over from the Yankees, he played four years with Boston (119 games in #7, 74 games in #6, and 211 games in #9). His best season was in #9, hitting .306 in '35.

There was one final time when #9 was worn on the field at Fenway. After Ted Williams died, on July 5, 2002, every player and coach wore a four-inch-high black #9 on their left sleeve for the rest of the season.

MOST OBSCURE RED SOX PLAYER TO WEAR #9—John Smith. The name sound familiar? In the case of this 1931 first baseman, his real name was . . . John Smith. John Marshall Smith, to be precise. Being a Washington, DC, native, perhaps he was named after the first chief justice of the Supreme Court. Just before his 25th birthday he found himself in a major league uniform, wearing #9, the second Red Sox player to wear the number. Could you compare Smith the hitter in 1931 to Ted Williams? No, but Ted was only 13 in '31. Smith's first game was September 17 and his last game was September 18—but he managed to appear in four games, all against Cleveland. Boston's Earl Webb set a major league record (which still stands), hitting his 65th double in the second game on the 17th. Smith played first base in both games of that doubleheader, going 0-for-3 and 0-for-4 (with one RBI). He was 1-for-4 in each of the two games on September 18, and he stole a base, too. He handled 46 chances, all putouts, without an error. His average was .133, but the Sox won three of the four games he squeezed into his two days in the sun.

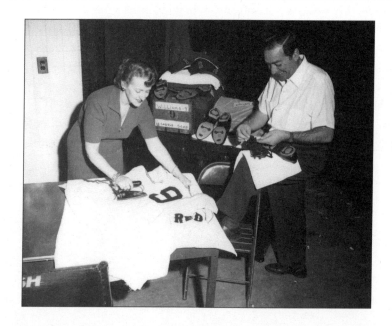

Nine Iron: Helen Robinson spent six decades as Fenway Park's switchboard operator. Originally hired by Eddie Collins, she started work on September 2, 1941—the month #9 Ted Williams secured his status as the last major leaguer to hit .400. Robinson, pictured with longtime clubhouse attendant Johnny Orlando, filled the time between calls by knitting sweaters for all the Boston ballplayers who were off to war. She also sewed the uniform numbers on the backs of the players' jerseys and, obviously, helped keep them ironed.

#10: Crisp Hawk Grove

The four Red Sox players who wore #10 and a world championship ring are **David McCarty** (2004) and **Coco Crisp** (2007), and both Jose Iglesias and John McDonald in 2013, though neither was on that year's postseason roster. For McCarty, 2004 was the middle of the three seasons he played with Boston as a first baseman–outfielder. He hit .286 for the Red Sox in 118 games over the three years, better than any of the other six teams for which he worked. He even pitched three times in 2004, with a very sharp 2.45 ERA—not surprisingly, the Sox lost all three games, but McCarty threw two shutout innings in the last game of the year, a 3–2 loss in Baltimore. He later served as an occasional co-host on the team's NESN postgame telecasts.

Crisp was a center fielder with a great name—and glove—who played in 361 games, hitting .271. Yet Crisp was eclipsed in the final weeks of 2007 when Jacoby Ellsbury broke in, batting .353 (and .438 in the World Series against Colorado, while Coco only got two at-bats). Crisp ended the 2007 ALCS with a sensational catch in "The Triangle," colliding with the wall as everyone in Fenway celebrated the refreshingly undramatic 11–2 win in Game Seven. Both Crisp and Ellsbury played center for the Sox in 2008, and had roughly equivalent seasons in some regards, though Ellsbury stole 50 bases and was clearly the flavor of the future. Crisp was wearing a Kansas City jersey come 2009.

Delving deeper into the past, the American League championship team of 1946 boasted a couple of #10s: pitcher **Jim Wilson**, who only lasted two-thirds of an inning that year, facing four batters and giving up two earned runs, and **Don Gutteridge**, who played a little infield and hit .234 in 47 at-bats. Gutteridge was perfect in the field at second base, but made four errors in eight games at third. For Wilson, it was the worst of his 12 seasons in the majors. Gutteridge also played a dozen big league seasons. Wilson wasn't on the World Series roster, but Gutteridge was 2-for-5.

The Hall of Famer of the group was **Lefty Grove**, enshrined in 1947 after a 17-year pitching career with the Philadelphia Athletics and the Red Sox resulting in 300 wins, 141 defeats, and a career 3.06 ERA. Seven times a 20-game winner for the Athletics (in 1931 he actually went 31–4!), he won 20 once for Boston. Still, in eight Red Sox seasons, when age and arm problems limited his effectiveness, Grove had an excellent 105–62 mark and led the league four times in earned run average during a great period for hitters in a great park for sluggers. He was an All-Star five straight years for the Sox.

After Montreal's AstroTurf ruined his knees and Wrigley Field's friendly confines restored his career, **Andre Dawson** landed on the soft grass of Fenway Park. Though well compensated—his $4.8-million salary was the highest on the team in 1993—the eight-time Gold Glove winner was relegated mostly to designated hitter in Boston. "The Hawk" hit just 29 home runs over two Sox seasons before concluding his Hall of Fame career in his native Miami with the Marlins.

It's a good thing that **Billy Goodman**'s uniform number wasn't determined by his field position. In 1950, he won the American League batting title (with a .354 average), but he was a player without a fixed location. He played all four infield positions, and 45 games in the outfield, too. He was a hot hitter on a hot-hitting team—so sizzling was his bat that when Ted Williams came back from his elbow injury, Johnny Pesky (batting .310) volunteered to take himself out of the Sox lineup so that Goodman (hitting .350 at the time) could accumulate enough at-bats to qualify for the batting title. Pesky's selflessness paid off, and Goodman won the crown. Over 11 seasons with the Red Sox, Goodman hit .306 (Pesky batted .313).

From 1963–1990, #10 belonged to backstops, starting with **Bob Tillman** and **Jerry Moses**, and then—for pretty much all of two decades—**Bob Montgomery** and **Rich Gedman**. "Geddy" (rarely confused with the lead singer of Canadian rock group Rush) hit .259 in his 11 seasons with the Sox, with highs in homers coming with 24 in 1984 and in average with .295 in 1985. He was behind the plate in the bottom of the 10th inning of Game Six of the 1986 World Series, when a ball went astray and allowed the Mets to tie the game. Was it a wild pitch (as the record shows) or a passed ball? The debate continues to this day.

In more recent years, **Scott Hatteberg** caught with #10 on his back (1997–2001) after breaking in with #30 and then #47. He caught more games than any other Sox catcher in 1997 and 1998, but he was strictly a backup the other years. He was traded to the Rockies for Pokey Reese on December 19, 2001, only to find himself "granted free agency" just two days later. Hatteberg reinvented himself as a first baseman with Oakland—where much ink was devoted to his superior batting eye in *Moneyball*—and he later played in Cincinnati. His average improved each time he moved to a new team, and don't tell Michael Lewis or Billy Beane, but his OBP and OPS (on-base plus slugging) were higher in Boston than Oakland. August 6, 2001, was his most dramatic day with the Red Sox: In back-to-back at-bats, he lined into a triple play, then hit a game-winning grand slam.

When **Carlos Baerga** joined Boston in 2002 after making the team as a spring training invitee, it presented an odd situation. He was himself owner of a ballclub in Puerto Rico, Los Vaqueros de Bayamon. He was a teammate of Rey Sanchez with the Red Sox but was Sanchez's employer in Bayamon.

For three wartime seasons, the Red Sox were right-hander **Pinky Woods**'s employer (13–21, 3.97 ERA), but those were the days when ballplayers needed to take other jobs in the offseason. "In 17 seasons of pro ball I've held roughly 34 offseason jobs," Pink once told *Baseball*

Digest. "I have been an agent for Yellow Cabs, installed a landscape sprinkling system, operated a restaurant, worked for Railway Express, been a librarian, a short-order cook, offered gift suggestions, held an apprentice license at a pharmacy, acted in movies, been a scenario writer, and become the recognized crossword puzzle expert of the Pacific Coast League." Ultimately, he found steady post-baseball work as a public relations man for a bank in Los Angeles.

Sox fans visiting Toronto had as long a look as you're likely to ever have of a home run hitter's jersey number, when **Tony Graffanino** took more than five minutes to complete his home run trot after hitting one out on September 14, 2005. Baserunner Gabe Kapler blew out his Achilles tendon running around second base, before it was clear that Graffanino had hit a home run. Once Kapler was taken out, and a courtesy runner inserted, Tony's trot resumed.

MOST OBSCURE RED SOX PLAYER TO WEAR #10—Rick Lancellotti had 5,394 minor league at-bats and briefly played for San Diego and San Francisco, but he was only with the Red Sox for four games in August 1990. Over the first three games, the first baseman handled 22 chances flawlessly. The 34-year-old Providence native got eight at-bats but didn't collect a hit and fanned three of his last four times up. In his final game, he didn't have an official at-bat but drove in a run with a pinch-hit sacrifice fly. He even pitched an inning for Pawtucket that same year; he'd pitched previously for Class AAA Hawaii . . . eight years earlier.

Hats Off

To Bob Montgomery, who flew airplanes and already had the dangerous job of catching professionally for the Red Sox, wearing a hat when he batted wasn't a big deal. But after his first year in the major leagues, the rules officially changed. In 1971, two years before the designated hitter became the law of the land in the American League, the major leagues passed a rule that all players must wear a helmet to bat. It sounds like—ahem—a no-brainer, but at the time sports headgear was not universal. In the far more dangerous National Hockey League, where goalies had only started wearing masks in 1959 due to resistance from hardliners like

Canadiens coach Toe Blake (who thought it restricted vision), helmets were not mandated for all skaters until 1979.

A "grandfather rule" allowed Montgomery to wear just a plastic liner inside his cap when he batted, though it didn't offer anywhere near the same protection as a fused plastic helmet. Starting Boston catcher Carlton Fisk not only wore a helmet in the field, he used a helmet with a left ear flap when he batted (this added protection over the ear was not made mandatory until 1983—also with a grandfather clause). As backup to a perennial All-Star, Montgomery's in-game exposure was relatively low. His last season with 100 plate appearances was 1975 and he was hit by only seven pitches during his career, including just once in his final four seasons. When Montgomery batted for the last time—bouncing into a double play on September 9, 1979—the helmet-less era for batters ended. He'd outlasted the other two players who'd used the grandfather rule to bat with a hat: Detroit's Norm Cash (final at-bat in 1974) and the last National League holdout, Philadelphia's Tony Taylor (1976).

Montgomery loved playing in Boston. According to author Bruce Markusen, Monty often told the press that he preferred being a backup for the Sox to starting in other cities. His loyalty was rewarded as Sox color commentator for 14 seasons on TV38 and he still occasionally appears on NESN.

#11: Fate Both Good and Bad

Two of the biggest hits in Red Sox history came off the bat of third baseman **Bill Mueller** in 2004. The first was his July 24 home run off Mariano Rivera in the bottom of the ninth inning, catapulting the Red Sox over the Yankees for a dramatic 11–10 win that some felt turned the season around for the Red Sox. This was the same game in which Jason Varitek and Alex Rodriguez got into it, kicking off a bench-clearing brawl immortalized in photos of Tek's glove in A-Rod's face which hang on many a Sox fan's wall. The second came in Game Four of the ALCS against those same Yankees. Facing elimination and looking at a sweep, it was the bottom of the ninth and the Sox were, once again, facing Rivera. Kevin Millar walked, pinch runner Dave Roberts stole second base, and Mueller singled in Roberts to tie the game. The Sox won in the 12th on a David Ortiz home run and never lost again in '04. Though he won a batting title for the Sox in 2003, Mueller will always be remembered in Boston for those two moments.

A couple of big games stand out in the brief visits that **Rico Brogna** (2000) and **Hideo Nomo** (2001) paid Boston. August 14, 2000: Turners Falls, Massachusetts, native Brogna, who had grown up fantasizing himself as Carl Yastrzemski or Carlton Fisk, was playing in just his 10th game with the Red Sox. He'd entered the game as a pinch runner in the eighth, but he was stranded in a 3–3 game. He stayed in at first base and came up to bat, hitting .188, in the bottom of the ninth after Tampa Bay intentionally walked two batters to face him with the bases loaded. With two outs and two strikes . . . you guessed it: grand slam. Nomo's biggest game was his first start for Boston. On April 4, 2001, Nomo struck out 11 and walked three in Baltimore—and he did not allow a hit. Nomo's no-no put him in company with numberless but timeless Sox alum Cy Young as one of five pitchers to hurl a no-hitter in each league.

Among the most beloved #11s, each to a different generation, were **Frank Malzone** and **Tim Naehring**.

A member of the Red Sox Hall of Fame, Bronx native Malzone signed with the Red Sox at age 17. He progressed through the minors, debuting late in 1955 (going 6-for-10 his first day as a starter in a September 20 doubleheader against the Orioles), but Malzone only became a first-string player in 1957. He won the first three Gold Gloves ever awarded at third base (1957–59), and was named to eight All-Star squads. His .292 average was 10th in the league that year and he finished seventh in the MVP tally. Malzone generally hit in the middle of the order, batting .276 (.296 at Fenway) and hitting 131 home runs in 11 seasons in Boston. A steady anchor at the hot corner, he played in 150 or more games seven straight years and led the league in double plays for a third baseman for five straight seasons. His 1,270 putouts top all Sox third sackers, 105 more than Wade Boggs.

Naehring thought a lot of his time in Boston. He constructed a 90-percent-to-scale replica of Fenway Park in Miamitown, Ohio. Though he later became head of player development for his hometown Reds, Naehring spent his entire professional playing career with the Red Sox—eight seasons in Boston, batting .282 and driving in an even 250 runs. Though star-crossed and injury-prone, Naehring was versatile; he played all four infield positions, mostly third base post-Boggs. **Alex Gonzalez** played just one infield spot—shortstop—but he played it exceptionally well whether he was wearing

#11 in 2006 or #13 in 2009. He committed only five errors in '06 for a .985 fielding percentage which stands as the best for his position in team history—even better than the man he wore #11 to honor: **Luis Aparicio**.

Unfortunately, one of the worst moments of Aparicio's Hall of Fame career came with the Red Sox. A strike had delayed the start of the 1972 season, and the truncated schedule played out with some teams playing a different number of games. That came back to bite Boston on October 2. In the top of the third against the Tigers, Aparicio was on first base when Carl Yastrzemski hit what would have been a triple had Luis not stumbled rounding third. Scrambling to get back to the bag, he found Yaz there and Yaz was ruled out. The Sox lost the game and—two days later—the division title, by a half-game, to the Tigers. Aparicio played one more year, and though it was the only one of his three Boston seasons when he wasn't an All-Star, he had his best Sox season with the bat: hitting .271, with 49 RBIs and 13 steals in 14 tries at age 39. Aparicio's #11 is retired throughout his native Venezuela.

Dave Stapleton will largely be remembered for two reasons. First, he'll be remembered for what he didn't do: play late-inning defense at first base when the Sox were trying to close out Game Six of the 1986 World Series at Shea Stadium. Mookie Wilson's grounder to first base should have been a routine play—and who knows what might have happened if they'd kept playing in the 11th inning and beyond. Second, for having one of the more unusual progressions in batting average over the years:

1980: .321
1981: .285
1982: .264
1983: .247
1984: .231
1985: .227
1986: .128

Going, going, gone .... After the 1986 Series, he never came back to the majors (though another Dave Stapleton, a pitcher, began his brief career the following year for Milwaukee).

Completing a trio of sorts, after Dom DiMaggio pulled a muscle trying to stretch an eighth-inning game-tying double into a triple in Game Seven of the 1946 World Series, **Leon Culberson** took over for Dom. Culberson was in center field in the bottom of the eighth when Harry Walker hit a ball that allowed Enos Slaughter to make a "mad dash" from first to home on what should have been a routine single. Had the swift and accomplished DiMaggio been in center field, Slaughter never would have dared, and history might have worked out other than it did.

Clay Buchholz, of course, has been something of an enigma for Red Sox fans. A first-round pick in 2005, he threw a no-hitter at Fenway Park in his second major-league start, on September 1, 2007. He's 73–51 with a 3.85 in nine seasons for Boston but it seems as though in odd-numbered years he's unable to pitch a full complement of innings due to extended stays on the disabled list.

MOST OBSCURE RED SOX PLAYER TO WEAR #11—Kim Andrew, part of the 1975 pennant-winning Red Sox, can look back at his major league career and say that he got on base every time up, never made an error, and batted .500 in the big leagues. That and 1,000 lire might have bought him a cup of espresso in Italy, which is where he was playing two years later. Andrew played just two major league games, both against the Yankees. The first was at Yankee Stadium on April 16, filling in at second base in the ninth inning and seeing no action. On April 19, the Yanks had an 11–0 lead after six innings so he was given a chance to play at Fenway. First time up, he reached on a fielder's choice. Second time up, he had an infield single in the bottom of the ninth, but it was not part of a miracle comeback. He was on base when the Sox spoiled Pat Dobson's shutout before a Bernie Carbo double play ended the game. Andrew was sent to Pawtucket to get more playing time, but he sprained his ankle badly and was sent lower down the ladder until he eventually wound up in Italy. After saying "ciao" to baseball, he began working as a FedEx driver and put in more than 25 years with the company.

How Low Can You Go?

There's long been a sense among amateur jersey numerologists that the lower the numeral, the more appealing the uniform number is to ballplayers. In other words, there's a tendency to select the lowest number available unless there's a compelling reason (say, avoidance of #13).

We decided to try to statistically analyze this data and see if there is any demonstrable "downward pressure." Tossing out the myriad reasons why a player would prefer one number over another—that's a subject for another survey—we looked at every Red Sox player who changed numbers at one point or another during his stay with the club. We acknowledge that the decision regarding assignment of numbers is often not a choice made by the player and there is also lot of randomness involved in the process, taking into account seniority, numbers worn for past teams, favorite numbers, and we could go on . . . that is, after all, what this book is for.

How many Red Sox players changed to a lower number, and how many changed to a higher number? Looking at every instance in which a player's number changed, either within the course of a season or in successive years, we found 340 instances that met these criteria. In 210 instances, the second of the two numbers was lower; in 130 instances, the second number was higher. So, given the chance, 62 percent went low.

There were some instances in which a player played in non-consecutive seasons. Michael Coleman, for example, played in 1997 and then again in 1999. He played as #44 the first time and #40 the second time. Such non-consecutive instances were not counted among the 340, but there were 39 cases in which a player's second stint was just one year later (in other words, only one year was skipped between stints). In 25 of those cases, the number in the second stint was lower. Again, even taking this expanded circumstance into account, it appeared there was a statistically significant downward trend.

What's it all mean? Players generally prefer lower uniform numbers . . . or at least the fellows doling out the jerseys do.

#12: Cheaper by the Dozen

The major league leader for most home runs hit by a pitcher is **Wes Ferrell**, #12 for the Red Sox, with 37 career homers. Four times he had two-homer games for the Sox, and on July 21 and 22, 1935, he won back-to-back games with home runs, the first of the two as a pinch hitter. A tempestuous player—even with his brother Rick serving as his catcher for much of his time in Boston—Wes once knocked himself unconscious with a punch to his own head, and another time walked off the mound in the midst of a game (much to the displeasure of manager Joe Cronin). Wes was 62–40 for Boston.

Earl Johnson was a true war hero. Unlike many ballplayers who played exhibition baseball during World War II, Johnson served in the Battle of the Bulge and was awarded a Bronze Star, a Bronze Star with cluster, and a Silver Star, also receiving a battlefield commission promoting him from sergeant to lieutenant. After the war, trading in #20 for #12, the swingman southpaw became the first Red Sox pitcher in 28 years to win a World Series game and the first ever to do so wearing a number. Johnson took over the number from outfielder **Pete Fox**, a 1944 All-Star who played in Boston for the last five years of a major league career he'd begun in 1933. Fox hit a solid .289 for the Red Sox. Bellhorn's .980 fielding percentage at second base for the Sox helped solidify a somewhat shaky infield.

An understated, quiet hero of another sort was **Pumpsie Green**. He had the honor—but also bore the brunt—of being the first African American ballplayer on the last major league team to integrate (sadly, that team was the Boston Red Sox). Pumpsie debuted in the majors on July 21, 1959—more than a dozen years after Jackie Robinson first played for Brooklyn and more than 2 1/2 years after Robinson had retired. All Pumpsie ever wanted was to be a ballplayer—not a symbol or someone to rally around. Pumpsie played four years for the Red Sox, hitting .244 as a middle infielder before being traded to the Mets as part of a swap bringing **Felix Mantilla** to Boston. "Felix the Cat" assumed the #12 mantle from 1963 through 1965, playing infield and outfield and hitting .287 with 54 homers during the three seasons. The next to wear the number was **Jose Tartabull**, an under-performing member of the 1967 Impossible Dream team with an occasional flair for the dramatic. Tartabull's steal of second on Opening Day led to the fifth run in a 5–4 win over the White Sox. He is best remembered as the father of Danny Tartabull (who hit 260 more home runs than his dad), but Jose made one throw in Boston that lives on: a game-ending outfield assist to Elston Howard at the plate on August 27. The double play ensured a 4–3 win (also over Chicago) at a key point in the season.

"Whistlin' Jake" Wade was a pitcher the Sox hoped would break big in 1939. He didn't, but he did bring a colorful nickname to the ballpark. The North Carolinian enjoyed imitating birds. As a sportswriter from Detroit once wrote, "He whistles like a mockingbird and he pitches like a kangaroo." Wade, not known for his control, didn't even last the full year—in 47 2/3 innings, he allowed 105 baserunners and posted a 6.23 ERA before flying away to the St. Louis Browns for cash.

One of the more infamous players to wear #12 was **Stan Papi**. He arrived a couple of months after the Sox had lost the bitter one-game playoff to the Yankees in 1978. In early December, the Sox sent left-handed pitcher Bill Lee to the Expos for Papi, a utility infielder who wasn't utilized all that much. He had been hitting around .230 for Montreal and had yet to homer in almost 200 career at-bats. He homered once for Boston and hit .188. Bill Lee had been 94–68 with a 3.62 ERA for the Red Sox, but "The Spaceman" was too much a free spirit and didn't suit the Red Sox management of the day. Papi's days in Boston were also numbered. He played all of one inning at third base in 1980 before he was traded to the Phillies several weeks into the season. (He was the "player to be named later" in a trade that brought Boston one year's part-time work from Dave Rader.) Papi wasn't part of the answer in Philadelphia, either; he was sold to Detroit before ever suiting up with the Phillies.

A quarterback's number in football, #12 seemed like a journeyman's number at Fenway—the majority of wearers from **Russ Scarritt** (1931) to **Dave Sax** (1987) held it for a year or less. Then it landed on the back of first-round draft pick **Ellis Burks**. The 22-year-old center fielder won the hearts of Boston fans from the start, and played for six seasons (1987–92) before being released. His best years followed in the National League, hitting over .300 in eight years with the Rockies and the Giants (in 1996, Burks led the league in total bases, slugging, and runs while hitting .344). He was a 1990 All-Star for the Red Sox, and when he returned to Boston briefly at the beginning of 2004, it was a feel-good moment for Sox fans. Burks—who wore #25 on his return—hit only .182 in 2004 with just one RBI (a game-tying homer), though he returned at the end of the year and had the rare distinction of his last two career at-bats coming in the same inning on October 2 in Baltimore. He was not on the postseason roster, but Boston's season ended wonderfully and Burks wound up with a world championship ring 18 seasons after he debuted for the Olde Towne Team.

Wil Cordero was, to be kind, troubled, and he was a player the Sox more or less had to shed. His 1996 season showed some promise, as did the first half of 1997, and Cordero was the first to hit a homer off the Coke bottles that for several years were fastened to one of the light stanchions atop the Green Monster. On June 11, 1997, however, he was arrested for assaulting his wife, Ana, with a telephone receiver and choking her. For game after game after his first two weeks back he was booed in Boston, until a key home run temporarily turned the boos to cheers. His wife tried to have the charges dropped, but the district attorney declined and Cordero was sentenced to a 90-day suspended prison term. In the end, the Sox felt they had no choice but to release him after the season. He played eight more seasons for five more teams.

Cordero's uniform number went to third-base coach **Wendell Kim**, a fan favorite for the way he *ran* to and from his position, but who became known as "Wave 'em In" Wendell for his aggressive approach toward sending baserunners home in hope of scoring. **Jed Lowrie** had a pivotal role in one of the happier waving episodes in recent Fenway memory when the rookie shortstop's single in the bottom of the ninth scored Jason Bay just ahead of the throw to clinch the 2008 Division Series against the Angels. (DeMarlo Hale was the coach waving Bay home.)

Of second baseman (and Boston native) **Mark Bellhorn**, the *Wall Street Journal*'s Darren Everson once wrote, "After posting a miserable .264 slugging percentage for his previous team, the Colorado Rockies, he was such an afterthought before the 2004 season that he was acquired by the Red Sox for a player to be named later—who was never named." The deal wound up being for cash. It couldn't have worked out much better for the Red Sox. Although he led the league in strikeouts with 177, Bellhorn came up with the big hit on several occasions. A .264 hitter—his slugging boosted to .444—he drove in 82 runs and scored 93 in 2004. During Boston's quest to overcome an 0–3 deficit dealt them by the Yankees in the ALCS, Bellhorn's three-run homer in the fourth inning of Game Six was the game-winning hit after the umpires conferred and ruled it a homer instead of a double— the first of two rightfully overturned calls that night (saints, and umps, be praised). By the time he hit another homer in the eighth inning of Game Seven the next night, the Sox already had an 8–3 lead and the Stadium was emptying of Yankees fans.

Bellhorn's two-run homer in the bottom of the eighth during Game One of the World Series against the Cardinals broke a 9–9 tie and won the game. He hit .300 in the Series. Released in August 2005, Mark was scooped up by the Yankees but only hit for .118 for them. His later play for the Padres and the Reds wasn't much better, but he will long be remembered in Boston for his contributions to the long-awaited world championship.

Mike Napoli was another #12 who played a big role in a World Series win, in 2013. He had one of the bushiest beards of that year's crew, and also drove in 92 runs during the regular season and seven more in the postseason, kicking off the World Series with a three-RBI double in the first inning of Game 1.

MOST OBSCURE RED SOX PLAYER TO WEAR #12—Lee Graham played three games in center field in 1983 with five putouts and one assist, but his best attempts to get a hit came to naught. He pinch-ran for Dwight Evans and scored in each of his first two games, but when he reached on an error in his first major league at-bat, he was thrown out stealing. Later in the game, he reached on another error—bunting home Chico Walker from third. He might have received credit for an RBI had the sacrifice been fielded cleanly, but he was robbed by the official scorer, who seemed determined to see that Lee never got a hit. He didn't. He got an RBI on a sac fly, but his last two opportunities ended up as mere outs.

Who's This Boob in Skip's Uniform?

How is it that **Eric McNair**—"Boob" to his friends—wore #4 during 1936? We don't know, but there really isn't much question about it. Number historian Mark Stang has 11 different Red Sox scorecards from 1936 and McNair's #4 (along with player–manager Joe Cronin's #6) is on every one of them. In 1937, the numbers are reversed on the 15 scorecards Mark has. McNair had worn #6 while with the Philadelphia Athletics (1933–35). Carl Reynolds had worn #6 for the Red Sox in 1935. Reynolds was traded to Washington in December 1935, so #6 was available. McNair was acquired by the Red Sox in January 1936, and presumably could have been offered the available #6. But instead Cronin—who as manager presumably had his way—took #6 (the shortstop's position) and had McNair wear #4. Maybe Cronin's subpar and injury-filled 1936 season grated on him and he wanted his old number back (he'd previously worn #4 with Washington). Cronin thus told McNair to take #6.

Cronin's biographer, Mark Armour (*Joe Cronin; A Life in Baseball*), offers an educated guess: Cronin switched to #6 when he dropped himself in the order. He moved back to cleanup in 1937, and stayed there until Ted Williams arrived. It could have been a superstition thing, too, as he had had an off-year in 1935, and an even worse year in 1936. The switch back to #4 coincided with a five-year run that saw Cronin hit .307 with 99 homers and 517 RBIs. McNair hit .292 in '37 and was traded to the White Sox two years later.

#13: Just Plain Unlucky

There's a long-standing cross-cultural superstition that 13 is unlucky. That belief is so prevalent that there's even a word for the fear of the number: triskaidekaphobia (harder to spell than even Mientkiewicz). The superstition is traceable back to ancient Persia, and likely didn't start there. Other numbers—for instance, four—have prompted other phobias; we understand that numerous Asian hotels will not have a fourth floor just as many American hotels will not have a 13th floor.

Given the avoidance of #13 from 1931 through 1989 (only three players wore it, and none of them for more than a season), the fact that the number has been worn almost continuously since 1990 is remarkable by contrast. Most of that time—a full decade—it was occupied by **John Valentin**. Val was a fifth-round Red Sox draft pick in 1988, a shortstop (and frequent third baseman) who hit .281 in 991 games for Boston.

In the postseason, Valentin shone, accumulating a .347 batting average in 72 at-bats, including two homers and seven RBIs in the record-setting 23–7 shellacking administered to the Indians in Game Four of the 1999 ALDS. And he's got an unassisted triple play to his credit. On July 8, 1994, at Fenway, he caught Marc Newfield's line drive, stepped on second, and tagged out Seattle's Keith Mitchell coming from first base. He was the ninth major leaguer to execute an unassisted regular-season triple play.

Bob "Fats" Fothergill was the first Sox player to wear #13, a number he brought over from the White Sox, where he'd worn it in

1932. Standing 5-feet, 11-inches, he's listed with a playing weight of 230 pounds. His shape must've been ideal for hitting—in 3,269 at-bats over 12 seasons, he hit for a .325 average, four times hitting above .350. The last season of his career was the one he played for the Red Sox, hitting .344 in '33, albeit in only 32 primarily pinch-hitting at-bats. Bill Ballou's list of Red Sox jersey numbers shows Skinny Graham as wearing #13 in 1934, but a thorough perusal of Boston newspapers on microfilm for the 14 games the Sox played once Skinny joined the team didn't find anything to either confirm or deny the number. Too bad—Bill was right to always love the idea that the number transitioned from Fats to Skinny . . . and it would've provided 13 Sox, instead of 12, who've worn #13. Triskaidekaphobia wins again.

Elden Auker was a bit of an odd duck as a pitcher. After six years of relative success with the Tigers, the submariner was part of a five-player trade in December 1938 in which the Red Sox unloaded Pinky Higgins (but not for good—see Chapter #5). Auker came to Boston with a record of 77–52 and a 4.26 ERA. He was only with the Sox for one year, but he developed a lifelong friendship with rookie Ted Williams and a number of other members of the 1939 team. He was a disappointing 9–10 (5.36 ERA) for Boston and sent to the St. Louis Browns in a cash transaction. He won 44 games over the next three years for the lowly Browns. He'd worn #13 for three years in Detroit. Although one book reports him as wearing #12 at one point for the Red Sox, this has not been verified. Thirteen extant score-cards with dates throughout the course of the season all show Auker wearing #13.

After Auker, no one wore #13 for 46 years, until **Reid Nichols** found it. It took him a few years to get to it, though. He spent four years coming up in the Red Sox system before making his debut in 1980, and from then through 1984, he wore #51—and had that number longer than anyone in Red Sox history. But in 1985, all of a sudden, he took on #13. His batting average had been dropping rapidly, from .302 to .285 to .226. We asked him why he changed numbers, and his response was succinct: "I'm not superstitious. Looking for a change." One thing changed: after appearing in 21 games, the Red Sox sent him to the White Sox for Tim Lollar. Nichols wore #20 in Chicago, and the change of Sox seemed to help at first, but then his average plunged almost 70 points in 1986.

Twice a New York Yankee (1997 and 2005) and implicated in a mid-game hair-cutting scandal as a Met (2003), **Rey Sanchez** was a .272 career hitter in nearly 1,500 games for nine teams. He played with the Red Sox in 2002: 100 games at second base and 10 at shortstop, batting .286. Boston got a good deal out of Rey for $700,000; he made more than three times as much the year before as a Royal and almost double the amount the year after as a Met. Vilified in the New York press for receiving a clubhouse haircut—the barber was supposedly Armando Benitez—in the middle of a 2003 blowout loss in St. Louis, Sanchez and his coif were banished to Seattle.

When Framingham's **Lou Merloni** returned for a third stint with his hometown Red Sox in 2003, he considered equipment manager Joe Cochran's list of available numbers and noticed #13. Lou had played with John Valentin and admired him, so he selected #13. By then he'd already shuttled between Pawtucket and Boston numerous times, played every infield position plus left field in Boston (wearing #50 and then #26), played for the Yokohama Bay Stars in Japan's Central League in 2000, returned to the Red Sox (and hit .320 as a part-timer), spent two more years on the Pawtucket shuttle, been snagged off waivers by the Padres in March 2003, and acquired by the Red Sox again that August. It was his third time—they say it's the charm—that he hitched up #13 with his Sox.

He appeared in just 49 games for the Red Sox and only hit .215, but the name of **Doug Mientkiewicz** will forever be honored in the hearts of Sox fans for catching an easy flip from Keith Foulke, thereby recording the final out of the 2004 World Series. Countless snakebitten Sox hearts jumped a beat, though, waiting for the ball to traverse from Foulke's hand until it rested securely in Mientkiewicz's glove. So many things had gone wrong over the preceding 86 years that it would have been no surprise had Mientky missed the ball entirely, a rally followed, and the Cardinals won four straight to snatch the Series away from the Red Sox. It didn't happen, though. It was a routine out, and Mientkiewicz (who had only arrived in Boston minutes before the July 31 trading deadline in a complicated four-team trade that sent away Nomar Garciaparra) found himself holding a prized souvenir. He held on to the ball, too, and became embroiled in a controversy over who truly owned the ball that clinched the World Series. In the end, a deal was worked out whereby he donated the ball to the Hall of Fame. In January 2005, the Red Sox sent Mientky and some money to the Mets for a proverbial—and far less valuable—bag of balls.

Immediately after Mientkiewicz, another #13 joined the team, Venezuelan first baseman–outfielder **Roberto Petagine**, who'd surfaced with four National League teams before spending six seasons in Japanese baseball from 1999 through 2004. He toiled in Pawtucket in 2005, hitting .327, and joined Boston in early August, batting .281 in 18 games. Beloved by the baseball cognoscenti for his high on-base percentage—.345 in the majors, which looked especially good when compared to his .227 career batting average—Roberto left Theo wanting and was released in spring training 2006. He had a final fling of low BA and high OBP in Seattle.

Alex Cora, a steady, reliable utility infielder, came to Boston from Cleveland in July 2005. He had started wearing #23 but moved to #13 during the 2006 season. In parts of four seasons, he hit .252 for the Red Sox. Once it seemed that Jed Lowrie had what it took to be a regular in the Red Sox infield, Cora's days were numbered. A badly injured left wrist kept Lowrie on the shelf for most of 2009, and the Sox reacquired **Alex Gonzalez**. His former #11 was already taken, so he selected #13. It wasn't considered an unlucky number in Venezuela, he said. Quite the contrary, it's been the lucky 13, worn by shortstop greats such as Davey Concepcion and Ozzie Guillen, among others.

When reliever **Billy Wagner** joined the Red Sox in late August, though, Gonzalez gave up #13, dropping the "1" and playing as #3. For his part, Wagner struck out the side in the first inning he pitched, on August 30. His 1.98 ERA in 15 games was good but his 18.00 ERA in two postseason appearances was more ugly than unlucky.

While with Tampa Bay, **Carl Crawford** had always seemed to tear apart the Red Sox—with his speed as a baserunner, his fielding, and his offense. He'd hit for a .296 average over his nine years with the Rays. "Why can't we get players like that?" fans wondered. And then they did. Coming off an All-Star season when he ranked seventh in MVP voting, suddenly his batting average plunged more than 50 points and he was the picture of "uncomfortableness" in Boston. When he was dealt to the Dodgers at the trading deadline in 2012, after only appearing in 31 games, there were few tears shed.

The next player to wear the number was **Hanley Ramirez**, in his second stint with the Red Sox (he'd had two at-bats in 2005 and struck out both times—that was the fullness of his prior role). He'd gone on to be Rookie of the Year the very next year—2006, for the Marlins—and NL batting champion (.342) in 2009, second in MVP voting. He was a career .300 hitter—who hit .248 in 2015, when he returned to the Red Sox. After July 5, he hit all of one home run. This from the man some thought could supplant David Ortiz as DH for the Red Sox.

MOST OBSCURE RED SOX PLAYER TO WEAR #13—A native of Ware, Massachusetts, this first baseman had a name that made him sound like a lumbering slugger from southwest Louisiana: **Billy Jo Robidoux**. He played part-time for Milwaukee and the White Sox, flirting with the Mendoza Line over 424 at-bats. Billy Jo was released by Chicago and signed by Boston in time for the 1990 season. He got into 27 games, accumulated 44 at-bats, hit one homer, drove in four runs, and batted .182.

Boston's Dirty Laundry

One person has sewn on the numbers of Red Sox uniforms for the last 40 years. Her name is Valentina Federico and since 1969 she's worked in a nondescript single-story block building on a side street in Somerville, not far from Ball Square. She walks to work each day from her home in Medford, and has done so since the first year both Billy and Tony Conigliaro played for the Sox. She's sewn on numbers for Yaz, Fisk, Dewey, Roger, and Pedro, for Papi and Manny, for Rice, Lynn, and El Tiante, for Johnny Pesky as a coach, for every member of the 2004 and 2007 world champion Red Sox, for "cup of coffee" players, and for the stars of several eras.

She couldn't be more unassuming, and still speaks with a strong Italian accent despite her many years in America. Working with "Vally" the last 31 years has been Neil DeTeso of Riddell All American, who has himself seen the company change hands more than once. We joined Neil at 5:30 A.M. on September 30 at Fenway's Gate D, as he pulled his Econoline van into the ballpark and picked up all the dirty uniforms—both the Blue Jays and Red Sox—from the night before. Neil has some 70 or 80 accounts in the Greater Boston area, mostly high schools and colleges, but he handles the Red Sox and Patriots as well. Around 6 AM, he pulled his van into the Somerville facility and we climbed out. He piled the jerseys and pants into a Star Market shopping cart and brought them inside to the washers and dryers.

Dustin Pedroia's pants had almost an inch-long tear in them, and some infield dirt on them. And pine tar. Pedroia and Kevin Youkilis are the "pine tar kids," Neil says. Facility manager Frank Marshall sprays Mr. Clean Febreze on the affected areas, then uses a high-pressure water hose to blow out the dirt and pine tar. Nomar Garciaparra had patch after patch put on his pants, but DeTeso says that Jose Canseco was the Sox player who was the roughest on uniforms.

Placed on top of the dirty laundry back in the clubhouse was a blank Red Sox jersey, size 48, and a large manila envelope from clubhouse man Pookie Jackson. Inside was a note saying that reliever Billy Wagner needed a new shirt, plus two numerals: a "1" and a "3."

Neil took the blank jersey and the numbers—made of tackle twill, with an adhesive backing—and placed the jersey on a small metal heat press. He positioned the numbers four inches down from the soutache on the back of the white home jersey, centering them. "Ten seconds at 375 degrees," he said, and the adhesive fixed the two numbers in place. He brought the jersey to Valentina who then used her sewing machine to stitch both numbers more firmly onto the shirt. It was then placed in a clear plastic bag and hung on a rack awaiting delivery back to the Red Sox clubhouse.

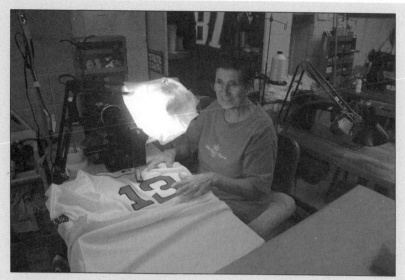

Valentina Federico has sewn on Red Sox numbers since before #13, Billy Wagner, was born.

The numbers used to be cut out of felt, and were stacked—a red number on top of a blue one, with the slightly larger blue one providing a border around the red numeral. Some of the old numbers were thick, almost like carpeting. Neil remembered how heavy the old Boston Bruins numbers were: "Those numbers, they would stand up by themselves."

The Sox had sent 37 jerseys and 50 pairs of pants that morning—luckily, September call-ups don't play enough to get that dirty. Valentina darned a patch onto the inside of Pedroia's pants. They were all washed and dried—as were the Jays jerseys—and all placed back in the van. At 8:30 in the morning, we drove back to Fenway, dropping off the clean uniforms in their respective clubhouses. In 31 years, DeTeso has never lost a jersey. The only time he returned one in less than improved condition was when one of Rick Dempsey's jerseys somehow got shredded in the dryer; he returned the evidence.

As of 2015, DeTeso still handles the cleaning and repairs, but a woman in Woburn does the actual sewing of the numbers.

#14: At Last

For future generations, #14 will forever be identified with **Jim Ed Rice**, Hall of Fame left fielder for the Sox from 1974 through 1989, when a deterioration of his vision brought his career to a sooner-than-anticipated conclusion. For a solid decade, he was one of the most feared sluggers in the game. Three times he led the American League in homers (39 in 1977, 46 in 1978, and 39 again in 1983), and twice he led in RBIs (139 in 1978 and 126 in 1983). The 406 total bases he recorded in his MVP year of 1978 were the most by any right-handed hitter since Joe DiMaggio, 41 years earlier. Had the rookie Rice not had his wrist broken by a pitch on September 21—less than three weeks before the 1975 World Series—there's every chance that the Red Sox would have prevailed in a Series that ran seven games.

Rice made everyone forget about **Ken Holcombe** and **Bill Werle**, **Bill Spanswick**, **Bob Duliba**, and even **George Smith**. The first four were pitchers with combined stats of 7–7 during the time with the Sox; Smith was a middle infielder who hit .213 in 1966. No one had worn #14 since Rice left the fold, though he himself wore it for the six years he served as hitting coach. As clubbie Joe Cochran said, players know their history and no one was about to ask for Rice's number. A few days after Rice was inducted into the Hall of Fame, the number was retired at a ceremony. Like Carl Yastrzemski's #8, a Sox player had worn #14 every year in Sox history until Rice first put on the jersey. Now it will be worn no more. Officially.

Ben Oglivie wore #14 just before Rice, but he only hit .235 in his first three years and the Sox swapped him for Dick McAuliffe. Who knew he'd hit .276 for Detroit and Milwaukee, share the 1980 home run crown, and club 225 homers during his 13 years out of a Sox uniform? **Jerry Adair** was an important ingredient in the run the Red Sox made to claim the 1967 pennant. Dubbed "Mr. Clutch" by Boston broadcaster Ken Coleman, Adair filled in for the injured Rico Petrocelli for a month and hit so well the Sox kept him busy at three infield positions, batting .291. The Sox were playing one game over .500 (22–21) before Adair arrived but 70–49 after the June 2 trade that brought him from the White Sox, who wound up three games behind Boston and cursing their luck.

Ike Delock wore #14 for nine years, longer than anyone not named Rice. Ike was a right-hander who went 83–72 with a 4.01 ERA during the lackluster years of the 1950s. He started with #29, and wore both #12 and #15 in 1953, but after returning to the Red Sox from duty in the Marine Corps in 1955, he wore #14 for the rest of his time with the team.

Backup catcher **Matt Batts** had the best baseball name among the #14 alums (he wore #5 in 1947). **Tom Carey**, a middle infielder who had played regularly with the St. Louis Browns in 1936 and 1937, became a utilityman with the Red Sox.

Wartime absences opened up opportunities for players like **Johnny Lazor**, who played for the Red Sox from April 1943 until September 1946. When Lazor first came up, he wore #82—as high a number as there was for the 20th century Red Sox. He switched to #14 and kept it through the war years. He really didn't play much in '44 and his 29 at-bats and .138 average in '46 meant he wasn't a key cog for the pennant-winning Sox.

In 1934, **Fritz Ostermueller** led the league with a 3.49 ERA in a hit-happy year when the league-average ERA stood at 4.50. Pitching for the 76–76 Red Sox—their best record in more than a decade—Ostermueller managed only a 10–13 record. But that was wearing #19. He dropped five digits to #14 the next year and suffered several injuries. Though he got more work in 1936, his stats were disappointing

(10–16, 4.88), and in 1937 he went under the knife. When Ostermueller came back for three more seasons with Boston, he switched to #21.

We'll leave with the strange story of **Curt Fullerton**. Born in 1898 in Ellsworth, Maine, he debuted in the major leagues with the 1921 Red Sox, tossing 15 1/3 innings in four games. He had the misfortune of pitching for a team that was rarely out of last place, but he did pitch for five seasons—from 1921 through 1925. His annual W–L totals were 0–1, 1–4, 2–15, 7–12, and 0–3, but it's noteworthy that his ERA improved each year: 8.80, 5.46, 5.09, 4.32, and 3.18. And then his major league career ended. Or so it seemed. He had played in the Pacific Coast League for Hollywood and Portland through 1931 and began 1933 playing for the Roslindale team in the Boston Park League. The Red Sox needed another arm and signed Fullerton on August 21. He appeared in six games and threw 25 1/3 innings—his 8.53 ERA wasn't big league good, but he stuck with it, traversing the minors from 1934 to 1938 in Kansas City, Dallas, Galveston, and Monroe, Louisiana. And then called it a day.

MOST OBSCURE RED SOX PLAYER TO WEAR #14—Undefeated on the mound, hitless at the plate—such was the story of **Joe Mulligan**. The native of Weymouth was a 6-foot, 4-inch right-hander who joined the team right out of Holy Cross about a month before he turned 21, appearing in his first game in relief on June 28, 1934. Number 14 appeared in 14 games, starting two, and threw one complete game. He finished his lone season with a 1–0 record and a 3.63 ERA. Any anxiety he had about his first big league start probably dissipated when Boston put nine runs across before he took the mound at Comiskey Park. The final was 16–3. This strikeout-to-walk ratio was backward, walking more than twice as many batters (27) as he fanned (13). Mulligan struck out almost as many times as he struck out others, whiffing 10 of the 12 times he stepped to the plate.

Most Valuable Sox

The Red Sox have been well represented as American League Most Valuable Player, winning the award at least once per decade since it was first given annually by the Baseball Writers Association of America in the 1930s. Boston's unnumbered Tris Speaker won the 1912 Chalmers Award, a predecessor to the MVP. Not counting Speaker—like Jimmie Foxx, Ted Williams, Carl Yastrzemski, and Jim Rice, a member of the Hall of Fame—nine different Red Sox players have taken home the MVP . . . and nine different numbers have been honored.

Of note, the only multiple MVP in Sox history, Ted Williams, won the Triple Crown in 1942 and 1947 but did not get the MVP either year. Carl Yastrzemski won the MVP in 1967, when he achieved baseball's last Triple Crown. Fred Lynn produced a major league first by winning both the MVP and Rookie of the Year in 1975. Roger Clemens claimed both the Cy Young and MVP in 1986.

Player	Year	Pos	Uni
Jimmie Foxx	1938	1B	#3
Ted Williams	1946	LF	#9
Ted Williams	1949	LF	#9
Jackie Jensen	1958	RF	#4
Carl Yastrzemski	1967	LF	#8
Fred Lynn	1975	CF	#19
Jim Rice	1978	LF/DH	#14
Roger Clemens	1986	P	#21
Mo Vaughn	1995	1B	#42
Dustin Pedroia	2007	2B	#15

#15: Dustin and the Cowboy

A surprising 53 different ballplayers have worn #15 over the years, second only to #28 (worn by 61 players). But among the list, few were truly popular players save **Kevin Millar** (2003–05) and **Dustin Pedroia** (since 2007). Pedroia shed #64 in time for his official rookie year, and won the Rookie of the Year with ease, winning 24 of the 28 first-place votes on the strength of his .317 average, often-spectacular fielding, and general all-around hustle.

Dustin Pedroia

Pedroia got the Red Sox off on the right foot by leading off the 2007 World Series with a home run to start the Sox on a sweep of the Rockies.

Ricky Trlicek	1994
Mike Macfarlane	1995
Milt Cuyler	1996
Shane Mack	1997
Mark Lemke	1998
Donnie Sadler	1999–2000
Craig Grebeck	2001
Casey Fossum	2002
Kevin Millar	2003–05
Ron Jackson	2006 (coach)
Dustin Pedroia	2007–15
Number of times this number was issued: 53	
Longest tenure: 6 seasons, Joe Dobson	

No believer in the sophomore slump, "Pedey" bumped his average up to .326 in year two, increased his runs scored from 93 to a league-leading 118, and his RBIs from 50 to 83. Pedroia also led the league in hits (213) and doubles (54). He secured 16 of the 28 first-place votes for MVP, the first Boston player to win the award since 1995 and the first Sox middle infielder to ever do so. His third season was set up for a letdown, but it wasn't a far drop. He batted .296, smacked 48 doubles, led the AL with 115 runs, and was voted to start the All-Star Game—though he passed that up to be with his pregnant wife, Kelli, in the hospital.

Millar was both a cowboy and an idiot for Boston. Originator of the "Cowboy Up" mantra which seemed to inspire the Red Sox to an AL pennant drive in 2003 (derailed only at the last minute in Game Seven of the ALCS), Millar became one of the self-styled "idiots" who brought the Holy Grail home in 2004. Anaheim has its rally monkey, but Boston fans in 2003 had "Rally Karaoke Guy"—a homemade video of a teen-age college freshman Millar dancing (sort of) to Bruce Springsteen's "Born in the USA." The video had first been played before a July 29 team meeting in Texas, and the Sox scored 14 runs that night. It wasn't long before it made its way up onto the videoboard at Fenway.

Acquiring Millar had ruffled some feathers. Theo Epstein scooped him up after he'd been signed by Japan's Chunichi Dragons in a deal that saw the Dragons pledge a certain sum to Millar's club, the Florida Marlins. When the Marlins put Millar on waivers, Epstein made his move. There was some concern that the deal would be voided, but Chunichi settled its claims and Millar joined the Red Sox, where he was an outspoken, fun-loving first baseman who drove in 96 runs and hit 25 homers in his first year.

Pedroia and Millar even showed some one-upsmanship when it comes to #15. Pedroia wrote in his book, *Born to Play*: "The last player who wore 15, Kevin Millar, was a clown. I love that guy. Millar is awesome and every time we play against him, I tell him, Dude, I'm the real one-five." In the clubhouse in 2009, one could see a bat Millar presented to Pedroia, inscribed: "From a 2004 champ to a 2007 champ, keep 'one-five' proud with the lasers." The bat was signed, "The only 'one-five,' Kevin Millar."

The first two men to don #15 produced unusual results on offense. **Earl Webb** was an outfielder with the Red Sox who wore no number at all in 1930, and hit .323. When the team began wearing numerals in 1931, he got #15 and boosted his average to .333 but he also made a lasting mark in the major league record books by hitting 67 doubles. There were some who accused him of forgoing a handful of triples to add to his accumulating doubles total, but maybe he was just playing it safe. Webb hit 30 doubles in 1930 and 28 in 1932—those combined totals are nine shy of his '31 output. He never hit as many as 20 in any other year. No one has hit as many doubles since and it's worth remembering that Webb hit his 67 during the days when teams played a 154-game schedule. Less than three months into the following season, Webb was traded in a fitting two-for-one swap.

Dale Alexander was part of the return from the Tigers (along with Roy Johnson) for Webb. Alexander immediately responded to his new surroundings by becoming the first Red Sox hitter to win a batting title. Alexander had averaged .331 in the three seasons he'd played for Detroit but was in the doldrums in 1932, batting .250 over the first 23 games (only 16 at-bats). After arriving in Boston, the rangy first baseman caught fire, hitting .372 in 432 at-bats, creating a combined year-end average of .367, three points higher than Philadelphia's Jimmie Foxx. Alexander dropped to .281 the following year. He played nine more seasons in the minors but never returned to major league ball.

It was June 10, 1938. **Lefty Lefebvre** was a rookie Red Sox pitcher signed out of Holy Cross just the day before. He swung at the first major league pitch he ever saw and homered. It was the only pitch he saw all year long. His pitching wasn't as good that day; he gave up six earned runs in the game's final four innings, surrendering two home runs. He appeared in 87 games over four seasons—including two games at first base for the '44 Senators—but Lefty never hit another four-bagger.

Another ballplayer who had that one shining moment was **Billy Rohr**. His came on April 14, 1967, at Yankee Stadium. Rohr was just one out away from a no-hitter in his first major league start when New York catcher Elston Howard stroked a clean single to right field. Rohr retired the final batter to complete the one-hit shutout. He only won one more game for Boston. Ironically, he'd be in the minors by the time the "Impossible Dream" got going that summer while Howard became the Boston catcher after an August deal with the Yankees. Rohr pitched one more season in the majors—for the '68 Indians—and he later became a medical malpractice lawyer.

A Red Sox player with few shining moments was catcher **Marc Sullivan**. He appeared in two games in 1982, two more in 1984, and 133 between 1985–87, batting just .186 overall before he was traded to the Astros for minor leaguer Randy Randle. Neither player saw major league action from that point on. Though it might seem unfair to mention it, Marc's father, Haywood Sullivan, was Red Sox GM and part-owner at the time he first broke in with Boston.

Joe Dobson wore #15 longer than any other Sox player. He'd worn #17 and #19 in his first three years. He helped build ships during the war, then entered the army. He returned in time to join the 1946 pennant winners, going 13–7 with a 3.20 ERA. That set the stage for his best year, 1947 (18–8, 2.95). The right-hander won 106 games for the Red Sox against 72 defeats, posting a 3.57 ERA with Boston.

MOST OBSCURE RED SOX PLAYER TO WEAR #15—There is a subset of obscure Red Sox who wore #15 and shared surnames with U.S. presidents: **Deron Johnson**, coach **Ron Jackson**, and, believe it or not, two **Nixons**—**Willard** and **Russ**. The most obscure, however, shared his name with the 28th president. **Duane Wilson** signed with the Sox in 1952, and finally got his moment six years later. On July 3, 1958, the southpaw started against the Baltimore Orioles and escaped with only one run charged against him, despite giving up eight hits and five walks in six innings. His one official at-bat was a strikeout, though he also laid down a sacrifice bunt. On July 12, he started the second game of a doubleheader but got just one man out—on a sacrifice fly that drove in a run. Though he wound up not taking the loss, two days later the Red Sox called up rookie Bill Monbouquette and Wilson saw no further action.

Red Sox Rookies of Renown

Since the Baseball Writers Association of America first started presenting the Rookie of the Year in 1947, six Red Sox have won the award. Rookie of the Year went to one player throughout the major leagues its first two years—the inaugural award was won by Jackie Robinson, who'd been rejected by the Red Sox after a sham tryout in 1945. In 1950, Boston became the first city to sweep the award: Walt Dropo of the Red Sox and Boston Brave Sam Jethroe, who'd been spurned by the Sox at the same tryout as Robinson.

Carlton Fisk (1972) was the first Rookie of the Year to win the award unanimously. Nomar Garciaparra also won every first-place vote in 1997. Fred Lynn (1975) was the first player named Rookie of the Year and a league MVP the same season; Dustin Pedroia (2007) is the only other Sox to win those two awards in a career.

Player	Year	Pos	Uni
Walt Dropo	1950	1B	#3
Don Schwall	1961	P	#37
Carlton Fisk	1972	C	#27
Fred Lynn	1975	CF	#19
Nomar Garciaparra	1997	SS	#5
Dustin Pedroia	2007	2B	#15

Fenway Park laced up the skates on New Year's Day 2010 and put up a few numbers while they were at it for the NHL Winter Classic. In addition to those familiar Sox numbers, some retired numbers went up temporarily to honor that day's host—and winner—the Boston Bruins: #2 Eddie Shore, #3 Lionel Hitchman, #4 Bobby Orr, #5 Dit Clapper, #7 Phil Esposito, #8 Cam Neely, #9 John Bucyk, #15 Milt Schmidt, #24 Terry O'Reilly, and #77 Ray Bourque. As the Hanson Brothers said in *Slap Shot*, "Give 'em the old-time hockey!"

#16: Gentleman Jim Lonborg

Carl Yastrzemski was the offensive motor that drove the 1967 Impossible Dream team to Game Seven of the World Series; **Jim Lonborg** was Boston's wheel man. The 25-year-old right-hander came into that season with a 19–27 career record and was carried off the mound a conquering hero on the final day. He was an All-Star, Cy Young winner, and had a 22–9 mark, but that win on the last day against Minnesota was the biggest game for Boston since the Sox lost the last game of 1949 at Yankee Stadium to miss the pennant by a game. Lonborg pitched three times in the World Series—taking a no-hitter into the eighth in Game Two—before fading in the deciding game on short rest.

Though nicknamed "Gentleman Jim," he didn't mind pitching inside and led the league by hitting 19 batters that year, perhaps helping him lead with 246 strikeouts as well. Though he pitched over 2,400 innings in a 15-year career, an offseason skiing accident that winter may have deprived him of having a spectacular career. He attended Tufts Dental School after his career ended and has a practice in Hanover. Still a fan favorite, he and his wife, Rosemary, have been deeply involved in the work of the Jimmy Fund in fighting cancer in children.

A decade after his brief career with Boston ended, another right-hander, **Gordon McNaughton**, was working as a postal clerk in Chicago. He'd only appeared in six games for the 1932 Red Sox, with a record of 0–1 and a 6.43 ERA. He struck out six, but walked 22. A former girlfriend, Mrs. Eleanor Williams, left policeman Barney Towey sleeping in the hotel room they had shared, and burst into McNaughton's room, where her former lover was shacked up with Mrs. Dorothy Moos. Williams shot and killed McNaughton, with Towey's service pistol. A "dice girl in a roadside tavern," she said she shot McNaughton because "he tried to dust me off."

Also shot by a former girlfriend was **Billy Jurges**, a shortstop with the Cubs in 1932. Fortunately, Jurges recovered, helped Chicago win the pennant that year, and played 15 more seasons. He went into coaching and was unexpectedly named Red Sox manager in July 1959, taking over from Pinky Higgins. After 11 months on the job, he left the team in June 1959, having won 59 and lost 63, but perhaps also having lost some of his health to the tension of managing. It was Higgins who replaced him.

Carroll Hardy, the man best known as the only player to pinch-hit for Ted Williams, pinch-hit for Yaz and Roger Maris, too. But his claim to fame came nearly a week before Williams's career ended, on September 20, 1960. Ted fouled a ball off his ankle and had to leave the game; Hardy batted for him and hit into a double play. Hardy hit .236 for the Red Sox in 788 at-bats.

Ellis Kinder, known as "Old Folks" because he'd only arrived in the big leagues on the eve of turning 31, served the Red Sox both as an accomplished starting pitcher (23–6 with a 3.36 ERA in 1949) and reliever (leading the league in both games and saves in 1951 and 1953). Author Mark Armour has characterized Kinder (who reportedly more than once pitched while heavily hung over) as "an early pioneer in the evolution of the ace relief pitcher." His eight years with the Red Sox resulted in a W–L record of 86–52. Kinder's tenure as longest-running #16 was stealthily challenged by **Kevin Romine**, a spare outfielder who hung around Fenway for seven seasons (1985–91), though he accumulated as much in the stats department as a mediocre everyday player might gather in one year: 630 at-bats, 30 doubles, 55 RBIs, 11 steals, .251 average, .306 OBP, and .325 slugging percentage. Hey, he got his pension, his salary increased each year, and his office had a nice view—who wouldn't want that job?

Pitching coach **Joe Kerrigan** (1997–2001) came across as an odd breed of baseball genius. Of course, he did have Pedro Martinez on the staff, Tom Gordon at his best, and a good corps overall. An early pioneer of sorts, Kerrigan spent hours viewing video and working statistics to make his points, earning him the moniker "The Professor"—later changed to "The Nutty Professor" by those who enjoyed mocking his techniques. As manager of the Red Sox, there was much to mock. Taking over for Jimy Williams late in 2001, he brought the Red Sox home at 17–26, taking the squad from three games out to 16 1/2 back before a superfluous season-ending streak let them finish over .500. And Kerrigan proved to be far from a soothing presence in the midst of a number of fractious players.

Far from fractious was **Rick Miller**, another one of those dual incarnation Boston ballplayers. A good guy with a good glove, the left-handed Miller debuted with the Red Sox in 1971 in #16 and wore it well from 1972 through 1977, primarily as a platoon and backup outfielder. He never hit above .283 or drove in more than 47 runs. The Red Sox released him after the 1977 season and he was picked up by California, where he played regularly for three years and improved at the plate. After the 1980 season, he was traded back to Boston with Mark Clear and Carney Lansford, while the Angels took Rick Burleson and Butch Hobson. Miller played five more seasons for the Sox wearing #3. He stepped up his offense and kept Boston ties to relocated Carlton Fisk—he married Pudge's sister Janet.

Veteran lefty **Tom Burgmeier** (1978–82) snagged Miller's number after he went to California. Burgmeier's 24 saves in 1980 placed him fifth in the American League and helped earn a berth on the All-Star team, but he was somewhat more frequently used as a setup man, compiling a 21–12 mark with Boston, a very good 2.72 ERA, and 40 saves in 213 games. On August 3, 1980, he became the first Red Sox pitcher to play another position since 1942 when he took over left field with the tying run up in the ninth inning in Texas; Skip Lockwood got a foul pop-up from Dave Roberts to end the game as Burgmeier stood in left field, presumably prepared to resume mound duties if Roberts got on and Mickey Rivers got up. Now that's a situational southpaw.

A flurry of #16 wearers (three of them in 2015 alone) catapulted the number into the "50-plus" ranks, with 51 Sox players having borne the number.

> **MOST OBSCURE RED SOX PLAYER TO WEAR #16—Lou Collier** only got into four games (in as many days) in '03 and batted .000. His only at-bat came on July 31 in Texas. He entered the game as a pinch runner, and was thrown out stealing, ending Boston's ninth inning. The score tied, 3–3, he got up to bat and grounded back to the pitcher to end Boston's 11th inning. Alex Rodriguez, apparently then at his most powerful, hit a grand slam to win it for the Rangers.

Cy Young

When counting Red Sox Cy Young winners, it's sort of unfair to exclude Cy Young. He did win the pitching Triple Crown for the franchise in its first season in a new league and he won 20 games six times, 30 games twice, had 10 straight complete-game wins in 1902, and threw the AL's first perfect game in 1904—and this was just during his eight years with the Sox. He never wore a uniform number, but his 511 wins in the majors (along with scads of other records) will never be surpassed. But being Cy Young he couldn't win the Cy Young because the Cy Young wasn't handed out until 1956, the year after Cy Young died.

Three Sox pitchers have won Cy Young Awards a total of six times.

Pitcher	Year	Uni
Jim Lonborg	1967	#16
Roger Clemens	1986, 1987, 1991	#21
Pedro Martinez	1999, 2000	#45

#17: Monster, Marty, and Marvelous Mel

Al Van Camp (1931) may have been the first to wear the #17 jersey, but the first to wear it with distinction was "Marvelous" **Mel Parnell** (1947–56). The left-hander won 123 games for the Red Sox, including a league-leading 25–7 in 1949. He had another 20-win season in 1953, his sixth straight 200-inning campaign. In the last of his 10 seasons with the Red Sox he threw a no-hitter, on July 14, 1956—the first Red Sox no-no in more than 50 years. (Howard Ehmke had tossed the last in 1923.) A native of New Orleans, Parnell played a role in integrating baseball in his home city when he invited the Red Sox and Indians to play a pair of games there during 1960 spring training.

Imposing **Dick Radatz** flourished in relief under Seattle Rainiers manager Johnny Pesky before joining the parent club in 1962. "The Monster" immediately made a mark for the Red Sox, leading the league in games (62), games finished (53), and saves (24). It was just too tempting to call on Radatz when things got rough, and when Pesky became manager in 1963 and '64, he was guilty of over-using his ace closer, one time using him for 8 2/3 innings of relief in a 15-inning game (just two days after he'd thrown six innings in a 14-frame affair.) As Leigh Grossman pointed out, it's ironic that—with his own career shortened by over-use—Radatz as a radio talk show host constantly bemoaned the babying of pitchers with pitch counts. But he was a fiery legend in Boston for a while; you don't often see pitchers who never started a game post records of 15–6 and 16–9 like he had in '63 and '64. Monster years indeed.

Second baseman **Marty Barrett** was, with good reason, named MVP of the 1986 ALCS, though he was even better in the World Series. He'd played in all but four games that year, hitting for a .286 average, scoring 94 runs, and driving in 60. But in the League Championship Series against the Angels, he hit .367 and drove in five. In the World Series against the Mets, he stepped that up by hitting .433 and driving in four more. Had the Sox come out on top, the World Series MVP wouldn't have gone to Barrett but rather Bruce Hurst, but as it turned out . . .

A superb fielder, Barrett played 167 postseason innings and never made a miscue. A little sleight of hand enabled Barrett to pull off the hidden-ball trick three times (twice in one month against Angels baserunners). Barrett held steady at second base from 1984–89, while the Red Sox went through half a dozen semi-regular shortstops, one of whom—Jody Reed—wound up replacing Barrett at second. Marty's brother Tommy Barrett (#33) played briefly for the Red Sox in 1992—a somewhat uncomfortable time, in that Marty was suing the Sox and team physician/co-owner Dr. Arthur Pappas for misdiagnosis of a knee injury and medical malpractice. Marty won a substantial settlement as a result of his lawsuit.

Cecil Cooper apparently bloomed later than the Red Sox were willing to accommodate. Lost to the Cardinals in the 1970 Rule V draft, he was returned to the Red Sox and played part-time for three seasons (1971–73), and then was a regular for the next three (including a .311 season in 1975 to help Boston break Baltimore's hold on the AL East). After batting .364 in the ALCS, Coop had just one hit in 20 plate appearances in the World Series. Following his best season production-wise in 1976, the Sox swapped him to Milwaukee to reacquire George Scott, whose best years were behind him. (Ditto for Bernie Carbo, who also returned in the deal.) Had they only known. Cooper was an All-Star Brewer five times, hit over .300 for seven straight seasons, led the league in RBIs in 1980 and 1983, and won two Gold Gloves at first base. The man who preceded Cooper in #17 was **Cal Koonce**, a reliever for the 1969 Miracle Mets. There wasn't much magic remaining in his arm by the time he hit Boston in 1970, but his exit a year later enabled the number to pass from Koonce to Coop. Cool.

Two-time Cy Young Award winner **Bret Saberhagen** was an attractive target for GM Dan Duquette, who was willing to be patient while Saberhagen tried to come back from a serious shoulder injury. He appeared in six games at the end of 1997, with the Sox losing five of those starts (though his own record was just 0–1). The patience paid off and Sabes was 15–8 in 1998, and then 10–6 with a 2.95 ERA in 1999. Further injury left him with just three midseason appearances in 2001, followed by retirement.

Hall of Famer **Herb Pennock** wore #17 in 1934, his final year in baseball. By then he'd come up with the Philadelphia Athletics, been snagged off waivers by the Red Sox in 1915, got hit harder and harder as the Sox of the 1920s got worse and worse, and was finally sent to the Yankees for $50,000 and three warm bodies in '23. Predictably, he thrived with Babe Ruth and the boys in New York, leading the league in winning percentage his first year there and claiming four World Series rings. "The Knight of Kennett Square"—a fancy reference to his Pennsylvania hometown—was a perfect 2–0 for the '34 Sox to finish with 240 career victories. He died in 1948, the same year he was elected to the Hall.

Joe Wood wasn't the ace his father Smoky Joe Wood had been. Though named Joe, he wasn't a junior since his father's given name was Howard. Joe's opportunity came in 1944, but it didn't last long. He appeared in three games and tossed 9 2/3 innings, in which time he gave up 13 hits, walked three, threw a wild pitch, and amassed an ERA of 6.52. He handled four chances flawlessly in the field, but unlike his dad—who batted .244 as a Sox pitcher before a dead arm transformed him into a productive Indians outfielder—the younger Joe was 0-for-2 at the plate.

Researcher Maurice Bouchard found that Oregon-born right-hander **Bill Sayles** had ancestors in the Massachusetts Bay Colony dating back to the 1620s, before Boston was Boston, and that Sayles also had the odd experience of playing baseball in the 1936 Olympics in front of an audience that included Adolf Hitler. After pitching exceptionally well for Little Rock early in 1939, he was called up to Boston where he found it tougher: in 14 innings of work, he gave up 14 hits, walked 13 more, and threw a couple of wild pitches. He allowed 11 earned runs (and two more) and had a 7.07 ERA before being demoted. Though recalled for September, he never saw further duty in Boston, historic or otherwise.

Speaking of Boston being Boston, **Manny Delcarmen** is one of that rare breed of Boston natives to play for the Red Sox. Locally grown, he's thrived in the fertile soil in the Sox pen, though his ERA climbed more than one run from '07 to '08 and again from '08 to '09. Other than Manny—this Manny—the only uniformed personnel to wear #17 since 2003 have been coaches. It's apparently a popular one for the coaching staff.

MOST OBSCURE RED SOX PLAYER TO WEAR #17—Ken Poulsen, a member of the 1967 Impossible Dream Red Sox, became obscure enough that the Red Sox themselves were unable to locate him when they arranged for the 25th anniversary celebration in 1992. When the Society for American Baseball Research (SABR) prepared *The 1967 Impossible Dream Red Sox* for the 40th anniversary of the team, a clue in Poulsen's biography—his father's name—enabled us to find him the night before the book went to print. He'd really never gone missing. And he's been in the record books all along. While Dalton Jones was off for a short summer stint in the Army Reserve, Poulsen had joined the Red Sox—long enough to collect five at-bats in five July games. He made outs the first four times up, but then doubled in his final major league at-bat. Looking back on it all in early 2007, Poulsen said, "Hell, I wasn't anything to begin with."

Adding It All Up

You might reasonably expect that the lowest total of uniform numbers (adding the numerals of the nine—or 10—players) would be in the earlier years, when there were no numbers yet retired. You'd be right.

The first official retirement came in 1984, though Ted Williams's #9 had been informally retired since 1961. The lowest possible total would be 1+2+3+4+5+6+7+8+9 = 45. Surveying the nearly four score Opening Days since 1931, this total was approached on two occasions, in 1939 and 1940 when the total was 49. Pitcher Lefty Grove wore #10 each year, and the only numeral missing was #6. The only difference in personnel those two years was right fielder Dom DiMaggio took over #7 from Joe Vosmik in 1940 and batted leadoff. Doc Cramer hit second, Ted Williams shifted to left field and was in his familiar three-hole spot, followed by Jimmie Foxx, Joe Cronin, Jim Tabor, Bobby Doerr, Gene Desaultel, and Grove.

Not surprisingly, the highest number is in more recent years, with an extra player added thanks to the designated hitter and half of the single-digit numbers now retired. In 2008, the season opened in Japan, and the uniform numbers totaled 282—despite Matsuzaka-san wearing the second-lowest number of all 10 participants: #18. Only Dustin Pedroia's #15 was lower, an oddity since pitcher numbers have always tended to be higher. Opening Day in 2009 saw a 10-person lineup totaling 255. By 2015, the most recent Opening Day prior to publication, a lot of lower numbers for the starters really brought down the total. Heck, it just barely passed 200.

1939 Opening Day Lineup:	
#8 Doc Cramer	CF
#7 Joe Vosmik	LF
#3 Jimmie Foxx	1B
#4 Joe Cronin	SS
#5 Jim Tabor	3B
#9 Ted Williams	RF
#1 Bobby Doerr	2B
#2 Gene Desautels	C
#10 Lefty Grove	P
#Total: 49	

2008 Opening Day Lineup:	
#15 Dustin Pedroia	2B
#20 Kevin Youkilis	1B
#34 David Ortiz	DH
#24 Manny Ramirez	LF
#25 Mike Lowell	3B
#44 Brandon Moss	RF
#33 Jason Varitek	C
#46 Jacoby Ellsbury	CF
#23 Julio Lugo	SS
#18 Daisuke Matsuzaka	P
#Total: 282	

2015 Opening Day Lineup:	
#50 Mookie Betts	CF
#15 Dustin Pedroia	2B
#34 David Ortiz	DH
#13 Hanley Ramirez	LF
#48 Pablo Sandoval	3B
#18 Shane Victorino	RF
#2 Xander Bogaerts	SS
#10 Ryan Hanigan	C
#11 Clay Buckholz	P
#Total: 201	

Then in 2015, manager **John Farrell** went in for hernia surgery and learned that he also had Stage 1 Non-Hodgkin's lymphoma and had to leave the team for cancer treatment as of August 11. Bench coach Torey Lovullo was interim manager in his absence, which lasted through the end of the season.

#18: Dice-K and Johnny Idiot

The only Red Sox player we're aware of who had his uniform number written into his contract is pitcher **Daisuke Matsuzaka**. It's not necessarily that he demanded it, but more that ownership was pleased to commit to it as a mark of their respect for the star pitcher brought to Boston (at a commitment exceeding $100 million). You may ask, what did his Japanese team, the Seibu Lions, do with the wheelbarrow full of loot—$51,111,111.11 to be exact—they received for the negotiation rights to "Dice-K"? They installed their country's widest scoreboard and made several other improvements to the Seibu Dome, including electronically heated toilet seats. Japanese custom puts a lot of stock in commode comfort. And

Daisuke Matsuzaka

another thing, as pointed out by the team's director of business operations, "If the bathrooms are nice and convenient, then you do not hesitate to buy another cup of beer."

Other Japanese customs include having your ace pitcher wear #18. It was the number Dice-K had worn for Seibu and he'd told the Associated Press, "I would like the number if it's vacant." He got it. On his first visit to Boston after signing with the Sox, he took in a Bruins hockey game—wearing a Bruins shirt with #18 on the back. His last work with the Red Sox in his rookie year was to win Game Three of the 2007 World Series. In 2008, #18 won 18 games, the most major league wins in a season by a native of Japan. The less said about 2009, the better.

Given the historic association of #18 with ace pitchers in Japan, it's no surprise that **Tomokazu Ohka** selected the number when it was available in 2001. When Ohka had first come up, **Reggie Jefferson** had #18, and held it from 1995–99. Jefferson was a much better hitter than some fans may recall: he had a .316 average over 1,518 at-bats in five seasons with the Red Sox, hit 50 homers, and drove in 215 runs. Somehow **Andy Sheets** and **Midre Cummings** snagged #18 in 2000, and Ohka stuck with #53. He only wore #18 for four months in Boston. At the 2001 trading deadline, Ohka (6–13 with the Red Sox) and a minor league pitcher went to Montreal for Ugueth Urbina.

When Matsuzaka-san first put on #18 in 2007, most fans thought not about **Willie Banks, Dustan Mohr,** or **Jason Johnson**, but of **Johnny Damon**. A man whose autobiography is titled *Idiot* (of course, the self-proclaimed name for the group of players who finally brought a championship back to Fenway), Damon wore #18 from his Boston arrival in 2002 through the 2004 world championship run. He drove in seven runs against the Yankees despite only batting .171 in the ALCS, but his home runs in the final games of both the Championship Series and World Series announced that the "curse" was indeed a load of hooey—and over forever. Damon appeared in commercials, got voted to start the 2005 All-Star Game, and hit .316 in his "contract year," after which he signed with the Yankees for a sum substantially more than Boston was interested in discussing. Damon's career-high 94 RBIs had given the 2004 Sox a big lift, but he mainly provided a tough out at the top of the order. In four years, he hit .295 for Boston, scored 461 runs, and led the team in steals each season.

There was, perhaps, a time that a major leaguer wore his minor-league uniform during a major-league game. **Carlos Quintana** was in Pawtucket when he got the call to report to Boston. In fact, he was at McCoy and in the game. An hour and half before the June 2, 1989, game at Fenway, Jim Rice decided to have surgery for a bone chip in his right elbow. Quintana had, in fact, already started playing that night—the PawSox had a doubleheader against Iowa, and hence an earlier start. Quintana wore #18 for Pawtucket. He'd already played a half-inning in the first game when he got the call. The *Boston Globe* reported, "The PawSox pulled Quintana out of the lineup at McCoy Stadium and sent him in uniform to Fenway Park, where he arrived just before the game." So he sat on the bench in his PawSox uniform. At the time, explains Joe Kuras, the PawSox and Red Sox unis were identical—same style, same color combos for letters and numbers. They both said "Red Sox" on the front. Quintana didn't play that night, but he did play in the Saturday afternoon game the next day. Did he wear the same uni, or was he supplied a brand new, if identical one? We may never know.

Ted Cox set a major league record by getting hits in each of his first six major league plate appearances in September 1977. He hit .362 for the month and was enticing enough to be the whipped cream on the prospect package (plus Rick Wise) sent to Cleveland for Dennis Eckersley before the 1978 season. Take away that first month and Cox hit .236 for four years for three clubs.

Frank Sullivan (1953–60), a 6-foot, 6½-inch, two-time All-Star right-hander, passed the jersey number to an even taller righty, 6-foot, 8-inch **Gene Conley** (1961–63). The Sullivan-for-Conley trade with the Phillies in December 1960 was one of the tallest trades in baseball history. Conley had a world championship ring from the 1957 Milwaukee Braves and three more from the NBA champion Boston Celtics (1959–61). Conley remains the only member of the Red Sox to play on a world championship basketball team. Conley also earned headlines galore with the Red Sox when he and Pumpsie Green walked off the team bus after a game in New York . . . and didn't come back. Pumpsie turned up the next day, but Conley only surfaced four days later—at one point, he apparently had presented himself at the airport wanting to fly to Israel but was denied boarding since he had no visa (or sobriety). He was 29–32 with the Red Sox in his last three years in major league ball.

Sullivan was an accomplished and under-appreciated pitcher who went 90–80 for Sox teams that were subpar. His 18 wins in 1955 were enough to lead the league—Sullivan added another W in the All-Star Game—but he was clearly in decline in 1960 (6–16, with a 5.10 ERA). Baseball was just the beginning of a life lived large; Sullivan's 2009 book *Life Is More than Nine Innings* shows a man with a zest for exploring what the world has to offer.

Imagine a guy named Yank pitching at Fenway Park today? Well, during World War II, warm bodies trumped rough names—and even rougher stats—so to the mound stepped **Yank Terry**, a product of Indiana (in case you thought he might have been a nefarious plant by Hitler or Tojo). During his wartime exploits in Boston, Terry went 19–28 with a 3.88 ERA. A Yank whose number was later retired in New York helped the Red Sox win a pennant. **Elston Howard**, whose ninth-inning single broke up Red Sox Billy Rohr's 1967 no-hit bid in April, was dealt to Boston in August and was instrumental in helping complete the Impossible Dream pennant chase. Howard tied for 17th in AL MVP voting (with Rico Petrocelli) despite hitting just .147 with the Sox. He had a pivotal two-run single in the ninth inning of Game Five against St. Louis and wound up second in career World Series games caught (behind former teammate and manager Yogi Berra). He rejoined the Yankees as a coach in 1969 and spent a decade there before he died of a rare heart ailment in 1980. The Yankees later retired his #32—the classy Howard hadn't bothered Sox coach Ed Popowski about #32 after the '67 trade.

Glenn Hoffman inherited a difficult job, taking over for Rick Burleson at shortstop. Hoffman got into 678 games in eight Sox seasons, though he knocked in only 197 runs and hit .245 in that span. By 1986, an irregular heartbeat reduced his playing time and he became the third-string shortstop. He was traded to the Dodgers for a minor leaguer in August 1987. His younger brother Trevor Hoffman became an ace closer for the Padres, saving more games than any pitcher in history and being named to six All-Star teams.

Carlos Quintana, one of only five Red Sox whose last name began with a "Q," was a quality hitter. He was tabbed as the starting first baseman for 1992 when tragedy intervened over the winter in his native Venezuela. Two younger brothers were shot and Carlos was rushing them both to a Caracas hospital when he crashed into a bridge abutment. The accident broke both his wife's legs and broke his arm and big toe. He missed all of 1992, opening the door for Mo Vaughn to move in. When Quintana came back in 1993, Mo was the man and Q hit 51 points lower than when he'd been the heir apparent.

"Every little thing's gonna be all right." The Bob Marley song played every time **Shane Victorino** came to bat in Boston 2013, 2014, and 2015. The "Flyin' Hawaiian" was a reggae devotee and the attitude expressed by the Marley song "Three Little Birds" seemed to capture the spirit of the magical 2013 season, which more or less began with the deadly bombing of the Boston Marathon in April and carried all the way to a World Series win that interrupted a string of three last-place finishes. Victorino won a Gold Glove in the outfield, and drove in 12 runs in the postseason—including the game-winning hits in both clinching games of the ALCS and the World Seeies. There was a grand slam in the bottom of the seventh of Game Six, which won the game and the ALCS against the Tigers, and then a three-RBI double in the third inning, the game-winning hit of the final game of the World Series against the Cardinals.

MOST OBSCURE RED SOX PLAYER TO WEAR #18—Walt Ripley never signed his Red Sox contract; he was 18 and his parents signed it for him while he was still a student at Deerfield Academy. The right-handed pitcher got into his first game on August 17, 1935, and his last game was September 11. Those were the only two games he ever played in the majors. He threw a total of four innings in relief, finishing games against the Browns in St. Louis and the White Sox at Fenway. He faced a total of 21 batters, walking three, and allowing seven others to get hits. With four earned runs in the four innings, his ERA is a perfect 9.00 (if you call that perfect). Ripley let his son, Allen, sign his own contract with the Red Sox 37 years later . . . believe it or not!

Long Tom's First Long Ball

"Long Tom" Winsett, #18, was the first Red Sox player who hit a regular-season homer while wearing a uniform with a number on it. Never heard of him? You're not alone. He wasn't in the starting lineup when he went deep on April 14, 1931, and he didn't hit another home run for five years . . . when he was a Brooklyn Dodger.

It was on Opening Day 1931 at Yankee Stadium, and the 6-foot, 2-inch Winsett was called on to bat for pitcher Ed "Bull" Durham. The Yankees had a 6–1 lead, in part due to a homer by Babe Ruth. The left-handed Winsett strode to the plate with Charlie Berry on base to face New York starter Red Ruffing, who'd been acquired from the Red Sox the preceding May, and who also wore #18.

For Winsett, it was only his second major league at-bat. He'd appeared once at the start of the 1930 season and struck out. Now back in the bigs a year later, he took an inside pitch from the right-hander for ball one. Arthur Siegel of the *Boston Herald* reported how Winsett handled Ruffing's second pitch: "He pulled it into the extreme right-hand corner of the right-field bleachers, and he and Berry trotted around the bases. The Yankees protested that it was a foul, but the umpires pleaded nolo and the homer stood for two runs." There were 70,000 witnesses, most of whom went home happy with the Yanks' 6–3 win.

Winsett's reputation seemed to precede him. Siegel dubbed Winsett "the youth who apparently cannot field but can hit." Eventually they weren't even saying that as the outfielder wound up hitting .197. He had 88 at-bats for the Red Sox over parts of three seasons, and only had one other extra-base hit, a double in 1931.

It wasn't long before another numbered Red Sox knocked a ball out of the park. It happened the next day, April 15, 1931, and it was hit by yet another player not in the starting lineup. In fact, it was the first homer hit by a pitcher wearing a numbered shirt. Jim Brillheart, #27, Boston's third pitcher of the game, collected his only career home run in the seventh (#9 Charlie Berry homered in the ninth in the 8–7 loss). Brillheart's two RBIs were the only runs he drove in as a Red Sox.

The first uni number homer in Boston came during a City Series exhibition game against the Boston Braves; #15 Earl Webb's blast traveled a reported 500 feet, 10 rows deep in Fenway Park's center-field bleachers. "No mightier homer has ever been registered at Fenway Park," declared the *Herald*'s Burt Whitman. The Braves, though they were just playing down the street from Braves Field, wore their numberless road unis. Cartoonist Bob Coyne's character Phil Phan observed, "Th' Braves couldn't number dere players 'cause th' Sox had dere number—huh?"

The first regular-season homer by a number wearer at Fenway also came off the bat of #15. Webb homered in the first game of a May 2 doubleheader against Washington. They lost the game but split the twinbill. Their uniforms may have had numbers, yet one number the '31 Sox never got to was .500. The sixth-place club lost 90 times and hit only 37 homers all year, with just seven numbered Sox providing the power. Webb led the club with 14, but that year he set the still-standing major league mark with 67 doubles.

#19: Hey Nineteen

Though #19 is known for being worn by favorite fall heroes **Josh Beckett** and **Fred Lynn**, in the days of yore it belonged to brothers. **Milt Gaston** and **Joe Heving** weren't brothers, but they were pitchers in the 1930s who had brothers who each caught for the Sox. Milt is fortunate to get into this book to begin with, but his brother Alex is left out (at least in the index); he hit in the .220s in the 1920s and never got a Red Sox number to wear. Milt pitched from 1929 through 1931, and was a 20-game loser in 1930 (a rare feat today but the struggling Sox of that era had 20-game losers each year from 1927–30). Given another chance, and a uniform number—he wore both #19 and #20—Gaston went 2–13 with a 4.46 ERA in 1931. For whatever reason, the White Sox wanted him, and it was in Chicago he ran his string to nine losing seasons in a row. Milt's fortune off the mound was much better than it was on it. He lived to be 100, dying 65 years after first being assigned his number.

Joe Heving was a right-handed relief specialist who went 31–11 with a 3.83 ERA from 1938–40. The *New York Times* called him "a Kentuckian who loved to tell hillbilly stories." He got a late start in the majors, debuting at age 29 with the New York Giants, but he got an early start on putting together a family. He was already a grandfather in his first year with the Red Sox, despite being only 37 years old at the time (insert favorite hillbilly joke here). Grandpa Heving played four more years with the Indians and a final year in 1945 with the Boston Braves. Joe's brother, Johnnie, caught for the Red Sox in 1924–25 and 1928–30, but he was taken off waivers in January 1931 by the Philadelphia Athletics, so he wore their uni numbers instead.

Bob Weiland was the player the White Sox sent to the Red Sox for Milt Gaston in 1931. It was not a swap of aces, mind you. Weiland pitched from 1932 into 1934 and went 15–35 before being traded to the Indians (with "Suitcase Bob" Seeds and $25,000) to get Dick Porter and Wes Ferrell, a pitcher later honored in the Red Sox Hall of Fame.

Speaking of trades that worked out, how 'bout that Beckett deal? Considered the ace of Boston's staff after he and Mike Lowell came over from the Marlins in a November 2005 trade, Josh Beckett had been the MVP of the 2003 World Series for Florida. He led the American League in wins with 20 in 2007 and was 4–0 in the postseason that year. Someone who seems to come through when he's needed most, including a 17–6 mark in '09, Beckett has been at the center of the post-2004 postseason runs . . . even if the deal did cost the Sox Hanley Ramirez.

What kind of cost that was was something debated at some length during the second half of the 2015 season. The number 19, though, belonged to **Kohi Uehara** by then. Koji turned 38 at the start of the 2013 campaign, yet relieved in 73 ballgames with a 1.09 ERA— and saved seven games in the postseason. In three seasons with the Red Sox, his combined ERA was 1.86.

Josh Beckett

No discussion of #19 can be made without Freddie Lynn. The center fielder was an immediate sensation when he and Jim Rice both broke in late in 1974. The "Gold Dust Twins" helped carry the Sox to the 1975 pennant. Lynn was selected as both Rookie of the Year and Most Valuable Player in the same year—the first player ever so doubly honored. He'd come in second in batting (.331) but ranked first in both slugging (.566) and OPS (.967). He drove in 105 runs (including 10 in one game!) and scored a league-leading 103 times. He won the batting title in 1979 with a .333 average, and he won four Gold Gloves with the Red Sox, too. In the 1975 postseason, he drove in seven runs, including a three-run shot in classic Game Six.

In Lynn's seven seasons with the Red Sox, he hit for a cumulative .308 average and drove in 521 runs. Fearing that they wouldn't be able to re-sign him, the Sox traded him to the Angels in January 1981. Though he was grew up in California and starred at USC, the lefty Lynn was born for Fenway Park. The change of home field wasn't good for his career; he never cracked .300 again (though he did hit .611 for the Angels in a losing cause in the 1982 ALCS).

Bobby Ojeda quickly claimed Lynn's number, shedding the #28 he'd been assigned in 1980. Over his six seasons with the Sox, Ojeda won 44 and lost 39. In 1986, the season following a winter trade to the Mets, he posted the highest winning percentage in the NL, and then shamelessly went on to beat the Red Sox in Game Three of the World Series—at Fenway Park, no less.

It was going to be **Brian Rose** and Carl Pavano as the anchors of the Red Sox rotation, or so it seemed. Neither panned out as planned, but at least Pavano helped bring back Pedro Martinez from the Expos (and Pavano's later disastrous contract with the Yankees didn't hurt the Sox, either). Rose was with the Red Sox for four years but turned out a disappointing 11–15 record with a 5.73 earned run average. He had one great stretch in May 1999, allowing just one earned run over three starts against the Yankees (twice) and the Indians. By July he fell apart. By the next July, he was a Rockie.

Irrepressible **Mickey McDermott** began pitching for the Red Sox while still a teenager, and put up a record of 48–34. His best year (18–10, in 1953, with a 3.01 ERA) allowed the Sox to get good value when they traded him to Washington for Jackie Jensen. He once talked with Jim Prime about his time with the Red Sox, expostulating, "Why don't they put my %$#& name on the wall? Batters hit the *&^% wall ninety million times thanks to me. I threw it, they hit it, and I ain't got my name on it or nothin'. I didn't even get a trophy, and Pesky got a freakin' pole named after him!" The son of a police officer (and minor league ballplayer), McDermott fudged his age when he signed at 15 for $5,000 and two truckloads of beer. McDermott was also "chosen unanimously by his high school graduating class as the man most likely to be found dead in his hotel room." Those were the stories that trailed the blithe southpaw, many of them freely espoused by the subject, though McDermott eventually went sober and died a few years later at 74 in a hospice in Arizona. "He told his wife that he was dying as a publicity stunt for the book," said Howard Eisenberg, co-author of McDermott's book, *A Funny Thing Happened on the Way to Cooperstown.*

Another Mickey (not as well remembered) who threw left-handed and whose given name was Maurice was **Mickey Harris**. What a difference a stint in the United States Army brought about. Harris was 8–14 with the 1941 Red Sox, then missed four seasons serving in the military during World War II—though he did pitch a perfect game in a Canal Zone Army League game for the Balboa Brewers in 1942. He came back to Boston (admittedly with a much better team) and was 17–9. So he lucked out by coming back to the best Sox club since World War I. Harris started two games in the 1946 World Series and lost both, though his ERA was a decent 3.72. Like many of the Red Sox staff, arm problems rendered Harris a disappointment in the years that followed.

Jerry Casale was probably best known for homering in his major league pitching debut on April 15, 1959, against the Senators. His three-run homer put the game away—just like customers later put the food away at the restaurant, Pino's, that he ran in Manhattan for many years after he left baseball. Casale was 13–8 on the mound as a rookie, 2–9 the next year, and drafted by the Angels in the expansion draft after the 1960 season. Check, please.

MOST OBSCURE RED SOX PLAYER TO WEAR #19—They couldn't even get the guy's name right—and it's not like it was Nicholas Polachanin, a.k.a. **Nick Polly**. Right-hander **Bill Humphrey** got the final two outs of a 10–4 loss in Philadelphia on April 24, 1938. The Associated Press box score called him "Humphreys." In his only other game on May 4—the ninth inning of another loss—the AP labeled him H'phreys, Humpreys, and Humpries . . . all in the same box score! The accompanying text called him Humphreys. No respect, no respect at all.

When the Numbers First Circled the Bases

Below is a list of the instances when a uniform number in Red Sox history first reached the home run category since the advent of numbers in 1931. Ten times pitchers were the first of a number to homer—odd given that there were only 42 years for that to happen before the DH rule. No pitcher since Gary Peters, #43, in 1970 has managed the trick, though Ron Mahay, #46, homered in his last game as an outfielder in 1995 before converting to a full-time pitcher. The numbers get higher and the names a little more recognizable as the list approaches the present.

*=pitcher.

1931
April 14: #12 Tom Winsett
April 15: #27 Jim Brillheart (seventh inning)*
 #9 Charlie Berry (ninth inning)
May 2: #15 Earl Webb
May 4: #3 Jack Rothrock (fifth inning)
#8 Urbane Pickering (later in the fifth inning)
June 22: #1 Bill Sweeney
September 3: #28 Marty McManus
1932
May 5: #4 Smead Jolley
June 15: #18 Roy Johnson
June 27: #7 Urbane Pickering
August 9: #6 Johnny Welch*
August 24: #17 George Stumpf
1933
May 7: #5 Johnny Hodapp
July 1: #22 Billy Werber

August 9: #26 Lloyd Brown*
1934
April 19: #2 Bill Cissell
May 14: #20 Billy Werber
May 19: #10 Lefty Grove*
June 5: #11 Gordon Rhodes*
June 6: #21 Lyn Lary
1935
May 24: #19 Moe Berg
Jun 14: #25 Bing Miller
June 22: #24 Oscar Melillo
September 2: #16 Jack Wilson*
1939
June 6: #13 Elden Auker*
1942
April 20: #23 Bill Conroy
June 23: #29 Oscar Judd*
June 30: #32 Tony Lupien

1943
June 20: #42 Babe Barna
1945
June 2: #14 Johnny Lazor
1946
April 22: #39 Eddie Pellagrini
June 11: #36 Pinky Higgins
1952
April 17: #37 Faye Throneberry
April 19: #31 Don Lenhardt
May 5: #30 Clyde Vollmer
July 31: #33 Del Wilber
1953
May 28: #38 Tom Umphlett
September 3: #34 Karl Olson

1955
May 11: #35 Billy Klaus
1965
May 2: #40 Mike Ryan
May 25: #41 Jerry Moses
1970
September 27: #43 Gary Peters*
1972
May 14: #44 Andy Kosco
1977
August 27: #49 Tommy Helms
1979
June 17: #50 Mike O'Berry

1982
May 28: #51 Reid Nichols
1989
July 23: #55 Randy Kutcher
1992
September 4: #45 Scott Cooper
1994
June 7: #47 Lee Tinsley
1995
May 26: #46 Ron Mahay
1996
July 18: #48 Jeff Manto
August 2: #56 Darren Bragg
September 25: #57 Rudy Pemberton
1998
July 18: #52 Donnie Sadler
2000
July 3: #54 Morgan Burkhart
2006
September 9: #64 Dustin Pedroia
September 17: #60 David Murphy
2009
August 2: #68 Josh Reddick
2012
May 14: #66 Daniel Nava
2013
September 7: #72 Xander Bogaerts
2014
September 24: #70 Garin Cecchini

#20: YOOOOOUUUK!

It was good thing that **Kevin Youkilis** wore #20. It's been a number that oddly seems to have an unusually less interesting collection of players who've borne it in years gone by. "Youk" has changed that. Though of Romanian Jewish background, he was well-known in baseball circles as "the Greek god of walks" because of the book *Moneyball*, and his strike zone discipline. He became a nearly instant fan favorite at Fenway, where crowds like Lou Merloni because they can shout "Looooouuuu!" and they like Youkilis because they can shout, "Yooooouuuk!" He has that "dirt dog" way of playing the game like Trot Nixon or Dustin Pedroia, and Boston fans love that as well. Plus he can hit! His average over eight seasons stood

Kevin Youkilis

at .287 and of course there are the walks, which make his OBP more than 100 points higher than his batting average (just barely—.388). And he has the power you'd expect from a god.

Fielding? Youk played the entire 2007 season without an error at first base, handling 1,080 chances cleanly. A Gold Glover at first, he can nimbly switch to third base as needed.

The man who wore #20 longer than any other—so far—was Havana-born **Mike Fornieles**, a right-handed pitcher who appeared in a league-leading 70 games in 1960, earning Fireman of the Year. Over seven Sox seasons, Fornieles was 39–35 and pitched with an earned run average of 4.08.

From Venezuela, we have **Tony Armas**, who led the AL in 1984 in three offensive categories: home runs (43), RBIs (123), and total bases (339). He was far from a Triple Crown, though, given his batting average of .268. Part of the problem was that he also led the league in strikeouts with 156. Armas nonetheless was named an All-Star, won a Silver Slugger, and finished seventh in the MVP voting.

He roamed in center field between Jim Rice and Dwight Evans through the 1986 season, when the emergence of Dave Henderson made him expendable. Tony Armas Jr. turned out to be more valuable than his dad—if only for what he was able to fetch in return. Boston sent the minor leaguer to Montreal with Carl Pavano for Pedro Martinez in November 1997.

Continuing our tour of the Caribbean basin, we find **Juan Beniquez** of Puerto Rico, who started with the Sox as a shortstop at age 21 and became an outfielder a couple of years later. He hit .274 over his four seasons with the Red Sox—and started all three games of the 1975 dynasty-derailing sweep of the Oakland A's in the ALCS. Beniquez didn't fully mature until the 1980s, batting .293 in five seasons in Anaheim. In all, he played 17 seasons with eight teams, all of them in the American League.

It's a long way from the Caribbean to Coalfield, Tennessee, but that's where **Sid Hudson** was born. A right-handed pitcher who toiled for the Washington Senators for almost a decade, he was traded to the Red Sox for Walt Masterson and Randy Gumpert during the 1952 campaign. He'd led the league in losses (with 17) in 1949, and his overall record with the Senators was 88–130. He fared only marginally better for Boston (16–22), but with a better ERA (3.73). After his retirement from pitching, Hudson scouted for the Red Sox for five years.

Walt Masterson, did you say? The man traded for Hudson was no relation to Justin—or Bat, that lawman of the Old West (though that would've been a great name for a ballplayer). Like Hudson, Walt Masterson broke in with Washington, and came to the Red Sox on June 13, 1949, for Mickey Harris and Sam Mele. He was then traded back to the Senators for Hudson and Gumpert on June 10, 1952. He pitched better for Washington—3.98 ERA compared to 5.02 for Boston—but he fared better in W–L percentage for the Red Sox. Yet had he been 4–3 in 1949 instead of 3–4, the Red Sox would have won the pennant. Think about that. Actually, it's probably better if you didn't.

One last pitcher to look at is **Mike Ryba**, two four-letter names that formed a four-letter trade that cost the Sox Al Brazle, who pitched 10 years for the Cards, winning 97 games. The pair pitched against each other in the 1946 World Series: Ryba in mop-up work in Boston's Game Four loss and Brazle taking the loss for St. Louis in long relief the next day. Ryba won 36 games for the Red Sox through the war years. His World Series appearance was the end of the road for him as a player; he went on to manage for five years in the Red Sox farm system.

Position players who favored round numbers included **John Marzano**. In six seasons of backup backstop work, he hit .232 for Boston, but in several regards his best year was his initial half-season in 1987. Marzano was a 1984 first-round pick who couldn't hit a lick, but he kept his club's star pitcher from getting hit . . . literally. In the July 6, 1991, game against the visiting Tigers, Roger Clemens hit John Shelby with a pitch in the top of the second and Shelby charged the mound wielding his bat. Before he could reach Clemens, Marzano felled him with a tackle from behind. The backup catcher providing backup for the Rocket's red glare.

Most of **Darren Lewis**'s success came in the National League, including most of an unrivaled fielding streak in which he committed no errors for his first four years in the big leagues, a span covering 2,410 innings of outfield play. He signed as a free agent with Boston at age 30 and played four years, the first two fairly full-time, then part-time in his final two seasons. He didn't provide much pop—a .256 average and 132 RBIs in 468 games with the Red Sox—but "D-Lew" was considered a classy guy liked by all (except volatile teammate Carl Everett, with whom he once got into a violent shouting match).

While #20 doesn't feature a superstar honor roll, there are some provocative names. There's a pair of unrelated Williamses of somewhat recent vintage: outfielder **Dana** and coach **Dallas**. Then there are names that seem like typos upon first glance: **Eddie Joost** (not Yost), **Lee Stange** (not Strange), and **Bob** (not Hugh) **Heffner**. The best name of the bunch belongs to a luckless lefty named **Jennings Poindexter**, who at least had the good sense to go with his middle name rather than his given first name of Chester, which rhymed a little too well with Poindexter. His teammates just called him "Jinx," and with an 0–2 record and 6.75 ERA in three career Sox starts, that might have been the name that fit best.

MOST OBSCURE RED SOX PLAYER TO WEAR #20—Do you remember **Larry Wolfe**? He appeared in 65 games in 1979–80, playing all four infield positions and even catching a game. We like to think we pay pretty close attention, and we don't remember him at all. Our choice here is **Mike Palm**. Palm hailed from Greater Boston. His Red Sox debut came on July 11, 1948, when he entered the sixth with two outs, then gave up three hits before recording the final out. He told us, "I was a little wild, you know—nervous as hell . . . in a big league uniform." He got 2 2/3 innings of relief work one week later, and only allowed one hit (though he walked three). He had one more appearance July 21. Two hits and two walks in 1 1/3 frames left him with a 6.00 ERA. He went back to Birmingham, where he won four games in the playoffs that year. After two more years in the minors, he called it quits. "I figured I wasn't going to be in the Hall of Fame," he said. "It was time to go to work."

First Sox Home Runs by Number: #1–20

The sidebars in Chapters 18 and 19 tell the who and when of the first home runs hit by players wearing certain numbers in Red Sox history. What follows are the debut home runs, from #1 to #20, with particulars about some of the more interesting. (See the others after Chapters #21 and #22.)

#1. **Bill Sweeney:** June 22, 1931

Why not start at the top? The first baseman's homer off Tommy Bridges in a 7–2 win over Detroit was his only one all year long and the last of his career. Sweeney hit five home runs in 1,050 at-bats.

#2. **Bill Cissell:** April 19, 1934

#3. **Jack Rothrock,** #8 **Urbane Pickering:** May 4, 1931

Two numerical home run debuts in the same game. Rothrock's solo shot in the fifth helped power a 7–5 road win over the Athletics. Pickering's three-run homer in the same frame was the bigger blow. Since Pickering wore three numbers that year, some have doubts about which number he wore in this game. We don't. Pick, who liked to switch numbers and homer on the road—all 11 career home runs were hit away from Fenway—was the first #7 to homer (also at Shibe Park).

#4. **Smead Jolley:** May 5, 1932

#5. **Johnny Hodapp:** May 7, 1933

#6: **Johnny Welch:** August 9, 1932

There are 10 pitchers who were the first to homer at a given number—a disproportionate amount given the DH and the fact that pitchers generally don't flex much hitting power. Welch, the first Sox pitcher to so christen a number, is in an even rarer club of pitchers with single-digit uniform numbers. His homer in Detroit was the only one of his nine-game career.

#7. **Urbane Pickering:** June 27, 1932

Urbane he may have been. That aside, Mr. Pickering was the first #3 to hit a homer, the first #7, and the first #8.

#8. **Urbane Pickering** (see #3 above)

#9. **Charlie Berry:** April 15, 1931

#10: **Lefty Grove:** May 19, 1934

Lefty's the only Hall of Famer to christen a Sox uniform number with a homer. His three-run shot gets bonus points for breaking a seventh-inning tie in St. Louis.

#11: **Gordon Rhodes:** June 5, 1934

#12: **Wes Ferrell:** July 13, 1934

Pitcher Wes Ferrell hit 17 homers for the Red Sox, a total later equaled by Earl Wilson. Ferrell's 37 career homers top every major league pitcher. Wes was the new guy, having arrived in a May trade from Cleveland, and pulled off a sort of double-double: he didn't just christen #12 on the 13th with one homer, but two. You could even say he added a triple-triple: the third pitcher to christen a number with a homer in '34 and the third in succession after Grove's #10 and Rhodes's #11.

#13. **Elden Auker:** June 6, 1939

Make that four numbers in a row christened by pitchers, though Auker's blast came five years after Grove, Rhodes, and Ferrell's '34 hat trick.

#14: **Johnny Lazor:** June 2, 1945

The 10-player, 14-year wait for this annually issued number is ironic since #14 is now retired for one of the team's greatest sluggers, Jim Rice. Given that there was a war on and Lazor's lack of power, it's almost surprising the feat didn't take longer.

#15. **Earl Webb:** May 2, 1931

Webb hit this homer in the same year he set the still-standing major-league record for doubles in a season: 67. If he had stopped at second base on this home run and refused to go any further, that might have given him 68.

#16: **Jack Wilson:** September 2, 1935

Another pitcher does the dirty work . . . and it wins the game. Wilson's walkoff blast to the center-field bleachers earned him the victory in the 11th inning in the first of two with Washington.

#17. **George Stumpf:** August 24, 1932

Stumpf played 118 games in the majors and this was his lone home run. It came off Hall of Fame pitcher Ted Lyons of the White Sox, but Lyons and the Pale Hose prevailed.

#18. **Tom Winsett:** April 14, 1931

#19. **Moe Berg:** May 24, 1935

A spy defeats a general. Moe Berg, a bona fide intelligence agent for the United States government, hit a home run off General Crowder on May 24, 1935, in the bottom of the fifth at Fenway. Boston won the war with the Tigers, 8–4.

#20. **Billy Werber:** May 14, 1934

The second of two numbers broken in by Werber. As you will see, he also was the first #22 to hit a homer for the Red Sox.

#21: Love 'em or Leave 'em

Do the Red Sox face a dilemma here? No one has worn #21 since **Roger Clemens** first donned it in 1984. It's been more than 30 years. As recently as 2007, the Red Sox had been courting Clemens, hoping he'd come back and wind up his long career back in a Boston uniform (and he would certainly bear the number he'd worn in his prime). As it worked out, his 6–6 record with the Yankees that year was nothing special, despite the rapture with which some greeted his return to New York. And then, oh my good graciousness, the steroids matter surfaced, and possible legal troubles for allegedly lying to the United States Congress. The seven-time Cy Young winner was a lock for the Hall of Fame before the scandal broke, and he likely would have worn a Red Sox cap into the Hall. The enduring image that most fans are left with is in a Yankees uniform, and perhaps that's going to be OK with Sox fans.

The Rocket was nothing but spectacular with the Red Sox for his first nine years, winning the first of his three Cy Youngs and the MVP of both the regular season and the All-Star Game in 1986 (you can't hope for much better than a 24–4 season). Four times he led the league in ERA while with Boston, twice in strikeouts, and twice in complete games. Five times he led the league in shutouts. We might also point out his pair of 20-strikeout games 10 years apart—1986 and again in 1996—the only two times it had been done in history to that point. All in all, he finished his Red Sox years with 192 wins; he is tied with Cy Young for the most ever by a Boston pitcher, and the opportunity to win one more and top Cy Young was part of the courtship.

It was his final four seasons with the Red Sox that were problematic. He was 40–39, seemingly a .500 pitcher, though closer inspection shows him second in the league in ERA in 1994 and seventh in 1996. Never a great communicator, Clemens was viewed through increasingly fractious lenses by a media he spurned. And he did turn up to spring training as much as 35 or 45 pounds overweight on a couple of occasions. When GM Dan Duquette said he hoped the Sox could sign Clemens, so he could spend the "twilight of his career" in Boston, it was unfairly distorted to sound as though Duquette believed he was already in his twilight years. Perhaps Clemens used that as motivation to revitalize his career, which saw him immediately win back-to-back Cy Youngs with the Blue Jays. Perhaps he used some other things, too. We may never know for sure. He did become a *bête noire* every time he came to Boston, where fans (perhaps rightly) felt he'd slacked off for several years and not given his best effort. And then had the effrontery to pitch for the Yankees, not only once but twice.

How did Roger get #21 in the first place? He told us that it was given to him by the equipment manager in Boston. "I guess because he knew I wore 21 at the University of Texas," he said. "The same thing in New York. A player on the Yankees already had 21 [Paul O'Neill], so the equipment manager had 12 laying there on my chair. After two or three starts, my oldest son called and said that he noticed no one was wearing 22. That was the number he had many times in baseball, basketball, and football. He did so because of Emmitt Smith. Emmitt is his favorite player."

Preceding the Rocket was **Mike Torrez**, who took the opposite route, pitching first for New York and then coming to Boston as a free agent. Torrez is so indentified with the Yankees in the minds of Sox fans that it may surprise some to realize he'd only pitched five months in the Bronx. Those five months ended with two wins in the 1977 World Series: Game Three and the final Game Six over the Dodgers. He was just 14–12 during the '77 season. For the Red Sox, Torrez pitched for five seasons (60–54, 4.51 ERA) but there's that one thing he'll always be remembered for: the pitch he served up to Bucky Dent in the single-game playoff for the 1978 American League East title. He took the loss in the 5–4 epic, even though it was Reggie Jackson's homer off Bob Stanley that made the difference in the end. It was the first of two 16-win seasons (he lost 13 both years), before flipping to a 9–16 season in 1980.

Hall of Famer **Juan Marichal** spent one year with the Red Sox, the penultimate one of his 16-year career, and posted a 5–1 record in 57 1/3 innings of work. In a mark of great respect for "The Dominican Dandy," when Pedro Martinez won his first Cy Young Award (for the Expos in 1997), Pedro gave the award as a gift to Marichal.

There are four more #21s who pitched six or more seasons apiece for the Red Sox. **Ray Culp** joined the club in 1968 after five NL seasons (and a subpar '67 with the Cubs due to arm problems), rebounding with a 16–6 year for the Red Sox. His 2.91 ERA was helped considerably by four consecutive September shutouts. He won 17 games in 1969, made the All-Star team, and the abysmal-hitting Culp even popped his only career home run. There was one exciting game in May 1970 when he struck out the first six batters . . . and there was a period in 1971 when he himself struck out eight times in succession.

Before Culp, there was **Arnold Earley** (1960–65). These were lean years for the Red Sox. He appeared in 208 games, but never fashioned a winning record. The closest he came was breaking even (1–1) in 1964. And before Earley, there was **Willard Nixon** (1950–54 and 1957–58), his stint broken by single-year stands by **Karl Olson** and **Johnny Schmitz** while Nixon, for whatever reason, took #15. Nixon was considered a "Yankees killer" (and also reportedly produced the best facsimile "Ted Williams" autographs). All nine of Nixon's major league seasons were with Boston, going 69–72 with a career 4.39 ERA.

Digging more deeply in the past, we find the first of the six-year men, **Tex Hughson**. A native Texan (now there's a surprise), Hughson played his whole career in Boston, from April 16, 1941, to a fateful October 2, 1949. In just his second season (1942), he led the league with 22 wins. The team let him down a bit in 1943 (the second of four straight seasons he posted an ERA of 2.75 or below), but he was 18–5 in '44 (and then into the navy in early August) and 20–11 in the 1946 campaign. He was hit badly in Game Three of the '46 World Series, though he pitched well in two other games. Then, after four years in a row averaging 257 innings a year, Tex's arm simply gave out. Like Boo Ferriss at the same time, Hughson pitched a few more years with a bad arm without much success. Joe Cronin may have overworked his work-horses; some point to Hughson and Ferriss as classic cases of why not to overtax a good pitcher's arm.

Pete Appleton had a 14-year career, though he only pitched 11 times for the Red Sox, in 1932 . . . but you won't find his name in a single box score. There's a reason for that. His name was **Pete Jablonowski** at the time. It was only after the 1933 season as a Yankee that he changed it to Appleton. The Sox were so bad back then that it's surprising more players didn't try an alias to hide their past.

While hitters are few and far between at #21, a future manager donned the number . . . for a day. Boston purchased Joe Rudi and Rollie Fingers from A's owner Charlie Finley on June 15, 1976. Don Zimmer, the third base coach and still a few weeks away from replacing Darrell Johnson as manager, accommodated Fingers by yielding his own #34, which Fingers wore in the Red Sox bullpen (according to Peter Gammons's *Beyond the Sixth Game*). The next day—neither Rudi nor Fingers ever seeing action—the sale was nullified by Commissioner Bowie Kuhn. The fortunes of the Yankees, the Red Sox, and maybe even the Royals and Dodgers (New York's postseason whipping boys) might have been different if Kuhn had just let the deal be.

MOST OBSCURE RED SOX PLAYER TO WEAR #21—Red Daughters only appeared in one game for the Red Sox, the 1937 home opener against the Yankees. Daughters came in as a pinch runner for Rick Ferrell in the bottom of the 10th inning, with the Sox down by two runs. He acquitted himself well on the basepaths, advancing a base at a time, and he experienced the thrill of scoring a run in an extra-inning Fenway Park Opening Day game against the Yankees. But he never had a major league at-bat and never appeared in another ballgame. And his run left the Red Sox one short of keeping the game alive.

First Sox Home Runs by Number: #21–#40

This is a look at the first home runs hit by uniform number in Red Sox history, the middle chunk: #21–40, with selected highlights:

#21. **Lyn Lary:** June 6, 1934

#22. **Billy Werber:** July 1, 1933

Holding down the #22 and #20 homer debuts (both against the White Sox), Werber was simply doing his part to justify Tom Yawkey's fiduciary faith: $100,000 of the new owner's money went to the Yankees for Werber and George Pipgras in May of '33. Werber's #22 consummation came off Sad Sam Jones at Comiskey Park—Pipgras got the win, making it a two-for-one Yawkey payday.

#23. **Bill Conroy:** April 20, 1942

#24. **Oscar Melillo:** June 22, 1935

The leadoff home run at Comiskey Park was the first home run with the Red Sox for the recently acquired "Ski." It was the 22nd and last of his career.

#25. **Bing Miller:** June 14, 1935

#26. **Lloyd Brown:** August 9, 1933

#27. **Jim Brillheart:** April 15, 1931

#28. **Marty McManus:** September 3, 1931

The year before he became Red Sox manager in midseason, McManus hit a three-run blast into the right-field bleachers off New York's Gordon Rhodes, the same pitcher who would later become the first #11 to homer for the Red Sox (June 5, 1934).

#29. **Oscar Judd:** June 23, 1942

#30. **Clyde Vollmer:** May 5, 1952

#31. **Don Lenhardt:** April 19, 1952

A Patriots Day inside-the-park grand slam in the opener propelled Boston to a double-header sweep of Cleveland.

#32. Tony Lupien: June 30, 1942

#33. Del Wilber: July 31, 1952

#34. Karl Olson: September 3, 1953

#35. Billy Klaus: May 11, 1955

At 26 years, this is the longest wait of any of the first 39 numbers. Klaus, the 12th player to wear #35, hit his first major league four-bagger to overcome a 2–1 White Sox lead.

#36. Pinky Higgins: June 11, 1946

The recently acquired Higgins, the first wearer of #36, was in his last year as a ballplayer. Ted Williams and Rudy York also homered as the Sox beat the Indians, 10–5, for their 12th win in a row.

#37. Faye Throneberry: April 17, 1952

A grand slam was the first home run hit by a #37, poled into the distant center-field bullpen at Washington's Griffith Stadium. Throneberry's second career homer would also be a grand slam, but Faye's fame wouldn't arrive until he'd left the majors and became known as the big brother of "Marvelous Marv" Throneberry, whose treacherous feats at first base and on the basepaths were the stuff of legend with the abysmal '62 Mets.

#38. Tom Umphlett: May 28, 1953

#39. Eddie Pellagrini: April 22, 1946

Greater Boston native Eddie Pellagrini hit a home run in his first major league at-bat. Pelly's home run was the game-winner against the Senators. Ted Williams told Pellagrini, "Eddie, that's the worst thing you could have done because now they're going to pitch you like they pitch me!"

#40. Mike Ryan: May 2, 1965

Just as many 30s waited until the '50s to get on this list, most of the 40s waited until the '60s to get going. Ryan homered in consecutive Tiger Stadium at-bats, a solo homer in the third off Julio Navarro and a two-run shot off Johnnie Seale in the fifth as the Sox swept a Motown twinbill.

#22: Sammy, Doc, Moose, Soup, and the Spy

Though never worn by a Red Sox star, #22 has many interesting stories to tell, from animal tales to cases of mistaken identity to recent yarns of a player hitting .322 in the final stop of a successful career (**Sean Casey**) and a journeyman infielder on his fifth team in five seasons (**Nick Green**). The two most intriguing tales, though, go back a ways and go behind the plate, to a catcher who ran a bowling alley that suffered an apparent gangland massacre, and another backstop who was an international man of mystery.

Sammy White was both a bowling proprietor and Boston's main catcher from 1952 through 1959. White hit .264—and on June 18, 1953, he became the only 20th century player to score three times in one inning—but his defense kept him around longer than any other #22. His catching was praised by pitchers, almost to the degree that Jason Varitek has been lauded in recent years. When the Sox tried to trade White, he retired instead—only to relent and put in two more years in the National League. Sammy White's Brighton Bowl became a murder scene in September 1980 when four workers were shot execution style in a robbery.

During the '55 season White decided—for reasons that even best friend Frank Sullivan can't recall—to wear #8 for a year. Into the breach stepped shortstop **Owen Friend**, who wore #22 through mid-June. It then fell to bonus baby **Jim Pagliaroni**, who signed with the Red Sox five days after Friend left and got into one August game while still only 17 years old.

The Red Sox were the last stop for 15-year major leaguer **Moe Berg**, but his true calling beckoned during World War II. Armed with a pistol and working for the OSS, predecessor of today's CIA, the former catcher was also given a cyanide capsule for himself. His mission was to assassinate German nuclear physicist Werner Heisenberg at a conference in Switzerland if Berg concluded the Nazis were on track to develop nuclear weapons. One doesn't usually think of ballplayers as erudite, but the Princeton grad was sufficiently conversant enough in nuclear physics—and German—to decide after talking with Heisenberg that Germany was not close to completing the bomb. Fluent in seven or more languages—and, as the story goes, "he couldn't hit in any of them," his .262 average with the Sox notwithstanding—Berg also did a little espionage work in Japan and in Latin America, as detailed at length in Nick Dawidoff's book *The Catcher Was a Spy*. We can report no spying on the parts of later catchers **Mike Ryan**, **Ernie Whitt**, **Eric Wedge**, or **Mike Stanley** (unless they were so good at it that no one's found out yet).

Bill Campbell (predictably nicknamed "Soup") came to the Sox as their first major free agent signing after players were freed from baseball's reserve clause. His market value was at an all-time high coming off 78 appearances and a 17–5 mark with a 3.01 ERA for the 1976 Minnesota Twins; he'd closed 68 games, a league- high. He was just about as good with the Red Sox the next year, closing 60 games and recording 31 saves (13–9, 2.96). Burnt out by overuse, he never threw more than 50 innings or saved more than nine games over the last four years of his deal.

Chuck Stobbs was a bonus baby who came up in 1947 not long after he turned 18. The lefty lost out on the opportunity to get the sort of seasoning that the minors can offer, because the bonus rule at the time required that a bonus signee be kept on the major league roster. For two full seasons, Stobbs said, "I wore the bench out." Finally, in 1949, he got starting assignments and recorded double-digit wins against single-digit losses for three years running. He was 33–23 for the Red Sox, though with a not-very-special 4.70 ERA due in part to his penchant for walking more batters than he struck out. After the 1951 season, he was traded to the White Sox.

You think it was difficult to fit Rich "El Guapo" Garces (see Chapter #34) into a Lowell Spinners jersey? Try **Wily Mo Pena**. Joe Shesta-kofsky said when he was working for the Spinners, Wily Mo came on a rehab assignment and there was no Spinners jersey large enough to accommodate him. So the team sent someone to the Souvenir Store across the street from Fenway, bought a replica jersey, and put some iron-on numbers on the back. Wily Mo had his number, but it wasn't a regulation jersey.

Working his way up through the Red Sox system since 1968, **Darrell Johnson** got his first major league managing post in Boston in 1974. He built on an 84-win rookie season by taking the Sox all the way to Game Seven of the 1975 World Series. Though he was named Manager of the Year, his players grumbled about his moves—such as leaving a spent Luis Tiant in too long in fabled Game Six and replacing Jim Willoughby with Jim Burton in the climactic ninth inning against Cincinnati the next night. After a 41–45 first half in 1976, and just two weeks following owner Tom Yawkey's death, Johnson was fired shortly after managing the AL All-Star team. Replaced by Don Zimmer in Boston, Johnson subsequently became the first manager of the Seattle Mariners.

From 1997 through most of 2001, **Jimy Williams** was at the helm in the Hub. He'd originally signed as a free agent with the Red Sox way back in 1964, but Williams only appeared in 14 major league games (for the Cardinals). He had a winning record every year with the Sox, and shepherded the team to the postseason in 1998 and 1999.

The coaching lines also deserve some notice at #22. Hitting coach **Ron "Papa Jack" Jackson** (2003–05) oversaw a couple of the most powerful offensive years in baseball history, with a 2003 team slugging percentage of .491 (eclipsing the 1927 Yankees' .489) and a club that led the AL (as it did once more in 2004) in batting average, runs, doubles, total bases, extra-base hits, and on-base percentage. Jackson wore #22 for three seasons, though there was one inning he didn't. Bill Ballou explained that during a game at Fenway in 2003, the clubhouse guy inadvertently put Jackson's #22 shirt into Mike Cubbage's locker and vice versa, and—with no names on the back of the home uniforms, naturally—no one noticed the mix-up until Cubbage had been in the third base coaching box for the first inning. They then changed shirts so each was wearing the proper number. (Cubbage normally wore #39.)

Larry Woodall (1942–47) is more remembered by history for what he didn't do—he didn't see Willie Mays. Boston had an option on Mays, a member of the Negro League Birmingham Barons, and Red Sox scout George Digby sang his praises. Woodall was asked to check out Mays, yet because Mays was black, Woodall apparently didn't even bother to attend a ballgame before sending back a negative report. He may have single-handedly cost the Sox a pennant or two, not to mention the chance of integrating the club more than a decade before Pumpsie Green finally did.

Jack Russell wore #22 in 1931, but you wonder why they ever assigned him a number. He was 6–18 in 1929 and 9–20 in 1930 (with a 5.45 ERA) for the last two Sox clubs without uniform numbers. Why would they bring him back again? The Sox did a lot of head-scratching things in those days, so Russell returned for another year and pitched as one might predict: he lost 18 games. And still Jack Russell, like a terrier of the same name hovering around the supper table, remained on the Fenway premises. Russell changed to #21 and went 1–7 for the Red Sox before they traded him to Cleveland. Believe it or not, though Russell was 12–21 in 1934 and '35, and the first half of 1936, the Red Sox acquired him once more. Given the chance to redeem himself, he went 0–3. Ruff!

Speaking of animals, an outfielder named Julius Joseph Soltesz arrived in Boston in 1934 going by the handle of **Moose Solters**. He had a solid rookie campaign with a .299 average, though he committed 15 errors in just 89 games in the field. After a slow start the next year, he was traded to the St. Louis Browns for infielder Ski Melillo, resulting in the Moose–Ski Swap of '35. Moose wound up finishing in the top 10 in the MVP voting that year while Ski batted .260 and committed 18 errors in 106 games at second base.

Lastly, a rat story. After the Red Sox released **Ed Jurak** in March 1986, he carped, "They never gave me a chance to show what I could do." He'd only been in the Red Sox system since he was drafted on June 3, 1975. In the four years he did play in Boston, his average declined from year to year, from .333 to .231. In 1984, he hit his sole major league home run, but that was also the year in which he made the play of his career. On May 22, there were two Indians on base in a scoreless game with Bruce Hurst on the mound. A rat came from around the Red Sox on-deck circle and headed to the mound, then veered off toward third. Jurak, the first baseman that day, scooped up the rat in his glove and stuffed him in a trash can in the dugout. "I was sort of unnerved when the rat came out," said Hurst, "I didn't make a move because I knew Ed had him all the way." The Tribe failed to score, and Boston plated three runs in the bottom of the inning to win, 7–1. Jurak's glove suffered a couple of bite marks, but he earned a real save.

MOST OBSCURE RED SOX PLAYER TO WEAR #22—Infielder **Doc Farrell** played eight years in the majors between 1925 and 1933. After spending 1934 with the minor league Newark Bears, he refused to report to the Pacific Coast League when the Yankees traded him with three other players (and four more to be named later) to the San Francisco Seals for Joe DiMaggio. Doc returned to the majors for one final fling, with the '35 Red Sox. His year was over on May 1, with stats reading four games, seven at-bats, two hits, one RBI. The one error he made in 12 chances helped the Senators to a five-run seventh-inning rally on April 26—Doc's final misdiagnosis, if you will.

First Homer Highlights: #41 to Infinity . . . and Beyond

This is the last of five total installments looking at the first home runs by uniform numbers in Red Sox history. What follows is a listing of this achievement since #40, with selected highlights. *Red Sox by the Numbers* vows to be as obsessive as any book written on the team. Here's continued proof.

#41. **Jerry Moses:** May 25, 1965

Moses finds the promised land in his second major league at-bat. The Sox hit four home runs at Fenway, but the eventual AL champion Twins hit five longballs in a 17–5 shelling.

#42. **Babe Barna:** June 20, 1943

#43. **Gary Peters:** September 27, 1970

The 10th and last pitcher on this list with a number-christening home run . . . unless you want to count #46.

#44. **Andy Kosco:** May 14, 1972

#45. **Scott Cooper:** September 4, 1992

There were seven players who wore #45 before Cooper went deep against Oakland's Dave Stewart. It took Cooper 112 games to collect his first major league home run. Jeff Bagwell, who was traded instead of Cooper for Larry Andersen in 1990, already had 28 HRs for Houston.

#46. **Ron Mahay:** May 26, 1995

Call this episode "Scab's Revenge." Replacement player Ron Mahay was playing center field in his fifth major league game when he put #46 on the board with the second of back-to-back homers against the Angels (Reggie Jefferson went first). It was also Mahay's last game as a position player. By 1997, he was back in the majors as a lefty reliever. He had a 26–11 mark and 3.86 ERA over 473 games through 2009. Mahay's 1995 homer was his last, though he's given up 70 of them.

#47. **Lee Tinsley:** June 7, 1994

#48. **Jeff Manto:** July 18, 1996

#49. **Tommy Helms:** August 27, 1977

#50. **Mike O'Berry:** June 17, 1979

#51. **Reid Nichols:** May 28, 1982

#52. **Donnie Sadler:** July 18, 1998

Frank Castillo held a 3–2 lead with runners on second and third in the top of the fourth and the Tigers hurler had to like that .161 hitter Donnie Sadler was coming up with two outs. Sadler launched a three-run blast, followed by another home run by leadoff hitter Darren

Lewis. After walking Midre Cummings, Castillo was yanked, only to see Nomar Garciaparra homer off his replacement.

#53. Nobody

Some 17 ballplayers have worn #53 for the Red Sox, but 12 of them have been pitchers (and all since the DH era) and the two hitters—Angel Santos and Anthony Abad—amassed a total of 33 homerless at-bats. So #53 is the lowest—but certainly not the only—number without a homer for the Red Sox: #59, #61, #62, #63, #65, #67, #71, and #73 to infinity are also homerless. But we have a few stops yet . . .

#54. Morgan Burkhart: July 3, 2000

Signed out of independent baseball, he got seasoning in the Red Sox farm system before getting the call to Boston in June 2000. In his seventh game Burkhart hit a three-run homer off Minnesota's Jason Ryan at the Metrodome. It was the fourth homer of the fourth inning, a nine-run frame as the holiday fireworks came early and indoors.

#55. Randy Kutcher: July 23, 1989

#56. Darren Bragg: August 2, 1996

Bragg had homered against Tim Wakefield earlier in 1996, but Boston acquired him from the Mariners for Jamie Moyer on July 30. Three days later, Bragg hit a leadoff homer against Rick Aguilera of the Twins.

#57. Rudy Pemberton: September 25, 1996

#58. Jose Iglesias: September 20, 2012

He only ever hit two homers for the Red Sox, one in 2012 and the other one the following year.

#60. David Murphy: September 17, 2006

Murphy hit his only Red Sox homer leading off the September 17 day game against Jaret Wright at Yankee Stadium. The Red Sox won the game, the first of a day/night doubleheader sweep.

#64. Dustin Pedroia: September 9, 2006

The highest number to hit a home run for the Red Sox, Pedroia's solo home run at Fenway put the Red Sox on the board in a game they lost to the Royals in 12 innings. Yet the Red Sox had the makings of a fine second baseman whose future—and uniform number (#15)—would suit his new city.

#66. Daniel Nava: May 14, 2012

It wasn't his first home run for the Red Sox. That was hit—a grand slam—on the first pitch he ever saw in the big leagues. He was wearing #60 at the time. The next year, he wore #66 and became the first Sox batter to hit one out and wear #66 as he trotted around the bases.

#68. **Josh Reddick:** August 2, 2009

After Reddick's December 2011 trade to Oakland, he realized his potential, hitting 32 homers for the A's in 2012. That was more than three times as many as he hit for Boston in three seasons of part-time play.

#70. **Garin Cecchini:** September 24, 2014

#72. **Xander Bogaerts:** September 7, 2013

His first and only home run in his first season, hit during the 18 games he wore #72. Starting with the 2014 campaign, the "X-Man" lopped the "7" off his jersey and wore #2.

#23: El Tiante

Things didn't start out all that well for players wearing #23. On March 1, 1932, **"Big Ed" Morris**, the second man in club history to don the number (outfielder **George Stumpf** had the initial honor), was being seen off to spring training at an Alabama fish fry when he was stabbed twice in the chest by gasoline station operator Joe White. He died two days later. Historian Jerry Fischer says Big Ed had peed in the peanut pot, and others took exception. It wasn't the first fracas he'd been in. An unconfirmed account had him being cut by a blade wielded by Sox teammate Merle Settlemire in 1928, when Morris, a 27-year-old rookie, won 19 games. The fish-fry assailant pled self-defense; he was sentenced to three years in prison but his conviction was overturned on appeal.

No one wore the number the year Morris died, but **Emile "Mike" Meola** tried his luck in 1933, winding up with an ERA of 23.14 in 2 1/3 April innings. He spent the rest of the year pitching in Jersey City for the Skeeters.

Bill Dickey was an All-Star catcher who played 17 years for the Yankees, hit .313, and was rightfully elected to the Hall of Fame in 1954. Bill's younger brother, **George Dickey**, was a catcher, too, in the Yankees' minor leagues. With Bill coming off his fifth straight .300 season, there was room for only one Dickey behind the plate in New York. When George came to the Red Sox in 1935, the club likely had high hopes for the switch-hitting backstop, but he wasn't his brother. George collected just one hit in 34 at-bats over two seasons before the Red Sox gave up on him. He later played four years for the White Sox and boosted his career average all the way to .204.

Two of the most char-ismatic pitchers the Red Sox have ever had are **Luis Tiant** and **Oil Can Boyd**. Both pitched in a World Series, one more memorably than the other.

Son of a Cuban pitching star unable to pitch in the majors due to discrimination, "Loo-ie" remains a fan favorite, and a fixture around Fenway. Tiant's twisting windup—he turned his back completely to the batter, the better to show off his "23"—inspired Jim Prime to write: "His windup was like a mini tornado and when the ball finally emerged from the funnel shaped twister, the batter was as befuddled as Dorothy on her way to Oz." He won 229 games and struck out 2,416 batters in his career. Three times "El Tiante" was a 20-game winner for the Red Sox, joining them in 1971 after six seasons in Cleveland and Minnesota. His 1.60 ERA for the 1968 Indians was the lowest in the AL since Walter Johnson's 1.49 in 1919.

For Boston, Tiant posted a 1.91 ERA in 1972. He won 18 regular-season games in 1975; his three-hitter against Oakland in the opener of the ALCS and his five-hitter against Cincinnati in the first game of the World Series set the tone for both series. His complete-game win at Riverfront Stadium in Game Four cost him a courageous 163 pitches, yet he still started epic Game Six and threw seven innings at Fenway (three days of rainouts provided rest).

Tiant threw a shutout in Game 162 in '78 to push the Sox into a fateful one-game playoff. That must-win two-hitter turned out to be his final game in a Red Sox uniform. Even though Tiant signed with the Yankees as a free agent in 1979, his popularity in Boston only suffered a temporary dip. He's in the Red Sox Hall of Fame, and could merit inclusion in Cooperstown. He rejoined the Sox in 2002 as a special instructor and full-time goodwill ambassador, plus the El Tiante Cubano sandwich is a Fenway must try. The 2009 documentary film *The Lost Son of Havana* portrayed his poignant return to his native land after 47 years away. If he ever is inducted into the National Baseball Hall of Fame, the Sox will no doubt retire his number. Until then, they've been assigning it with some frequency—eight times in the first years from 2011 through 2015.

When Oil Can was called up to Boston, excitement gripped the town. Boyd never fulfilled the hopes of the fans, but few players do. He carried himself with such élan that he remained a favorite for years despite an aggregate record of 60–56 with a 4.15 ERA from 1982–89. His best year was 1986, when he was 16–10, despite being suspended by the Red Sox for throwing a tantrum after being passed over for the All-Star Game. He was 1–1 in the ALCS, but four first-inning runs did him in during Game Three of the World Series against the Mets. Had John McNamara given Boyd the ball in Game Seven, rather than entrusting it to Bruce Hurst on short rest, who knows how '86 might have ended?

Dennis Boyd's nickname "Oil Can" represents a Mississippi expression for a can of beer. The mention of it brings to mind **Tom Brewer**, another right-hander who—like Boyd and Tiant—also served eight seasons with the Red Sox. Brewer pitched in 241 games, but appeared in 305, never pinch-hitting (he had a .228 career on-base percentage) but pinch-running a full 64 times (though he only stole two bases). Brewer was 91–82 with an even 4.00 ERA; his best year was 19–9 (with a 3.50 ERA) in 1956. He could have gone for 20 wins, but the team told him to take off the last game of the season in order to spare his ailing arm and that as far as they were concerned, he was a 20-game winner. After baseball, he worked 25 years for the South Carolina Probation Office.

Dave Morehead threw the last no-hitter at Fenway Park until Derek Lowe's 2002 gem. Morehead allowed only one Cleveland baserunner—a second-inning walk—on September 16, 1965, beating future Sox #23 Luis Tiant. The ninth-place Sox drew just 1,247 fans for the no-no (including one of this book's authors). Morehead lost his final two games of '65—getting knocked out in the second inning in his next start—and led the league with 18 losses against 10 wins. His five wins in 1967 helped Boston win the pennant, and he threw 3 1/3 innings of no-hit relief in the World Series (though we're compelled to mention that he walked four of the 14 batters he faced).

Catcher **Johnny Peacock** began as a mule trader and wound up a college trustee. In between, he caught eight seasons for the Red Sox, five wearing #23. He accumulated a .274 average over 1,440 plate appearances for Boston, and hit one home run. Behind the plate, he was, in the words of Boston sportswriter Jack Malaney, "a very acceptable receiver." Higher praise from Lefty Grove: "He's my idea of a hustling ballplayer." Not a bad epitaph.

Let's look at a trio of players who each contributed a few big plays. The first, **Clyde Vollmer**, a.k.a. "Dutch the Clutch," was a slugger whose career contained one concentrated burst of power. In July 1951, he hit 13 homers and drove in 40 runs. He'd only driven in 38 total the year before, and only knocked in 50 in '52. The 40 in the one month represented 47 percent of his 1951 production of 85 RBIs.

The Red Sox were hoping **Tom Brunansky** would be a slugger. Eight straight years he'd hit 20 or more homers with the Twins and Cardinals, twice topping 30, but when he got to Boston he hit 15, 16, and 15, and then 10 in a 1994 return. He's best remembered for a play that half the park didn't see, and was never even captured on TV—a sliding catch in the right-field corner by the Pesky Pole to clinch a berth in the 1990 playoffs. Oakland swept the ALCS in four games, and Bruno was 1-for-12.

After being released by other teams three seasons in a row, **Brian Daubach** signed as a free agent with Boston a week before Christmas in 1998. As a lefty-swinging first baseman/DH, from whom little was expected, Dauber bashed 21 homers and drove in 73 runs in 110 games. For the four years he played with the Red Sox, he had consistent numbers, charting 20–22 HRs each year and 71–78 RBIs. The 30 games he played in a reprise with the 2004 team were subpar.

Shortstop **Julio Lugo** was one of three Red Sox to wear #23 in 2009. He was traded the day the Sox got **Adam LaRoche**, but he wasn't traded for LaRoche (or **Joey Gathwright**, who signed as a free agent).

The Sox wound up getting Chris Duncan and another player from St. Louis for Lugo, though Boston was on the hook for the gargantuan salary owed the disappointing shortstop. He was much better as a Cardinal, however, and then hit .400 in the Division Series.

As a utility player for Johnny Pesky in the two years Johnny managed (1963–64), **Dick Williams** (wearing #16) was no great shakes. After two championship seasons managing Boston's Triple A affiliate in Toronto, he was named manager of the 1967 Red Sox at age 37. He whipped the Sox into fighting shape and skippered them into the World Series. He later led both Oakland and San Diego to pennants, the only major league manager to win pennants for three different teams (plus two consecutive world championships with the A's). He was recognized by the Hall of Fame's Veterans Committee and inducted into Cooperstown in 2008.

MOST OBSCURE RED SOX PLAYER TO WEAR #23—Neill Sheridan appeared in two games one week apart: September 19 and 26, 1948. "Wild Horse" Sheridan was put in to run for Bobby Doerr in a 6–6 game on September 19. No one knocked him in, and the Tigers won the game. His second appearance came one week later, batting for Boo Ferriss in the top of the ninth of a game the Sox were losing to the Yankees, 6–2. He slammed the first pitch out of the ballpark, but it was foul. He was called out on strikes. Boston baserunner Birdie Tebbetts, perched on second base during the at-bat, told Sheridan that the last pitch was definitely not a strike, but there was nothing to be done about it. He never got another chance.

Change of Fortune: 1946

Perhaps there's nothing as cruel in baseball as a player who labors through the bad years with a team only to be traded in the midst of the club's renaissance season. Sometimes the player has to be let go to bring in new blood to help reach the pennant, and sometimes the need for new blood pushes the faithful vet out the door. That number he wore with pride for years in Boston might be worn by the new guy standing on the field for the World Series player introductions.

Using transaction data from baseball-reference.com, here's a look at players who began a pennant-winning year in Boston and ended it somewhere else, and vice versa. We very much appreciate the World Series champions of 1903, 1912, 1915, 1916, and 1918—plus the 1904 AL champs who were spurned by the Giants, their would-be World Series dance partners—but this sidebar and the five that follow deal with the six World Series Red Sox teams of the uniform number era. It starts with 1946, the lone World Series chance for Ted Williams and his Sox mates. "In" and "Out" are the categories for those coming and those leaving during the season. This list does not include transactions before or after the season or minor league players promoted or demoted. Players are listed in order they arrived . . . or left.

Player	Pos	Trans.	Uni #	What Happened
Bob Klinger	P	In	37	After two years in the military in World War II, he was signed in May and became a relief ace. Took the loss in Game Seven.
Pinky Higgins	INF	In	36	Purchased from Detroit in May, he played all seven World Series games. It was his last action in the majors.
Bill Zuber	P	In	26	Here's a switch: A pitcher goes from the Yankees to the Sox and winds up in the World Series. Went 5–1 in '46.
Don Gutteridge	INF	In	10	Here's the rarest of birds: This fellow played in the World Series for both the St. Louis Browns and Red Sox. Hit .400 in '46 Series.
Wally Moses	OF	In	24	After his purchase from the White Sox, Moses hit .206 the rest of the season but .417 in the Series.
Tom Carey	INF	Out	14	A Sox utility man before the war, he was cut in July '46 to make room for Moses.
Frankie Pytlak	C	Out	24	His number went to Moses. Another pre-war Sox player's career ended in the summer of '46.

#24: Dew the Man

It was Dewey and Manny, Bootin' Buddin, and a dentist. Right fielder **Dwight Evans** was Dewey, natch. He started out with #40 but soon changed to #24 as a tribute to Willie Mays. Evans was the best defensive Red Sox right fielder anyone can recall (no one still alive remembers Harry Hooper from the 1910s). Evans earned eight Gold Gloves. It doesn't show up in an extraordinary number of assists, but that's largely because baserunners and coaches chose not to challenge his arm.

When Joe Morgan hammered a pitch into the Red Sox bullpen in the top of the 11th inning of Game Six of the 1975 World Series, it might have been all over . . . save for Evans, who reached into the pen and caught the ball, then fired to first base to double up an astonished Ken Griffey. The longer he played, the better he became on offense, his home run totals tending to climb from age 29 through 35 (the four times he drove in more than 100 runs all came in his early to mid-30s). The only man to play in both the 1975 and '86 World Series, Evans hit .292 in the former, .308 in the latter, and started all 14 games. After the 1990 season (his 19th with Boston), his numbers fell off sharply. The Red Sox released him and he spent a so-so year with the Orioles. The numbers added up over time; Evans hit 379 homers for the Red Sox and his 2,505 games was second only to Yaz.

Manny was . . . Manny. **Manny Ramirez**. Sprinting out to left field with an American flag clutched in his hand on the evening he was naturalized as an American citizen. Taking a visit (and maybe a leak) inside the scoreboard during a pitching change. Letting his dreadlocks grow and grow. Throwing out 17 baserunners in 2005 with a quick and accurate arm. But mostly hitting home runs, 274 of them for the Red Sox alone. American League batting champ in 2002 (.349), hitting .312 all told over his eight years in Boston—with a .999 OPS (on-base percentage plus slugging). He led the league with 43 homers in 2004 and was named World Series MVP that same year. He seemed to set his own schedule at times, taking days off or taking it easy, and more or less forcing the Sox to trade him in 2008 in what most considered to be a shameful sitdown in pursuit of a bigger payday. He arrived in Los Angeles and lit up the NL for the Dodgers (wearing #99), but "Mannywood" fans felt aggrieved when he was suspended 50 games for a positive drug test in '09.

Shortstop **Don Buddin** may have been more maligned than he deserved. *Globe* sportswriter Bob Ryan suggested he be given a vanity license plate marked "E-6." He was called "Bootin' Buddin" in part because he got off on the wrong foot, committing 18 errors in his first 40 games, though he only made 11 more the rest of the 1956 season. Two errors in the July 13, 1958, game led to seven unearned runs, and he led the major leagues in errors two years running—1958, and 1959. Pinky Higgins, who managed Buddin in Boston and Louisville, seemed to have a soft spot for him and probably started him more often than his play warranted. In five Red Sox seasons, Buddin batted .244—not bad for a shortstop of his era, but not particularly good either. Maybe contact was the problem. Not only did he walk a lot (.359 OBP for the Sox), but he was also in the top four in strikeouts in '58 and '59. It was the near-merciless hounding from the fans that really made his spot on field an insupportable proposition.

The dentist was catcher **Doc Legett**. Back in Doc's era (1934–35), dentists were far more common on the team than in recent years.

Among the other confirmed dentists who played with the Red Sox: Fred Anderson, Doc Farrell, Jack Hayden, Dick Hoblitzell, Jim Lonborg, Doc McMahon, Doc Prothro, and Jack Slattery. There are indications that both Pete Appleton (aka Pete Jablonouski) and Doc Gessler may have practiced dentistry as well. In Legett's case, he was a dentist before coming to the Red Sox. He broke into baseball with the Boston Braves and hit .180 in 81 at-bats. In three seasons with the Sox, he batted 43 times and drove in two runs.

Five years after an uneventful debut as a Pirate, **Leo Nonnenkamp** finally got his first major league hit for the Sox on May 6, 1938. Red made the Red Sox as the fourth outfielder, chosen over brash 19-year-old Ted Williams who was expected to benefit from a season of seasoning in the minor leagues. All 69 of Nonnenkamp's big-league hits were for the Red Sox: six doubles, two triples, and 61 singles. Like Don Buddin, Nonnenkamp had an eye, walking 33 times to boost his OBP to a respectable .348. Between him and Ted Williams, they drove in 150 runs in 1939, but 145 of them belonged to The Kid. After a hitless stint with the 1940 Sox, he spent a couple of years in the minors, a tour of duty with the navy, and one postwar season in Double A before becoming a letter carrier for the post office.

Wally Moses was a slightly built, left-handed leadoff batter. Picked up by the Red Sox for the 1946 pennant drive after the White Sox placed him on waivers, the outfielder exclaimed, "I'm glad to get my nose out of the mud." He contributed defensively during the World Series against the Cardinals, and hit .417 as well (largely because of his four-hit Game Four.) He was in the on-deck circle when Boston's Tom McBride made the final out of the Series. Moses hit .250 overall in 216 games with Boston, distinctly deficient compared to his time with the Athletics and White Sox. **Gene Mauch** ended his playing career with a bang in Boston. After hitting .220 in five stops in the National League, Mauch hit .275 with the Red Sox in his last go-round as a player in 1956–57 before embarking on a 26-year managing career. **Kevin Mitchell** was another matter. Returning from a cranky stint in Japan, the former NL MVP hit well enough—.304 in 104 plate appearances—but the idea of teaming him with Jose Canseco in the outfield did not help the pitching staff. The deadline trade of Mitchell, a "symbolic albatross" (so said the *New York Times*), resulted in more outs for Boston pitchers.

Catcher/first baseman **Mike Stanley**'s career seemed like a yo-yo between archrivals Boston and New York. After six years with the Texas Rangers—catching Nolan Ryan's final no-hitter—he was granted free agency and signed with the Yankees early in 1992. From then through mid-2000, he had two stints with both rivals sandwiched around 98 games for the '98 Blue Jays. In five seasons with the Yanks and five seasons with the Sox, he knocked out exactly 391 hits for each team. Because he had 53 more at-bats for Boston (out of a combined total of 2,797), his average was .285 for the Yankees and .274 for Boston. He hit 73 homers for the Red Sox and 72 for the Yankees with 263 RBIs for New York and 254 for Boston. Head to head in the 1999 ALCS, he hit .222 for the Red Sox against the forces of evil.

What a difference a digit makes. Whereas eight different players have worn #23 since 2009, no one has worn #24 all that time. It really can't be out of reverence for Manny Ramirez or Freddie Wenz. Maybe it's just one of those little mysteries.

MOST OBSCURE RED SOX PLAYER TO WEAR #24—There was no shortage of alliteration in the early years #24 adorned a Boston uniform: **Lou Legett** (1934–35), **Stan Spence** (1940), **Herb Hash** (1941), **Bill Butland** (1942), 1943 catcher **Danny Doyle**—not to be confused with '75 pennant-winning #5 Denny Doyle—plus **Lou Lucier** (1944) and **Harley Hisner** (1951). The last man on that list out-obscures them all. Right-hander Hisner got the ball from manager Steve O'Neill to make his first start in the last game of the 1951 season against the Yankees. He threw six innings in New York and gave up three runs on seven hits, all singles—one of which was the last regular-season hit by Joe DiMaggio. Hisner walked four batters, but he did strike out Mickey Mantle twice. He even collected a hit, though he suffered the loss as the Sox never scored. Hisner almost made the team in 1952 but was cut "two hours before the end of spring training" by Boston's new manager, Lou Boudreau. Hisner never made it back to the big leagues.

Change of Fortune: 1967

A look at in-season transactions during the Impossible Dream 1967 pennant-winning season proves that every little bit helps when you win the pennant by one game. A devastating injury to Tony Conigliaro left the Red Sox seeking a right fielder in a four-team battle for the pennant. Boston wound up getting both a new right fielder and catcher in August. The list below details in-season transactions—categorized by "In" and "Out"—but does not include deals before or after the season or minor league players promoted or demoted. Players are listed in order of transaction in '67.

Player	Pos	Trans.	Uni #	What Happened
Jerry Adair	INF	In	14	Hit .291 as Red Sox leadoff man after June deal with White Sox for Don McMahon and minor leaguer Bob Snow.
Don McMahon	P	Out	44	Journeyman pitched in postseason twice before '67 and twice after.
Gary Bell	P	In	39, 45	After a decade with the Tribe, he came to Boston, went 12–8, and pitched in his only World Series.
Don Demeter	OF	Out	4	Dealt to Indians with Tony Horton for Gary Bell. Finished his career in '67.
Tony Horton	1B	Out	11	Got a lot more playing time with Cleveland. Hit 27 homers in 1969 but had other troubles (see Chapter #30).
Dennis Bennett	P	Out	28	Don't know which is the bigger insult: getting dealt to 101-loss Mets or being traded for a AA outfielder with no home runs (Al Yates).
Norm Seibern	1B	In	4	Batted 50 points higher in Boston after his purchase from Giants; too bad that was still only .205.
Elston Howard	C	In	18	A Yankee imported for Sox pennant chase. Didn't hit after August trade, but Howard helped the staff.

Player	Pos	Trans.	Uni #	What Happened
Bob Tillman	C	Out	10	Sox sent two minor leaguers to Yankees for Howard and sold Tillman to New York the same week.
Jim Landis	OF	In/Out	15	Sox quickly saw why Tigers released Landis and did the same a week after signing him in August.
Ken Harrelson	OF	In		Landis was cut as Hawk swooped in after controversial release by A's. Harrelson didn't hit in '67 but would later.

#25: Tony C.

The player most identified with #25 may always remain **Tony Conigliaro**. The hometown hero homered in his first at-bat at Fenway Park, reached 100 career home runs at a younger age than any other player, was a local pop singer, and was a heartthrob to a legion of young women who began to flock to Fenway as he became established. Tony C. took an aggressive stance in the batter's box . . . and his career was shattered by a fastball to the temple as the Red Sox were making their run in 1967. It's another of those "what if" moments in Red Sox history; had Tony been healthy and in the World Series, the outcome might have been tipped in Boston's favor. It took a year and a half—and a great deal of courage—for him to mount a comeback.

Even with impaired vision, he hit 20 homers in 1969 and 36 in 1970. After three years out of baseball, he attempted a second comeback in 1975, made the team against all odds, and was—however briefly—a part of another Red Sox pennant-winning season. Trying to return to the team as an announcer in 1982, he suffered a heart attack and slipped into a coma. He died at age 45.

When **Mike Lowell** was with the Marlins, seven years before being traded to Boston along with Josh Beckett, Lowell was named the 1999 winner of the Tony Conigliaro Award, given to the ballplayer who "best overcomes an obstacle and adversity through the attributes of spirit, determination and courage." In Mike's case, it was testicular cancer. (Boston teammate and fellow cancer survivor Jon Lester won the award in 2007.)

Lowell, well aware that he shared #25 with Tony C., set a Red Sox team record at the hot corner, making just six errors and posting a .987 fielding percentage in 2006, better than Rico Petrocelli's .976 in 1971. Through 2009, Lowell's career fielding percentage is the best of any third baseman major league (minimum 1,000 games). Lowell was the Most Valuable Player of the 2007 World Series, batting .400, and reaching base in exactly half of his plate appearances. He scored six times and drove in the winning run in the 2–1 Game Two victory. The 120 runs he knocked in during the regular season helped get the Sox there.

Troy O'Leary wore #25 for his seven seasons with the Red Sox. The steady, if unspectacular, outfielder hit 28 homers and drove in 103 in 1998 and had two .300 seasons (1995 and '97). There was one spectacular day that Indians manager Mike Hargrove would rather forget: Game Five of the 1999 AL Division Series. With the series on the line and Cleveland ahead in the top of the third, 5–3, Hargrove walked Nomar Garciaparra to load the bases and face O'Leary. Grand slam. As if that wasn't enough, with the score tied 8–8 in the seventh and John Valentin on second, Hargrove ordered another intentional walk to Nomar. A three-run homer for O'Leary was enough to win the game. Hargrove was subsequently fired despite having led the Indians to five straight division titles.

A Boston versus Cleveland winner-take-all game that didn't go so well occurred on October 4, 1948. **Denny Galehouse**, 36, the oldest starter on the staff, was tabbed to start the one-game playoff for the AL pennant at Fenway. The more obvious choices to start were Mel Parnell (15–8) and Ellis Kinder (10–7), both well rested. Parnell had already beaten the Indians three times, and Kinder was on a recent roll.

Manager Joe McCarthy may have recalled an earlier long relief stint in which Galehouse had done well against the Tribe—but the manager seemingly had forgotten the two times since then that Cleveland had hit him hard, *and* Galehouse's last two poor performances, *and* his warming up in the bullpen for most of the previous day. Giving Galehouse the game ball was a gamble that failed . . . utterly. He allowed four runs and was yanked in the fourth inning. The Sox lost, costing them the chance for an all-Boston World Series against the Braves. What if McCarthy had started Parnell? Or Kinder? One thing that is known: Galehouse never started another game.

Dizzy Trout pitched 14 seasons for the Tigers before arriving in the nine-player swap in June 1952 that brought George Kell to Boston and sent away Johnny Pesky and Walt Dropo. Like Trout, **Orlando Cepeda** played just one season in Boston. The future Hall of Famer became the second designated hitter ever; Yankee Ron Blomberg beat him to that historic first at-bat at Fenway on April 6, 1973. Designated to hit, that Cepeda did: 20 homers with a .289 average and 86 RBIs.

Jeremy Giambi wore #25 because he couldn't wear #7. Trot Nixon had it. Mickey Mantle was the favorite player of John Giambi, father of Jason and Jeremy, and his two sons always wore numbers adding to 7. The Red Sox liked Jeremy's on-base percentage and hoped he would fill a gap for them in 2003. Instead, he had the worst (and last) season of his career, hitting just .197 in 50 games—but his weak showing and early departure opened the door for one David Ortiz, who'd originally been intended as Giambi's backup.

Reliever **Mark Clear** pitched for the Red Sox for half a decade after coming from California as part of a pretty big-name, multi-player trade in December 1980. He joined Carney Lansford and Rick Miller coming east, while Rick Burleson and Butch Hobson headed west. Lansford promptly won the AL batting title while the right-handed Clear had a good curveball and an 8–3 season, He followed that with a career year in '82 (14–9, with a 3.00 ERA). He lost it the next year; his ERA ballooned to 6.28, and he struggled with control, walking more than one batter an inning in both of his last two seasons. Clear missed a chance to take part in 1986, when Boston traded him to Milwaukee for infielder Ed Romero. **Mace Brown** got into a World Series for the Red Sox at the end of his career. He spent three seasons in Boston in the 1940s—plus two years out of town in military service. Brown led the majors with 43 appearances in '43 and pitched—though not well—in his final career appearance in the '46 World Series.

MOST OBSCURE RED SOX PLAYER TO WEAR #25—Some sources cite **Red Daughters** as wearing #25 in 1937, and he apparently did so on the bench late in the season, but the only game in which he appeared was the Opening Day game, wearing #21. Likewise, **Gene "Stick" Michael**—yes, the former Yankees infielder and current Yankees executive—was on the major league roster of the Red Sox from the start of the 1976 season until he was released on May 4. He spent 26 days without seeing a moment of game action. In August 2009, Michael confirmed that the 1976 *Red Sox Yearbook* was correct—he indeed wore #25 while never leaving the bench. Michael's 973-game career may not have been obscure, but finding him in the shadows of the Red Sox dugout took some digging.

Change of Fortune: 1975

"Never had two teams in a championship been more evenly matched, but there had been much more than routine excellence on display," Mark Frost wrote of the epic 1975 World Series between the Reds and Red Sox in his 2009 book, *Game Six.* "Stars had delivered under pressure, unknowns had turned into heroes, and millions of fans with no rooting interest in either team had been brought back to baseball by the extraordinary drama the two teams created."

The '75 Reds and Red Sox had three players apiece inducted into the Hall of Fame, plus plenty of All-Stars to go round. Yet two seemingly minor in-season moves by the Red Sox for an infielder and reliever helped the club claim its first division crown, sweep the three-time defending world champion Oakland A's in the ALCS, and take the favored Big Red Machine to the final inning of the seventh game before falling.

Player	Pos	Trans.	Uni #	What Happened
Denny Doyle	2B	In	15	Picked up from Angels and hit .298; was also solid in postseason.
Tim McCarver	C	Out	33	Carlton Fisk came back and someone had to go. You know McCarver had something to say about this.
Player	Pos	Trans.	Uni #	What Happened
Jim Willoughby	P	In	38	A July Fourth present: St. Louis owed the Sox a player and gift-wrapped Willoughby, who proved a key reliever down the stretch.
Dick McAuliffe	3B	In	3	Three-time Tiger All-Star cost Red Sox Ben Oglivie. Re-signed after being cut by Boston at the end of '74, he was cut again exactly one year later.
Tony Conigliaro	OF	Out	25	The one bitter spot of the 1975 season: Tony C. batted .123 in Boston and .203 in Pawtucket in his final comeback.
Deron Johnson	1B	In	15	Red Sox got him from White Sox in late September. He batted .600 but wasn't eligible for postseason.

#26: Chicken and Doughnuts

One of the first men to wear the #26 was a professional clown, **Al Schacht**, a coach in 1935. "The Clown Prince of Baseball" reportedly made much more money clowning than he had as a player or coach. And then almost half a century later came first-ballot Hall of Famer **Wade Boggs**.

The sideshow that always seemed to surround Boggs might have made fans forget that he was a five-time batting champion. A lengthy romantic liaison with one Margo Adams became a national sensation with Boggs confessing to being a "sex addict." And all the time people had just thought he was addicted to chicken, his ritual meal before every game, one of his many precisely timed daily practices. These sounded quaint at first, but after his Margo confession, it made one wonder if other habits were timed to the second. His wife, Debbie—apparently tired of making chicken and dealing with his B.S.—ran over him with her van. When approached by a knife-wielding assailant, Boggs said he escaped by willing himself invisible. He played 1,625 games during his 11 seasons with the Red Sox and hit for a cumulative .338 average. Boggs led the league in reaching base eight straight years—so

Wade Boggs

whatever he was doing off the field didn't seem to hurt his batting eye. He later played for the Yankees and Tampa Bay, becoming the first player to homer for his 3,000th hit; it was the last of his 116 career home runs. Boggs wanted a Devil Rays cap depicted on his 2005 plaque in Cooperstown—he played all of 213 games there—but the Hall of Fame justly said no and stuck a "B" on him.

After all that Boggsian drama, it's not surprising #26 was worn 13 times post-Boggs. Yet no one had worn it for seven years after Boggs's former Yankees teammate **Ramiro Mendoza** donned it in Boston in 2003–04. (Mendoza's last appearance with the Red Sox resulted in taking the loss in the 19–8 shelling in the '04 ALCS that preceded the comeback for the ages.)

Then it somehow became "available" again, for **Scott Podsednik**. Starting in 2013, uber-utilityman **Brock Holt**—the "Brock Star"—put the number on his back. And on June 16, 2015, he hit for the cycle, something no Red Sox player had done since John Valentin in 1996.

In December 2015, it was announced that #26 would be retired, honoring Wade Boggs, in a ceremony to be held during the 2016 season. On being informed of the team's decision, Boggs issued a statement saying, "I am so humbled and honored to be among the greatest legends to ever put on a uniform for the amazing city of Boston. To say that your number will never be worn again is the highest honor an athlete can receive. Thank you."

There have been some interesting characters who would do both Al Schacht and Wade Boggs proud. There was the only Red Sox player to be raised in a communal utopian society, **Bill Zuber**. "Goober" Zuber was born and raised in the Amana Colonies in Iowa, a right-handed pitcher who was 6–1 for the Red Sox at the end of his career in the late 1940s.

Another #26 was a tail-gunner on a Royal Canadian Air Force bomber: **Phil Marchildon**. Shot down over the North Sea at night—Marchildon and just one other crew member survived—he was captured and spent eight months as a POW at Stalag Luft III. He returned to the Philadelphia Athletics after the war, amassing 68 wins before being released in July 1950. He spent 19 days with Boston, appeared in one game, faced seven batters, walked two, and gave up one hit. A run scored. Five days later, he was released.

Combining excellent pitching with some power at bat was **Earl Wilson**, whose 17 homers equaled Wes Ferrell for most by a Red Sox pitcher. (Doesn't seem like anyone else will be joining that exclusive Boston club.) Wilson clubbed one of those homers in his June 26, 1962, no-hitter; that third-inning homer broke open a scoreless game against Bo Belinksy of the Angels. Wilson had one two-homer game, and he became the last Red Sox pitcher to hit a home run in extra innings when his leadoff homer off Jim Palmer in the top of the 10th inning beat the Orioles on May 18, 1966.

Combining decent pitching with double cheeseburgers was **Reggie Cleveland**, who didn't come from a communal society but did hail from Saskatchewan. A doughnut almost cost him his life when his car overturned in a Storrow Drive tunnel on June 30, 1975. He had reportedly been reaching into the back seat for a doughnut when his car flipped; he received 15 facial stitches. And that was his best year with the Sox. Cleveland—oh, we had to look it up; Reggie had a 6–6 lifetime mark against Cleveland—was 46–41 with the Sox, averaging 4.04 runs allowed per nine innings pitched. The first Canadian to start a postseason game, he got a no-decision in Game Two of the 1975 ALCS and lost Game Five of the '75 World Series.

Framingham favorite **Lou Merloni** wasn't wearing #26 when he hit a home run in his first career at-bat—a game-winning blast on May 15, 1998, with his parents in the stands celebrating their 33rd anniversary ("Loooouuuu" wore #50 for that occasion)—and Hollywood native

Freddy Sanchez wasn't wearing #26 when he won the 2006 batting title (he was in Pittsburgh by then, having been traded to the Bucs in the Jeff Suppan deal of 2003). **Joe Rudi** was assigned #28 in 1976 but never wore it in a game the first time he was acquired by the Red Sox, because the sale of All-Stars Rudi and Rollie Fingers to Boston by Oakland owner Charlie O. Finley was voided by Commissioner Bowie Kuhn. Rudi arrived for real in a 1981 trade with the Angels for Fred Lynn (Frank Tanana came with Rudi), and wore #26. Rudi hit .180 in 122 Boston at-bats and returned to Oakland after the season—this time of his own free will.

MOST OBSCURE RED SOX PLAYER TO WEAR #26—**John LaRose** pitched on September 20, 1978, during the final push of a season so tight the Yankees and Red Sox wound up playing a single-game playoff (the so-called Bucky Dent game). LaRose might have made a difference, but he was told to take a seat. The Tigers were up, 3–0, in the fifth inning and there were runners on first and second with nobody out. He walked the first batter to load the bases, but the next batter was cut down at home plate and he got out of it with an inning-ending double play. Unfortunately, he also pitched in the sixth and gave up a three-run homer. After putting on the first two men in the seventh, he was pulled out. Both men scored and the Tigers romped, 12–2. The Sox lost only once more the last 10 games of the season until the single-game playoff. During that tragic epic, LaRose and Bob Stanley were both warming up in the Boston bullpen when Dent hit his homer. Torrez walked Mickey Rivers. Stanley was called in. Zimmer sent the message to the bullpen: "LaRose, sit down." John and his career 22.50 ERA took a seat. Permanently.

Change of Fortune: 1986

All four of Boston's World Series Game Seven defeats were truly painful, but this may have been the toughest to take. Getting to the postseason for the first time since 1975 required help from outside sources, especially during the season when the Sox needed an upgrade at shortstop and another outfielder—they got both at the same moment. The 1986 Sox also got Tom Seaver for the last 16 starts of his remarkable career. Players who arrived and departed in '86 are listed as "In" and "Out." This list, however, does not include transactions before or after the season or minor league players promoted or demoted. Players are listed in the order the transactions were made during the season.

Player	Pos	Trans.	Uni #	What Happened
Tom Seaver	P	In	41	If only he'd been well enough to pitch in Game Six at Shea. Alas knee, alas fate . . .
Steve Lyons	IF	Out	12	Psycho goes to the South Side for Seaver in June Sox swap.
Dave Henderson	OF	In	40	The August deal with Seattle landed Boston an October hero.
Spike Owen	SS	In	5, 12	An absolute heist: Owen and Hendu for one rookie shortstop, two Mikes, and John Christensen.
Rey Quinones	SS	Out	51	He made a lot of errors, didn't show enough stick, and had no speed.
Mike Brown	P	Out	27	A former second-round pick, he spent parts of five seasons in Boston.
Mike Trujillo	P	Out	45	A Rule V pick, he did all right with Sox and had two decent years in Seattle.

#27: Pudge

Contemplating #27 will inevitably and forever start with **Carlton Fisk**, since it's his number that's retired and affixed to Fenway's right-field roof facade. Jason Varitek has surpassed him in a number of categories as catcher for the Red Sox, but Fisk was a New Englander and will forever be remembered for that indelible moment: urging his ball fair until it clunked off the foul pole affixed to the Green Monster in the bottom of the 12th inning to win Game Six of the 1975 World Series. It's been shown hundreds and hundreds of times on television and will be shown hundreds and hundreds of times more.

In Fisk's rookie year of 1972 he became the first player to ever win the Rookie of the Year Award by unanimous vote. Fisk was a tough player behind the plate and some of his confrontations with certain members of the New York Yankees helped stoke the rivalry between the two teams. After 11 seasons with the Red Sox, he had played in 1,068 games with a .284 average and 162 homers. It still remains a bit of a mystery how the Red Sox could forget to mail Fisk his contract renewal until two days after the deadline; the oversight made Fisk a free agent. He signed with the White

Carlton Fisk's game-winning home run in Game 6 of the 1975 World Series.

Sox, but #27 wasn't available, so he reversed digits when he switched Sox, becoming #72. He put in 13 seasons for Chicago and set several records for longevity by a catcher. Fisk was voted into the Hall of Fame in 2000, the right Sox represented on his plaque.

Another local guy made good is "Monbo," **Bill Monbouquette**, from Medford, Massachusetts. He had the misfortune of pitching for the Sox during the down years. By the Impossible Dream year of 1967, Monbo was—of all places—at Yankee Stadium trying to hang on in the bigs. He maintained a 3.69 ERA with Boston and had 96 of his 114 career victories for the Red Sox, including double-digit wins for six straight years (his 20–10 record in 1963 came for a 76–85 club). Monbo struck out 17 Senators in a 1961 game, second only to Bob Feller's record at the time (18 K's). He also threw a no-hitter in 1962 against the White Sox, edging Early Wynn in a tight 1–0 duel. A good friend to Pumpsie Green when the Red Sox integrated in 1959, Monbo drew a line in the sand when coach Del Baker used the "n" word. Monbo was blunt with Baker: "I'm going to tell you something. I'll knock you right on your ass. I don't care if you're the coach or not. You don't do things like that!"

Greg Harris was a switch-pitching pitcher, but he had the misfortune of playing for Red Sox management at a time when they didn't have a sufficient sense of humor (or history), and so his ambidexterity as a pitcher was never put to the test in Boston. Even when, in 1990, he led the league by appearing in 80 games, never once was Greg A. Harris (middle initial used in box scores to differentiate Gregory Allen Harris with contemporary non-ambidextrous hurler Gregory Wade Harris) allowed to release his inner southpaw. Only the Expos afforded him the opportunity. On September 28, 1995, Cincinnati led Montreal, 9–3. In the top of the ninth, Harris got Reggie Sanders to ground out to first and then, utilizing a special glove, started pitching left-handed. He walked the first batter, but got lefty-swinger Ed Taubensee to ground out catcher to first, and switched back to throwing right-handed to retire Bret Boone on a comebacker. No one had pitched using both arms in an inning since 1888 . . . and it turned out to be the final weekend of Harris's 15-year career. He was 39–43 with Boston—often taking the subway unrecognized to Kenmore Square and walking to Fenway—and held a 3.91 Sox ERA, along with a talent that could have lessened pitching changes, driven opposing managers to distraction, and made him a lot of money . . . but a weapon doesn't work if it's never used.

Here's a test. Which pitcher do you know more about: **Mike Brown** or **Skinny Brown**? Neither is well-known today, but Mike was the first of nine #27s right after Fisk—not *that* long ago—and he lasted five seasons with the Red Sox. Mike was a second-round draft pick, a right-handed pitcher, mostly a starter, who was 12–18 with a 5.57 ERA (he would have had a marginally winning record but for his 1–8 season in 1984). Hal "Skinny" Brown was signed by the Red Sox but first played for the White Sox—selected by Chicago in the 1950 Rule V draft, he was returned to his prior club, the Seattle Rainiers of the Pacific Coast League, then traded to Chicago after the season. He pitched for the White Sox for parts of two years. In February 1953, the White Sox really wanted Vern Stephens, so they packaged Brown with Marv Grissom and Bill Kennedy. He wound up 13–14 with a 4.40 ERA in Boston.

Charlie Wagner was one of the longest-serving members of the Red Sox in history, working for the club until he died. Known as "Broadway" Charlie Wagner, he was Ted Williams's roommate when The Kid came up in 1939 because of the veteran's sober and serious nature, plus the fact that he—like Ted—went to bed early and got up early. From his signing as a player in 1934 until the day he died while scouting for the Red Sox in the summer of 2006, Wagner spent more than 70 years with the Red Sox, including parts of six seasons with the "varsity." (It's hard to imagine hurler-hating Teddy Ballgame rooming with a pitcher, but non–night owls were hard to come by in the late 1930s.) Charlie had just started coming into his own in 1941 (12–8) and 1942 (14–11), but World War II intervened—as it did for his roommate and young men throughout the world. Wagner served in the navy, in the Philippines and New Guinea, and developed dysentery, which really did him in as a pitcher. After going 1–0 (with a 5.87 ERA) in 1946, he went into scouting for the Red Sox. When the Sox finally won a world championship in 2004 (he was in St. Louis to see the final game of the Series), Charlie Wagner opened the 2005 season at Fenway by saying "Play ball!" into the pre-game microphone. On August 30, 2006, he presented the Charlie Wagner Scholarship Award between innings at a game in his hometown of Reading, Pennsylvania. He made his way outside and expired while waiting for the driver to arrive and take him home.

From Broadway to Hollywood. Infielder **Lou Stringer** was perhaps not the clothes horse that Wagner was, but the former Cub concluded his six seasons of major league ball with the Red Sox (1948–50). He then returned whence he had come: the Hollywood Stars. Stringer hit .246 in 69 at-bats over parts of three seasons with the Red Sox. In his offseasons, he worked as an automobile salesman but also appeared in some Hollywood films, particularly those with baseball themes such as *The Jackie Robinson Story* and *The Monty Stratton Story*. He told us that he got tired of standing around on movie sets doing little or nothing most of the time, so he went back to where the action was: selling cars. The Corvette he once sold Elvis was, he said, an underwhelming experience. "He called and ordered it over the phone." Stringer drove it out to his place, and swapped it for a check. "He was nice, but I don't think he said 20 words while I was there." The King has left the building . . . with the car keys.

MOST OBSCURE RED SOX PLAYER TO WEAR #27—We thought this one was going to be a squeaker, with **Tex Aulds** (1947), **Kip Gross** (1999), **John Michaels** (1932), **Dick Midkiff** (1938), **Ed Phillips** (1970), and **Stan Royer** (1994) all solid candidates. But the last name we checked was the hands-down winner: **William McWilliams**. He pinch-hit for pitcher Ed Morris and made an out in the second game of a pair the Yankees swept from Boston on July 8, 1931. Three days later, there was another doubleheader, in Washington. He was retired again as a pinch hitter in the ninth inning of the first game as the Sox were swept that day, too. Three years later, Bill McWilliams suited up in the majors again, but it was in the NFL for the Detroit Lions.

Change of Fortune: 2004

Following a bitter defeat to the Yankees in Game Seven of the 2003 ALCS, the Red Sox came into '04 armed with a new manager, Terry Francona, plus a workhorse starter and post-season stud, Curt Schilling. Help was needed in-season, though, and Sox GM Theo Epstein proved he was not afraid to trade a star if it meant bringing the Sox closer to the championship that had eluded the club since 1918. This list does not include players already with the team, promoted or demoted from the minors, but the "In" and "Out" categories list the players who came to town or were sent walking for this idiot's delight season.

Player	Pos	Trans.	Uni #	What Happened
Curt Leskanic	P	In	30	A reliever who'd thrived at Coors Field, he was released by the Royals in June. He got the Game Four win against the Yankees.
Jimmy Anderson	P	In/Out	46	Lefty reliever came from the Cubs for a minor leaguer and was released a month later with a 6.00 ERA.
Pedro Astacio	P	In	39	This Coors vet didn't have much left, though the Sox kept him in the system through October.

Player	Pos	Trans.	Uni #	What Happened
Ricky Gutierrez	2B	In	16	Went from Mets to Cubs to Sox in '04. He played 21 games in Boston but didn't make the postseason roster.
Terry Adams	P	In	53	Came from Toronto in July. Like Anderson, had a 6.00 ERA, but he was 2–0 in 19 games . . . only to miss the postseason roster.
Dave Roberts	OF	In	31	Given the other deal that day, no one thought anything of this trade with the Dodgers. He'd come in handy, though.
Nomar Garciaparra	SS	Out	5	Boston icon sent to Cubs in four-team deadline swap that shook the Nation.
Orlando Cabrera	SS	In	36, 44	He came from Montreal in the Nomar deal, hit .379 in the ALCS, and wound up a World Series champion.
Doug Mientkiewicz	1B	In	13	In from Minnesota in the Nomar deal, former gold medalist wound up with the ball from golden moment and wouldn't give it back (for a while).
Mike Myers	P	In	36	Side-winding lefty specialist was cut by Seattle in August and grabbed by the Sox. He got into 25 games, threw five postseason games, and returned in '05.
Sandy Martinez	C	In	58	Purchased in September, he was insurance and an easy policy to cancel.
Phil Seibel	P	Out	53	He pitched twice in April—the only two games he ever pitched in the majors—and was released in late September.

#28: Watch Your Back . . . Or What's On It

By one standard, #28 is the most popular number in Red Sox history: some 58 different players have worn it. Read another way, of course, that means that players who were #28 don't tend to stick around too long or trade it in for a number they like better. History shows that it's more that they haven't stuck around that long. There are 18 years in which two or more players have worn #28, and five years in which it's belonged to three or more. Four players wore it in 1951 (**Tom Wright**, **Aaron Robinson**, **Mel Hoderlein**, and **Karl Olson**). **Steve Crawford** finally put an end to that, wearing it for parts of seven seasons.

Crawford was a 6-foot, 5-inch right-hander from Oklahoma signed by the Red Sox after he went undrafted in 1978. His Sox stats have a lot of zeroes: his first year (1980), he was 2–0. In 1981, he was 0–5. In 1982, he was 1–0. He spent 1983 in Pawtucket (no one wore #28 that year), but Crawford returned to go 5–0 in '84. By the time he wrapped up work with Boston in 1987, he was 19–13 with a 4.15 ERA. Later, he pitched parts of three seasons with Kansas City. His winless '81 pretty much put an end to his time as a starter, but he became a fairly effective reliever and his 12 saves even led the '85 club. His most prized memories are likely the wins he

Steve Crawford	1980–82, 1984–87
Steve Ellsworth	1988
Jeff Stone	1990
Bob Zupcic	1992–94
Greg Litton	1994
Derek Lilliquist	1995
Eric Gunderson	1995–96
Mike Benjamin	1997–98
Pat Rapp	1999
Tim Young	2000
Bernard Gilkey	2000
Marcus Jensen	2001
Doug Mirabelli	2001–07
David Ross	2008
Dave Magadan	2009–10 (coach)
Adrian Gonzalez	2011–12
Greg Colbrunn	2013–14 (coach)
Robbie Ross Jr.	2015

Note: Oakland's sale of Joe Rudi and Rollie Fingers to the Red Sox was disallowed before either man got to play in a game, though they were assigned uniforms. Rudi was assigned #28.

Number of times this number was issued: 61

Longest tenure by any given player: 7 seasons, Doug Mirabelli (389 games) and Steve Crawford (173 games)

recorded in 1986 in the ALCS against the Angels (after Dave Henderson homered, the Angels tied it up and Crawford was the pitcher of record after Hendu's 11th-inning sacrifice fly), and in the World Series against the Mets (his Game Two win at Shea came after Roger Clemens departed too early to qualify for the win; Crawford faced six batters, giving up just one single).

Doug Mirabelli may have set a record of sorts, being let go by Boston on five different occasions. Originally acquired in trade from Texas for Justin Duchscherer in mid-2001, he was granted free agency just five days after the Red Sox won the 2004 World Series. Four weeks later, the Sox re-signed Mirabelli, whose most marketable skill was his ability to catch knuckleballer Tim Wakefield. That skill brought him back in 2006 when—after Josh Bard struggled with Wake's knuckler—the Sox packaged Bard, Cla Meredith, and some money to the Padres to bring Mirabelli back. He arrived in dramatic fashion, actually changing into his uniform in the back of a State Police car as he was driven from the airport to Fenway Park, just in time to get into the game. All that fuss for a guy who went 0-for-4 that evening and hit .191 for the year (with 11 passed balls). He re-signed and helped Boston win another World Series in '07. Granted free agency once more, he signed again but was released during spring training . . . the fifth time he'd been sent packing. Adding up the time he spent in a Boston uniform (always #28), he hit .238, homered 48 times, and drove in 160 runs. Oddly, he was also a .238 lifetime postseason hitter. With the Red Sox, he had 66 passed balls; he can thank Wakefield for that. Jason Varitek can thank Mirabelli from saving him years of aggravation behind the plate trying to box the knuckler.

It says a lot about #28 that a backup catcher and a mop-up guy have spent the most time wearing it. Who else of note has tugged on the shirt? Provocatively nicknamed pitchers **Cot Deal** and **Riverboat Smith** are interesting if not middling. And what of **Greg Litton**? Signed as a free agent in 1994 after hitting .299 in Seattle, he was paid approximately $200,000 for one RBI. It's painful to recall the two days in Fenway Park limbo at #28 by All-Star left fielder **Joe Rudi**, whose 1976 sale by Oakland (with Rollie Fingers) was voided by buttinsky commissioner Bowie Kuhn. To be fair, Kuhn also kept Vida Blue from similarly being sold to the Yankees in the "best interests of baseball."

The Rudi/Fingers deal might have transformed Red Sox history in any number of ways, but it was not to be. During the offseason of 2010, heading into 2011, the Sox signed both Carl Crawford and **Adrian Gonzalez**. It was "A-Gon" who wore #28—and he performed pretty much just the way the Sox had hoped. His 213 base hits led the majors in 2011. He hit .338 (second in the league) with 117 RBIs (third in the league). And yet he lacked the color that Boston fans have come to love from their players. When he and Carl Crawford were both traded to the Dodgers in August 2012, Gonzalez already had 86 RBIs and was hitting an even .300—but fans weren't that sad to see him go.

Did you know that #28 once belonged to **Jack E. Robinson** in Boston? Well, he played at the same time as *the* Jackie Robinson, the pioneering infielder once given a sham tryout at Fenway, but most never noticed that Jack E. Robinson played in the majors. The Red Sox right-hander threw four innings over three games during one week in May 1949.

How about two second-generation pitchers for the Red Sox? **Allen Ripley**, whose father Walt Ripley pitched two games in 1935 (wearing #18), and **Steve Ellsworth**, whose father Dick wore #36 in 1968 and 1969. Allen doubled his father's career innings total in his first game—an eight-inning effort in Cleveland on April 10, 1978—and wound up throwing 137 2/3 innings with a 5–6 record and 5.36 ERA before being sold to San Francisco prior to the 1980 season. Dick Ellsworth came to Boston after nine years in the National League and put up very good numbers (16–7, 3.07 ERA) in his one full season in Boston before a six-player deal dispatched him to Cleveland in early 1969. Dick's son

Steve, the one who wore #28, played hard to get. The Twins selected him in the seventh round of the January 1980 draft and he did not sign. The Indians selected him in the third round of the June 1980 draft and he did not sign. When the Red Sox made him a first-round pick (ninth overall) in the June 1981 draft, he signed. Unfortunately, the Sox came to wish he'd signed with Minnesota or Cleveland. Steve's career was just eight games long, and he was 1–6 with 27 earned runs in 36 innings (that translates to a 6.75 ERA).

A pair of characters kept #28 occupied for half a dozen years: **Dennis "The Menace" Bennett** (1965–67) and **Albert "Sparky" Lyle** (1967–71). Bennett arrived in Boston from the Phillies in exchange for Dr. Strangeglove (a.k.a. Dick Stuart) in November 1964. Bennett was 12–13 overall with Boston before he was sent to the Mets. Two Bennett incidents are reported in *Tales from the Red Sox Dugout*. There was the time he resolved an argument with roommate Lee "Mad Dog" Thomas as to which of them would turn out the light in the room—by shooting out the light with one of the guns he carried. Another time, when he had to cross the country to attend a teammate's wedding, he traveled for free by having a stewardess friend lock him in the plane's toilet for the flight, with an "out of order" sign to protect him. Whether he was packing a pistol for the flight, we don't know.

Sparky Lyle debuted with the Red Sox about a week after Bennett was traded. He was 1–2 in '67, and not involved in the World Series that fall. In five seasons with the Red Sox, he pitched exclusively in relief, going 22–17 with 69 saves and an excellent 2.85 ERA in 260 games. Why would the Red Sox trade away a pitcher like that? Bill Lee believes Lyle was traded because he'd dropped his pants and sat on Tom Yawkey's birthday cake (a recurring stunt he was apparently famous for doing). "The next day Lyle is shipped off to the Yankees and here comes Danny Cater," said the Spaceman. The 1972 trade happened about a month after Yawkey's birthday (February 21), so that was either a tardy celebration or a tweaked memory. Lyle blew out the candles in the American League for most of his seven seasons with New York. Lyle was 57–40 with a 2.41 ERA and 141 saves for the

Yankees, plus a 3–0 postseason mark in 1977, the year he became the first AL reliever to win the Cy Young.

Finally, the only member (so far) of the Red Sox who was born in Poland was a #28: **Johnny Reder**. Born in Lublin, he played 10 games at first base and one at third in 1932; he made one error at each position. At the plate, he was 5-for-37 (.135) with six total bases, six walks, and six strikeouts. He went on to become chief engineer at the J&J Corrugated Box Company in Fall River, Massachusetts, the city where he died in 1990. His obituary in the *Fall River Herald News* states that he "was also considered one of the top professional soccer players in the country and was named a soccer All-American." He had been a goalie for the New York Marksmen (1929–30) and the New York Yankees(!), who were somehow also called the New Bedford Whalers, in 1931, before coming to the Red Sox to play baseball.

MOST OBSCURE RED SOX PLAYER TO WEAR #28—Alex Mustaikis of Chelsea, Massachusetts, was a right-handed pitcher who played for a month in 1940. He threw an even 15 innings, but faced 76 batters—that's a bad sign already. In the 15 innings, he gave up 15 hits. And he walked 15 batters, too. He also gave up 15 earned runs! Hoo boy. Somehow his record was only 0–1, though the 9.00 ERA tells it all. He was better at the plate, batting .333 with two hits and three RBIs.

Change of Fortune: 2007

The Red Sox thought they needed bullpen help in 2007 and the Eric Gagne trade blew up in their faces. As much as any of the six American League pennants won in the uniform number era by the Red Sox, this one required the least in-season tinkering. (And was able to withstand the good deal gone very bad with the acquisition of supposed bullpen help.) This list does not include deals made before the season—though getting Josh Beckett and Mike Lowell from the Marlins and Daisuke Matsuzaka and Hideki Okajima from Japan certainly helped. "In" and "Out" are the categories for those brought in or shipped out during the season, but it does not include players brought up or demoted from the minors (although Rookie of the Year Dustin Pedroia and Jacoby Ellsbury were stellar). The result was Boston's second World Series sweep since 2004.

Player	Pos	Trans.	Uni #	What Happened
J.C. Romero	P	Out	32	Lefty had a 3.15 ERA but allowed too many runners (WHIP 1.950). Released in June, he prospered with the Phillies.
Kason Gabbard	P	Out	61	Was 4–0 as a Sox starter before being sent to Texas with David Murphy and Engel Beltre for Eric Gagne.
David Murphy	OF	Out	44	A first-round pick, he got the chance to play with Texas.
Eric Gagne	P	In	83	The former Cy Young winner was a total bust in Boston. The '07 Sox were good enough to win in spite of him.
Joel Pineiro	P	Out	36	Red Sox tried to make him a reliever. Sent to St. Louis for a minor leaguer, Dave Duncan worked his magic.
Bobby Kielty	OF	In	32	Picked off waivers from Oakland in August, he played 20 games for the Red Sox and homered in the World Series.
Wily Mo Pena	OF	Out	22	Traded to the Nationals in August for Chris Carter. Sorry, but good riddance.
Royce Clayton	SS	In	11	For reasons unclear, he ended his 11-team, 17-year baseball odyssey with six hitless September at-bats for Boston.

#29: Foulke Hero

"**S**wing and a ground ball, stabbed by Foulke. He has it. He underhands to first. And the Boston Red Sox are the world champions. For the first time in 86 years, the Red Sox have won baseball's world championship. Can you believe it?"

Joe Castiglione's call of the play that ended the 2004 World Series focused, of course, on the grounder that Edgar Renteria hit back to **Keith Foulke**, who tossed underhanded to Doug Mientkiewicz for the final out in St. Louis. Foulke became a short-lived hero, and some have said that he ruined his career, giving his all in 2004, since he was never the same pitcher after that. His 2004 ERA was 2.17 in 83 regular-season innings. That October it was 0.00 in the ALDS, 0.00 in the ALCS (appearing in five of the seven games), and 1.80 in the World Series, with Foulke earning a win in Game One and finishing each of the four World Series games.

Foulke had led the American League in appearances (67) and saves (43) the year before with Oakland. Might he have made enough of a difference to hold off the Yankees in 2003 and prevent the Sox from losing in seven during that year's ALCS? We'll never know but

Theo Epstein and the baseball operations staff went after him in earnest the moment he became a free agent that fall. He had a bit of a public relations problem in Boston, with some of his candid statements coming across poorly. It didn't sit too well when he said he didn't even like baseball (what he decried was all the downtime that goes with the game) and grumbling about "Johnny from Burger King" booing him when he wasn't doing well (his 2005 ERA was 5.15 and the remark seemed to snidely put down fans making the $6.75 per hour minimum wage while he was working on a $30-million or so guaranteed contract). But his performance in 2004 was an MVP-caliber year and one that many Red Sox fans will never forget.

Shea Hillenbrand could also rub people the wrong way. The 3B/1B/DH played for Boston in 2001 and 2002, breaking in with a .263 rookie season and 49 RBIs, blossoming in his sophomore year to .293 and 83 RBIs. Things were looking up, and he was hitting .303 near the end of May 2003 when he was traded to Arizona for pitcher Byung-Hyun Kim. Why the trade? It might have something to do with enmity between him and Epstein, whom he had called a "faggot" on a radio show some days earlier, demanding a trade, while expostulating, "They don't know what they have with me . . . You've heard of Jeff Bagwell?" Hillenbrand hit .267 in Arizona. His replacement, Bill Mueller, won the American League batting title. Similarly egocentric comments from Shea saw him quickly ushered out of Toronto and Anaheim.

Adrian Beltre was frankly a "rental" for a year in 2010, and he led the league in doubles, drove in 102 runs, and hit .321. He also smashed into two different teammates, most notably Jacoby Ellsbury, who only played in 12 games that year after his collision in the field with Beltre.

Is there something about #29 and a running of the mouth disorder? Well there was a man who lived his life as a former #29 and only death parted him from the lie. It began when baseball historian David Lambert telephoned to console **Bill Henry**'s widow after reading about the Red Sox pitcher's passing. She replied that Bill was sitting right there in the living room. The upshot of this "reports of my death have been greatly exaggerated" moment was that another man, who had recently died, had posed as Bill Henry for more than 20 years. He'd convinced his wife and friends that he'd been the 16-year major league veteran pitcher. He looked enough like the real Bill Henry to pull it off; both were left-handed, 6-feet, 2-inches tall, and of similar age. The widow and friends of the fraudulent Henry were left confused, but for the real Henry's friends and fans who'd read the first story, it was a bigger save than any of the 90 he had as a big leaguer from 1952 to 1969.

Another player who didn't die—but had a brush or two with death—was **Rogelio "Roger" Moret**. The Puerto Rican lefty broke in with Boston in 1970 at age 20 and had two excellent won-loss seasons: 1973 (13–2) and 1975 (14–3). That culminated in an impressive 41–18 mark and 3.43 ERA in Boston, plus a 1–0 record and 0.00 ERA in the '75 post-season. His low point for the Red Sox, however, came on August 5 that year. Scheduled to start that evening, he crashed his car into a parked trailer on I-95 at 4:30 in the morning . . . in Connecticut, over 90 miles from Fenway. He did not make his start, though he did win six of his last eight decisions. A few years later with Texas, he fell into a catatonic state in front of his locker and was sent to a neuropsychiatric clinic.

The Red Sox had traded Moret after the '75 season for another odd bird of a #29: **Tom House**. As a pitching coach in Texas, he advocated that his charges throw footballs—strange enough, but Nolan Ryan liked it and credited House with getting him in the best shape of his career in his 40s. In 2005, House admitted that he was one of the earliest athletes to take steroids. "I tried everything known to man to improve my fast-ball, and it still didn't go faster than 82 miles per hour," House told the Associated Press. "I was a failed experiment." For the Red Sox, he appeared in 44 games over parts of two seasons, and won one game each season. The most noted steroid incident involving #29, however, was **Manny Alexander**, a .211 hitter with four home runs for Boston in 2000. His Mercedes was stopped by police in Dorchester after he lent it to a clubhouse attendant. The glove compartment contained syringes and steroids and the major leaguer let the high school kid take the heat.

A player who made the briefest of appearances, then came back after nearly five years away to be a regular, was **Jim Pagliaroni**. He signed with the Red Sox at age 17 and got into one game that summer, taking over defensively for catcher Sammy White on August 13, 1955. With the Senators winning, 18–8, Pagliaroni (wearing #22) hit a sacrifice fly to give him zero at-bats and one RBI. The next time Pagliaroni played for the Red Sox was August 1, 1960, and he got that long overdue official AB. He popped up. Pag played through 1962 for the Red Sox before being traded with Don Schwall to the Pirates for Dick Stuart plus Jack Lamabe. Pag hit .254 in his four years with the Red Sox; he hit .254 for the Pirates for five seasons.

In 1967, with the Red Sox battling for the pennant right down to the final game of the season, Uncle Sam had other plans for rookie reliever **Bill Landis**. With just four games remaining in the season, he was plucked from the bullpen and sent to Fort Polk, Louisiana. The only way he got to see the World Series was on TV. "My commanding officer was from Boston and he let me watch all the games on television in the rec room," Bill explained. His service commitment done, Landis pitched in 1968 to a 3.15 ERA; he threw 101 games in a Red Sox uniform and compiled a 9–8 mark and a 4.50 ERA.

A player who didn't go to war was **Oscar Judd**. Consequently, he was able to play for the Red Sox throughout World War II. He was Canadian, though that didn't matter as much as that he was 34 years old before the 1942 season began, and thus above the age of men being called to serve. Judd was a southpaw and didn't have the best control, but in 1943, against depleted rosters, he went 11–6 with a 2.90 ERA. He only got into nine games in 1944, losing his number temporarily to **Clem "Steamboat" Dreisewerd**, who subsequently joined the service. Judd was put on waivers on the last day of May 1945, three weeks after Germany surrendered.

MOST OBSCURE RED SOX PLAYER TO WEAR #29—Of the 46 players and five coaches who've worn #29, **John Lickert** stands out—or, depending on your view, doesn't stand out. In 1981, he appeared once behind the plate but never stepped into the batter's box as a hitter. He caught Mark Clear for the ninth inning, as the Sox beat the Yankees. And that was his career—but luckily for him, that September 19 game was nationally televised as *Game of the Week* so all of John's family and friends were able to see his work. Lucky for all involved that catchers get a lot of screen time. It would have to last.

The Great Oakland Laundry Theft

Rogelio Moret wore #29 throughout his six-year Red Sox career—except for one night. According to the commemorative book of the 1975 season, *Diary of a Winner*, after the Red Sox game in Oakland on May 12, "Thieves robbed the Sox clubhouse during the night." Seventeen jerseys and four pairs of pants were made off with—among the jerseys was Moret's. It had been Half-Price Night at the Oakland Coliseum, and someone apparently thought the bargain ticket included all the laundry one could grab. The Red Sox also reported a few uniforms stolen out of the clubhouse in Anaheim in the series that immediately preceded the trip to Oakland. (And it wasn't even Half-Price Night at the Big A!)

The night following the Oakland pilfering, May 13, Rick Wise started for the Red Sox and left in the seventh trailing the A's, 5–4. In came Moret . . . wearing Luis Tiant's #23. Neither the southpaw's penchant for pitching out of trouble nor El Tiante's mojo rubbed off. Taking over with a runner on second with one out, Moret got Reggie Jackson to pop up, and then walked Joe Rudi intentionally to face another lefty, Billy Williams. The 36-year-old Williams launched a three-run homer. Sal Bando followed with a walk, and pinch runner Matt Alexander stole on Moret. He issued his second intentional walk—and third base on balls of the inning—to Gene Tenace before retiring Claudell Washington to finally finish the seventh. The 9–5 loss was charged to Wise.

Moret had only pitched in four games in '75 when he left Oakland, including a perfect two-thirds of an inning in Oakland the previous night wearing his own jersey. His ERA for the year stood at 6.75 ERA—for those counting at home, a 26.87 ERA as a #23—but that was the low water mark of the year for Rogelio. Back in #29, he put together a marvelous 14–3 season and 3.60 ERA. He led the league with an .824 winning percentage and won 10 times as a starter after a promotion to the rotation, where he did not have to clean up anyone else's mess . . . or put on anyone else's clothes.

Change of Fortune: 2013

After winning two championships in quick succession, the Red Sox had a run of not so great luck that saw them miss reaching another World Series by one game in 2008, get swept in the 2009 Division Series, and then miss the postseason three straight years. The 2011 finish was so bad, the Sox lost both a nine-game lead and manager Terry Francona, who'd won the first Sox world championships since the First World War. An odd interlude with Bobby Valentine lasted a year, finishing in last place, and new manager John Farrell, traded from Toronto to Boston, helped the Red Sox reach the postseason once more, worst to first. How did they get back to this lofty perch and end up in Duck Boats yet again? In part, thanks to a perhaps unprecedented number of transactions in the 12 months beginning in October 2012. Take a gander at the personnel on this list, which only includes players coming in from other organizations or being shipped out over the course of the year (hence "In/Out" designations in chart).

Player, Pos	Trans	Uni#	What Happened
Nate Spears, OF-IF	Out	71	In changing the club from top to bottom, the Red Sox let go Spears; that same day they dumped Bobby Valentine.
Rubby De La Rosa, P	In	62	One of players to be named later in contract clearinghouse deal that shipped Adrian Gonzalez, Carl Crawford, and Josh Beckett to the Dodgers in August 2012. Rubby debuted in Boston as a reliever a year and a day after deal.
Allen Webster, P	In	64	Also came east in Dodgers deal and served as Sox starting pitcher in 2013. But like Rubby, Webby did not see postseason action and the two would again be traded together—to Arizona for Wade Miley.
Guillermo Quiroz, C	Out	62	Clearing out roster room at end of 2012. The Sox got very busy.
Jason Repko, OF	Out	16	Repko let go. The last major-league stop with an .091 finale for this No. 16.

John Farrell, MGR	In	53	In the oddest transaction of all, the Red Sox made their first-ever trade for a manager. As you can see, there were plenty of transactions made between October 2012 and 2013, but this deal with Toronto was as key as any trade. (See Mike Aviles)
Mike Aviles, SS	Out	3	Good enough to trade for a manager who would win the next World Series. J.D. Drew took Aviles's place in John's Farrell's new Boston order.
Che-Hsuan Lin, OF	Out	67, 85	When you wear No. 67 and 85, you may not be long for The Town.
Aaron Cook, P	Out	35	After surviving on the mound for a decade in Denver, Cook put up a 5.50 ERA at Fenway in the last year of his career.
James Loney, 1B	Out	22	After the big trade with the Dodgers, he was a place setter for a short meal at Fenway. Loney was a better fit in Tampa Bay.
Daisuke Matsuzaka, P	Out	18	Much ink was spilled and yen spent on the promise of Dice-K. He won 50 games and had a 4.52 ERA for the Red Sox, winning his lone World Series start and getting a ring as a 2007 "rookie." He re-emerged in the majors with the Mets in 2013 and later returned to the Japanese League he so famously fled. No posting fee required on the way back home.
Scott Podsednik, OF	Out	26	Working his way up from the minors, the Podfather of Dice-K. ended his career with a .302 average in 63 games for the Red Sox. Maybe it was a soft .300, but it's a nice curtain call for a singles hitter.

Vicente Padilla, P	Out	44	When this many players from a team never play again in the majors, it's a clear sign how bad the previous year was—and Padilla had a pretty decent 2012 for someone who'd pitched little in relief for a decade.
Cody Ross, OF	Out	7	It wasn't his last year as a major leaguer, but 2012 was his last year as an everyday outfielder. His 22 home runs were second-highest in his career and third on the team.
David Ross, C	In	3	Out with one Ross, in with another. No relation, but long-in-the-tooth backup backstop became a key contributor in the 2013 postseason. He had a few key hits and started all four Red Sox World Series wins against the Cards.
Scott Atchison, P	Out	48	Useful reliever with low ERA and injury history wound up a Met.
Zach Stewart, P	Out	47	Started twice for the 2012 Red Sox, lost both, and a 22.24 ERA. No surprise seeing him in the "out" category.
Rich Hill, P	Out	53	Southpaw reliever had a 1.83 ERA for the 2012 Sox before becoming a free agent, getting knocked around, coming back to Fenway in '15, and posting a 1.55 ERA—as a starter.
Danny Valencia, 3B	Out	23	Valencia was squeezed out of Boston after hitting just .143 in 2012.
Jonny Gomes, OF	In	5	Kind of guy you'd want in your foxhole, except maybe for that long beard. But with Sox down in the World Series and with Game Four tied, Gomes hit a three-run blast and Boston never trailed again.
Jonathan Diaz, OF	In	76	He would be a pinch runner and not got a hit in his brief Boston apprenticeship in 2013.

Shane Victorino, OF	In	18	"The Flying Hawaiian" signed as a free agent and was loved in Boston for his hard-nosed play and Gold Glove, but maybe not by opponents who drilled him more than any AL player. Knocked in 12 runs in 14 postseason games.
Ryan Dempster, P	In	46	Boston was the last stop in a 15-year big-league career and ended in his only championship locker room. Timing is everything.
Koji Uehara, P	In	19	Had a 1.09 ERA in 73 games and was even better in October. He had one hiccup in Tampa but saved the next game, was MVP in the ALCS, and fanned Cardinal Matt Carpenter to bring Boston its eighth world championship.
Joel Hanrahan, P	In	52	Wait, it was supposed to be Hanrahan getting that World Series-clinching K after coming over from the Pirates, but his arm gave out after 7 1/3 innings and he didn't pitch again in the majors.
Brock Holt, IF-OF	In	26	No, wait again. That wasn't the Joel Hanrahan deal; it was the Brock Holt deal. The versatile Texan made his AL debut in '13 as a fill-in and soon progressed into a Brock Star.
Mark Melancon, P	Out	37	The Pirates got a pretty good player back in the Brock Holt deal. It is no coincidence that in the reliever's first three seasons in Pittsburgh, the Pirates made the postseason each time after a 20-year drought with Melancon saving 100 games and posting a 1.85 ERA.
Stephen Drew, SS	In	7	Showed some pop and some glove. Compared to his Mendoza Line-challenged seasons that followed, Drew's .253 average in '13 was like Ted Williams.

Mike Napoli, DH	In	12	Another big beard and big postseason. Homered for only run off unhittable Mike Verlander in Game Three of ALCS.
Mike Carp, 1B	In	37	For a guy purchased from Seattle in spring training, Carp played plenty and drove in a run off the bench in the World Series. Carp Diem.
Ryan Sweeney, OF	Out	12	Sweeney seemed to do many of the things Mike Carp did, only not as well and with less power. So Sweeney became a Cub.
Brandon Murphy, 3B	In	23	But teams need depth, so when Ryan Sweeney left, the Sox signed Murphy, who'd been cut by Texas.
Pedro Ciriaco, SS	Out	23	When Brandon Murphy came up wearing 23, it was after Ciriaco was shipped to San Diego. All part of the circle of life in the majors.
Matt Thornton, P	In	38	The first sign that a team thinks it's serious is they acquire a left-handed reliever, whether he's good or not.
Jake Peavy, P	In	44	Jose Iglesias and a host of minor leaguers went to Detroit and Chicago to bring Jake Peavy to Boston for the stretch run. Peavy, who'd reached postseason just once in a long career, spent two straight years with world champions: the '13 Sox and '14 Giants.
Brayan Villareal, P	In	60	Came in Jake Peavy deal, pitched to one batter, walked him. And that was that.
Jose Iglesias, SS	Out	10	Iglesias was Tigers regular shortstop as replacement for suspended PED abuser Jhonny Peralta, who was allowed to come back for the postseason. That ridiculous loophole has since been covered.

Quintin Berry, OF	In	50	Late August acquisition from Royals to try to nail down the division. He batted just eight times, but hit .625 with one homer and four RBIs. Nailed it.
Clayton Mortensen, P	Out	59	Sent to Kansas City for Quintin Berry. Yet to make it back out of the minors, with a K.C. team suddenly stacked.
John McDonald, SS	In	10	Lyme, Connecticut kid who played at Providence College in the mid-1990s, finally got to play at Fenway—a nd celebrate—at age 39.

#30: From Awfulman to Sigh Young

When you get into the 30s, you start finding a lot of coaches, managers, and pitchers. The man who wore #30 the longest was a coach, **Tom Daly**. He'd spent most of his playing time with the White Sox and Cubs, but he coached the Red Sox for 13 years (1933–46), and even served as best man at Johnny Pesky's wedding. His biggest baseball moment might have been when he was 18 on a round-the-world exhibition tour with the White Sox and Giants in 1914. At the Chelsea Football Grounds, in England on February 26, playing before some 30,000 curious Englishmen, Daly was asked by King George V to hit a home run. "I'll do the best I can, Your Majesty," he replied. He then hit the first pitch of the 11th inning out of the park for a White Sox win in front of the king. Your wish is granted, my liege.

Representing the Tudors was lefty **John Tudor** (1979–83), a Red Sox third-round draft pick who found his way to back-to-back 13-win seasons in 1982 and 1983, making him sufficient trade bait to bring Mike Easler over from the Pittsburgh Pirates. With a mark of

78–40 *after* he left the Red Sox, the southpaw went 21–8 (with 10 shut-outs and a 1.93 ERA) for the 1985 Cardinals, winning two games in that year's World Series. But the short-tempered Tudor cut his left hand punching a fan (a rotary fan in the clubhouse) after exiting his Game Seven loss to the Kansas City Royals.

Kansas City Athletics fans probably felt the same sense of loss Sox faithful felt with Tudor when bemoaning the development of **Jose Santiago** in Boston. Unlike Tudor, though, Santiago hadn't shown much promise when he was sold to the Red Sox after the 1965 season. He'd been 1–6 over parts of three seasons with a 5.27 ERA. In Boston, he won an even dozen games each of the next two years, with nearly identical ERAs (3.66 and 3.59). The won and loss records reflect overall team performance—the 1966 Red Sox finished a half-game out of last place in the 10-team league and Santiago was 12–13; the 1967 Sox won the pennant and Jose was 12–4. With Jim Lonborg resting after clinching the pennant on the last day, Santiago lost a tough 2–1 World Series opener to Bob Gibson; the one Red Sox run was Santiago's home run in the third inning (his only other career homer had come that year against Detroit). Santiago lost again to Gibson in Game Four. It was just bad luck to draw Gibson both times—his home run accounted for the only Sox run over two games.

The announcement of .194-hitting, right-handed swinging **Bob Bailey** as a pinch hitter chased Cy Young southpaw Ron Guidry from the seventh inning of the epic 1978 one-game playoff against the Yankees. Bailey's 16-year career ended a few minutes later with a strikeout against Hall of Fame reliever Rich Gossage.

Another hard luck pitcher was **Matt Young,** who endured a psychological condition that inhibited him from throwing to first base, but he's best remembered for throwing the no-hitter that wasn't on April 12, 1992. A leadoff walk by Cleveland's Kenny Lofton, who took advantage of Young's "move" and catcher John Flaherty's major league debut by stealing second, then third, and scoring on an error: 1–0 Indians. In the third, two walks, and then two force outs with the lead runner advancing twice: 2–0 Tribe. Young had still not given up a hit, and never did. The Red Sox scored one run—despite nine hits—and because the game was in Municipal Stadium, there was no need for the Indians to bat in the bottom of the ninth. Five months later, MLB revoked no-hitter status from Young because he only threw eight innings, even though the game remains in the record book as a complete game and he never yielded a hit. They weren't just picking on Young, who didn't record a win in '91 before getting hurt; 50 pitchers in all lost no-hitters by MLB decree, including the 12 perfect innings in 1959 by Pittsburgh's Harvey Haddix ('71 Sox pitching coach, #33). A 2001 ESPN.com poll listed "Sigh" Young in Boston as the third-worst free-agent signing ever. Kick a guy when he's down, why don't ya.

Psychological problems did in **Tony Horton**. He debuted in Boston five months before he turned 20, playing left field for the 1964 Red Sox, the same year another teenage Tony (Conigliaro) broke in. Horton hit .294 in his second year, with some power, filling in after Gary Geiger broke his hand. He switched to #11 in 1966, but Horton spent most of the year in the minors since George Scott was playing so well at first base. In 1967, with Dick Williams looking for pitching help, GM Dick O'Connell traded Horton and Don Demeter to Cleveland for Gary Bell. It was with the Indians that Horton developed most of his stress-related symptoms, which included him crawling back to the dugout after a foul popup. He later survived a suicide attempt. All indications are that Tony was able to pull his life together and have a successful career in the non-baseball world, in business.

Another player who seemed not to live up to his baseball potential was **Matt Clement**. A closer look at his record reveals that he never had a winning record in the seven NL seasons before he was enticed to Boston by a contract in excess of $25 million. On July 26, 2005, Clement was struck in the head by a vicious line drive off the bat of Tampa Bay's Carl Crawford. Clement came back quickly, and won his next three decisions, but he lost his last three. He only started 12 times in 2006 before needing shoulder surgery. He signed on with the Cardinals and then the Blue Jays, but Clement never pitched another major league game. He announced his retirement in April 2009.

Haywood Sullivan wore three different numbers in his playing career as a member of the Red Sox, including #30 in his final year,

1960. He was an odd player, literally, catching every other year—1955, 1957, and 1959—before playing six times as many games in the even-numbered 1960 than the other three seasons combined. Given that he'd batted .000, .000, and .000 the first three times around, you did wonder what it was the Sox saw in him. Perhaps the .161 he pounded out—four extra-base hits!—in 1960 made their investment all seem worth while. Seeing Sullivan at the top of his game, the Washington Senators snared him in the 1960 expansion draft and then traded him two weeks later to the Kansas City Athletics. Sullivan must have been a courtly gentleman because Tom and Jean Yawkey seemed almost to "adopt" him as the son they never had. After T. A. Y.'s death, J. R. Y. seemed to like him so much that he was given co-ownership of the Red Sox in 1978. He remained in that capacity through the 1993 season. The year after he became co-owner, the Red Sox drafted Haywood's son Marc (#15), a veritable Johnny Bench compared to his dad with a .186 average in Boston in 137 career games caught.

Slugger **Sam Horn** was a first-round draft pick designated to become a DH, and he jumped into the majors in the second half of the 1987 season, swatting 14 homers in just 158 at-bats. Trouble was, he struck out 55 times. With Jim Rice getting the lion's share of the playing time in '88 and '89, there wasn't much room for Sam, who hit .148 both years and was released. He homered 23 times for the O's in 1989 but struck out 99 times in 317 at-bats. He lives on in Red Sox Nation as the namesake for the "Sons of Sam Horn" Web message board that's been frequented by Curt Schilling and owner John Henry. Ka-pow!

The signing of **Jose Offerman** by GM Dan Duquette mystified observers. Why was the switch-hitting second baseman given a lavish salary? And why for four years? His first six seasons with the Dodgers had been mediocre, but then—and this is what Duquette no doubt noticed—he seemed to flourish in Kansas City, hitting .306 over three seasons with a .385 on-base percentage. It was the OBP that "The Duke" cited when announcing the signing. Both figures were fairly close to those of recently departed Mo Vaughn, but Offerman had only hit 22 homers in the previous nine years. And he'd already earned the nickname "Awfulman" for the 42 errors he committed back in 1992. He only committed 43 in three years with Boston, but the Awfulman name was just too appealing to drop and his play on the field—or the base-paths, where he was 0-for-8 in stolen base attempts in 2000—did little to overcome it. When last seen with a bat in his hands he was wielding it in an independent league melee in Bridgeport in one of the ugliest scenes this side of Juan Marichal's 1965 tirade. Somehow, Offerman was subsequently deemed manager material in the Dominican Winter League. Maybe Dan Duquette put in a good word for him.

MOST OBSCURE RED SOX PLAYER TO WEAR #30—Jim Byrd appeared in back-to-back games for Boston, on May 31 and June 1, 1993. The shortstop was hitting .175 with 12 errors in just 45 games in the minors but Luis Rivera, Mike Greenwell, Cheo Garcia, and Steve Lyons were all injured. It was never intended that Byrd would stay more than a few days. He didn't. He was inserted to run for Andre Dawson in the eighth inning against the Royals; the box score records Byrd as "pr-dh." He made it as far as second base on a wild pitch. Boston lost, 5–3. The next day, again, Byrd came in to run. Again, he didn't score. Again, Boston lost to the Royals (4–3 this time). Immediately after the game, Greenwell was activated and Byrd was sent back to Pawtucket. He did not return.

There's nothing like experience in the dugout. When Arthur Giddon last served as batboy, it was 1923. He performed the job for the Boston Braves, but advice from the commissioner, Judge Kenesaw Landis, pushed him toward law. He always followed the Red Sox and asked what he wanted as he approached his 100 birthday, Giddon reflected that he'd like to be a batboy again. On April 25, 2009, Giddon got his wish. Wearing a uniform with his age and "Big Pappy" on the back, he went back to work. And got to meet the other "Big Papi."

#31: The Steal of the Century

There are far greater players who have worn #31, a cancer survivor turned World Series hero, the only Canadian in the Hall of Fame, and coaches of Cooperstown caliber: **Bobby Doerr** and **Herb Pennock** (dealt with earlier in Chapters #1 and #17, respectively), plus another coach who hit .440 during the Grover Cleveland administration, for corn sakes. But with a chapter title this obvious, you know, we know, everyone and their brother knows the identity of the man who put "The Steal" in the lexicon for a franchise known for its lack of speed and systematic opposition to "small ball." It's as obvious now as it was on October 17, 2004. But what Red Sox fan wouldn't want to hear the particulars one more time?

The Red Sox were losing to the Yankees in Game Four of the ALCS in the home ninth, 4–3. The failure to score meant elimination, a sweep at the hands of the hated Yankees, and losing the pennant to New York for the second year in a row. The Yankees had already won the first three games of the series, and they had Mariano Rivera, the best closer in the history of baseball, on the mound. But Kevin Millar walked, and in came **Dave Roberts** to run for him. A spare outfielder acquired for a minor leaguer at the trading deadline, Roberts had stolen five of seven bases since arriving from the Dodgers. Everyone knew he was going for it. He indeed went for it and barely beat Jorge Posada's throw . . . but he was safe. Bill Mueller followed with a single to center and Roberts scored to tie the game and set the stage for a comeback for the ages. Roberts also ran for Millar the next night and again scored the tying run with Rivera on the mound. That Roberts never played another game for the Red Sox can be construed as immaterial or perfect.

Jon Lester was a hero in Boston's next run to the title. One of the many homegrown pitchers the Red Sox have developed in recent years, Lester

Jon Lester

was a second-round pick in the first year under new ownership in 2002. His ERA improved each of his first three years, and the left-hander put up some very nice W–L totals: 7–2, 4–0, and 16–6. This despite being diagnosed with anaplastic large cell lymphoma and cutting short his rookie year, which began 5–0, to undergo chemotherapy. Cancer-free, he beat the Rockies in Game Four to clinch the 2007 World Series. He threw a no-hitter on May 19, 2008. Just over a year later, he took a perfect game into the seventh against Texas before it was broken up by Michael Young, who had the only two hits in Lester's complete-game win. Every time Boston kicked the tires on another team's star, Lester's name came up, but the southpaw stayed—a wise choice—and by the end of the '09 season (15–8, 3.41 ERA), many Sox observers were anointing him the team's ace. When the time came, former Red Sox GM Theo Epstein—who had moved on to run the Chicago Cubs—signed Lester as a free agent and brought him to Wrigley Field to pitch for the Cubbies. (Boston had in the interim traded him to Oakland for the last two months of the 2014 season, getting Yoenis Cespedes in exchange.) Maybe he didn't feel he was wanted in Boston anymore. In any event, the Cubs made him a better offer.

After two Red Sox heroes of October, here's Calvin. **Calvin Schiraldi** was taken eight spots after University of Texas teammate Roger Clemens in the first round of the '83 draft. After parts of two seasons with the Mets, he came to Boston in the eight-player trade that sent Bobby Ojeda to New York. Schiraldi pitched exceptionally well down the stretch, with a stellar 1.41 ERA, nine saves, and 51 innings in just 25 appearances following his callup in late July of '86. Three of his four wins followed blown saves, though, which might have served as a bit of a warning. He lost Game Three of the ALCS in the bottom of the 11th, but it was the only earned run he gave up in four games and six innings against the Angels. When facing his former team in the World Series, he earned a save in Bruce Hurst's 1–0 win in Game One, and then had a week off. In fateful Game Six, he allowed the Mets to tie it in the bottom of the eighth on a single, two bunts, and a sac fly. The Red Sox took a two-run lead in the top of the 10th, but after recording two quick outs, three consecutive singles gave Schiraldi a "deer in the headlights" look as he was removed in favor of Bob Stanley. Suffice it to say, Schiraldi wound up taking the loss . . . and he suffered another in Game Seven after entering a tie game in the seventh. Six earned runs in four innings and an 0–2 record in World Series play. (Insert curse here.) Though 8–5 in 1987, Schiraldi's ERA was exactly three runs higher than in '86, to go with ballooning walk and longball totals. In early December he and Al Nipper were sent to the Cubs for Lee Smith.

After a good sophomore season with the Expos, right-hander **Dustin Hermanson** began to decline . . . but the Cardinals still traded for him and paid him a salary just shy of $6 million. Why, they might have asked themselves, after he went 14–13 for them with a 4.45 ERA. So they traded him to the Red Sox for three minor league prospects. (The Red Sox assumed his salary, of course.) Soon Boston was also asking, why. In his first start, on a cold rainy day in April, he slipped off the mound. It was painful just to watch. He injured his hamstring so badly that he wasn't able to pitch again until July 20. And after that one relief stint, his next appearance came on August 22. That April game was postponed due to rain, so it officially never occurred. By year's end, he'd only thrown 22 innings, contributed one win to the Red Sox (and lost one, too) and was saddled with a 7.77 ERA. A sad story. The Red Sox declined his $7 million option for 2003—he went to St. Louis, believe it or not—and the Sox were ready to turn over #31 to another person. **Robert Person**.

Twelve coaches and one manager have worn #31. A couple were pals of Ted Williams, even if they were pitchers. **Frank Shellenback**, Ted's manager in 1936 and '37 with the Pacific Coast League's San Diego Padres, was a former spitballer—back when the pitch was legal. **Paul Schreiber**, who served the longest stint of any Red Sox pitching coach (1947–58), wearing #45 from 1952–54 and #34 his last four years. He often threw extra batting practice to Williams, which The Kid loved more than ice cream.

But if you really wanted to get Teddy Ballgame's attention, a .440 batting average on your résumé was sure to do it. Hall of Famer **Hugh Duffy** achieved the highest average in major league history with the Boston Beaneaters in 1894, with 237 hits in 539 at-bats. Duffy also led the NL in home runs, RBIs, doubles, total bases, and slugging that year, capturing the Triple Crown before anyone knew what it was. Before uniforms bore numerals, Duffy managed the Red Sox (1921–22). In 1939, the 20-year-old Kid, who certainly loved to talk hitting, listened to the 72-year-old Rhode Islander. Sir Hugh told him, "Son, you've got form and power. But the form is most important. With it you get the power. Don't monkey with your form."

A Hall of Famer whose career was monkeyed with in Boston was **Ferguson Jenkins**. For six seasons in a row, he was a 20-game winner for the Cubs (1967–72) and was a 25-game winner for the Texas Rangers in 1974. In the wake of the loss in the '75 World Series, the Red Sox traded three players to Texas to get him. Jenkins won 22 games for the Red Sox, but it took him two years to do it (12–11 and 10–10, though his ERA was a combined 3.47). Traded back to the Rangers, he went 18–8 with a 3.04 ERA in 1978. Had the Sox had a happy Jenkins on the mound in '78—or gotten back something more useful from the Rangers than John Poloni (his contribution was one win at Pawtucket)—perhaps there wouldn't have been the need for a playoff against the Yankees that year. One of the reasons Jenkins might not have prospered in Boston was manager Don Zimmer. It was Jenkins who gave the name to the Buffalo Head Society of the club's more free-thinking Sox players such as Bill Lee and Bernie Carbo. Jenkins claimed that the buffalo was the dumbest animal of all, and hence he thought of a buffalo when Zimmer came to mind. Fergie was elected to the Hall of Fame in 1991, the only Canadian native in the Hall.

MOST OBSCURE RED SOX PLAYER TO WEAR #31—Ontario's **Peter Hoy** was a 6-foot, 7-inch left-hander signed by the Sox in the 1988 draft. He debuted as the second of eight Red Sox pitchers who worked in the 19-inning game in Cleveland on April 11, 1992. Hoy threw the sixth inning, allowing two hits but no runs. Four of his five appearances that spring were either one-run affairs or extra-inning games, netting him a hold (in his debut), a blown save, and two games finished . . . all in 3 2/3 innings. His 7.36 ERA, however, was a tad large. Hoy's time with Boston ran its course after six weeks, a brief yet exciting career in the bigs.

What Do Uniform Numbers Mean to the 2009 Red Sox? Part One

Uniform numbers are sacred to some players, others are superstitious, others don't care one way or the other. And with all of them inhabiting one locker room over the course of a season, Bill Nowlin talked with all uniformed personnel of the 2009 Red Sox to see what their uniform numbers meant to them: the players, coaches, and other support staff. We spoke with everyone who wore a number. With 52 players, six coaches, and one manager, that's a lot of reasons. Broken down into nine segments—innings, if you will—follow this numbered serial in sidebars through Chapter #39.

Why the 2009 Red Sox? Because that's when the first edition of this book came out, and we did a comprehensive round of talking with all the players on that year's year. It still stands as a representative cross-section of the thoughts and considerations that go into uniform number assignments—even if it is sort of a time capsule at this point. We'll add a few thoughts from some of the 2015 Red Sox, too.

As a rule, the more veteran players have more of a say in their choice of numbers, but even then one finds exceptions. With all the player movement from team to team, many prefer to wear the number they wore previously. For instance, **J. D. Drew** said, "I had number 7 my whole career. Trot [Nixon] had left. I came in. That number was available, so I stuck with it. I didn't want to make any changes. Much like other teams that I've left, I've had no problem with the guy taking the number once I leave and I don't think Trot had any ill feelings with it, either."

When **Mark Kotsay** came to Boston, the number he perhaps logically should have taken was #28, but his pattern had been disrupted in 2008 when he wore #11 in Atlanta. "It just seemed like a good number at the time. The numbers that I've worn, I usually increment them by 7. I went from wearing number 7 to 14, 21, and then to 11. Number 28 wasn't available. It was my eleventh season in the big leagues." So he selected #11 and kept the same number after he was traded to the Sox in August. Math may not have been a strong suit for Kotsay (2008 was actually his 12th season), unless he meant that it was his 11th *full* season in the majors.

Reliever **Ramon Ramirez** said of #56, "When I was playing with [the Royals], they gave it to me there. I like it. I like the number. There's no reason. When I came here, he asked me what number. I say 56."

Josh Beckett had worn #21 with the Florida Marlins when he'd been the MVP of the 2003 World Series. Acquired by Boston after the 2005 season (with Mike Lowell), and still just 25 years old when he joined the Red Sox, Beckett perhaps felt it presumptuous to request #21 with Boston. Players do have a sense of history of some numbers, said equipment manager Joe Cochran, and #21 was long associated with Roger Clemens. No one has worn the number since The Rocket left Boston after the 1996 season, and at the time Beckett arrived, the Sox were still hopeful of enticing Clemens back to Beantown. Asked why he chose #19, Beckett said with a straight face, "I like it because Mike Lowell used to wear it. No, I'm just joking. I had it in high school. That's the only significance."

Brad Penny took #36 when he signed as a free agent coming off rehab in late 2008. His preference from previous stops, #31, wasn't available (**Jon Lester** had #31), so Penny picked from the numbers available to him. There was one he skipped over. "I'm not going to take 21," he said.

Lester started with #62 when he first joined the Sox and now wears #31. Did he just cut his original number in half? Did #31 have another meaning to him? "Not really, I had 13 in high school. When I got to pro ball, when I was in A ball, I just got 31. Somebody else had 13. I wanted to get 31 because I had it in the minor leagues, but there's no significance to it." After Penny was released in late August (landing in San Francisco and reclaiming #31), the Sox brought up **Paul Byrd** from Triple A. For the second year in a row, Byrd was able to wear #36. "That's been my number since '01," he said. "Kevin Cash had it last time." Cash. Penny. Sort of a money thing? "There ya go!"

#32: Lowe Budget

For 40 seasons (1955–94), this number was monopolized by coaches. Once outfielder **Don "Footsie" Lenhardt** let go of it, it was taken in succession by the "mega-firm" of Baker, Orkie, Malmberg, Runnels, Popowski, Williams, Jackson, Harper, Torchia, McNertney, Hebner, and Allenson. Three of the coaches served very brief stints as Red Sox interim managers: **Del Baker** (2–5), **Pete Runnels** (8–8), and **Eddie Popowski** (6–4). Some were more noted for other things, usually for having played for the Red Sox (**Len Okrie, Stan Williams, Tommy Harper, Gary Allenson**, and Runnels). **Richie Hebner**, a corner infielder with power who played in eight postseasons in the two-division era, was renowned for his offseason job: digging graves in the Boston suburb of Norwood. "I like to tell people I'll be the last person to ever let them down." Nice.

The #32 torch then passed to outfielder **Wes Chamberlain** for his brief time in Boston in 1995; his last game was June 7. Though he kept playing in the minors and independent league ball, he never returned to the big leagues. Entrusted with the sacred coaches' numeral, he hit .119 in 42 at-bats.

Mike Stanton wore the number for a couple of seasons, pitching so-so relief in Boston. He did help the Red Sox reach the postseason in 1995, but it was his seven seasons with the Yankees when the southpaw excelled. Acquired from the Washington Nationals the last week of the 2005 season (wearing #37), Stanton added one appearance to his eventual career total of 1,178, second all-time to Jesse Orosco.

It was **Derek Lowe** who really did #32 proud, coming over from Seattle with Jason Varitek for Heathcliff Slocumb. (While the 1990 deal of Jeff Bagwell for middle reliever Larry Andersen in 1990 can never be undone, getting two All-Stars for one washed-up reliever is a little karma coming back east.)

Not only was Lowe's no-hitter in 2002 the first at Fenway since Dave Morehead's 1965 gem, but "D-Lowe" pulled off an unparalleled trifecta in 2004: he was the winning pitcher in the final game of the American League Division Series, the American League Championship Series, and the World Series. The one that officially ended the 86-year drought was his last game donning Red Sox jersey #32.

Lowe's first full year with Boston was as a starter in 1998 and that didn't work too well (3–9, 4.02 ERA). Converted to a reliever, he was 6–3 with 15 saves in 1999 with a 2.63 ERA. Further transitioning in 2000 and becoming a full-time closer, he led the league finishing 64 games and with 42 saves, this time with a 2.56 ERA. In 2001, his ERA deteriorated by almost a full run, so—why the heck not?—he was re-converted to a starter, and became a 20-game winner (21–8, 2.56 ERA). Though the Red Sox did exceptionally well in both 2003 and 2004, Lowe's ERA went the other way. His postseason performance notwithstanding, he was only 14–12 with a 5.42 ERA during the '04 season. There were intimations that the night life was taking up too much of his time. The Red Sox made a healthy offer to him, for close to what he accepted with the Dodgers, but it was perhaps time to for both parties to move on.

The only other player to make any kind of a splash since was **Bobby Kielty**, who made his moment count. After being released by Oakland at the trading deadline in 2007, he signed as a backup outfielder with the Red Sox a week later. He hit .231 in 52 late-season at-bats. But his moment came in October. After seven innings in Game Four of the World Series, Kielty led off the eighth pinch-hitting for Mike Timlin. The first pitch he saw from Brian Fuentes—boom! Home run. Red Sox lead 4–1. It mattered; the final score was 4–3. He's got a 1.000 batting average in World Series play, a 4.000 slugging percentage, and a 5.000 OPS.

It took Eddie Popowski 30 years in the minors before he had his first opportunity to appear in a big league game, but the first year he did, the Red Sox won the pennant. He first signed with the Red Sox in 1936, and began playing second base for Hazleton in 1937. A broken hand in 1941 led to the suggestion that he take over the team and was his first experience in managing, which he began in earnest in 1944. Pop managed for a long list of teams (in sequence): Roanoke, Scranton, Lynn, Oneonta, Louisville (coach), Greensboro, Montgomery, Greensboro again, Albany, Allenton, Alpine, Minneapolis, Johnstown, Winston-Salem, Reading, and Pittsfield—all in the Red Sox system. He coached for Dick Williams in 1967, and when Williams was fired nine games before the end of the 1969 season, Popowski ran the team. He also managed the last game of '73. He continued to work for the Red Sox right through spring training 2001, and died later that year. Like Charlie Wagner and Johnny Pesky, Eddie Popowski was pretty much a Red Sox lifer.

MOST OBSCURE RED SOX PLAYER TO WEAR #32—Stew Bowers played parts of three seasons for the Red Sox (1935–37), a right-handed pitcher with a winning record (well, OK, it was just 2–1, but still). Signed by Herb Pennock, "Doc" Bowers appeared in 11 games that first year, collected one base hit, got his two wins, and forged a 3.42 ERA. He didn't pitch many times the next year, but his time on the mound seemed long given his 9.53 ERA. And in 1937, he appeared just once, on May 18, as a pinch runner for pitcher Johnny Marcum and scored one of four runs in a Red Sox rally. (The Indians scored four times in the ninth to win.) In a 2001 interview, Bowers talked about the three times he was asked to pinch-run in a career prematurely ended by arm trouble. "Well, I could carry the mail, as they say."

What Do Uniform Numbers Mean to the 2009 Red Sox? Part Two

Some players pick numbers in tribute to a particular ballplayer. **David Ortiz**, for instance, wears #34 in honor of Kirby Puckett, one of the greatest players in Twins history. Ortiz started his career with Minnesota. (Any notion that he wears it because Don Zimmer wore it for the Red Sox would be sheer poppycock.) **Julio Lugo** took #23 because of Ryne Sandberg. "He used to wear number 23. That's why I wear it." Asked about the great Boston pitcher who'd once worn #23, he replied, "Luis Tiant. That's a different era." Lugo was traded to St. Louis on July 22 (he took #23 on the 24th). Lugo's #23 was taken by **Adam LaRoche**, and worn for the nine days he was with the Red Sox; he didn't really have a specific reason for #23, other than it was pretty close to his Pirates number (#25). When he landed with the Braves, he took #22 for the same reason, and because he wanted to honor his former teammate Marcus Giles. After LaRoche left, the number lay dormant until **Joey Gathright** was brought up from Pawtucket on September 1. Did he have a choice? By that point in the season, not really. "It was already here when I got here," Gathright said. "I know it used to be Lugo's number. I didn't get a choice, but we usually do. It's not a bad number." **Casey Kotchman**, who came from the Braves in the LaRoche trade, was shown a list of numbers to choose from and selected #11. "I wore it in high school," he told us. "My dad wears it also. He manages a short-season team in Orem, Utah."

Another player who wears a number associated with his father is **Manny Delcarmen**. He had #57 when he first broke in with Boston, and pitching coach Dave Wallace had #17. "My dad had it when he played [in the Phillies system in the 1970s]. Every time he played baseball—even in over-30 ball—he always had it, so every time I played in Little League and stuff, I always wanted it. I had it through high school. I had it in the minors. When I first called up, I asked Dave Wallace, 'I'd like 17.' He thought I was joking around. Then it was already the end of the season, so he gave it to me for the following year."

Tim Wakefield's choice of #49 should come as no surprise: "I wore it because Charlie Hough wore it. It was available when I was in Pittsburgh, too." He explained that he'd originally worn another number with the Pirates, but once he converted to become a pitcher he wore the number worn by fellow knuckleballer Hough. And **Jason Bay** took #44 with another player in mind. "When I was growing up, my idol was Eric Davis of the Cincinnati Reds. When I got traded here, Joe Cochran called me and said, 'You've got the choices of three numbers between 45 and down.' It was an easy decision." **Brian Anderson** felt fortunate to be offered #32 when he arrived. He'd worn it in Chicago, and even back in school playing basketball. "I wear it because I was such a huge fan of Magic Johnson. It was a nice gesture on their part [the Red Sox]. I mean, I don't want to be too caught up in it, but it's nice to have it."

Chris Woodward was happy to be wanted by a major league club after being claimed on waivers from Seattle last August 7. He was assigned #3. Equipment manager Joe Cochran hadn't asked him. "He's worn a single-digit the last four or five or six years, so I just gave him number 3." Woodward, a fan of low numbers, was surprised and pleased. Long ago he'd been assigned #11 and that "felt kind of big on me," he explained, demonstratively stretching his shoulders uncomfortably. When he'd first come up with Toronto, he'd had #31 and he didn't like it at all. After eight days with the Red Sox, however, Woodward was designated for assignment. He agreed to go to Pawtucket and was recalled on September 1, but by then Alex Gonzalez was wearing #3. Woodward got #30. Presumably it weighed heavily upon him, and less than two weeks later he was outrighted back to Pawtucket to make room for Daisuke Matsuzaka on the 40-man roster. Yet Woodward returned to Boston a third time—still in #30—when Nick Green had a back issue. Woodward finally got a hit in a third stint in six weeks with the club. He finished the season batting .083 in 12 at-bats, but it ended happily: his wife had a child at the end of the year and he saw the Red Sox advance to the postseason. Though he didn't make the postseason roster, Woodward was pretty busy at home with baby #3.

The visiting bullpen door, open during Red Sox batting practice, showing the 380-foot mark.

#33: Boo-Tek

Boo Ferriss missed the plate with his first 11 pitches in the major leagues on April 29, 1945. Lucky for him there was a war on. Since most of manager Joe Cronin's talent was fighting in Europe, the Pacific, or on training bases scattered across the globe, his options for bringing in someone better were rather limited. And his club was already 1–8. Ferriss got a pop-up, walked the next batter on four pitches, and then fell behind 3–0 on the fifth batter . . . but he induced a double play and went on to pitch a complete-game shutout. He even collected three hits himself. In his next start, he shut out the Yankees. He finally let in a run in his third game—after 22 1/3 innings of shutout ball to start his career—and won his first eight games. In that string, he beat every team in the league at least once and four of the wins were shutouts. He was on his way to a 21–10 record (2.96 ERA), despite the fact that the Red Sox were a seventh-place team. In 1946, the Sox won the pennant and Boo was a big part of that (25–6, 3.25). He threw a 4–0 six-hitter in Game Three of the World Series, but he couldn't pull it off in Game Seven. He allowed three runs, saw the Sox tie it, and watched from the dugout as they lost on Enos Slaughter's "Mad Dash."

Despite his given name of David, he's still listed in the phone book as Boo. Bats left, throws right—but Ferriss believed he could also have thrown left-handed if given the chance. His right shoulder is what did him in during the 1947 season. He battled through a couple more seasons, yet he was never again the same pitcher. Ferriss threw his last pitch in the majors at age 28, and later became the club's pitching coach (1955–59). A star at Mississippi State before the war, Ferriss coached at Delta State for 26 years. He guided the Statesmen to 639 wins, but his best-known decision as a coach was cutting enthusiastic would-be outfielder and future bestselling author John Grisham, telling him "to stick with the books." A member of the Red Sox Hall of Fame and several other Halls, the an-

Jason Varitek

nual award for the top collegiate baseball player in Mississippi is named after him.

Jason Varitek, the first captain the Sox have had since Carl Yastrzemski and Jim Rice, is an intense leader second only to Carlton Fisk in many people's minds as the best catcher in club history. (He's even surpassed Fisk in several franchise categories at the position.) Pitchers can't seem to say enough about the way "Tek" calls a game, and even though there's a lot of luck in pitching a no-hitter, it may not be pure coincidence that he's been the man behind the plate in four no-hitters, the most of any catcher ever. He came over with Derek Lowe in the Heathcliff Slocumb trade in 1997, and has been an All-Star three times, a world champion twice, and won both a Gold Glove and Silver Slugger. After his retirement, the Red Sox hired him as a Special Assistant to the General Manager. Tek and Pedro.

Serving a much shorter term as Red Sox catcher was a man better known today for his broadcast work: **Tim McCarver**. Sox fans who follow his Fox Sports commentary believe he's extremely biased against the Red Sox. He played against them in the '67 World Series, guiding the Cardinals pitching staff but hitting just .125. Purchased by the Red Sox from St. Louis in mid-1974, maybe he didn't appreciate being released in late June 1975, a few months before the Red Sox worked their way into the World Series. He was batting .306 for Boston, but Carlton Fisk was coming off the DL and the Red Sox preferred Bob Montgomery and—this may have been what got to him—Tim Blackwell. McCarver got a good gig as Steve Carlton's personal catcher in Philadelphia and then slid into the broadcast booth. His obvious statements and belabored points have created, oh, a handful of detractors, from Deion Sanders dousing him with water (repeatedly) to shutuptimmccarver.com (which features a ticket-seeking Red Sox fan holding up a sign: "Please don't make me have to listen to Tim McCarver tonight!!").

Another odd ex-Sox is **Jose Canseco**. Though he helped the Sox fend off the Yankees for the '95 division title, his 0-for-13 ALDS in Cleveland's sweep was an ugly ending to an otherwise good year for both Canseco and the club. He'd come pretty far from the man who'd endured singsong chants of "steroids" at Fenway during the 1988 Championship Series . . . but chalk one up for the hecklers. We learned later (from Jose himself in his book *Juiced*) that the groundlings had it right. He averaged 26 homers in his two years in Boston, and batted .298 (he missed about a third of each season due to injuries). After manager Kevin Kennedy was fired in '96 and Canseco pouted, the Sox weren't so interested in keeping Jose around and sent him back to Oakland for John Wasdin, whose career ERA was 5.81 at the time. One of Canseco's more memorable moments at Fenway came in a visiting uniform. With the Rangers—managed by Kennedy—getting blown out on May 29, 1993, Canseco volunteered to pitch an inning. He allowed three walks, three runs, and missed three months after he blew out his arm.

Varitek with his "C," which he wore from 2005–11.

After Canseco and before Varitek, there was pitcher **Steve Avery**. The third overall pick in the 1988 draft, Avery was spectacular at age

21 in helping the Braves win the first of their record 14 straight division titles and then earned NLCS MVP. By the time he was a free agent after the '96 season, Jimy Williams was Red Sox manager and he'd worked with Avery in Atlanta. But Williams may have been a little too close to Avery. The southpaw missed almost all of May and June, and he wasn't cutting it after returning from the DL. Four straight losing starts in August bumped him from the starting rotation. With 17 starts under his belt, it became known that Avery's contract had a provision that guaranteed the second year of his contract (around $4 million) if he made 18 starts. Suddenly, Jimy asked him to start on September 25. His ERA was 6.77 at the time. He lasted five innings and left the game without having given up a run in an eventual Red Sox win. A nice effort but not a $4 million start. Williams had apparently been given a direct order not to start Avery, but start he did and the Sox had him for another year. He had his final double-digit win season in '98—at $400,000 per win—with a 5.02 ERA that was the highest of anyone on the staff with at least 10 starts.

Tom Barrett had the odd circumstance of joining the Red Sox a year after his brother, Marty, the club's long-time second baseman, had left as a free agent following a dispute regarding a misdiagnosis by the club's trainer (see Chapter #17). Tom's reason for leaving Boston? A malady known as triple-0-itis, or hitting .000. He did walk twice in six plate appearances, but his 1992 arrival came too late to benefit from hitting specialist **Walt Hriniak**, who spent a dozen years on staff at Fenway despite a method diametrically opposed to the one espoused by best-damned-hitter emeritus Ted Williams (in simplified terms: Walt advocated swinging down on the ball and Ted favored the opposite approach). Hriniak, a disciple of legendary hitting coach Charlie Lau, had his own set of disciples in Dwight Evans, Rich Gedman, and Wade Boggs.

Sal "The Barber" Maglie won pennants with all three New York teams in the 1950s (before two moved), yet he was saddled with a sad staff in Boston as the 1960s arrived and his job description changed. As pitching coach of the Red Sox under six different managers (he spent 1963–65 out of baseball), the club finished seventh, sixth, eighth, ninth, and then (in 1967) first! Both Bill Monboquette and Earl Wilson threw no-hitters in 1962, and both credited Maglie for helping them become better pitchers, as did The Monster, Dick Radatz. And '67 Cy Young winner Jim Lonborg praised Maglie, too: "He taught me the importance of the brushback pitch. He said you had to be able to throw very hard *inside*, and create intimidation, because the more you threw inside, the farther away the outside part of the plate looked to the batter." (They didn't call Maglie "The Barber" because he liked to cut hair.) Maglie left with some bitterness, in that manager Dick Williams fired him the very day after the World Series. Maglie kept all his information in his head, and Williams wanted it written down—a difference in philosophies that eventually led Maglie to his next stop, where his wisdom would be written down by someone else (and not favorably): Seattle Pilot Jim Bouton in the landmark book *Ball Four*.

Len Okrie spent two years apiece as a coach in #32 and #34, but one game as a player in #33. The catcher struck out in his only Sox (and last career) at-bat in April 1952. **Del Wilber** took over #33 and backup catching duties a few weeks later after his purchase from the Phillies. His talent, however, was as a pinch hitter par excellence. Check out the Wilber chronology from May 1953:

- May 6: Wilber hit a pinch-hit homer in the seventh for Boston's only two runs in a 6–2 loss to Chicago.
- May 10: The next time Wilber was asked to bat, he pinch-hit another home run, in a losing battle against the Yankees, 7–4.
- May 11: Three swings, three home runs. It was just an exhibition game against the New York Giants at the Polo Grounds, but Wilber swung at the first pitch and hit it to the roof of the third deck in left.
- May 20: In the bottom of the 14th inning, the St. Louis Browns were worried about making the 6 P.M. train out of town. When Wilber was announced, a Boston sportswriter turned to Browns owner Bill Veeck and said, "Don't worry. You fellows can catch your 6 o'clock train to Cleveland. This guy always hits a home run when he comes in as a pinch hitter." On a 3–1 count, Wilber hit it into the screen in left field. Right on time.

MOST OBSCURE RED SOX PLAYER TO WEAR #33—We didn't tell the whole truth before about who came between Jose Canseco and Jason Varitek at #33. It wasn't just Steve Avery. **Kirk Bullinger** wore it after Avery left, but not for long. Bullinger appeared in just four games in June for the 1999 Red Sox, facing nine batters in two full innings of work. He filled the role of situational righty during his brief stay, never completing a full inning and removed each time in favor of a lefty (once for Rheal Cormier and three times for Mark Guthrie). Jimy Williams kept him busy, or vice versa.

What Do Uniform Numbers Mean to the 2009 Red Sox? Part Three

A couple of other 2009 Red Sox players wore numbers associated with Sox stars of the past #5 and #25. **Rocco Baldelli** told us about why he wore #5. "I had it in Tampa. My rookie year, I had 5 with Tampa. I always liked the low numbers, and most of them were already used. There were only a couple available and I've had 5 since. I'm from this area [Baldelli is a native of Woonsocket, Rhode Island]. I know that Nomar had that number for a long time and no one had had it since he played here. So I wasn't going to ask for it." GM Theo Epstein knew Rocco had worn #5 and telephoned Baldelli to offer it to him.

Number 25 had been worn by Tony Conigliaro. **Mike Lowell** recounted how he got the number: "When I got traded over here, Joe Cochran was asking me what numbers, and I didn't really know what [was] taken. I said, 'I'm thinking about number 25,' and he said, 'I usually give it to a veteran guy, because it was Conigliaro's number. And you won the Award.'" In 1999, Lowell—a survivor of testicular cancer—had been named the winner of the Tony Conigliaro Award, a national award instituted by the Red Sox in honor of recently deceased Tony C. The award is given each year to a major league player "who has overcome adversity through the attributes of spirit, determination, and courage that were trademarks of Tony C."

Lowell continued, "So I accepted [#25] and I've stayed in touch with Richie Conigliaro. He left a message for me in '07. He said he was really proud that I was the one wearing his brother's number. That has a nice feel to it."

#34: Popeye, Papai, and Big Papi

Forty seasons passed between the time outfielder **Karl Olson** and infielder **Scott Cooper** donned #34; it was the domain of coaches and managers for the period between 1954 and 1993. The best known of these—and most successful—was **Don Zimmer**. Following two last-place seasons managing the woeful Padres, Zim served as third-base coach under Darrell Johnson from 1974 through the 1975 World Series and the half-season that Johnson survived afterward. Promoted to replace Johnson on July 19, 1976, Zim managed the team until the last few days of the 1980 season.

Zimmer took the reins just after Tom Yawkey died and Red Sox ownership went through a rocky time until Jean Yawkey and allies righted the ship. Needless to say, there was more than a little frustration as well for fans. After the near-miss in '75 and close second in '77, there was the truly maddening '78 season. The team had a 14-game lead over the Yankees in mid-July that year, before blowing it entirely, sinking into second, and recovering at the very last minute—only to lose on a Bucky Dent home run in the single-game playoff against the Yankees.

Layered throughout all this was the counter-culture, which was affecting baseball a decade after it had first impacted American society. The '60s arrived in baseball in the late '70s. Waving the freak flag for the Red Sox were Bill Lee, Bernie Carbo, Ferguson Jenkins, Jim Willoughby, and Rick Wise. A baseball lifer like Zimmer was steeped in the ways of hierarchy and adherence to hidebound ways in the game. And here was Bill Lee talking about sprinkling marijuana on his pancakes. The aforementioned players were the core of the Buffalo Head Society, effectively an anti-Zim cabal in the Red Sox clubhouse. Affectionately known as "Popeye" for his resemblance to the spinach-eating sailor, the Buffalo Heads re-dubbed him "Gerbil"—an even less-flattering depiction—and undermined Zim in the press and the clubhouse. Yet the Sox had a .575 winning percentage under Zimmer, including 91 wins or more in each of his three full seasons with the club. It remains a legitimate question whether a Terry Francona–type manager who works to bridge gaps might have evoked more from the team and held onto first place one of those three summers (1977–79). Zimmer became manager of the Texas Rangers in 1981 and, in a reversal of the circumstances of 1976, was replaced by Darrell Johnson in mid-1982. Zim finally won a division title with the Cubs in 1989.

Until David Ortiz came along, Zim's eight seasons wearing #34 ranked first. Señor Ortiz broke more than one team record.

Much more popular in the Sox clubhouse and much more successful in October was David Ortiz. Not without ample justification did Red Sox ownership bestow on "Big Papi" the title "Greatest Clutch Hitter in the History of the Red Sox"—the plaque actually delivered to him after winning the September 6, 2005, game with a ninth-inning home run. Admittedly, it was based on a small sample size, but in his first five seasons with the Red Sox, Ortiz came through time after time with big hits at key moments. Originally a castoff from the Twins, he was signed by the Sox as a backup to Jeremy Giambi. Hard to believe.

On one day alone, Ortiz staked a claim to be remembered forever. The date was October 18, 2004. There had been a foreshadowing in the bottom of the 10th inning of the October 8 game against the Angels, when Ortiz hit a two-run homer to win the game—and the Division Series—from the Angels. The ALCS saw the Yankees beat Boston three games in a row, and the were poised for a sweep in the ninth inning of Game Four. A Kevin Millar walk, "The Steal" by Dave Roberts, and a Bill Mueller single tied it to force extra innings. In the bottom of the 12th, Ortiz homered to win the game and keep Sox hopes alive. The hit came after midnight, early in the morning of the 18th, and there was another elimination game that very evening—one that ran into the 14th frame. A couple of walks brought him up with two outs, and he battled through a 10-pitch at-bat before stroking a

David Ortiz

single to center to bring in the winning run. This time it was before midnight, so twice on the same date Big Papi had come up big and staved off elimination. The Red Sox went on to win that series—you may have heard—and sweep St. Louis in the World Series. The heroics continued, and in 2006 Ortiz even set the all-time single-season Red Sox record with 54 home runs, eclipsing Jimmie Foxx's long-standing 50.

Come 2007, Ortiz led the league in on-base percentage, then drove in three runs in the Division Series, three more runs in the League Championship Series, and four runs in the 2007 World Series. He added a second ring to his collection. But he wasn't done yet. World Championship-wise, there came also 2013 when he upped the ante again—three RBIs in the ALDS, four RBIs in the ALCS, and six RBIs in the World Series (with a staggering .688 batting average—11 hits in 16 at-bats.) There were those five times he actually made an out, but who's quibbling? He was the World Series MVP.

Was Big Papi all washed up the year he turned 40, in November 2015? All he did was hit 37 homers and drive in 108 runs.

Al Papai was no Big Papi, though he stood only an inch shorter. The St. Louis Cardinals signed Papai, who was 0–1 for them in 1948. Put on waivers, he was claimed by the St. Louis Browns. His Sportsman's Park address remained the same, but his former employer wound up with 96 wins and his new one lost 101 times (11 of those attributable to Papai, who walked 81 while striking out just 31). That he was waived again isn't a surprise; why another 96-win team would want him is a good question. But the Sox sought help in the bullpen. He was 4–2 in 1950, but his 6.75 ERA was almost two runs a game worse than he'd managed with the lowly Browns. Boston put him on waivers in early July and he returned to St. Louis . . . with the Cardinals. His second tour wasn't any more successful.

Another big player for Boston was "El Guapo," **Rich Garces**. The portly Venezuelan right-hander got the number after a 1996 deal with the Expos sent slender New Brunswick native **Rheal Cormier** closer to home (the southpaw would join Garces in the Fenway pen in 1999–2000 wearing #37). El Guapo—"the handsome one"—spent the last seven seasons of his career as a setup man and fan favorite in Boston. People enjoyed his good humor and identified with his roly-poly body type, but they loved his results: 23–8 with a 3.78 ERA in 261 Sox games. Jon Goode of the Lowell Spinners told us that when Garces went to the Spinners on a rehab assignment in 2001, they didn't have any uniforms big enough to fit him so someone was dispatched to Fenway Park to collect one of his jerseys. El Guapo played for the Spinners in his #34 Red Sox uniform . . . as if he wasn't already easy enough to spot. A couple of years after his release, Garces was reported missing and feared kidnapped—unfortunately, not an unknown occurrence in Venezuela, as happened to former Sox reliever Ugueth Urbina's mother (see Chapter #41)—but El Guapo turned up in no worse shape, save for maybe a headache, after returning from a 10-day beach party.

For a team that was the last to integrate by bringing African American Pumpsie Green on board in 1959, the Sox were the first to field a Mexican native (Mel Almada) and had other Latinos and Native Americans as early as 1908. The first Native American manager in the big leagues? Boston's **Rudy York**. York had worn #3 as a Red Sox first baseman in 1946, and came up big in the July 27 game with two grand slams and a total of 10 RBIs. In the '46 World Series, his 10th inning homer in Game One and his first-inning homer in the Game Three shutout both provided the margin of victory. He worked as a coach for the Sox (1959–62), and when GM Bucky Harris fired manager Pinky Higgins, York was tabbed to run the club until a replacement could be found. Billy Jurges was installed the next day. York managed the July 3, 1959, game—a 6–1 loss in Baltimore. The *Globe*'s Clif Keane wrote, "Manager for a day—but Rudy York was beaten tonight before he could put on his war paint."

Babe Martin was born Boris Michael Martinovich, the son of a professional wrestler, Iron Mike Martin (Bryan Martinovich). A catcher for the Browns from 1944 through 1946, he was taken in the 1947 Rule V draft by the Red Sox and was therefore required to spend all of 1948 and 1949 on the major league roster. Martin could have benefitted from catching regularly in the minors, but he instead sat on the bench for a team that was in the running for the pennant until the last day both years. (He batted .500 in his four at-bats in 1948 and went hitless in his only two at-bats in 1949.) They finally let him go in July 1950, selling him to Detroit. His only other major league action was four more plate appearances for the Browns in 1953. It would have been better for all parties if the Sox had just let Babe stay with St. Louis in '47.

MOST OBSCURE RED SOX PLAYER TO WEAR #34—Curiously, every game **Mel Deutsch** appeared in went extra innings. He debuted in relief of Boo Ferriss on April 21, 1946, throwing 4 1/3 innings before he got lit up in the seventh for three runs. The Sox won 12–11 in the 10th on a Ted Williams single. The rookie next relieved Earl Johnson in the eighth inning on April 23, recording two outs, but the Senators scored six runs off three relievers in the top of the 11th. Deutsch took over for Tex Hughson and helped hold the Browns on May 7. The Sox—and Clem Dreisewerd—got the win on a Leon Culberson grand slam in the 14th inning, Boston's 12th win in row. The Red Sox wound up winning 15 straight, but Deutsch didn't see it. The Sox trimmed the roster the day after his last appearance and Deutsch went down to Louisville, never to return to the majors.

What Do Uniform Numbers Mean to the 2009 Red Sox? Part Four

Much as we hate to put all the pitchers from Japan in one basket . . . but numbers mean much more in Japanese culture than in the United States. We're told that **Daisuke Matsuzaka**'s #18 is even in his contract. Why? Pure numerology. Interpreter Masa Hoshino explained Matsuzaka's reasoning. "Number 18 has traditionally been what's called the 'ace number' in Japan. It's usually the number 1 pitcher on a team. The one I know for sure was Masumi Kuwata, who wore number 18 for the [Yomiuri] Giants, but I think it goes back earlier than that. There's no equivalent here. I guess 21 or 45 in a Red Sox uniform."

Jeff Yamaguchi, who works closely with **Hideki Okajima**, checked with the relief star and reported, "When he signed with the Red Sox, he wanted to wear number 28, but the number was taken by Doug Mirabelli, so he said, 'How about 37?' because he was wearing 37 when he was a rookie with the Tokyo Giants. The number 37 was open, so he took it. He likes it."

There is respect on a ballclub for past greats, hence players shying away from Roger Clemens's #21. Manny Ramirez wore #24 from 2001 to July 31, 2008. It remained unused the rest of '08, but it was snapped up by new Red Sox reliever **Takashi Saito**. The number, however, was taken only after talking to Manny, a teammate of Saito's with the Dodgers for the last two months of '08. Interpreter Masa Hoshino said, "People have asked him in reverse, 'Why would you take such a weighty or loaded number here?' The Red Sox had shown him a list of numbers that were available and that was one that stood out. He did speak to Manny through one of the Dodgers' interpreters to make sure it was cool, and Manny was very positive about it. He said, '24 is a lucky number in red and 99 is a lucky number in blue, so if it's available to you, take it.'"

#35: Major Magic

Careful. It seems that #35 is a place where Sox fans start to lose their bearings. It begins with 1937 righty **Joe Gonzales** out of USC, not to be confused with the 21 Jose Gonzalezes who later played minor league ball, plus the one who reached the majors, and the two Joe Gonzalezes who never made it. Then there's **Loyd Christopher**—just one "L," thanks— not to be confused with Christopher Lloyd, best known for playing Jim Ignatowski on *Taxi* and Doc Brown in *Back to the Future*. Don't forget **Don Gile**, which looks a little like **Rich Gale**, which rhymes with **DeMarlo Hale**. There's **Russ Gibson**, not to be confused with Cardinals ace Bob Gibson, who fanned Russ in his only two at-bats in the 1967 World Series. There's coach **Goose Gregson**, not to be confused with Hall of Fame reliever Goose Gossage. And every Red Sox fan worth their salt should know which **Joe Morgan** is which: there's ESPN blowhard, '75 Game Seven bloop-hitting "Little Joe" and the man of the same name known as "Walpole Joe."

Unlike Cincinnati's two-time MVP of the same name, Joseph Michael Morgan was three inches taller, a dozen years older, and couldn't hit. Signed by the Boston Braves a few months before they bolted to Milwaukee, Morgan batted .193 over four seasons with five teams. Jean Yawkey finally put her foot down regarding some of the shenanigans that had gone on under John McNamara (whom she also realized had likely cost the Sox the 1986 World Series). GM Lou Gorman offered the sudden managerial vacancy to Morgan, who'd spent more than a decade as manager in Pawtucket Red Sox and 3 1/2 years as third base coach at Fenway. Morgan took it but said that "interim" wasn't a word with meaning to him. The team won 12 in a row and 19 out of the first 20 games under Morgan. He famously stood up to Jim Rice, suspending him for three games. The Sox had been nine games out of first place before "Morgan's Magic" and reached first after the 19–1 run. There they stood at season's end and "interim" still wasn't part of Morgan's vocabulary.

Walpole Joe's popularity after '88 was such that the understated, laconic New Englander developed a following that enjoyed just hearing him talk. And though his teams failed to win even one postseason game—getting swept by Oakland in the 1988 and 1990 ALCS— Morgan's men won division titles by one and two games, respectively. That's no simple magic trick. He had a regular-season record of 301–262.

Preceding Morgan and McNamara was "The Major," **Ralph Houk**. Major was no honorary rank. He received several medals and was wounded at the Battle of the Bulge. Listed as "Missing in Action," Houk turned up with three days' growth and a bullet hole in his helmet; he rose from private to major before returning to civilian life as a minor league catcher. After spending parts of seven years backing up Yogi Berra, he took over from Casey Stengel and won world championships his first two years as manager. He took over as Yankees GM and fired Berra after one year and one pennant. Houk later returned to the dugout, managing the Yankees for 11 years in all, plus five heading up the Tigers. He replaced Don Zimmer in Boston, running the club from the strike-split year of 1981 through 1984, going 312–282 (1,619–1,531 career).

Though **Billy Herman** spent more games wearing #35 than anyone other than Morgan, his tenure is a time most Red Sox fans would rather forget. Voted to the Hall of Fame in 1975 as an NL second baseman, Herman was one of Pinky Higgins's cronies, tarred by simple association with Higgins, but perhaps not without cause seen as ineffectual. He wasn't a drinker like Higgins, but "preferred talking golf to baseball and carried his clubs with him throughout the 1965 season" [*Red Sox Century*]. His '65 club—ballclub, not golf club—couldn't break 100 (losses). He was fired the following year, eventually replaced by Dick Williams, who made sure the Red Sox mindset was strictly baseball.

The Red Sox entered the final game of both 1948 and 1949 needing just one win to claim the pennant. **Windy McCall** made both those teams out of spring training. He appeared just once in '48, an April 28 start in which he lasted just 1 1/3 innings, allowing a three-run homer to Joe DiMaggio—enough for Windy to lose the game. It's manifestly unfair to suggest that there would have been no need for the single-game playoff had the Sox won that game, so we leave it. He appeared in five games in '49, all in relief; in 9 1/3 innings he surrendered 12 earned runs, though his 11.57 ERA was progress over his 20.25 the year before. Windy didn't help, but his 0–0 record leaves him blameless for how things turned out in '49.

Charlie Bevis has written that shortstop **Billy Klaus**, at 5 feet, 9 inches, and 165 pounds, was "a small-stature, dirt-dog ballplayer who scrapped and clawed through every inning to try to secure victory for his team." After nine years in the minors, the lefty-swinging shortstop hit in 51 of his first 61 games and the Red Sox made a move, coming from 14½ games out of first to just 1½ back on August 10. When he started to cool off, so did the Sox. The AP's Joe Reichler, a friend of Ted Williams, wrote that Klaus had been more important to the Red Sox than Ted himself during the drive. Klaus finished second to wunderkind Cleveland southpaw Herb Score for Rookie of the Year and was 13th in MVP voting. The Sox were so enamored of Don Buddin, though, that Klaus was bumped to third base in 1956. His numbers steadily declined.

Back in 1995, when **Matt Stairs** was 27 and with the Red Sox, he hit .261, mostly as a pinch hitter. He had one at-bat in the postseason that year and struck out. Built a bit like a beer keg—somewhat fitting given that his native St. John, New Brunswick, is home to the Moosehead Brewery—Stairs has played with 11 clubs through 2009. He got a World Series ring at age 40 for the Phillies, contributing a game-winning homer in the 2008 NLCS, and was back in the Series again in 2009.

You get an idea how popular #35 is among players when the immortal **Hipolito Pichardo** (8–4, 3.97 in 2000–01) can wear it for all but the first of his 10 seasons in the majors. But #35 was good enough to be a backup number for **Rickey Henderson**. Henderson had previously asked Willie Mays if he could wear number #24—unofficially retired since Willie's swan song at Shea Stadium—when Rickey had been a Met, yet in his 24th season in the majors, he let Manny be Manny and just took #35 upon joining the Red Sox in 2002. "Rickey Time" had begun in 1979 with him wearing #35 in Oakland before switching to #24 the next year and keeping it for all but a few weeks of his remarkable yet nomadic Hall of Fame career (four stints just with the A's). Rickey broke at least 50 major league records in his one season with the Red Sox. They were all his own records, including those he previously set for steals, walks, and runs. No matter, he moved on to the Dodgers—wearing #25 (#24 was retired for Walt Alston)—and broke those records one last time at age 44.

MOST OBSCURE RED SOX PLAYER TO WEAR #35—Al Richter got in two seasons for the Red Sox, accumulating an .091 average. He had a single and walked three times in 1951, but he more or less canceled out those by grounding into three double plays. His one appearance in 1953 was filling in at shortstop for an inning in a tight game. He made two plays flawlessly, but that was Richter's brief stint in the show. Later in life, Richter had a show of his own and spent seven years hosting *Spotlight on Sports*, which aired before television's Sunday *Game of the Week*.

What Do Uniform Numbers Mean to the 2009 Red Sox? Part Five

You'd think a player who'd worn one number for two decades of major league success would have some attachment to it. **John Smoltz** himself never really much cared one way or the other about #29. It was just a number assigned him by the Braves, with no particular significance. During his 2009 stay in Boston, Smoltz confessed, "I actually tried to change it for a long time, but they wouldn't let me do it." The Red Sox wouldn't, either. **Dave Magadan** gave up the #29 he'd worn in Boston since 2007 figuring Smoltz would want it (Magadan took #28). Despite the veteran pitcher's ambivalence about uniform numbers, Smoltz appreciated Magadan's gesture and took up the number he'd worn since 1988 (he briefly wore #57 when he first broke in as a rookie). Smoltz's pitching numbers with the '09 Sox (2–5, 8.32 ERA) looked a little too much like those as an '88 Braves pup (2–7, 5.48), and Boston let the 42-year-old hurler go in August. Once Smoltz's designation for assignment period expired, Magadan put on #29 the next day. (Since 2005 Cy Young winner Chris Carpenter already had #29 in St. Louis, Smoltz took #30 when he signed with the Cardinals on August 19.) As for Magadan, who broke into the majors in #29 in 1986, he'd given up #29 once before. "I was 29 my rookie year with the Mets. I gave that number up for Frank Viola [acquired in 1989]. Went to 10. I picked 28 because my wife's birthday is January 28."

Brad Mills is another coach who has given up his number for another player, albeit not a star of the caliber of Smoltz or Viola. "I like the single-digit numbers," #2 said. "My favorite number is 9, but here in Boston, I don't think you're going to get that one; 2 was next and nobody wanted it then, back when we got here in '04. I gave it up for Willie Harris [in 2006]. He asked me for it, and so I was nice and thought, 'Well, yeah, I'll do that for you.'" There was no payment of $25,000 or anything like that, just a coach willing to accommodate a ballplayer. How did Mills end up with #31 the year he ceded #2 to Harris? "I didn't really pick it. It's one they had left. I said, 'It looks good to me. I'll do it.'" Looks like he'll be keeping #2, only in Houston. Mills was named Astros manger after the 2009 season.

First base coach **Tim Bogar** picked #10 for a reason. "It was either 10 or 13," he said. Bogar explained that he knew Coco Crisp had worn it with the Red Sox, and having been a coach with Tampa Bay when the Rays and Coco had a run-in during 2008, the number just stood out in his mind when he came to Boston and needed a number. Strength and conditioning coordinator **David Page** chose #67 very deliberately. "I was born in Boston and grew up in Maine. 1967. The Impossible Dream. You know how it is with the team you grew up with," Page said. "I was three. I barely remember it. We were living in Malden. I can barely remember Yaz Bread. I've got the album [*The Impossible Dream* LP]. That's why."

Bullpen coach **Gary Tuck** (#57) says there's no number that means enough to him to try and pick another. Tuck says there's no number that means enough to him to try and pick another, but he knows that Bernie Williams wore #51 his entire career, and that Ichiro Suzuki wears #51 because Bernie was one of his idols. Uniform numbers mean nothing to pitching coach **John Farrell** (#52) or batting practice pitcher **Ino Guerrero** (#65). Coach **Alex Ochoa**'s #77 was picked for him. He quickly came to appreciate it, though. "I like it because I like the number 7 so that means I've got two of them." Bullpen catcher **Mani Martinez** wears #88, but was totally nonplused to be told it was the highest number in Red Sox history. "That doesn't matter," he shrugged. "They just gave it to me."

Manager **Terry Francona** has worn eight uniform numbers in the majors since 1981 and had long since stopped caring what he wore by the time he was hired in Boston. "They just said, 'Here's what we have' and I just said, 'You give me whatever.' I've been with so many teams and had so many numbers . . . It doesn't mean a thing. I've never been enamored with having to have a number." Francona wears #47, though most fans would be hard-pressed to name his number because of the pullover he always wears over his jersey.

#36: Flowers, Flash, Penny, Cash

Short-timers have dominated #36 in recent years, with 11 different players wearing the numbers in the first nine years of the 21st century. The first post-Nomar, post-Curse shortstop, **Orlando Cabrera**, wore the number upon arrival in Boston in August 2004, but he quickly switched to #44 and that's what he's wearing in all the celebration photos. And few would recall **Bobby M. Jones** of the 2004 world championship team, or **Joel Pineiro** of the 2007 champions.

Tom Gordon is still remembered widely, though, and not just as a key figure in Stephen King's 1999 book *The Girl Who Loved Tom Gordon*. Well, he should be remembered. Gordon's first two years with the Red Sox he was a starter, but near the end of 1997 he began to work as a closer. He had a 97–89 record to that point, mostly as a starter, with more career shutouts (4) than saves (3). Ten days later, he'd doubled his career saves total and never started again. In 1998, he set the Red Sox record with 46 saves and also led the American League. That year also began a streak that resulted in 54 consecutive saves (a major league mark broken by Eric Gagne as a Dodger in

2003). Shortly after Gordon's streak ended, a serious elbow injury cost him the second half of 1999 and resultant surgery put him out for all of 2000. The Red Sox released him, but the resilient "Flash" mounted a comeback, making the All-Star team with two different clubs since leaving Boston and alternating between setup man and closer.

There are only three players other than Gordon who wore the number for as many as three seasons. **Aaron Sele** was the most recent of the trio, and the one for which the Sox held the highest hopes. A first-round draft pick in 1991, he was thought to possess the stuff that could make him the best homegrown Sox starter since Roger Clemens. By June 1993, Sele was in Boston and putting up promising numbers (7–2, 2.74), but he added over an earned run per game in 1994, was hurt most of 1995, and mediocre in the two years after that (20–23 in 1996–97 with an ERA over 5.00). He was widely perceived as lacking in intestinal fortitude and even Clemens reportedly called him "gutless." Boston finally gave up on Sele and traded him to Texas for Damon Buford and Jim Leyritz, but the Sox had to throw in Mark Brandenburg and Bill Haselman to get the Rangers to bite. Though his ERA was nothing special, he revived his career, winning 37 games in two seasons with Texas. Sele never really stuck any place, working for five more teams over the next eight years.

There's a touch of the pastoral in #36, with **(Ben) Flowers** in the **(Jack) Spring**—never mind that they combined for one win in the 1950s. There's a sing-song, nursery rhyme quality as well. **Billy Muffett** never sat on a tuffet—that we know of—but he came over from the National League and went 6–4 with a 3.24 ERA in 1960 for Boston. That fell off to 3–11 (5.67) the second year, and one poor start in 1962 frightened the Red Sox away.

The year after Muffett left, a tomato came flying in. **Jack Lamabe**, called "Tomato" for his ruddy face, was 7–4 with a 3.15 ERA, but like Muffett, he deteriorated the next year (9–13, 5.89). And, following the Muffett pattern, Tomato didn't make it through his third season, falling to 0–3, 8.17. He did help the Red Sox in 1967, though . . . as a reliever for the St. Louis Cardinals. He entered a 4–4 tie in Game Six, allowed the Sox two runs, and took the loss.

A third-round draft pick in 1989, catcher **Eric Wedge** singled in his first at-bat in the majors in the penultimate game of 1991. He re-joined the Red Sox in late August 1992, his 1.000 career average on the line, and hit an even .250 with five homers and 11 RBIs in 81 plate appearances. That November, he was drafted by the Colorado Rockies in the expansion draft, but Wedge appeared in just nine games over the next two years (hitting .182) and was released. The Red Sox re-signed him, but he never made it back to play in major league ball. He did, however, become manager of the Cleveland Indians (2003–09). He earned AL Manager of the Year in 2007, though Boston victories in the last three games of the ALCS put a speck of tarnish on the trophy.

David Cone is usually thought of as a Yankee or a Met, but he won a Cy Young Award as a Royal and a World Series as a Blue Jay. He also had a decent 9–7, 4.31, season for the Sox at age 38. **Eddie Yost** would have been a highly- compensated superstar today with his 1,614 walks and steady play—he held many career defensive marks at third base before Brooks Robinson—but "The Walking Man" became a fixture a few feet on the other side of the bag as third base coach for the Sox. His eight years in #36 were matched only by **Eddie Popowski**, who preceded Yost in the coaching box.

Paul Byrd came on to help the team at the end of the 2008 season and again in the waning weeks of 2009, though if his latter visit was notable for anything it's because both times he took the number of a "money man" of sorts: **Kevin Cash** and **Brad Penny**. Count your change.

MOST OBSCURE RED SOX PLAYER TO WEAR #36—Boston native **Dick Mills** was drafted in the first two amateur drafts, but spurned both the Phillies and Pirates before getting drafted by his hometown team the third time—that's the charm—and signing with the Sox in 1966. Mills debuted in Cleveland on September 7, 1970, throwing three innings in relief, allowing a run on four hits. Six days later, he came into a game the Orioles led, 7–1, inheriting a one-out, bases-loaded situation. Mills misplayed the first ball hit his way for an error allowing one run to score. He then walked in a run and hit the next batter, forcing in another. After striking out the fourth batter, consecutive singles drove in three more runs. Six O's runs scored on his watch, but Mills was not charged with even one earned run (though it was his own error that made the runs unearned). Still, he never pitched again in the major leagues. His 2.45 career ERA is deceiving; his .500 lifetime fielding average is revealing.

What Do Uniform Numbers Mean to the 2009 Red Sox? Part Six

A couple of younger players given low numbers, for whatever reason, when they first arrived with the major league team were **Jed Lowrie** and **Kevin Youkilis**. Lowrie says that in 2008 spring training, before the team decamped to open the season at the Tokyo Dome, "I was 80-something, and then right before we went to Japan, they gave me 12. Yeah, it's not bad." Youk was asked how he got #20. "Oh, that was in my locker. When I was up in Toronto [his major league debut was against the Blue Jays in May 2004], that was my number. I always stuck with it. It's an honor just to get a number, so I stuck with it."

Clay Buchholz was assigned #61 when he broke in, and was wearing the number when he threw his no-hitter on September 1, 2007. He's stuck with it ever since. **Michael Bowden** was just glad to get a number, and had #64 in his two stints with the Sox. That number was also the starting point for **Dustin Pedroia**. He switched from #64 to #15 because "it was the lowest number that was kind of available. I'm not a very big guy. I usually like single digits. I'm not very big and a two-digit number looks bigger on you." Actually, #3 was available, but as he explained in his book, *Born to Play*, "Mark Loretta had just worn 3, and Edgar Renteria before him. So I took number 15."

Nick Green joined the Red Sox for the 2009 campaign and was assigned #22. Joe Cochran had done his research. "The last time I was in the big leagues [2007], I wore 22. With Seattle. I started with number 20. When I first came up with Atlanta, that was the number they gave me there. A really good number. I liked it. You can't get 20 here!" But #22 worked out nicely. "I like it." Sean Casey had liked #22, in 2008. He'd wanted #21 but was discouraged in that regard. "They said I couldn't get 21, so I said, '22?' and they said, 'Yeah.'" Told that when Roger Clemens went to New York, he'd worn 22, Casey responded, "Oh, did he? Oh, sweet!"

Jonathan Van Every was up and down with the Red Sox in 2008 and 2009. "The first time I came up, in May [2008], I was 30. I guess somebody came over and I got caught in the uniform shuffle—they took my number. I wasn't here. And then when I came back up, they just gave me whatever was left over." Van Every had been up for one game on May 14, 2008. Essentially, he wore Kevin Cash's number for the day. Cash had worn it as recently as May 11 and then again on the May 17. When recalled in August, Van Every was assigned #60. When we spoke with him, he'd just been activated for the April 24, 2009, game and was once more assigned #30, even though his locker nameplate still read "60—Van Every."

Jason Varitek was #47 when he first joined the team in 1997, but when Rod Beck joined the Red Sox in 1999, Beck wanted #47 and the young catcher willingly acquiesced to the veteran pitcher. Tek took the recently available #33 and has worn it ever since, earning the addition of the letter "C" for Captain to his uniform front.

#37: Not All There

It might seem that #37 gives a touch of idiosyncrasy, given that two of its bearers were **Jimmy Piersall** and **Bill "Spaceman" Lee**. Even its current occupant, **Hideki Okajima**, is a little nonconformist in his ways—as a glance at his dyed hair would indicate.

Tragedy made good. That's the Jimmy Piersall story. *Fear Strikes Out* was the name of his autobiography and the film made about his life. A center fielder with great range, the Waterbury, Connecticut, native signed with the Red Sox in 1948. Piersall got his feet wet in Boston two years later, becoming a regular in 1952, but he suffered a nervous breakdown during the season, foreshadowed by some bizarre behavior on the diamond. It was a time when mental illness was kept under cover as much as possible; in his case it was a condition we would now call bipolar disorder. After treatment in a sanitarium, which he describes in his book, Piersall returned to play a full 1953 season and quite a few more years after that. In eight seasons as a popular figure with the Red Sox, he hit .273—well above the league average at the time. He played 17 seasons of major league ball and later worked as a coach, in management, and as a long-time broadcaster for the White Sox.

We could write a whole book about Bill Lee, but why should we when he's already written a few about himself? Fans lap them up because he's always been an entertaining ballplayer, one who so evidently plays for the love of the game. The first time he arrived at Fenway Park, he reportedly looked at the Green Monster and asked, "Do they leave it there during the games?" A 22nd-round draft pick, he won 17 games three years in a row. Starting two games in the 1975 World Series, he threw 14 1/3 innings with a 3.14 ERA, though his bloop pitch Tony Perez crushed in Game Seven is one all of New England wants back.

The personality clash the free-spirited "Spaceman" had with manager Don Zimmer was a deep one, but Zim may have cost the Sox the 1978 pennant by refusing to let Lee start even one game after August 20. In his 11 2/3 innings over three September relief stints, the lefty allowed only two earned runs. And then after the '78 season, Lee was traded to the Expos for utility infielder Stan Papi. Lee won 94 games for the Red Sox against 68 losses, with a 3.46 earned run average. Papi hit .188 for Boston. Lee went 16–10 for the Expos in 1979. Lee was inducted into the Red Sox Hall of Fame in 2008.

Carlos Pena is one player the Red Sox wish they still had wearing #37. A graduate of Northeastern University, he was in many regards a hometown boy. Born in the Dominican Republic, he moved to Haverhill as a teen and went to high school there before ending up at Northeastern and playing in the Cape Cod League. The Rangers grabbed him in the first round of the 1998 draft and he reached the majors in 2001. Traded that winter to Oakland, he was dealt again the following summer to Detroit. Released by the Tigers and then the Yankees in 2006, the Red Sox immediately signed him after Triple A Columbus clipped him. Pena hit .459 in 11 games in Pawtucket and was brought up at the end of August. He played a series in Oakland and then, in his third game at Fenway (September 4), Pena hit a walkoff homer against the White Sox in the bottom of the 10th inning. With Kevin Youkilis to man first base, the Red Sox concluded they didn't need Pena—and winning the World Series in 2007 proves they did not—but they could have hardly predicted that, after signing with Tampa Bay in '07, he would suddenly knock in 121 runs and collect 46 home runs (11 more than anyone on the Sox and 45 more than he'd hit in his limited Boston engagement the previous year). Pena hit three homers against Boston in the 2008 ALCS and led the league with 39 homers in '09.

If the Red Sox had Pena when Okajima joined the team, the Japanese lefty certainly would have settled for another number . . . or figured out an interesting swap. One of the few ballplayers born on December 25 (though perhaps it was still Christmas Eve in America when he was born in Kyoto), Okajima was signed by the Red Sox on November 30, 2006, a couple of weeks before Boston won the right to sign Daisuke Matsuzaka from the Seibu Lions.

Okajima spent 11 years with Tokyo's Yomiuri Giants, then played one year with the Hokkaido Nippon Ham Fighters. The southpaw struck out one batter per inning over most of his career in Japan, something he's come close to in Boston. As soon as the Sox signed Matsuzaka, Okajima knew he would be playing in his fellow countryman's shadow, but as he said through a translator in spring training, "I'm willing to be a hero in the dark." The very first pitch he threw in the regular season was pounded for a home run, but he proved an excellent setup man for the Sox, entering games with his own special rock-style "Oki Doki" walk-on music. He pitched in 60 games for the third straight year in '09 and went 6–0.

Don Schwall was the 1961 American League Rookie of the Year, but his reign only lasted the one year and his time with the team lasted but two. After three years of minor league ball (two

Hideki Okajima, talking to Japanese school kids at the Tokyo Dome in March 2008.

years in D ball and one full season in AAA), Schwall arrived in Boston in late May and got everyone's attention by winning his first five starts. His overall numbers that year were superb: 15–7, 3.22 ERA. His second year was not. Schwall went 9–15 with a 4.94 ERA and was traded to the Pirates (with Jim Pagliaroni) to land Dick Stuart and Jack Lamabe. In five NL seasons, Schwall barely won as many games as he did in two for the Sox.

MOST OBSCURE RED SOX PLAYER TO WEAR #37—Congratulations, **Earl Snyder**. A native of New Britain, Connecticut (the longtime Double A home of the Sox), Snyder got a World Series ring for appearing in one game. He'd played 18 games for the Indians in 2002, batting an even .200 with 21 strikeouts in 55 at-bats. The Red Sox picked him up on waivers in early 2003, but he didn't see the major leagues until August 18, 2004, when he played third base and batted ninth against the visiting Blue Jays. The Sox scored four runs in the first; Snyder struck out leading off the second. He grounded into a double play in the fourth and flied to center in the sixth. In the bottom of the eighth, with Boston ahead, 6–2, and Bill Mueller on second base, Snyder singled to left field but Mueller was cut down at the plate. Snyder was granted free agency on October 4, so he watched the playoffs as an ex–Red Sox. He never played again in the majors, but he gladly received the ring for his last day of work.

What Do Uniform Numbers Mean to the 2009 Red Sox? Part Seven

Jonathan Papelbon embraces everything about the major league life, all the way down to his uniform number, #58. He was happy to get a high number, and often wears a T-shirt spelling out his number in Spanish: cinco ocho. "It was the number that was given to me, man. I've always worn a 50s number and I asked for a 50s number in spring training of my rookie year. I liked playing linebacker. I like the linebacker position. I'm a football fan and linebacker's my favorite position. And then when I go out there and pitch, I've gotta be like a linebacker. No holds barred."

Dustin Richardson is 6-foot-6, 220 pounds, and at home in #54. "Oh-oh, do I look like a linebacker?" he asked. "I didn't have any say in the number. It was just waiting for me. I tell you what: so far it's successful. I'll take it!"

Number 46 was waiting for **Jacoby Ellsbury** when he arrived at Fenway Park at the end of June 2007. (After the '09 season, he made a move to #2.) Pitcher **Hunter Jones** found #62 awaiting him for his debut. Asked if, given the choice, he would pick something else, he replied, "I like this number." The same was true for **Gil Velasquez**, who's enjoyed a few stints with the Red Sox going back to late 2008. "It was in the locker. Oh, man, I don't care what number they give me. I'm happy to be here! I'm glad." **Javier Lopez** had #48, but he also had nothing to do with picking it. Is he happy with it? "Absolutely," he said. "I kind of like it. I kind of like the even number, ending in an even number like that." **Chris Carter** was given #54. "It was just given to me two years ago. I don't think you get any say in it unless you actually make the team out of spring. It's a good number. I was a linebacker in high school." **Jeff Bailey** had the same reaction—#55 was just what he was given.

George Kottaras did get a choice, but he had to earn it. Kottaras had worn #68 for three September 2008 games. When he made the team out of spring training, he was offered a choice and selected #16. "They just said it would be a good idea to try and change your number. My number was very high. My number doesn't really . . . I don't have like a certain number that I must have. It was something that was available." The number was still available when he was recalled in September. Kottaras, who saw plenty of time behind the plate the first four months of '09, was sent down after the trading deadline acquisition of Victor Martinez. He played in nine September games and 48 overall.

#38: The Bloody Sock

Curt Schilling came back to Boston on a mission. Back to Boston, since he'd originally been drafted by the Red Sox in the second round in 1986. While still in the minors, the Red Sox made a move to bolster the team for the 1988 stretch drive and traded for Baltimore starter Mike Boddicker. To get him, they had to give up both Schilling and Brady Anderson. Schilling was traded again to Houston and then the Phillies. He finally got in a full year's work in 1992, placing fourth in the National League with a 2.35 ERA and leading the league with a WHIP of 0.990 (less than one hit or walk per inning pitched). A year later, the world was asking why this kid had been traded so often. He emerged as an ace to help the Phillies make their first postseason appearance in a decade. He was MVP of the NLCS and tossed a shutout to send the World Series back to Toronto, where it ended on Joe Carter's home run. He had back-to-back 300-strikeout seasons (on the way to a career total of 3,116). Dealt to Arizona in 2001, he recorded a 22–6 record, a 2.98 ERA, and was co-MVP of the World Series with Randy Johnson.

Knowing they would lose him to free agency, the Diamondbacks traded him to Boston after Theo Epstein convinced Schilling to waive his no-trade clause in perhaps the most analyzed Thanksgiving dinner since 1621.

Schilling announced—in a Ford ad—that he was coming to Boston to win a world championship. And he did his part: 21–6 during the regular season, plus a win in each round of the curse-bustin' postseason. It wasn't easy, though. Schilling had to leave Game One of the ALCS due to an ankle injury, and only pitched Game Six (in obvious pain) after an unprecedented surgery in which Dr. Bill Morgan sutured skin from his leg to deep connective tissue near the bone in order to hold in place a dislocated tendon in his right ankle. Under the pressure of pitching, some blood seeped around the stitches and stained Schilling's sock—it became known as "the bloody sock" and is on exhibit in Cooperstown. Schilling threw seven innings of one-run baseball at Yankee Stadium to take Game Six. The surgeons had practiced the technique on a cadaver and the Dr. Frankenstein creation captured the attention of the whole country. Schilling went through with the procedure, to his lasting credit. He won a World Series game in 2007, a few weeks before his 41st birthday. Because of shoulder problems, it turned out to be his last game.

Jeff Gray's medical issues came at age 28 and were severe enough to end his career. Released by the Phillies, he came to Boston and was impressive as a setup man for closer Jeff Reardon in 1990 and 1991, enjoying a breakthrough season in '91 with an ERA of 2.34 in 61 2/3 innings of work. After a routine workout prior to the July 30 game against the Rangers, Gray suffered a stroke in the Red Sox clubhouse. Reports indicated that it took a fair amount of time before an ambulance arrived. He later attempted a comeback, but he could never fully get his fastball back. He ultimately announced his retirement in January 1994.

Jim Willoughby became a quick one-line lament in the sad annals of Red Sox history. In his fourth season with the Giants, he'd converted from starter to reliever and that's how the Red Sox used him in 1975 after he arrived on July 4 as the "player to be named later" from an earlier trade. He appeared in 24 games, going 5–2 with a 3.54 ERA. During the World Series against the Reds, the Ed Armbrister bunt play cost him a loss, but he appeared in three games without giving up an earned run. He mowed down the Reds 1–2–3 in the top of the eighth in

Game Seven. The score was tied, two outs, and none on in the bottom of the eighth, and manager Darrell Johnson batted Cecil Cooper for Willoughby. Cooper, a .311 hitter during the season, was 1-for-18 in the Series; he fouled out to third base. Johnson called on rookie Jim Burton, whose 2.89 ERA in 53 regular-season innings of work was better than Willoughby's, and the Reds scored the deciding run of the Series. There's no way to know if Willoughby would have succeeded, but many have pondered the possibilities. Peter Gammons reported that three months later, he was in a bar watching a Bruins game, when an older man turned to him, mumbled, "How the hell could he have taken out Willoughby?" and then passed out. Now that's Boston before The Curse was broken!

Johnny Murphy, one of the great pre-war relievers, was sent packing by the Yankees after seven world championships. He finished his career in Boston in 1947 and then joined the front office. He eventually returned to New York and became general manager of the 1969 Miracle Mets. Bespectacled Boston native **Skip Lockwood** was a third baseman who couldn't hit, but he converted to pitcher and became a solid reliever. A Seattle Pilot, an original Brewer, a last-place Angel, and a post-Murphy Met, Lockwood excelled for plenty of losers, but by the time he skipped home to the 1980 Sox his arm was all but shot.

Just like Ted Williams, **Don Gile** went out with a bang: a home run in his last time up in the majors. Though there wasn't the attendant excitement of Ted's last game just two years earlier, Gile's blast was a walkoff homer in the bottom of the ninth against the Washington Senators to earn a split in the 1962 season-ending doubleheader. Author John Updike did not pen, "Hub Fans Bid Gile G'bye," but getting any offense out of the first baseman was certainly newsworthy. Before that day, he'd appeared in 16 games with 34 hitless at-bats. His first time up he singled, but by the end of the first game, he'd walked once and struck out twice. Gile didn't get a hit his first three times up in the nightcap. Finally, in the ninth, his home run and a heady .049 average ended the season and his four years in Boston.

Todd Benzinger was one of those players who come along every few years. A lot of people fall in love with a prospect's perceived potential, buy T-shirts with the kid's name and number on the back, and then watch as he fizzles out or departs for other locales. A fourth-round pick in 1981, Benzinger worked his way up from A ball to AA to three years with AAA Pawtucket. He never hit much above .250 in the minors until 1987, when he batted .323 and got "the call" to Boston near the end of June. He stuck with the Red Sox and batted a very respectable .278, playing almost exclusively in the outfield. In 1988, Benzinger played plenty of first base, but he hit only .254. He figured in a multi-player trade with Cincinnati that brought Boston Nick Esasky. Benzinger's nine-year career ended with a .257 overall average, plus one world championship as a 1990 Red. Who knows where all those blue Benzinger T-shirts are today?

A bit of a Benzinger from an earlier era may have been **Gene Stephens** (1952–60), not to be confused with Vern Stephens (1948–52). Vern wore #5 while Gene wore #38 when they were both on the same club. Gene also wore #10, but he was in #36 when his claim to fame occurred. A .204 hitter in 1953, Stephens had three hits in the seventh inning on June 18 against the Tigers as the Sox scored 17 times that inning at Fenway en route to a three-touchdown victory, 23–3. The only other player to ever have three hits in an inning did it 50 years later: Boston's Johnny Damon—back when he was Boston's.

The jury's still out on **Rusney Castillo**. The Red Sox paid a staggering amount of money to acquire the athletic Cuban outfielder as a free agent. After his first 90 games, he was hitting .262. He looked to be part of a relatively young new outfield for the Red Sox, with Mookie Betts and Jackie Bradley Jr., but he was also trade bait, too. He is, after all, the only major-leaguer ever named Rusney.

MOST OBSCURE RED SOX PLAYER TO WEAR #38—John Leister, not to be confused with Jon Lester. And Leister, wearing #38, was no Curt Schilling. Leister started six games in 1987, and relieved in a couple more. In 30 1/3 innings, he gave up 31 earned runs on 49 hits and 13 walks (one intentional). He finished 1987 at 0–2, with a 9.20 ERA. Three years later, the Sox gave him another chance in April, twice against the Brewers for a total of 5 2/3 innings. Five more runs, three of them earned. He wound up with a career 8.50 ERA and, not surprisingly, no wins.

What Do Uniform Numbers Mean to the 2009 Red Sox? Part Eight

When fireballing pitcher **Daniel Bard** was called up to Boston in mid-May 2009, it might have crossed someone's mind to give him 100 in recognition of his 100-mph fastball. (It had been sported by 100-year-old batboy Arthur Giddon in April.) Bard wound up with #60, and he was honest enough to admit—between the lines—that he wouldn't mind having a lower number. "You'll notice that all the guys here, all the pitchers who get called up, have 60-something. Justin Masterson is 63. We'll see how the rest of the season plays out." Bard added, "I'm not a big number guy," and that he was happy to have any number in the major leagues "for now." He'd worn #31 in Pawtucket, but acknowledged that Jon Lester had a secure hold on that one. "I don't think it's going anywhere."

When asked why he'd given Bard #60, equipment manager Joe Cochran said he assigned it because "it was there." Cochran tends to save lower numbers for possible veterans who might come over from another club, but he said that not a lot of thought went into choosing #60 as opposed to some other number. **Aaron Bates** was given #50 and **Dusty Brown** #59 for the same reason: they were there. **Marcus McBeth** was assigned #59 the two times he came up—and, though he never saw duty, the number was held for him, so when Brown was recalled on September 9, he was assigned #50 (Bates had been optioned back to the Pawsox in mid-July). "Not bad. Better than 59," he allowed. "I'll take it!"

Josh Reddick was happy enough to get #68. "It's just a number. It doesn't matter to me. As long as I have a jersey, that's all that matters to me." Joe Cochran acknowledged that the high number raised an eyebrow or two. "A couple of people asked me why such a high number. It worked out. There's a method to the madness. With the waiver wire coming and all that, he didn't have any big-league time." There are two numbers Joe doesn't give out: #66 and #69.

Reliever **Fernando Cabrera** echoed Reddick's sentiment. "In spring training, they gave me 53 and as soon as I got called up, they keep me with the same number. I'm happy to be here. It's not about the number. It's good to be here!" The same was true with **Billy Traber**; he had #40 in spring training, so when he came in—for all of one game—that's the number he received. Likewise **Enrique Gonzalez**. Why did he get #51? "I don't know. I go to spring training and he gives me that number. I was 49 with the D-Backs, and 48 and 52 with the San Diego Padres." Like the others, he said he was just happy to be here. Obviously, it's a sentiment expressed a lot, but it's refreshing to know how many major league players cherish the opportunity.

#39: GREENIE

Ridiculously difficult shoes to fill? Think about becoming left fielder for the Red Sox following Ted Williams (1939–60), Carl Yastrzemski (1961–77), and Jim Rice (1975–86). That was what **Mike Greenwell** had to do. Three Hall of Famers in a row had manned the patch of grass in front of the fabled Green Monster for over almost half a century. Thanks to the designated hitter, and Yaz's ability to play first base, there was a long overlap allowing Rice to become established. Thanks to the DH for Rice, Greenwell was able to start as far back as 1985 before taking over the lion's share of the work in left. It wasn't until his eighth game in September 1985 that Greenwell finally collected his first hit, but it was a home run—in the 13th inning, a game-winner. His second hit was a homer, too, and so was his third. Finally, he collected a lowly single in his 14th game, but it was an RBI single, one of three singles that day.

Greenwell made the postseason roster in 1986 (going 1-for-5 with a walk), hit .328 as a rookie the next year, and let loose in '88, taking over left field full time and hitting .325 with 119 RBIs and 22 homers. He was credited with the game-winning hit 23 times, a full 25 percent of the 89 Red Sox wins that year, an AL record. That was his best year and might have been an

MVP year if Jose Canseco hadn't become the first 40–40 man—40 HRs and 40 steals—however dubious it seems today given Canseco's admitted steroid use. Twenty years later, Greenwell said he had considered taking steroids as a player but didn't because his wife, a nurse, "Told me she'd kill me if she caught me doing it." If only more baseball wives had been so hands-on.

Greenwell never had another MVP-caliber season, but he was very good, posting a .303 average in a career spent entirely with the Red Sox. Among his distinctive moments: he hit for the cycle, played an inning as catcher, drove in every Sox run in a 9–8 win, and hit two inside-the-park homers off the same pitcher (Greg Cadaret) in successive seasons. "Gator" also helped convince the Sox to relocate spring training to Fort Myers, his hometown. Yet when it became clear that the Red Sox planned for someone else (Wil Cordero) to play left field starting in 1997, Greenwell pulled a Manny Ramirez of sorts. Though the Sox were still mathematically in the '96 wild card hunt, Greenwell—along with soon-to-depart Roger Clemens—began packing, took down his locker nameplate, and said he wouldn't be coming back. Playing part-time, he said, "would be degrading . . . I want to go where I'm respected." He wound up in Japan, retiring after just seven games because of a broken foot. Greenie, who became a successful stock car and truck racer, was inducted into the Red Sox Hall of Fame in 2008.

Number 39 was available for Greenwell because of the departure of catcher **Gary Allenson**. Allenson had come up in the Red Sox system at the right time, since Carlton Fisk's rib injury caused him to have to DH rather than catch in 1979. Allenson caught 104 games to Fisk's 39, but Allenson hit just .203—though he doubled the percentage of runners thrown out by Pudge. Allenson's batting average leapt to .357 in 1980, in just 70 at-bats, but his average kept dropping the more he played. Eventually, it was at .118 and Allenson went into minor league managing—something he was still doing in 2009 (for Triple A Norfolk in the Orioles system). He served as a Sox coach (1992–94), wearing #32 since Greenwell had his old number.

As with Greenwell, **Creighton Gubanich** had to wait a bit for his first hit, but when it came, it was a big one. Gubanich appeared in two early season games before making his second start, on May 3, 1999; he got his first hit: a grand slam in the top of the first inning in Oakland. He also was hit by a pitch and singled before being replaced by Jason Varitek late in the game. It was the only home run of his brief yet productive 18-game major league career, and it's one he will always remember.

Years earlier, Boston-born **Eddie Pellagrini** hit a home run that he never forgot: a homer his first time up in Fenway Park. It was one of only six home runs he ever hit for his hometown team. An infrequently used utility infielder in 1946 and 1947, he hit .211 the first year and .203 the second. He often said that he "led the league in stolen towels" those first couple of years. The Red Sox really wanted Vern Stephens and Jack Kramer from the St. Louis Browns, so they packaged Pelly, five other players, and $310,000—plus an undisclosed number of towels— to cinch the deal. After eight seasons, 20 homers, and a lifetime .226 average, Pellagrini settled in to become baseball coach at his alma mater, Boston College.

Dave Sisler was famous for his name. Son of Hall of Famer George Sisler (who twice hit over .400) and brother of Dick, an All-Star as a Philly "Whiz Kid" in 1950, Dave was the smart one. He attended Princeton on an academic scholarship, yet he was—as he told inter- viewer Rick Huhn—more a "thrower than a pitcher." Sisler went 24–25 with a 4.79 ERA in 94 games over four seasons with the Red Sox, and 38– 44 (4.33) in seven seasons in the majors before retiring. He eventually became vice-chairman of the investment firm A.G. Edwards. While Sisler began his career in Boston as the tail end of a baseball family, **Ray Boone** was the opposite. He batted .205 for the '60 Sox in his sixth and last stop in the majors, but he developed a cottage industry of big league Boones: his son, Bob, and grandsons, Bret and Aaron, together went to 10 All-Star Games (not counting Ray's two) and collected nine Gold Gloves.

Tracy Stallard told us that #39 had no significance to him; it was just the number they gave him—and took from Boone. Stallard's time with the Red Sox would have been likewise insignificant except for number 61. October 1, 1961, was the last day of the season, and Roger Maris sat on 60 home runs at Yankee Stadium. Maris drilled a fourth-inning Stallard pitch for the record-setting home run to pass Babe Ruth's 1927 mark. That homer to Maris was the only run allowed in a 1–0 loss; he went 2–6 with a 5.08 ERA in his other appearances. He allowed no runs in either 1960 (four innings of work) or 1962 (one inning), and when Stallard and Pumpsie Green were traded to the Mets after the 1962 season, he left the Sox with a 4.71 career ERA. He lost a league-leading 20 times for the not-yet-amazin' Mets, despite a much-improved 3.69 earned run average.

A four-time All-Star and a key part of the Impossible Dream team in 1967, **Gary Bell** came from Cleveland on June 4 that year. "Ding Dong"—his name *was* Bell—had been 1–5 with the Indians, but he went 12–8 with a 3.16 ERA after the trade, and he had a loss and a save in three World Series outings. The following year, Bell put up a 3.12 ERA but the '68 Sox sequel was disappointing and Bell's 11–11 record reflected that.

Mike Garman, drafted with the third overall pick in '67, won all of two games in Boston, but he was good trade bait for several clubs: the Sox (in the 1973 Reggie Cleveland deal), the Cardinals (for six-time All-Star Don Kessinger in 1975), and the Cubs (in the Bill Buckner trade in 1976). Garman's value didn't translate internationally as the Dodgers received two Montreal pitchers for him in '78 and neither won a game in L. A.

MOST OBSCURE RED SOX PLAYER TO WEAR #39—This one really is a dead heat, between **Bob Scherbarth** and **Moose Morton**. Both appeared in just one game. Scherbarth, a catcher, was put in defensively late on April 23, 1950. He caught one inning and then was pulled for a pinch hitter. At least he got to touch the ball. Scherbarth explained to us that he appreciated the opportunity, "Even though I didn't play or anything, they got me in one inning just so I'd get my name in the book. It was the greatest thing that ever happened to me—just to put on the Red Sox uniform. The Red Sox, they treat you like you're a . . . I never felt so good in my life as I did when I got up there." Morton's game was on September 17, 1954, and he was a catcher, too. His father, Guy Morton Sr., had been a major league pitcher for the Indians. In the third inning, Sox manager Lou Boudreau sent Morton to bat for Frank Sullivan. Facing lefty Dean Stone, Morton struck out on three pitches, swinging at each one. "I didn't feel anything particularly about it," he told Richard Tellis. "It was just another day's work. I had struck out before." He would not get to strike out again . . . at least not in the majors. Carlos Peguero put in a bid to be in the running in 2015, but it's hard to beat a couple of guys who only played in one game. Carlos played in four.

What Do Uniform Numbers Mean to the 2009 Red Sox? Part Nine

Is there a number to be feared? Number 13, perhaps? Not at all, says **Alex Gonzalez**. It's even considered a bit of a lucky number by Venezuelan shortstops. Tomas Perez wore it for a while; Edgardo Alfonzo, who played mostly second and third base, wore it for his first couple of teams. Omar Vizquel wears it. "I picked it," A. G. said. "There's a lot of shortstops wore that number. Ozzie [Guillen]. [Dave] Concepcion. Some places it's bad luck but I don't believe that." So why did he switch to #3? "Pookie asked me for it," he said of clubhouse attendant Pookie Jackson. "It doesn't matter, the number." Closer **Billy Wagner** thinks so.

Wagner was the #13 Pookie was speaking on behalf of. Activated on August 27, Wagner had been traded by the Mets a few weeks after his return from major arm surgery the previous fall. Wagner had worn #13 since his days at small Ferrum College in southwestern Virginia. Wagner is kind of small himself for a pitcher. And he's never forgotten. "Five feet, 10 inches and I wasn't supposed to . . . nobody had any expectations of me going to pro ball. They gave [#13] to me. It just kind of stuck." Was he surprised to find that someone had given up the number for him when he came to Boston? "Yeah, I really was." Had he realized that Gonzalez was wearing #13? "Well, my kids knew it. I mean, I couldn't care less what they gave me. When you get traded, and coming back and stuff, you can't really sit here and demand anything. You're just happy to be here. It's nice of him. I know it meant a lot to Gonzo." Fortunately, Gonzalez started hitting even better right after he switched to #3. Wagner noticed. "I'm just glad he's had a couple of pretty good games. I'm pretty happy about that."

With young players, the number issue generally seems less complicated. **Justin Masterson** was simply handed #63 and put it on. "That's what they gave me. In spring training, I had number 70, which I thought I'd get, but then they gave me 63. They just said, 'Here's the number.' It's grown on me. I like it." After Masterson was traded to the Indians in the **Victor Martinez** deal, that freed up 63. When the Red Sox brought up **Junichi Tazawa**, he took on the number. "He's got Masterson's number," Cochran said. "He was 86 in spring training."

Now, as to Martinez, a native of Venezuela, he'd actually begun his major league career with #63 and then took #20 before landing #41 with Cleveland in 2004. "That was a funny story," he said. "When I signed with the Indians, we got the academy in Puerto La Cruz. They have those guys who came and play here in the United States, so before those guys leave they always give everything—you know, batting glove, whatever—they give to guys like us. You know, [players] just arriving. In those academies, we used to wear T-shirts . . . with the Indian logo and number [logo on breast, heart side], I remember, one of those guys gave me a T-shirt that was number 41. He give it to me and I start wearing it, and I start hitting and hitting and that's how I start wearing number 41." Victor's son has his own child-size #41 shirt. As soon as he heard his father was being traded to Boston, he asked, "What number are we going to wear with Boston?" Was the boy happy to learn it was #41? "Oh yeah, really happy. He's four years old." From Cochran's perspective, it was easy. Nothing had to be changed: "Even with his catcher's gear, it's already stitched in there." The number 41. Perfect.

#40: Belonging Nowhere

ALL TIME #40 ROSTER

Player	Year
Bill McKechnie	1952–53 (coach)
Buster Mills	1954 (coach)
Russ Kemmerer	1955
Frank Baumann	1955–56
Bob Chakales	1957
Mike Ryan	1964–65
Rollie Sheldon	1966
Galen Cisco	1967
Ken Harrelson	1967–69
Carlton Fisk	1969
Billy Conigliaro	1970–71
Dwight Evans	1972–73
Rick Wise	1974–77
Frank Tanana	1981
Calvin Schiraldi	1986
Dave Henderson	1986
John Dopson	1989–93
Sergio Valdez	1994
Erik Hanson	1995
Herm Starrette	1996 (coach)
Robinson Checo	1997–98
Mark Guthrie	1999
Michael Coleman	1999
Sang-Hoon Lee	2000
Tony Cloninger	2002–03 (coach)
Cla Meredith	2005
Alejandro Machado	2005
Ken Huckaby	2006
Bartolo Colon	2008
Billy Traber	2009
John Lackey	2010
Curt Young	2011 (coach)
A.J. Pierzynski	2014

Number of times this number was issued: 33
Longest tenure by any given player: 5
seasons, John Dopson

No one wore #40 until 1952. Only a handful of people had even worn anything above the 30s until the whole coaching staff got high . . . numbers. Pitching coach **Bill McKechnie** crashed through the barrier with #40, followed by first base coach Earle Combs (#41), Oscar Melillo (#42), George Susce (#43), and Paul Schreiber, (#45). Newly installed manager Lou Boudreau himself wore #4. One detects a pattern here.

It would be 15 years before a notable player donned the digits. **Ken Harrelson** turned up in Boston at the end of August 1967, snapped up and signed three days after he'd been released by the Kansas City A's—though kicked off is more like it. His sudden change of scene resulted from what could be politely termed a "personality clash" between Harrelson and A's owner Charlie O. Finley. Harrelson publicly dubbed his owner a "menace to baseball" and when he failed to turn up at a press conference to apologize, ties were severed. The timing was perfect for the Red Sox. Boston was desperate to replace some of the power lost after Tony Conigliaro's tragic beaning in the middle of August. Some punishment for Harrelson! His salary leapt from $12,000 a year to $150,000.

Harrelson struggled at first, hitting just .200 for the Sox in 1967 (he'd been batting .305 for K.C.), and he didn't help at all in the World Series

(1-for-13). He found his Bay State legs in '68 and led the American League with 109 RBIs. His 35 homers were also a career high. Harrelson, who developed an alter ego known as "The Hawk," was a counterculture sensation in Boston sports circles, with his Nehru jackets and all. He was traded to the Indians in a six-player deal at the start of the 1969 campaign. He was so popular that fans picketed Fenway Park and Hawk initially said he'd rather retire than leave Boston. Things were worked out; he played in Cleveland through 1971, when he quit baseball to pursue a professional golf career. He later became a White Sox broadcaster in 1981, a position he still holds today.

Rick Wise arrived with Bernie Carbo in a trade with the Cardinals for Reggie Smith and Ken Tatum after the 1973 season. Wise was an experienced right-hander who'd won 16 or more games the three prior seasons, and had been an All-Star two of those seasons. He threw a no-hitter and homered twice on June 23, 1971. Though he wouldn't have to hit now in the AL, it was nice to have that on your résumé.

Wise was asked to pitch the third game of the year in Boston, with temperatures in the 30s, after a 12-day layoff. He threw a complete game, but he later tore his triceps and 1974 became a more or less lost season (3–4, 3.86). In 1975, though, Wise was a big part of the pennant-winning Sox, going 19–12 with a 3.95 ERA and 17 complete games. He won the third and deciding game of the ALCS and was the pitcher of record when Carlton Fisk's home run won Game Six of the World Series. After two more double-digit winning seasons for the Red Sox, he was sent to the Indians in the Dennis Eckersley deal. So #40 lay dormant for six of the next seven years, filled only in 1981 by three-time All-Star southpaw **Frank Tanana**, who had one disappointing season with the Red Sox. Starting in 1989, **John Dopson** kept the number warm longer than anyone—five seasons—but his pedestrian numbers in Boston as a starter (26–30, 4.29 ERA) and only logging a little over 5 1/3 innings per start made sure the bullpen stayed warm as well.

Calvin Schiraldi started wearing #40 in 1986 but gave the number to **Dave Henderson** when he arrived from Seattle on August 19 with Spike Owen. Henderson played a huge role in the 1986 playoffs, to say the least. It was Papi-esque (and we don't mean Stan Papi). Henderson only hit .196 with one homer in the last six weeks of the regular season, but with the Red Sox facing elimination in Game Five of the ALCS, Hendu was the last hope. Down three games to one, trailing by a run, man on first, two outs, top of the ninth—boom! His long home run off Donnie Moore gave the Sox the lead. They couldn't hold it, but that was taken care of when Hendu faced Moore again in the top of the 11th and hit a sacrifice fly. Schiraldi closed out the game. Henderson's home run two weeks later should have iced Game Six of the World Series, but we know how that turned out. After batting .234 with 25 RBIs in 1987, he was traded to San Francisco and later became an All-Star in Oakland.

Billy Conigliaro wore both #1 and #4 when he first came up in 1969. His brother Tony had hit a home run in his first Fenway Park at-bat, on April 17, 1964. Billy made his own mark by homering in his first Fenway start on April 16, 1969, and then he hit another his next time up that day. The Conigliaros wound up with the most homers of any BoSox bro duo, beating out Wes and Rick Ferrell, 78–47. Billy hit 22 home runs in his career with the Sox, but his average dropped each season so that by 1971 he appeared in fewer games than Joe Lahoud. (Historical note: That's not a good sign.) Just a few days after the 1971 season ended, Tommy Harper became Boston's right fielder in a 10-player trade that sent Milwaukee both Lahoud and Billy C., along with Ken Brett, Jim Lonborg, George Scott, and Don Pavletich. It was quite the housecleaning.

Could Bill Lee, a practicing Buddhist, be reincarnated (while still alive) as Korean left-hander **Sang-Hoon Lee**? That's the question posed in *Red Sox Threads*. The Korean Lee was the first to have played professionally in Korea, Japan, and the United States. With his long hair dyed orange, the latter Lee was introduced to the media at Fenway, and said, "Bill Lee was crazy. So am I." At this point in time, the Red Sox were cornering the Korean market; they had signed six of the 14 Koreans in American organized baseball. Lee relieved in nine games in Boston in 2000 and finished the year with very good 3.09 ERA. But come 2001, back in Pawtucket, his 5.43 Triple A ERA in 43 games raised flags. The Sox weren't crazy; they started looking elsewhere.

You think **Cla Meredith**'s name is spelled crazy? It beats his given name of Olise. The reliever debuted in Boston less than a year after being drafted out of Virginia Commonwealth. He entered a tie game on May 8, 2005, with two outs and two on, and walked the first two batters he faced. He surrendered a grand slam to his third batter. The fourth laced a double before he finally got out of the inning with an 81.00 ERA. Meredith would settle down, albeit elsewhere. The panic trade to get back Doug Mirabelli because Josh Bard couldn't catch Tim Wakefield netted San Diego both Meredith and Bard.

MOST OBSCURE RED SOX PLAYER TO WEAR #40—Dan Shaughnessy often called **Robinson Checo** the "Dominican Mystery Man" because it often seemed hard to pin down where he actually was. In both 1997 and 1998, Checo pitched for four different ballclubs in the Red Sox organization. This was after a career in which he played in the Dominican Summer League, on the Hiroshima Carp's minor league team in Japan, and with the China Times Eagles in the Taiwan Major League. He got in some work with the big team in Hiroshima but then "retired" (his sham retirement was to enable him to play in the United States). The Red Sox signed him and he debuted in September 1997. Checo started twice and saw action in three other games, tossing 13 innings in all (1–1, 3.38). He lost both his starts in 1998 and his 9.39 ERA inspired little confidence. He toiled in the system the rest of the season and was released in December. He signed with Detroit but was soon traded to the Dodgers, the mystery finally ending for him in Albuquerque.

What Might Have Been

Andy Gilbert was the first Red Sox player to wear #42 and it was in '42. He went to war, returned, donned the number, and batted one last time, but by all rights that uniform number should have been occupied when Gilbert returned.

Jackie Robinson had a tryout at Fenway Park almost two years to the day before he debuted with the Brooklyn Dodgers. Boston city councilman Isadore Muchnick threatened to block the "blue laws" waiver that allowed Sunday baseball in Boston if the Red Sox did not begin to offer opportunities to black ballplayers. A tryout was scheduled, then cancelled, then put back on after an article by influential and infamous columnist Dave Egan. Three Negro

League players arrived at Fenway on April 16, 1945: second baseman Marvin Williams of the Philadelphia Stars, outfielder Sam Jethroe of the Cleveland Buckeyes, and Robinson, then a shortstop for the Kansas City Monarchs. The display lasted about 90 minutes, punctuated by an epithet hurled from a mysterious voice at empty Fenway (a detail not revealed until eyewitness Clif Keane mentioned it 34 years later). There was praise from coach Hugh Duffy, but the Red Sox never followed up with any of the trio. Robinson, of course, became the first player in the 20th century to break the color line in 1947. He was voted Rookie of the Year in that season, MVP in 1949, and is installed in the Hall of Fame. Jethroe became Rookie of the Year in 1950 with the Boston Braves. And the Red Sox were the big losers. The Sox were the last team to integrate, waiting 14 seasons after the sham tryout to actually put Pumpsie Green on the field at Fenway. By then, Robinson, who'd led the Dodgers to six pennants, had been retired for two years.

Things can change. On April 15, 2009, there were 42s everywhere as the Red Sox took the field in Oakland to celebrate the 62nd anniversary of Robinson's major league debut. Rather than just a few players wearing the number he wore in Brooklyn, all uniformed personnel throughout the major leagues—even the umpires—wore #42 for the day. This was one time you couldn't tell the players *with* a scorecard—and probably about as close as a modern-day fan could get to experiencing how people in the stands figured out who was who before uniform numbers were introduced. Of course, you wouldn't have known Terry Francona was wearing #42 instead of his customary #47, since he was also wearing his ever-present pullover. Tim Wakefield threw a complete-game 8–2 win. The starting nine (or starting 42s, if you will): Jason Bay, J. D. Drew, Jacoby Ellsbury, Nick Green, George Kottaras, Mike Lowell, David Ortiz, Dustin Pedroia, and Kevin Youkilis. First base coach Tim Bogar and third base coach DeMarlo Hale (wearing #42 for the third year in a row) manned the coaching boxes.

Mo Vaughn was the last member of the Red Sox to wear #42 on a daily basis. Like every other major leaguer who wore #42 at the time it was retired throughout organized baseball in 1997, Vaughn had the option to wear the number for the rest of his career. To Vaughn, it was a validation, since he very consciously wore it to honor Robinson. "He's the reason why Barack Obama gets elected," Vaughn said in a 2008 NESN interview. "He's the reason why the integration of anything and anybody has happened."

A laundry basket in the Red Sox clubhouse after Jackie Robinson Day on April 15, 2016. The jerseys would later be sold to benefit the Red Sox Foundation.

#41: Of Dragons and Pens

A 58-year-old man on a visit to Boston steps onto the T and is immediately greeted by a stranger. "Hey, Dragon! How are you doing?" the driver hollers. "My friend couldn't believe it," **Dick Drago** told Herb Crehan about a visit to Boston in 2003. "I hadn't pitched for the Red Sox in over 20 years and people still recognized me. I love Boston!"

The former Royals right-handed starter arrived in Boston after the 1973 season in exchange for Marty Pattin. Drago split his time between starting and relieving in 1974, but by 1975 he was used almost exclusively at the final innings, finishing 34 games while only starting twice. His 15 saves helped get the Sox into the postseason and his two saves in the ALCS helped get them into the World Series. He bore the loss in Game Two, coming in for Bill Lee in the top of the ninth. Two hits drove in a pair of Reds to even the Series. In Game Six, after Bernie Carbo's three-run homer tied it in the eighth, Drago held Cincinnati scoreless for the next three innings. Rick Miller pinch-hit for him, so it was Rick Wise who threw the top of the 12th and got the win on Pudge Fisk's home run. Yet in his second tour in Boston—after surrendering Hank Aaron's 755th and final home run in 1976 as an Angel—Drago had a chance to pick up the win in another all-time epic. In the one-game playoff against the Yankees at Fenway Park on October 3, 1978, Drago retired Thurman Munson to end the top of the ninth, keeping it a one-run game. Drago gets a win for the ages if either Hall of Famer Jim Rice or Carl Yastrzemski puts a ball out of sight just this one time . . .

A Hall of Fame pitcher who toiled briefly for the Red Sox was **Tom Seaver**, who closed his playing career as #41 in the latter of half of 1986. Perhaps the reason he's in the Hall of Fame wearing a Mets cap has to do with his 198–124 (2.57 ERA) record with the Metropolitans rather than his 5–7 (3.80) record with the Red Sox. The Mets retired #41 in 1988—the only player's number retired by that franchise is for "The Franchise." The number was certainly up for grabs in Boston. **Mike Smithson** had been drafted by the Sox in 1976 and traded to Texas, only to return in '88 for his last two years of mediocrity (16–20, 5.83).

Jeff Reardon's best season with the Red Sox was 1991, when he saved 40 games and had an ERA of 3.03. A native of Dalton, Massachusetts (the same town whence came future GM Dan Duquette), Reardon went 8–9 with 88 saves for the Red Sox. "The Terminator" seemed to be losing his touch in 1992 just as he was surpassing Rollie Fingers's record for most saves in history—back when the mark stood at 342. The Sox moved Reardon while he still had value, sending him to the Braves at the end of August for two prospects who never panned out.

In an unfortunate incident apparently attributable to a mixture of a dozen anti-depressants he was taking to try to cope with the death of his son from a drug overdose, Reardon robbed a jewelry store in a Florida mall (claiming to be armed, though he was not). He then simply walked to a nearby restaurant. He was tried and found not guilty by reason of insanity, and began a course of treatment.

Former Red Sox reliever **Ugueth Urbina** is still in prison, sentenced in March 2007 to 14 years incarceration for the attempted murder of five workers on his ranch in Venezuela. Urbina, whose mother had earlier been dramatically freed after a five-month kidnapping ordeal, simply snapped. The workers had reportedly been swimming in his pool when Urbina and four other men turned up unexpectedly and attacked the swimmers with machetes and tried to set them afire. Ugueth Urtain Urbina—all his siblings' first and middle names also started with "U"—had come to Boston from Montreal at the trading deadline in 2001. He saved nine games the rest of the year (with a 2.25 ERA) and dialed in 40 in '02. The Red Sox decided to go with their rueful "closer by committee" approach in 2003 and let Ugie go.

There's a lot less drama in the story of **Jim Corsi**, and he's probably grateful for that. A Newton native who still lives in the area, Corsi has worked as an occasional broadcaster on NESN and is a popular guest at Fenway's Autograph Alley. Like all the #41s above who aren't in the Hall of Fame, Corsi was a right-handed reliever. In three seasons with the Red Sox (he spent 10 years in the bigs) he appeared in 134 games, going 9–7 with a 3.35 ERA. He threw three scoreless innings against the Indians in his lone postseason in the 1998 ALDS, allowing just one hit and a walk.

The lefty in the group, **Wilbur Wood**, signed out of nearby Belmont High School in 1960. His fastball and curve were ordinary enough that he pitched just 36 times over four seasons in Boston, accruing no wins, five losses, and three uni numbers (he also wore #19 and #28), plus a 4.85 ERA during the most dominant period for pitching since the Dead Ball Era. Sold to the Pirates and then traded to the White Sox, ageless knuckleballer Hoyt Wilhelm advised Wood to just throw his flutterball. It worked. In 1972, Wood would start more games (49) and log more innings (376 2/3) than any pitcher since the early 1900s. In 1973, he became the last hurler to start—and, incidentally, lose—both games of a doubleheader. And this came after he set a since-broken mark of 88 appearances as a reliever in 1968. Yep, local kid Wood made good . . . wearing the wrong Sox.

The first Colombian to play for the Red Sox was shortstop **Jackie Gutierrez**, who impressed fans (and apparently scouts) with his hustle and style afield. After several years in the minors, he debuted in five late-season games in 1983. His .300 average was far higher than anything he'd done in the minor leagues. Gutierrez played 151 games for Boston in 1984 and hit a very respectable .268 with 17 extra-base hits; his 12 stolen bases led the team by a mile. In the field, though, he committed 31 errors. Glenn Hoffman, whom he'd replaced at short, wound up shouldering more of the load in 1985. Jackie's average plunged to .218, and his fielding was even weaker. That December he was traded to the Orioles for Sammy Stewart, another former Red Sox pitcher currently in prison (see #53).

The best Beantown hope for #41 arrived in 2009. **Victor Martinez** came over in Cleveland's summer fire sale in return for prized pitching prospects Justin Masterson, Nick Hagadone, and Bryan Price. A switch-hitting, three-time All-Star catcher, who also plays first base, Martinez hit .336 in his 56 games after the trade. "V-Mart" has the best middle-of-the-order sock from a Sox backstop since Pudge Fisk.

John Lackey came to Boston to high expectations, but after a mediocre 2010 (with #40) he totally soured with fans the following year, with a 6.41 ERA. One thing he needed was Tommy John surgery, if not a new P.R. firm. He did come back in 2013 and had a 3.52 ERA, despite a losing record in wins and losses. Come the postseason, though, he came through came through well, winning one game in each of the three rounds, including the final game of the World Series, in which he worked 6 2/3 innings allowing just one run.

MOST OBSCURE RED SOX PLAYER TO WEAR #41—Unemployed free agent **Dan Smith** was signed by the Red Sox on June 2, 2000, and pitched on June 3 and June 7, both times facing National League teams in interleague road games. He pitched well in Philly, getting four of five men out, but things unraveled in Miami. In two innings he allowed two hits, two walks, and, oddly, three sacrifice flies. The Sox were already behind before Smith came in, so he didn't bear the loss, though he did earn a demotion and was released after the season. He fared better against NL teams in an Expos uniform . . . but not a lot better, going 7–12 with a 5.17 ERA.

Sox by Any Other Name

There are players one associates primarily with other teams, but who nevertheless spent a season or two, or maybe three, with the Red Sox: Don Baylor, Jose Canseco, Frank Tanana, Dizzy Trout, and even Hall of Famers Ferguson Jenkins, Tony Perez, George Kell, and Luis Aparicio, just to name a few. Lou Boudreau played the last games of his Hall of Fame career in Boston in 1952 and then remained as manager. Long before there were numbers, there were a couple of Hall of Famers who hung 'em up close to home with the Sox: Worcester resident Jesse Burkett retired back in 1905, and Jack Chesbro from cozy Conway, Massachusetts, a 41-game winner in New York in 1904, who pitched once in 1909 for Boston. Then there were players who were Red Sox property (however briefly), but for one reason or another never played for the major league team: Jeff Bagwell and Rollie Fingers come to mind. Often.

And finally, there are those players who actually did play for the Red Sox, but who spent so little time in Boston, it's surprising to see their names in this book—even a future Cooperstown enshrinee who spent a few weeks in a Sox uniform in 2009. Here's our top 10 numbered Sox shocks who spent a year or less in Boston near the end of their distinguished careers, listed from most games with the Sox to least. (+ indicates those whose last career game was as a Red Sox; **bold** denotes Hall of Fame inductee.)

Orlando Cepeda, 142 games: #25 (1973)

+John Olerud, 87 games: #19 (2005)

Heinie Manush, 82 games: #7 (1936)

Rickey Henderson, 72 games: #24 (2002)

Al Simmons, 40 games: #8 (1943)

Bobby Thomson, 40 games: #25 (1960)

+**Tom Seaver**, 16 games: #41 (1986)

Juan Marichal, 11 games: #21 (1974)

John Smoltz, 8 games: #29 (2009)

+Gary Gaetti, 5 games: #6 (2000)

#42: Mo Money

Mo Vaughn was the last Red Sox player to wear #42 on a daily basis before it was retired in honor of one of Vaughn's heroes: Jackie Robinson. Vaughn was easily the best of the 21 Sox players to wear the number (**Oscar Melillo**, a coach, wore #42 back when Jackie Robinson was still with the Dodgers).

Selecting Vaughn, a Norwalk, Connecticut, native and record-shattering slugger at Seton Hall, in the first round of the 1989 draft paid off handsomely for Boston. "Hit Dog" captured the AL MVP in 1995, leading the league in RBIs with 126 in a strike-shortened season (18 games lost); he'd knock in 143 over a full season in '96. For six seasons in a row (1993–98), he was in the top 10 in slugging percentage. The first baseman/DH batted .304 in his eight seasons with the Red Sox, hitting substantially higher over his final five seasons—an impressive feat given his girth, gait, and the overshift defense often employed against him. It seemed almost inconceivable that the Red Sox would ever let him go. He was a much-loved, gregarious, charitable, larger-than-life figure, a New Englander who was very comfortable playing in Boston. When it came time to re-sign him, though, things became thorny. Vaughn emphasized "respect" and his taped phrase "It's not about the money" is still played over radio talk shows whenever some athlete starts talking about respect when money issues arise. Vaughn claimed that the Red Sox had hired private detectives to follow him around, presumably to get dirt on him and drive his price down. He did himself no favors when he was arrested for DWI and hitting a disabled car in an early morning drive home from the Foxy Lady strip club he was known to patronize. The Red Sox finally just let him walk after the 1998 season and he signed with the Angels (who later traded him to the Mets) at a salary that over the next six years doubled what he'd made in Boston.

Vaughn's better years were behind him, though. In his Angels debut, he tumbled down the dugout steps trying to catch a foul popup and sprained his ankle. The injuries piled up: he lost the first part of 1999, all of 2001, the last five months of 2003, and all of 2004. Vaughn had been a real presence in the Red Sox lineup, intimidating the opposition and often coming up with the big hit. Perhaps his most memorable moments came in his last Sox season: a walkoff grand slam in the home opener to cap a seven-run, ninth-inning comeback from a 7–2 deficit; almost winning the batting title at .337; and the two homers he hit in Game One of the 1998 ALDS, driving in seven runs in the 11–3 win over the Indians. Vaughn was inducted into the Red Sox Hall of Fame in November 2008.

Bobby Darwin had a very long wait to get into his second major league game. He pitched once as an Angel in 1962 and then not again until 1969, with the Dodgers. He led the American League in strikeouts for three straight years (1972–74). That would have been wonderful, except that 1969 was the last time he pitched. From 1971 on, he was an outfielder. By the time he got to the Red Sox, he was hitting too much like a pitcher. His .188 average in parts of two seasons got him traded from the Red Sox to the White Sox.

Sonny Siebert was a home run–hitting pitcher of sorts. In his sixth season with the Indians, he was traded to Boston in time to win 14 games in 1969. The right-hander was 57–41 with a 3.46 ERA over parts of five seasons. He only hit .199 in his Boston years, but he clubbed six homers in 1971 alone. He was the last Red Sox pitcher to have a multi-homer game, knocking in all three runs and tossing a shutout to boot on September 2, 1971. The pitcher who preceded Seibert in #42 could certainly hit: **Ken Brett**. We hear his brother George was pretty good with the stick, too.

Ken Brett batted .262 for his career with 10 home runs: three HRs with the Red Sox, three as a Pirate, and four in successive starts with the 1973 Phillies, a major league record. The White Sox often went without a DH when the lefty-swinging—and throwing—Brett was on the hill. The first such instance came at Fenway on July 6, 1976. He went hitless batting ninth in a complete-game loss (ironically, Bobby Darwin was DH for the Red Sox and tripled—and fanned twice). Boston had been taken with "Kemer" Brett's pitching when they chose him with the fourth overall pick in 1966. He pitched twice in the 1967 World Series a few weeks after turning 19, the youngest Series pitcher in history. Brett, who also wore #36, #15, and #18, was sent to Milwaukee in the 10-player Tommy Harper trade just after the 1971 season.

Chuck Rainey was likewise a first-round choice by the Red Sox. The right-hander spent four years in Boston (1979–82) compiling a 23–14 record and a 4.38 ERA, and was traded to the Cubs for **Doug Bird**, who had led the NL in earned runs and homers allowed in '82. In the last stop of his 11-year career, he compiled just a 1–4 mark and 6.65 ERA with the Red Sox.

Rob Woodward was a New Hampshire man who appeared in parts of four seasons with Boston but spent far more time each year in Pawtucket. He put together a 4–4 record and 5.04 ERA in exactly 100 innings pitched. **John Trautwein** was another short-time pitcher, throwing only 16 innings and allowing 16 earned runs for a sort of perfect 9.00 ERA. The second man and the second-to-last man to wear #42 both wore the number for their last at-bats in the majors 47 years apart. **Babe Barna** hit .170 and socked the first homer by a #42 in '43 and **Jim Pankovits** never even got to bat. The Astros veteran filled in twice defensively at second base in 1990 and that was that.

MOST OBSCURE RED SOX PLAYER TO WEAR #42—It wasn't a memorable trade that sent .210-hitting backup catcher Lou Berberet to Detroit for right-hander **Herb Moford**. An .027 hitter in 1958 (1-for-37), Moford wasn't much of a pitcher, either—he arrived in Boston with a 5–10 career mark for the Tigers and Cards. For the Sox in 1959, he started twice and lost both with an 11.42 ERA. Moford didn't resurface in the majors until the '62 Mets put him on their inaugural roster. He pitched seven times in April—all losses—and took the defeat in the first Mets extra-inning game in history. Even the worst team in the 20th century knew when to say goodbye.

Don Gile's Numerical Theory

Red Sox catcher/first baseman Don Gile (1959–62) started out with #35 and was later given #38 at a time when few players wore numbers in the 40s and no one seemingly got such a number by choice. He recalled what life was like on the roster bubble under manager Mike "Pinky" Higgins.

"I think any of the rookies or second-year players were just happy to be there and your number didn't mean a thing," Gile said. "The most important thing was don't get called into Mike Higgins's office. 'And bring your play book with you!'" Triple A, here I come!

"I can say, among the rookies, in spring training, we felt the lower your number the better your chance to go north with the club. When you get into the high 30s, you better have one hell of a spring, and if you were in the 40s, forget it."

Gile played 31 games over four seasons with the Red Sox, hitting .150. He spent a fair bit of time with Minneapolis and Seattle—both Triple A affiliates of the Sox.

What Do Uniform Numbers Mean to Some of the 2015 Red Sox?

OK, we've waded through 2009. Very late in the 2015 season, we had the opportunity to catch up with a few of the players from that year to ask them about their numbers. When Jackie Bradley Jr. was in spring training with the Red Sox in 2013, he was assigned #74. He wanted a lower number. Why? He told the Boston Globe, "With 74, I'd never get any calls from the umpires." He didn't specifically select #25, though. He said it was just given to him. He'd had 44 before, and that, too, was just the number given to him. He did know that it had been Tony Conigliaro's, or he learned it soon after he was given it.

It's not only batters who have to worry about getting calls from umpires; pitchers do, too—but that didn't faze Dalier Hinojosa, who was with the Red Sox briefly (as in 1 2/3 innings). Hinojosa had been signed out of Cuba in late 2013, and pitched in one game for the Red Sox, on May 3, 2015. He wore #94. To date, it's the highest number to be worn by a Red Sox player. No, he wasn't born in '94. It was the number he wore with the Cuban national team. He faced nine batters for Boston, walking three of them (those umpire calls?) but striking out two. He was plucked off waivers by the Phillies and was 2–0 (0.78) in 18 games (23 innings) for the Phils before the year was done. He wore #94 for them, too.

We asked Hanley Ramirez why he wore #13. "Why? Because that was the only number left." "That's not true," we said. There's #95." "I'm not a wide receiver," he said back. Actually, he said, he picked 13 because that's the number he'd worn with the Dodgers and it was available.

Travis Shaw was given #47 and said he was happy enough with it: "It works for now." Dustin Pedroia said the same thing. "They just gave it to me. Nothing behind it."

Mookie Betts? "That was just what they gave me from the start. I had some family members buy the jersey, so. . . ." That would make it more difficult to change it, of course. "Are you thinking of changing it someday?" "Ahhh, it seems like it's been all right, so. . . ."

The litany started to get a little uninteresting. Brock Holt: "I did not choose it. It was just given to me when I got traded over." "Did you ever look into the history of it?" "I know it was Wade Boggs's. I caught some flak on Twitter when they found out I was number 26. They thought I picked it." Here he sets the record straight.

The two young catchers had better stories. Blake Swihart said, "I was 71 when I got to spring training this year, but when I got here this year, that's what they gave me." "They didn't ask you?" "Not really. I think when older guys come over—get traded over—they ask them what they want." "It was Luis Tiant's number, I guess you know." "Yeah. But it was just given to me. I like it, though." Christian Vasquez was on the DL for all of the 2015 season. He'd had

#55, but late in the season, he was spotted rehabbing at the park and wearing a #7 jersey. We asked, "You've got number 7 this year." "Yeah, I changed it this year from last year. I like Ivan Rodriguez. He used 7. So . . . it was available and I took it." Some people just take the lowest number available, but that wasn't his motive. Nor was it what influenced Xander Bogaerts to ask for #2. That was because of his admiration for another #2, a certain New York shortstop named Jeter.

Some of the Sox players in spring training 2015 had numbers but we never saw them on the big-league roster. A quick look at those who didn't make it:

31 Dana Eveland P
39 Felipe Paulino P
40 Humberto Quintero C
41 Mitchell Boggs P
61 Bryan LaHair IF
62 Zeke Sprull P
72 Luke Montz C
74 Keith Couch P
75 Miguel Celestino P
80 Sean Coyle IF
81 Matt Spring C

That's not to mention some, such as Edwin Escobar and Quintin Berry, who had previously been with Boston but did not return in 2015.

#43. WHAT THE ECK?

Dennis Eckersley. "The Eck." Hall of Famer. The man who helped bring Bill Buckner to the Red Sox. He started with Cleveland at age 20, won the *Sporting News* 1975 AL Rookie Pitcher of the Year honors, and threw a no-hitter in his third season. Cleveland traded him to the Red Sox just before the 1978 season began—and he became a 20-game winner for the Red Sox, helping propel Boston to the final game of the year, the Monday afternoon playoff against the Yankees. Unfortunately, Eck wasn't pitching that day (he'd pitched Saturday and won four times in the final two weeks). Eck led the league in strikeout-to-walk ratio and had a 2.99 ERA, placing fourth to Ron Guidry in the Cy Young voting.

Eck had a very good year in 1979 with the exact same ERA, but then began to flounder for a number of reasons, several of them off-the-field. Boston traded him to the Cubs for Bill Buckner, a good trade for the Red Sox at the time (though it's a lot harder to justify now). After the Cubs sent Eck to Oakland, the A's converted him to a closer and he blossomed, averaging more than 35 saves a season, winning both the 1992 AL Cy Young Award and AL MVP. He pitched in 14 League Championship Series games for Oakland, with a 1.50 ERA, and was MVP of Oakland's sweep of the Sox in 1988. He pitched in three consecutive World Series, recording a save but setting in motion the lasting image of Kirk Gibson's oft-replayed homer at Dodger Stadium in '88. Eckersley spent two years in St. Louis before returning to Boston for his final major league season in 1998. He went 4–1 in a setup role, with a 4.76 ERA, recording his 390th save and 1,071st appearance. In 2004, he was voted into the Hall of Fame. He lives in the Boston area and is a frequent co-host on NESN postgame broadcasts.

Alan Embree was a nice midseason pickup in 2002, arriving in a trade from San Diego. He stayed through two very exciting years, 2003 and 2004, before being released in mid-2005 (and snapped up by the Yankees). The lefty reliever's Boston record doesn't seem special (8–9, 4.69 ERA), but he had better than a 3–1 K–to–BB ratio. And he was better in the postseason. In his first 10 postseason games, he did not allow an earned run. In Game Seven of the 2003 ALCS, he's the man Grady Little called in ... after he finally decided Pedro Martinez had had enough. Embree kept an inherited runner from scoring, but the 5–2 lead Boston had opened the inning with was gone. Too Little too late.

The only two runs Embree ever gave up in the postseason while wearing his Red Sox jersey came in Game Three of the 2004 ALCS as the Yankees boosted their lead from 15–6 to 17–6. Embree was just taking his turn in the shelling—and it made for a better story later. As the Sox made their improbable comeback, Embree pitched in Games Four, Five, and Seven without allowing a run. He also held the Cardinals scoreless in the 2004 World Series. Not a bad guy to have around!

Left-handed starter **Gary Peters** spent his last three seasons in Boston. After 11 years with the White Sox, he donned new Sox in December 1969. He was 16–11 and 14–11 his first two Boston seasons (4.06 and 4.37 ERA, respectively). Lefty **Kevin Morton** had a lot in common with fellow 1991 rookie Mo Vaughn. Both were natives of Norwalk, Connecticut, teammates at Seton Hall, and chosen in the first round of the 1989 draft (Vaughn was the 23rd pick; Morton the 29th). But that's where Mo and Mort parted company on the diamond. The southpaw never pitched again in the majors after going 6–5 with a 4.59 ERA in '91.

How often does a rookie with a 1–2 record pitch the ninth inning of a tied World Series Game Seven? For relievers, won and loss stats are sometimes fairly meaningless, but back in 1975 managers generally went with pitchers in that situation who had more than one career win. **Jim Burton** never got another; in fact, he pitched just once more in the majors after losing Game Seven to the Reds.

A first-round draft pick in 1971, Burton debuted in Boston on June 10, 1975, appearing in 29 games. He started four times, resulting in his only two losses. The southpaw's lone win came after taking over for Dick Drago, a reliever making his last career start. Burton's 2.89 ERA and 2-to-1 strikeout-to-walk ratio both indicate the help he provided in '75. His only appearance after Game Seven came in 1977, closing out a contest Baltimore led, 10–0. Ironically, he took over from Jim Willoughby, the man he relieved in Game Seven, to New England's everlasting regret.

Here's a father and son story, involving **George Susce**, or more precisely George Cyril Methodius Susce and George Daniel Susce (the father perhaps giving his son a more merciful middle name). G. C. M. Susce coached for the Red Sox from 1950–54, and became the first man to don #43 in 1952. He'd been with the Indians since 1941, but when George the younger signed with Boston's Louisville farm club late in 1949, Cleveland fired his dad. The Indians had wanted the junior George, and even offered more money, but the young man really preferred the Red Sox (and opined that perhaps it wouldn't be a good idea for father and son to be in the same organization). The elder Susce accepted a job as Red Sox bullpen coach in 1950. A year after G. C. M. left Boston, boy George debuted with the Red Sox; one of his wins was a one-hitter against the Kansas City A's, where his father now worked. George Daniel (18–14, 4.23) wore #41 and #27 in his three-plus years with the Sox.

If the Susces had an agent to represent them, things might have worked out another way. Not necessarily better, but different. It's just a curiosity that when David McCarty (#10 for the Red Sox, 2003–05) was a kid growing up in Houston, his idol was left-handed reliever **Joe**

Sambito of the Astros. Sambito wound up with the Red Sox in 1986 (2–0) and 1987 (2–6), appearing in an even 100 games. His 6.93 ERA in '87 resulted in his release by the Red Sox. When McCarty was claimed off waivers from Oakland in August 2003, and then signed as a free agent, who represented him? Joe Sambito. From idol to agent.

MOST OBSCURE RED SOX PLAYER TO WEAR #43—Neither **Tom McCarthy** nor **Carlos Castillo** pitched much for the Red Sox; they each had better chances with the White Sox. Born in Lundstahl, Germany, McCarthy debuted with Boston on July 5, 1985. John McNamara gave him three assignments: two bad, one good. McCarthy wound up with the White Sox and his 3.61 ERA looked much better. Castillo, a Boston native, debuted with the White Sox in 1997, though his cumulative 10–7 mark and 5.03 ERA out of the bullpen resulted in his release after three seasons in 2000. The Red Sox claimed Castillo and he finished his major league career the following year with his hometown team, pitching in the city where he'd gotten his first chance. Castillo threw two innings of mop-up work in a 13–8 loss in Chicago.

A Hall of Fame Number

Hall of Famer Dennis Eckersley arrived in Boston at age 23 just before the 1978 season following a trade with Cleveland. A 20-game winner in Boston, he later reinvented himself as the game's top closer in his native Oakland. He returned to the Red Sox for his final year, fittingly, at age 43. Now a studio analyst at NESN and TBS, Eck and *Red Sox by the Numbers* discussed how he wound up with #43 on his back.

RSBTN: Did the number mean anything to you?

ECK: It does now. It didn't at the time. It never changed, once I got here. When I was in Cleveland before, it was 37, but when I got to Fenway, Bill Lee was 37. It could have changed everything.

RSBTN: And before him, Jimmy Piersall.

ECK: Maybe that was a blessing, huh? To not have 37 . . . . I never thought much about numbers. They just sort of gave you one when I got to Cleveland. I was just happy to be there.

And so when I got here, they didn't have 37, so I just got over it. When you first got to the major leagues years ago, you'd get jewelry that had "37" on it, and like that. As soon as you changed teams, and changed numbers, that went down the tubes. But I stayed with 43 the rest of the time. Then I got traded to the Cubs, right, in '84. When I got there, 43 was a rookie. They were going to send him down soon, so I didn't want to grab it. So I took 40, see? Took 40 and the first time I pitched, I completed the game and they loved me. I lost, 4–3, but they needed nine innings and I gave it to them. Then they got rid of the kid, so I took 43. [Rick] Sutcliffe came and he took 40 and he won 14 in a row. Won the Cy Young that year.

#44: BIG DEAL

Some of Boston's best-known #44s arrived in splashy trades. None made a bigger splash than the three-team deadline deal in 2008 that sent Manny Ramirez to Dodger Stadium and brought back **Jason Bay**. The quiet

Jason Bay

Canadian made an instant impression by taking over left field in the wake of Manny's upheaval. Though everyone would nod and agree that it wasn't fair to compare the two, everyone did anyhow.

Bay had been traded by the Expos, Mets, and Padres before he finally got to play in Pittsburgh, where he was the 2004 NL Rookie of the Year. An All-Star two years later, Bay seemed to have plateaued at empty PNC Park. He was revitalized by the festive Fenway atmosphere and playing for an organization that specialized in actually *not trading* its best assets. Bay batted .293 with nine homers in 49 games for the Red Sox in '08 and he reveled in his first taste of the postseason. He hit .412 against the Angels and slid across the plate with the winning run to clinch the Division Series. He amassed his fourth 30–100 season in 2009, finishing second in the AL in RBIs, made his third All-Star team, and had already amassed almost an RBI per game while someone else was finishing up a 50-game suspension for taking women's fertility drugs (and calling himself Man).

Before Bay was **Brandon Moss**, the outfielder and occasional first baseman whose home run in the top of the ninth on Opening Day 2008 tied the game at the Tokyo Dome. The Red Sox went on to win in 10 innings. His sunrise homer—the broadcast started before dawn on the East Coast—was the first home run ever hit by a Red Sox player on another continent. Back in the United States, Moss managed just one more Sox home run before becoming part of the July trade that brought Bay east and sent Manny west. Moss landed a full-time job as an outfielder for the Pirates. Bay signed with the mets in 2010.

Think Moss's time in Boston—49 games—was short? Many have worn #44 for far less time, starting with **Ben Steiner**'s three games in 1946. **Joe Trimble**, taken in the November 1954 Rule V draft, was returned to the Reds in May after a grand total of two hitless innings for Boston. Oufielder **Andy Kosco** played 17 games and hit .213 after a mid-August trade with the Angels in 1972. **Joel Finch** was 0–3 in 15 games in '79. **Rudy Pemberton** hit a scalding .512 in 13 games in 1996; given more time the next year he hit .238. **Michael "Prime Time" Coleman** was not ready, hitting .167 after Pemberton was let go. The thumper of this group was **Butch Huskey**; picked up in a 1999 deadline deal with Seattle, he hit .266, homered seven times, and knocked in 28. We'll end this competition here. Though Huskey might have played four fewer games than Moss, who played parts of two seasons, Butch hits the bonus with six postseason games and 10 at-bats (.200).

Don McMahon was the first to actually wear #44 for more than a few days, logging exactly one year: He was traded from Cleveland to

Boston on June 2, 1966, for Dick Radatz and dealt by the Red Sox to the White Sox for Jerry Adair on June 2, 1967. McMahon was 9–9 with the Red Sox with a 2.82 ERA. Adair helped the Sox win the pennant, but McMahon went 5–0 as Chicago pursued the Olde Towne Team until the final days of the season.

Jim Dorsey, the next to wear the number for multiple seasons, also arrived via a big trade. In January 1981 he came to Boston from the Angels with Joe Rudi and Frank Tanana for Fred Lynn and Steve Renko. While the 6-foot, 7-inch Dorsey was the biggest of the players involved, his stat lines were the most modest—some might say heinous. Finally seeing major league action for Boston in 1984, he posted a 10.12 ERA; he doubled that the following year to 20.25. Perhaps fearing a 40.50 ERA in 1986, the Red Sox simply released him.

Wes Gardner, who came over with Calvin Schiraldi in the eight-player Bobby Ojeda trade with the Mets, took over #44 in 1986, and kept it for five seasons. The one year Gardner really got some innings, 1988, he put up a 3.50 ERA and an 8–6 won-loss record. He went 3–7 each of the next two years, winding up his Boston tenure with a 17–26 mark and 4.93 ERA.

Danny Darwin did not arrive in Boston through a trade; he was a free agent. His Boston stretch took him from age 35 through age 38 (1991–94) of his 21-year career, and saw him post a 34–31 mark, with an unremarkable 4.14 ERA. The year before Darwin became a free agent, he'd led the National League with a 2.21 ERA, which followed a 2.36 in 1989, with identical 11–4 marks both years. So Sox GM Lou Gorman signed him up . . . and Darwin got hurt while accruing a 3–6 mark (5.16 ERA) in 1991. He had one exceptional year for the Red Sox, leading the '93 club in wins (15) innings (229 1/3) and and allowing the fewest runners per nine innings in the league (1.068). He also took a no-hitter into the eighth inning at Fenway before settling for a one-hit shutout. Southpaw starter **John Curtis**, a first-round pick in 1968, liked the double numbers. He began in #44 in 1970 and moved down to #22, pitching four Sox seasons in all for a 26–23 mark and 3.65 ERA. He was then dispatched to St. Louis in the Reggie Cleveland deal.

Kevin Kennedy succeeded Butch Hobson as Red Sox manager in 1995. Kennedy's record of 171–135 gave him a .559 winning percentage, sufficient to rank eighth on the list of Red Sox managers. He was one of those figures who gains the nickname "Red Light," meaning that when the red light of a television camera goes on, he's in front of it. Perhaps this was good training for his later work as a sportscaster with Fox Sports and for the Tampa Bay Rays. Of his hiring, *Red Sox Century* succinctly states, "[GM Dan Duquette] hoped to hire a big name like Oakland manager Tony LaRussa [but] settled on the glib Kevin Kennedy, who had managed in Texas for two years before the players tuned him out and revolted." Funny, he lasted two years in Boston and was in charge when Mike Greenwell left the team early, Roger Clemens departed soon after the season, and Jose Canseco was, well, Jose Canseco. The Red Sox acquired Canseco at Kennedy's request, and sent him to Oakland once they fired Kennedy. One could advance the argument that some of his players managed Kennedy more than he managed them.

Some men just come in, do their job, and win. Shortstop **Orlando Cabrera** arrived in Boston in the four-team trade that sent Nomar Garciaparra to the Cubs. Cabrera was freed from the final season of Montreal baseball hell and wound up with a World Series champion. The Cartagena, Colombia, native hit .294 in the portion of the regular season remaining in 2004. Though his error rate that season was a little higher than people may recall, O. C. was error-free in the postseason. He really shone offensively in the ALCS against the Yankees, batting .379 and driving in five runs (and three RBIs in both the ALDS and the World Series). In one of the most unfortunate decisions of the Theo Epstein Era, the popular Cabrera was granted free agency and the Red Sox signed fellow Colombian Edgar Renteria to a huge four-year deal (he lasted one year with the Sox). Cabrera, meanwhile, has helped his teams reach the postseason in all but one year since.

Another popular player was **Gabe Kapler**, who played on a Sox world champion, managed the team's Class A club in Greenville, and then returned to life as a big league player with Milwaukee and Tampa Bay. Purchased from Colorado in mid-2003, he made an immediate impression going 7-for-9 with seven RBIs in his first two games and finished his Sox season with a .291 average. The Red Sox released him on December 21, surprising a lot of fans, but then signed him again the very next day. He played through the 2004 season, only to be released again the day after the Red Sox won the World Series. This time they didn't sign him again until July 15, 2005 (after he'd begun the season with Tokyo's Yomiuri Giants). It was in this third sign-and-release stint that he adopted #44. On August 8, 2005, the Sox made history of sorts by playing Kevin Youkilis, Adam Stern, and our man Gabe in the same game (though none of them started). The Red Sox became the first American League team to ever have three Jews on the 25-man roster at the same time. *Mazel tov*!

MOST OBSCURE RED SOX PLAYER TO WEAR #44—Bob Gallagher's career was certainly obscure, but he was quite popular. The grandson of former Red Sox manager John "Shano" Collins (1931–32), manager of the first Sox team to wear numbers, Gallagher played just seven games for the Red Sox, in 1972, and didn't have a hit. (He batted .220 in three seasons in the NL.) Yet he was happy to be grandfathered in at Fenway. "I was received very well because of him," Bob said of Shano. "A lot of people remembered him . . . respected that background. There's such lore in Boston. I got more attention than I deserved."

Last Fenway Hurler Homer

The last pitcher wearing a Red Sox uniform to hit a home run at Fenway Park was Marty Pattin, #33. On September 26, 1972, Pattin had a 15–12 record going into the game, and the Red Sox held a one-game lead over the Tigers in the race for the pennant. There were nine games to go for the Sox. Carl Yastrzemski hit a two-run homer in the first inning for an early 2–0 lead over Milwaukee (an AL East team way back when). Pattin made it 4–0 with his two-run homer in the second inning, but there was still plenty of game—and season—to go.

Pattin held a 4–2 lead in the eighth when the Brewers struck for three unearned runs, the tying and go-ahead runs crossing the plate on a homer by former Sox slugger George Scott. The loss was tragic. Because Detroit didn't play that night, the Sox lost a half-game in the standings. They finished a half-game behind Detroit during that uneven schedule year because of the 1972 strike. Sigh.

Let's try to focus on the pitcher's home run, though. It was his second of the year and of his career. It would also be his last; and many more AL pitchers would be in the same boat when the designated hitter rule became the law of the land in 1973. Some would say that's a good thing because it removed the .123 hitters of the world like Pattin (but that's a whole 'nother argument). Red Sox pitchers got to swing the bat again when interleague play began in 1997, but only on the road since the DH is always used in AL parks in both interleague play and the World Series. On May 20, 2006, Josh Beckett homered in Philadelphia, the first 21st century home run by a Sox hurler; #19 homered in Philly again in 2009.

#45: PEDRO

Pedro Martinez was one of the greatest pitchers Red Sox fans will ever see. Already holding a newly minted Cy Young Award for his 1997 work with the Montreal Expos, GM Dan Duquette traded Carl Pavano and Tony Armas Jr. for Pedro, and then signed him to the lucrative long-term deal the Expos could not afford. It was money well spent. Pedro won the Cy Young Award for the Red Sox in 1999, and captured the pitching Triple Crown to boot. He posted a 23–4 record, with 313 strikeouts, and a 2.01 ERA. During one stretch in August and September, he struck out at least one batter in 40 consecutive innings and fanned at least 10 batters in eight consecutive games.

No one thought Pedro could put up better numbers than he had in 1999, but he did just that. Opposing batters only hit .167 off him, a major league single-season record (topping, by one point, Luis Tiant's 1968 mark). Pedro posted the lowest on-base percentage against (.213) in 116 years. His ERA was just 1.74 in a year when the league average was 4.91. For the second year in a row, he

David Ortiz and Pedro Martinez

was unanimously selected for the Cy Young. He missed much of 2001 with arm problems, but he rebounded to lead the AL in ERA for two seasons, earning his second 20-win season in '02. After seven years with the Red Sox, his totals were spectacular: 117–37, 2.52 ERA, and 1,683 strikeouts (an average of 10.9 per nine innings). In 2003, he was poised to be the winning pitcher over the Yankees in Game Seven of the ALCS, but even after accepting all the congratulations of his team-mates for a job well-done, manager Grady Little sent an exhausted Pedro back out—and left him in until New York had tied the score. His sub-par season in 2004, though good by most standards (16–9, 3.90 ERA), was his last for the Sox. He ended his epic stint in Boston with a victory in Game Three of the World Series. Worried that Pedro wouldn't be the pitcher he had been, the Red Sox allowed themselves to be out-bid by the Mets. He had just one Pedro-esque season as a Met, yet many injuries later could still perplex NL lineups when all was

Pedro's 45 in position on the right-field roof facade between Jim Rice and Jackie Robinson.

right, even throwing seven shutout innings for the Phillies in the 2009 NLCS before losing twice in the World Series.

In 2015, Pedro was inducted into the National Baseball Hall of Fame.

There's Pedro and there's everyone else. His #45 was retired by the Red Sox as well. It's now out of circulation forever—but there was plenty of pre-Pedey action. The first two players to wear it possessed names that could get your mouth washed out with soap in your stricter Sox families in the '70s: **Dick Pole** and **Don Aase**. **Jim Wright**'s name wouldn't get you in trouble with mom, but he wasn't that great, either. Rule V pick **Mike Trujillo** spent two years at Fenway in the mid-1980s; Hanover, New Hampshire's **Rob Woodward** wore #45 for two of his four partial Sox seasons in the late 1980s; and **John Doherty**, **Greg Pirkl**, and **Walt McKeel** each held the number for a spell in 1996.

Now if Jerry Reed the singer—the wise-cracking, Buford T. Justice–evading trucker in *Smokey and the Bandit*—had been with the Red Sox in the late 1980s, there'd have been some stories to tell. This here **Jerry Reed**, the righty reliever with a 2–1 mark and 4.80 ERA in 1990, did such a poor a job he was cut in August. So the Red Sox got right serious about finding someone for their contending club's bullpen. They located a fellow in Houston named Larry Andersen.

The story goes that the player the Astros really wanted for Andersen was **Scott Cooper**, but the Sox scouts liked Cooper, so Boston GM Lou Gorman talked Houston into taking the third baseman three years behind him in the Red Sox system: Jeff Bagwell, a Boston native

who'd grown up a rabid Red Sox fan in Connecticut. "Our house was one of those places where you couldn't mention the word Yankees when you came inside the front door," Bagwell recalled. But this isn't about the 449 homers that Bagwell hit—all with Houston—it's about Cooper, the first #45 who was *not* a right-

handed reliever. He had a smooth left-handed swing, hit 27 home runs over three years, and batted .284 in 399 games (committing 51 errors). Cooper wore #34 as Boston's representative in both the 1993 and 1994 All-Star Games; the latter season Bagwell was an Astros All-Star . . . with 27 homers and a .348 average at the break. Bagwell was named that year's National League MVP; Cooper was traded to St. Louis.

Now how about a story where nothing was expected from a player? **Luis Aponte** never advanced out of A ball in four seasons in the Red Sox minor league system. So in 1976 the right-hander retired to his native Venezuela, where he developed "an amazing forkball" while with the Maracaibo team, the Petroleros de Zulia. The Sox signed him again and in 1980 he played for the Bristol Red Sox (AA), the Pawtucket Red Sox (AAA), and—in September—the Boston Red Sox. He spent most of 1981 in Pawtucket and pitched four innings of the 32-inning "longest game"; Señora Aponte didn't believe his story about the game running until after 4 AM, and she locked him out of the house. He returned to the ballpark and slept in the clubhouse. He spent '82 and '83 in Boston, and after four years and 85 games, had a 3.02 career ERA in the big leagues. That'll help you sleep nights.

MOST OBSCURE RED SOX PLAYER TO WEAR #45—Lots of competition for this award, but **Matt Murray** gets the nod for being a Boston native, never winning a game, and rarely getting anyone out. Drafted in the second round in 1988 by the Braves, he threw 10 2/3 innings with an 0–2 mark and 6.75 ERA after his 1995 callup to Atlanta. On August 31, he was the player to be named later to complete the July 31 trade that had sent Mike Stanton to the Red Sox and two minor leaguers to Atlanta. Shipped north, Murray first entered a game wearing #45 on September 8 in Yankee Stadium. New York had a 5–0 lead—a walk, a single, and two doubles later, it was 8–0. On September 25, having already clinched a playoff berth, the Sox deemed it safe to try Murray again. He started against the Tigers and got through the first two innings with ease, but the third was a career-ender.

Where'd You Get That Ring?

Diehards know the 2004 world champion Red Sox roster from top to bottom. The top is very familiar; this is the bottom. How many of these 17 members of the 2004 club do you recall? There are a few recognizable names but even those are a little foggy when it comes to an '04 memory. Here's a hint: none played in that memorable postseason, and none appeared in a major league game with the Red Sox after '04. We included their uniform numbers and position because you really can't tell some of these guys apart without some identification. We also included the number of games played so you don't feel so bad about not recalling them.

Terry Adams, 19 games (#53) Pitcher

Abe Alvarez, 1 game (#59) Pitcher

Jimmy Anderson, 5 games (#46) Pitcher

Pedro Astacio, 5 games (#39) Pitcher

Jamie Brown, 4 games (#52) Pitcher

Ellis Burks, 11 games (#25) Designated Hitter

Frank Castillo, 2 games (#37) Pitcher

Andy Dominique, 7 games (#39) First Base

Ricky Gutierrez, 21 games (#16) Second Base

Bobby M. Jones, 3 games (#36) Pitcher

Byung-Hyun Kim, 7 games (#51) Pitcher

Mark Malaska, 19 games (#46) Pitcher

Anastacio Martinez, 11 games (#67) Pitcher

Sandy Martinez, 3 games (#58) Catcher

Joe Nelson, 3 games (#57), Pitcher

Phil Seibel, 2 games (#53) Pitcher

Earl Snyder, 1 game (#37) Third Base

It's OK, we had to look them up, too.

#46: Full Steam Ahead

"The Steamer" defined #46 for a generation. **Bob Stanley** was a New Englander, a native of Portland, Maine, and a first-round pick in 1974. Stanley pitched his entire 13-season career with a big "46" on his back for the Sox. He started 85 of his 637 Red Sox games, but he was primarily a reliever and a very good one at that, often pitching several innings at a time. In 1982 and 1983, he combined to throw 313 2/3 innings out of the bullpen over 112 games. His best season might have been his second, 1978, when he was 15–2 (2.62), almost entirely in relief (he had just three starts).

Passed ball or wild pitch? Opinions differ, but it was charged to Stanley as a 10th-inning wild pitch and it set the stage for the Red Sox to lose Game Six of the 1986 World Series to the Mets. For many fans at Fenway, especially those in the bleachers, the high point of many a lazy summer game might have been when a beach ball got loose on the field, Steamer grabbed a bullpen rake, then vigorously pounded it until it punctured. Of course, this only prompted a few more beach balls to bounce his way.

"Way Back!" Not the sort of nickname a pitcher would want, but **John Wasdin** gave up enough home runs that broadcaster Jerry Trupiano's "way back, way back" radio call transformed him into Way Back Wasdin. When Oakland wanted Jose Canseco back, the A's sent some hard currency and this former first-round draft pick (who'd been 9–8 with a 5.81 ERA). Over parts of four seasons for the Red Sox, Wasdin appeared in 170 games (starting 16) and was 19–16 with a 4.66 ERA.

Though the longballs he surrendered stayed on fans' minds, Wasdin wasn't as homer-happy as it seemed: he gave up 54 home runs in 339 2/3 innings, a little over 1.4 home runs per nine innings, and his ERA was below league average each year in Boston. But Way Back Wasdin he'll always be.

On the subject of way back, Martin Van Buren was the eighth president of the United States; yet in a seeming paradox, he was the first president born as an American citizen and the only one to date for whom English was a second language (he grew up speaking Dutch in Kinderhook, New York). **Jermaine Van Buren** was also born an American citizen (in Mississippi), almost 200 years after the eighth president (see sidebar). The Red Sox bought him—Jermaine, that is—from the Cubs and he appeared in 10 games in 2006, throwing 13 innings while allowing 17 earned runs. On the bright side, he was 1–0. Less encouraging was his 11.77 earned run average. **Gar Finnvold** had a name that sounded like English wasn't his native tongue, but the Floridian's 5.94 ERA in eight 1994 starts spoke clearly enough.

Jacoby Ellsbury (left) is also a native of America—but he's a Native American as well. The Oregon native arrived at Fenway at the end of June 2007 and hit .353. Though Ellsbury appeared in just 33 games

Jacoby Ellsbury

during the season, he played 11 postseason games and batted .438 in the World Series as the Red Sox swept the Rockies. Coco Crisp never got his job back. Ellsbury led the AL in steals the next two seasons, swiping 120 bases in that span, and breaking the club's single-season mark in 2009. He also became the first Sox runner with a straight steal of home in 15 years. That he did it on national TV against the Yankees was a bonus. After the 2009 season, he swiped uniform #2.

A so-called "replacement player," **Ron Mahay** spent the 1995 spring exhibition season with the Red Sox while the players were still on strike. He was therefore shunned by some of the more fervent Players Association backers. He was a center fielder as #46 in the five games he played after the strike was settled in 1995. When next summoned to the Red Sox in 1997, Mahay was a pitcher (wearing #57). The position change didn't help him attain MLBPA acceptance, but his 4–1 mark and 3.00 ERA put him on the path to financial success, southpaw style.

After **Paul Campbell** wore #46 in 1946, no one tried it on again until 1974 (not even a coach). Campbell, a first baseman from Paw Creek, North Carolina, had appeared in his first game (wearing #37) on Opening Day 1941, though he didn't bat that year. In 1942, Campbell appeared in 26 games (wearing #15) with only one hit. After three years in the army, he returned in 1946 and collected three more hits, bumping his Boston average all the way to .098. Four decades later, switch-hitting rookie **Dwayne Hosey** saw his average go from .338 in 68 at-bats in 1995, to just .218 in 78 tries in '96—the last at-bats he saw in the majors.

MOST OBSCURE RED SOX PLAYER TO WEAR #46—Steve Barr pitched a complete game 7–4 victory over the Indians in his October 1, 1974, debut. The next year, he appeared in only three July games for the pennant-winning Red Sox. He was hit hard, though his 2.57 ERA looks none the worse for wear—an identical WHIP of 2.57 tells the rest of the story. In his first outing he held the Orioles scoreless in an inning of work, despite three walks and a single (one runner was thrown out trying to steal). He started his next time out but was tagged for six runs (only one earned). A second start was his last: 4 1/3 innings, three more runs (again, only one earned). He was 1–1 with the Red Sox and that sounded good to Texas, which brought in Barr, Juan Beniquez, and PTBNL Craig Skok in exchange for Fergie Jenkins. Barr's 5.59 ERA in '76 with the Rangers—not to mention 2–6 record—proved more indicative of what he could do.

Positively Presidential

No matter your political views, a president's name gets your attention. Players are listed alphabetically and we'll leave it to you to recall which president they share a name with, though if this book had an obscure category for presidents as well as ballplayers, Franklin Pierce, Rutherford B. Hayes, Zachary Taylor, and Martin Van Buren just might qualify.

This list only follows surnames, but original Red Sox outfielder Thomas Jefferson Dowd may be the only Sox player named after a president; 1912 Sox pitcher Benjamin Harrison Van Dyke just misses, though he was seemingly named after a presidential candidate (Harrison was elected the 23rd president when Master Van Dyke was four months old). Ike Boone was a Sox outfielder in the mid-1920s, when Major Dwight D. Eisenhower was still stuck in the Panama Canal Zone. Truman "Tex" Clevenger began his 1954 term (uniform #26) at Fenway shortly after Harry S. (chief executive #33) left Washington. John Truman Wasdin was born on a military base the same year the former president died.

There have been no Washingtons in Red Sox lore, but two Boston ballplayers have gone by Adams, one for each of the Massachusetts-born presidents of that name. The most popular presidential name in Sox history? Johnson defeats Wilson. Recount!

To show we play no favorites, players born before uniform numbers are also included, as are coaches and managers. Numbers are listed by years worn.

Player	Number	Years
Bob ADAMS	—	1925
Terry ADAMS	#53	2004
Bullet Joe BUSH	—	1918–21
Chris CARTER	#54	2008–09
Reggie CLEVELAND	#33, 26	1974–78
Lu CLINTON	#4, #19, #24, #6	1960–64
Frankie HAYES	#25	1947
Al JACKSON	#32	1977–79 (coach)
Conor JACKSON	#36	2011
Damian JACKSON	#2	2003
Ron JACKSON	#5	1960
Ron D. JACKSON	#22, #15	2003–06 (coach)
Reggie JEFFERSON	#18	1995–99
Bob JOHNSON	#8	1944–45

Player	Number	Years
Brian JOHNSON	#61	2015
Darrell JOHNSON	#33, #22	1968–69, 1974–76 (coach, manager)
Deron JOHNSON	#30, #15	1974–76
Earl JOHNSON	#20, #21	1940–41, 1946–50
Hank JOHNSON	#18, #16	1933–35
Jason JOHNSON	#18	2006
John Henry JOHNSON	#48	1983–84
Kelly JOHNSON	#7	2014
Rankin JOHNSON	—	1914
Roy JOHNSON	#18, #3, #4	1932–35
Vic JOHNSON	#16, #34	1944–45
Bill KENNEDY	#18	1953
John KENNEDY	#12	1970–74
Kevin KENNEDY	#44	1995–96 (manager)
Otis NIXON	#2	1994
Russ NIXON	#22, #5, #15	1960–65, 1968
Trot NIXON	#7	1996, 1998–2006
Willard NIXON	#21, #15	1950–58
Jeff PIERCE	#56	1995
Harry TAYLOR	#35, #12, #23	1950–52
Scott TAYLOR	#56	1992–93
Jermaine VAN BUREN	#46	2006
Alex WILSON	#63, #30	2013, 2014
Archie WILSON	#32	1952
Duane WILSON	#15	1958
Earl WILSON	#36	1959–60, 1962–66
Gary WILSON	—	1902
Jack WILSON	#20, #16, #18	1935–41
Jim WILSON	#16, #10	1945–46
John WILSON	—	1927–28
Les WILSON	—	1911
Squanto WILSON	—	1914

#47: TITO

Terry Francona

Terry Francona is known as "Tito" (after his father, an All-Star outfielder in the 1960s); he's won as many World Series as any Sox manager (Bill Carrigan also won two titles in the 1910s), and is the second-winningest manager in Sox history (only Joe Cronin has more victories). But one thing he'll never be known as is "Ol' Number 47." *Red Sox Magazine* presents his photo and number in every issue and numerous Web sites list this information as well. Yet it's a rare day that you'll ever see it on the back of his uniform. Under MLB strictures, he wears the numbered jersey every day—MLB spot-checked Francona, believe it or not, in the middle of a Yankees-Red Sox game—but it's unseen under the pullover that he always wears, for medical reasons (circulation problems).

Before coming to Boston in 2004, he was probably best known for being Michael Jordan's minor league manager. Fans weren't necessarily expecting much from Francona, and some looked skeptically at his four losing seasons with the Phillies (1997–2000). But he had the horses in Boston, plus his best pitcher from Philly (Curt Schilling), and Francona demonstrated a true talent for open and supportive communication with the diverse array of player personalities he'd inherited. Francona, of course, won the World Series his first year in Boston and then another in 2007. He amassed 565 wins with the Sox through 2009, more than halfway to Cronin's 1,071 on the all-time list.

The man who was almost MVP of the 1986 World Series, **Bruce Hurst,** was a left-handed starter from Mormon country. The Shea Stadium scoreboard inadvertently flashed congratulations to the Red Sox for winning the World Series late in Game Six before the last-minute push by the Mets gave them back-to-back wins and the title. Hurst had been designated the MVP, but it was not to be. Hurst was 1–0 in the ALCS and 2–0 in the World Series, and held a 3–0 lead after five innings in Game Seven. He finally tired, and left with a 3–3 tie. In Games One and Five combined, he'd given up just two earned runs.

Hurst didn't fare as well in the 1988 postseason, going 0–2 against Oakland, but it was hardly his fault alone: he allowed just two runs in each start. His regular-season record that year was 18–6, compared to 13–8 in 1986, but his 3.66 ERA in '88 wasn't up to par with his 2.99 mark from two years earlier. All in all, Hurst won 88 games for the Red Sox before leaving as a free agent. He simply wasn't interested in re-signing with a Red Sox team that seemed beset with unsavory scandals at the time (such as the Wade Boggs/Margo Adams revelations). He followed his stay in Boston with four solid seasons in tranquil San Diego.

Manager Don Zimmer declared that pitcher **Bobby Sprowl** had "ice water in his veins." Or at least that was Zim's reason for selecting to start Sprowl instead of Bill Lee to stave off the "Boston Massacre" in September 1978. Lee, of course, was in Zimmer's doghouse. With the Yankees having won three straight at Fenway and Boston's lead down to one game on September 10, Zimmer tapped Sprowl for his second major league start. It didn't last long: two-thirds of an inning. (Lee pitched scoreless mop-up relief.) This was the same Sprowl who during spring training had been shot in the right arm while he slept in his Winter Haven hotel room. A doctor in an apartment next door said he thought he heard prowlers. Sprowl was just grazed (apparently not losing too much ice water) and released from the local hospital. The Sox sent him to Houston the following June.

Tom Murphy and **Rob Murphy** weren't related, but both Murphs wore #47 for the Red Sox. Both were first-round picks—with other organizations—who wound up in the Boston bullpen, pitched for two years, and moved on to other locales. Right-handed Tom twirled for six teams (1968–79) and Rob, a lefty, spent time with eight clubs (1985–95).

In 1998, right-handed closer **Rod Beck** appeared in exactly half the games of the Chicago Cubs (81) and finished 70 of them, earning 51 saves and recording a 3.02 ERA. The Red Sox got him for Mark Guthrie at the trading deadline in 1999, and young catcher **Jason Varitek**, in his first full year with the Red Sox, gave up #47 so Beck could feel more at home. Beck pitched well in the 1999 and 2000 regular seasons; he lost Game One of the 1999 ALCS to the Yankees, though, when the first batter he faced, Bernie Williams, homered to win, 4–3.

Korean right-hander **Sun-Woo Kim** was one of several pitchers signed when the Red Sox seemed to try and corner the market in Koreans. He'd pitched for his country's Olympic team and in 1995 World Junior Baseball Championship competition in Fenway Park at age 17, where he was noticed by Boston GM Dan Duquette. In 2001, Sunny Kim was 0–2. In 2002, he was 2–0. Come July, the Sox traded Kim and Korean minor league pitcher Seung Song to the Expos for slugger Cliff Floyd.

Theo Epstein decided to pick up lefty relief specialist **Scott Sauerbeck** from the Pirates for Boston's 2003 stretch drive. Sauerbeck didn't pitch well, to say the least—17 hits in 16 2/3 innings, plus 18 bases on balls, four hit batsmen, and one wild pitch. That all added up to a WHIP (walks and hits per inning pitched) of 2.100. But Sauerbeck's arrival caused a disturbance in the numerical order of things: the Scott Sox Swap of 2003. Sauerbeck had never worn any number except #47. But **Steve Woodard** had worn that number for the Sox that season before heading back to Pawtucket. Red Sox equipment manager Joe Cochran thought that Woodard might be recalled, so he held back the number. Sauerbeck took the closest number: #48. When Scott Williamson arrived, seven days after Sauerbeck, he presented a new problem.

Williamson had always worn #48. The new Scott settled for another number, #36. After about a week, Cochran made both Sauerbeck and Williamson happy by freeing up #47 for Sauerbeck, and then Sauerbeck ceded #48 to Williamson. Everyone was happy, except presumably Woodard, who was 1–0 with the Red Sox but never made it back to the big leagues.

MOST OBSCURE RED SOX PLAYER TO WEAR #47—For several years now, the Red Sox have provided a former player before each game at Autograph Alley, so fans can meet Sox alumni and collect a free autograph. Next time you see **Bill MacLeod** at Autography Alley, you'll know that this left-hander from Gloucester was the first member of the Sox to wear #47. That might be all you two have to talk about. In his debut on September 13, 1962, he retired the one Tiger he faced with the Sox down, 8–0. MacLeod got a more important relief assignment in Washington on September 22, entering in the bottom of the 11th. He whiffed two, but the next inning he could not get his man, surrendering a walkoff double to the equally obscure Bud Zipfel. MacLeod walked off a major league field for the last time with a loss and a 5.40 ERA.

They'll Manage

Joe Cronin managed the most games in Red Sox history and—not surprisingly—has the most wins of any Sox manager, with or without a uniform number. The most wins by a manager prior to the adoption of uni numbers at Fenway Park was 489 (against 500 losses) by Bill Carrigan, the only multiple World Series–winning manager in Sox history until Terry Francona, who also won 744 regular-season games.

Thanks to Cronin, #4 has more wins than any number in franchise history. He wore #6 for a season (1936), but that was more than made up for by Lou Boudreau, hired by Cronin after he moved up to general manager. Boudreau had worn #4 as "Boy Manager" of the Indians, and he donned it in Boston while adding 229 wins and 232 losses to the #4 ledger for grand total of 1,226–1,068 (.534). That number was retired in 1984. The number worn by the most managers is #35 by Ralph Houk, Joe Morgan, Billy Herman, and Johnny Pesky (a combined 742–730).

Joe McCarthy chose to wear a uniform with no number during his reign (1948–50), yet he has the highest winning percentage of any Red Sox manager in the uniform number era (.606).

For the record, Jake Stahl's .621 winning percentage (144–88) in the numberless 1910s is the best in franchise history. And about the record, Boston's is 7,029–6,310 (.527) since they stitched on the numbers in 1931. Despite five world championships, the franchise's record was 2,267–2,298 (.497) before uniform numbers—though you can fault that to a far from roaring '20s at Fenway.

Uni #	Last Name	First Name	Years Managed	Wins	Losses
—	McCarthy	Joe	1948–50	223	145
1,2	McNamara	John	1985–88	297	273
3,2	McManus	Marty	1932–33	95	153
3	Little	Grady	2002–03	188	136
4,6	Cronin	Joe	1935–47	1071	916
4	Boudreau	Lou	1952–54	229	232
5	Higgins	Pinky	1955–59, 1960–62	560	556
16	Jurges	Billy	1959–60	59	63
16	Kerrigan	Joe	2001	17	26
17	Hobson	Butch	1992–94	207	232
22,35	Pesky	Johnny	1963–64, 1980	147	179
22	Johnson	Darrell	1974–76	220	188
22	Williams	Jimy	1997–2001	414	352
23	Williams	Dick	1967–69	260	217
25	Valentine	Bobby	2012	69	93
27	Harris	Bucky	1934	76	76
30	Kasko	Eddie	1970–73	345	295
30	O'Neill	Steve	1950–51	150	99
31	Collins	Shano	1931–32	73	134
32	Baker	Del	1960	2	5
32	Popowski	Eddie	1969, 1973	6	4
32	Runnels	Pete	1966	8	8
34, 23	Zimmer	Don	1976–80	411	304
34	York	Rudy	1959	0	1
35	Herman	Billy	1964–66	128	182
35	Houk	Ralph	1981–84	312	282
35	Morgan	Joe	1988–91	301	262
44	Kennedy	Kevin	1995–96	171	135
47	Francona	Terry	2004–09	744	552
53	Farrell	John	2013–15	246	240
			Total since 1931	7029	6310

David Ortiz and Hanley Ramirez greet Jake Gyllenhaal and Boston Marathon bombing survivor Jeff Bauman. Each threw out the first pitch on Patriots Day, April 18, 2016.

#48: The Lower Forty-Eight

The Red Sox tried to keep things all in the Martinez family when they signed Pedro's older brother **Ramon Martinez** and their younger *hermano*, Jesus. Pedro's arrival in Boston had helped trigger a warm relationship between the broader Hispanic community and the Red Sox, with fans bearing Dominican flags at Fenway. Ramon had been a 20-game winner in 1990, tossed a no-hitter in 1995, and sported a 3.64 ERA and a record of 123–77 after 11 seasons as a Dodger. He had shoulder surgery during the 1998 season, but the Red Sox still ventured for a reunion of the brothers Martinez in September 1999 (Ramon and Pedro had previously spent 1993 together in L. A.). Ramon's four starts at season's end and his average of six innings per start in the postseason showed some promise. He won 10 games in 2000, though he allowed more than six runs per nine innings. His option was too expensive and the Sox let him go. Jesus Jaime Martinez (all three brothers had the same middle name) pitched for Boston's advanced A Florida League farm club in Sarasota (1–2, 5.23); like both of his brothers, he'd started in the Dodgers organization. Jesus played 10 years in the minors, but nary a day in the majors.

The hitters are pretty scarce at #48. Much-sought-after catcher **Kelly Shoppach** went 0-for-2005 in Boston (15 at-bats, to be precise), and the Sox took the next good offer, which landed Coco Crisp, Josh Bard, and David Riske at Fenway while Shoppach—plus ballyhooed Andy Marte—

wound up in Cleveland. There was also infielder **Arquimedez Pozo**, whose name alone was far more interesting than his .192 batting average in 25 games. Another infielder, **Chuck Goggin**, had spent a little time in the National League, getting his first career hit in the same game Roberto Clemente achieved his 3,000th and, tragically, final hit. Goggin fanned in his only at-bat for the 1974 Sox, but he did start a double play at second base on a grounder by Rich Coggins: a Coggins-to-Goggin DP. What makes Goggin truly stand out is the Bronze Star he earned as a Marine in Vietnam in 1967—he also received a Purple Heart.

Mostly, #48 is about relief pitching. The fringiest breed is the "Left-Handed One Out Guy" and **Tony Fossas** is one fringy LOOGy. Born in Havana but raised in Boston, he was often summoned to try to just get one out. With the Red Sox overall, he faced 699 batters in 239 games—often, it took three batters for Fossas to get one out. The Sox kept coming back to Fossas, whether in the bullpen or in negotiations; he was signed, released, re-signed, released, re-signed, and released again. Over the three consecutive contracts, he recorded a serviceable 3.98 ERA.

Former NL Rookie of the Year **Scott Williamson** arrived in Boston at the 2003 trading deadline (to learn about the Scott Sox Swap, see Chapter 47). Two really bad outings hurt Williamson's stats with the Red Sox in the regular season, but he was lights-out in the ALDS. Pitching all five games against Oakland, he faced 19 batters and fanned eight, allowing two hits and no runs. He gave up a homer to Ruben Sierra in Game Four of the ALCS against the Yankees, but the Sox won the game. It was the only hit he allowed in three innings of work in the series . . . sure wish Grady Little had found a place for him in Game Seven. Anyway, Williamson returned in '04 but was recovering from surgery while the Sox celebrated.

The pitcher wore #48, not the catcher. Both lefty specialist **Javier Lopez** and backup catcher Javy Lopez were on the club for one stretch in 2006 but the Red Sox never saw fit to make them batterymates, even for just one batter. To ensure they could tell one from the other, they assigned them different numbers. Lopez the catcher wore #18. Meanwhile, #48 went to the pitcher Lopez, who'd arrived in a trade two months before the other Lopez caught on. To remove confusion and a suddenly puny .190 hitter, the Sox jettisoned the catcher a month after getting him. Javier Alfonso Lopez threw well for three seasons, with ERAs of 2.70, 3.10, and 2.43. The 2009 Red Sox had a strong enough pen that Lopez became the extra man and was outrighted to Pawtucket in May.

Left-hander **John Henry Johnson** was justifiably proud of his Native American heritage. "Being an Indian is important to me," he told the *Sporting News* in 1978. "They're the ones who made America." He spent two years with the Sox in the mid-1980s, going 4–4 with a 3.62 ERA, mostly in relief. Lefty **Tim Lollar** took #48 after coming from the White Sox in a deal for Reid Nichols. Lollar went 5–5 the rest of the year, which would be his final year in the majors, he picked up a pair of 1.000s in '86: Lollar went 2–0 on the mound and 1-for-1 at the plate. A career .234 hitter with eight home runs in the National League, he batted for Rey Quinones against Dan Quisenberry in the ninth inning of a tight game in Kansas City on August 12. He singled but was stranded.

After the highs of the 1986 season, followed by the crashing thud of fifth place (20 games out of first place), the Sox decided they needed a better closer in 1988. In an inspired deal, Boston shipped Al Nipper and the somewhat snake-bitten Calvin Schiraldi to the Cubs for **Lee Smith**. For the previous five seasons, Smith had ranked in the top four in saves, including 36 to place second in 1987. When the Sox signed The Terminator (Jeff Reardon) in December 1989, they had the two relievers who would hold the all-time saves record over the next 15 years (Smith broke Reardon's mark in 1993 and Trevor Hoffman eventually topped Smith's 478 saves in 2006). Yet, having both Smith and Reardon was overkill. Boston flipped Smith to the Cardinals for Tom Brunansky; Smith had four straight 40-save seasons.

Reliever **Larry Andersen** was secured with a more immediate need in mind. The Sox acquired the 37-year-old righty at the end of August from the Astros, who weren't going anywhere and were willing to give up the free-agent to be in exchange for a minor league third baseman, who could have been Scott Cooper but turned out to be Jeff Bagwell. Andersen, who began in #40 before switching to #48, had a wonderful 1.23 ERA, but it was in just 22 innings of work. He earned one save and blew three others. Of the 15 games in which he appeared, the Sox went 7–8. Oakland swept the ALCS in four straight—Boston scored only once in each game—with Andersen taking the loss in Game One. He signed with San Diego while 1990 was still on the calendar. Bagwell, on the other hand . . .

MOST OBSCURE RED SOX PLAYER TO WEAR #48—Vic Correll began his career with the Red Sox, playing just one game, but a bittersweet game it was. Correll caught the 4–1 win in Detroit on October 4, 1972, which closed the AL East deficit to a mere half game. Sadly, that's where the season ended. It had begun with a strike, and teams that year played less than a 162-game schedule—one of the games sliced off the schedule by the labor dispute was an early season Tigers–Sox game. Detroit played 156 games, with an 86–70 mark. The Red Sox played one less game, and were 85–70—hence the half-game deficit. The season finale meant nothing since Detroit had already clinched. Correll had two hits and drove in a run; he went on to play 409 games in seven reasonably obscure seasons in the National League.

The Wearing of the Green

With green jerseys and caps but red longsleeve undershirts, red piping, red warmup jackets, and red socks, it looked like Christmas in April on 4/20/07. The Red Sox wore green jerseys in tribute to the recently-deceased Red Auerbach of the Boston Celtics. It's both poignant and ironic that the Red Sox would don green to honor Red. The Red Sox donned the green again on 6/20/08 to honor the 17th NBA title by the Celtics.

#49: WAKE

Signed by the Pirates as a first baseman after setting the Florida Tech home run record, **Tim Wakefield** was sent to Watertown in the New York-Penn League. He hit .189. That wasn't going to cut it. Even though he played six games as a third baseman in 1989 at Augusta, he'd also begun to pitch and got into 18 games. He never looked back. In 1991, he was 15–8 with a 2.90 in Double A. He and his knuckleball made an immediate impression in the majors in 1992, with a record of 8–1, a 2.95 ERA, and two complete-game wins over Tom Glavine in the NLCS for the Pirates (the second was the last postseason win for Pittsburgh, incidentally). He sagged the next season, was sent back to the minors, and was released in 1995 spring training. The Red Sox signed him and a beautiful relationship began. Wakefield wowed everyone. He went 14–1 out of the blocks, including six complete games, and finished at 16–8. He placed second in the league with a 2.95 ERA, and third in the Cy Young voting. His one game in the postseason was a loss to Cleveland. Wake's next big year was 1998; lo and behold, the Sox got back in the playoffs. Once more, he lost his one postseason game, again to the Indians. After three years with losing records, he had a 2.81 ERA in 2002. In 2003, he lost an ALDS game, then won two against the Yankees in the ALCS before being victimized by Aaron Boone in Game Seven.

Wake's postseason ERA—even with his Pittsburgh heroics—is a poor 6.75 to go with a 5–7 mark, but that's far from the full story. His strengths had been keeping the club in contention and a willingness to work out of the bullpen on short notice. Due to start Game Four of the 2004 ALCS, the Sox were losing Game Three in a horrific blowout and Wakefield threw 3 1/3 innings so the bullpen wouldn't be overly

Tim Wakefield

taxed. Wakefield threw another three innings in relief in Game Five, pocketing a win when David Ortiz drove in the deciding run in the 14th. The longest-serving member of the current Red Sox, by a big margin, Wakefield has a unique contract allowing the Red Sox to extend him each year for a predetermined "hometown discount" of $4 million.

Wake had taken over as the all-time Sox leader in losses and walks, but in 2009 he passed Roger Clemens for most starts in club history (his final total of 430 exceeded Roger's 382) and at the time of his retirement stood third in wins (186), just six wins behind Clemens and Cy Young (each tied at 192). He ranked first in innings (3,006). It was long true that Tim Wakefield was as durable and unselfish a pitcher as any to wear a Red Sox uniform, but the numbers don't lie: Wake's also among the best.

First to wear #49 was Natick native **Pete Smith**, a right-handed pitcher from Colgate University. He had a good enough year with the Seattle Rainiers in Triple A to earn a September 1962 start with the Red Sox. It didn't go well. He gave up eight earned runs in 3 2/3 innings and lost. The '63 Sox were in no position to be picky and gave him six chances to make good. He wasn't. **Craig Skok** followed Smith's career line and achieved the same 0–1 record in Boston; unlike Smith, Skok pitched for a couple of other teams and got in the win column.

Steve Dillard followed Skok, and—like Smith—played in just one game his first year, but it was a 1975 game, thereby making him a member of the team that won the pennant (even if he watched the proceedings on TV). Dillard's debut was as Sox second baseman on September 28, the meaningless season finale. He had hits his first two times up in the majors. Unlike Ted Williams in 1941, Dillard saw his average go *down* to .400 by making outs his last three times against Cleveland. But .400 is still .400. Was it a mistake to trade up for shiny #3 for 1976? There's no way to know, but we do know that the highest average he ever collected after that was .283 as a '79 Cub. His career ended with a 1–for-26 slump with the White Sox, dragging his 1982 average from, believe it or not, .400 to .171 in the final month of what was his final season.

There have only been four Red Sox players born in Europe in the uniform number era: Tommy McCarthy (Germany), Johnny Reder (Poland), Bobby Thomson (Scotland), and **Wilhelmus Remmerswaal** (The Netherlands). Any competitive athlete would be glad to bear the nickname "Win" but perhaps even more so for a pitcher. Win Remmerswaal was a right-hander who—unlike fellow Dutchman Bert Blyleven—learned the game in his native land. Signed by scout Charlie Wagner as an international free agent, Win got his first pro win for Winter Haven in 1975, the year after he signed. He finally reached the majors in late 1979, picking up a win in his second game thanks to a well-placed relief appearance in a 19–5 crushing of the Brewers. After starting off with Pawtucket in 1980, he came back to Boston in late June and appeared in 14 games—yes, Win finished his major league career with a winning record (3–1, 5.50) before hurting his arm. In 1981 he played for Pawtucket and for Parma in Italian baseball. He had substance abuse problems even before returning to Europe; he wound up living on the street in Holland, finally being found in 1997 with pneumonia, pleurisy, and in a coma. He surprised doctors by recovering, but he suffered brain damage and has been wheelchair-bound ever since.

Fortunately taking a different route in life, **Al Nipper** was a righty starter for most of his five seasons with the Red Sox. Nipper put up better numbers than fellow rookie Roger Clemens in 1984. That changed. Nipper racked up a record of 42–43 (4.62) and his only postseason appearance resulted in a loss to the Mets during Game Four of the 1986 World Series. Nipper was shuffled to the Cubs with Calvin Schiraldi in the trade to get Lee Smith. Nipper later returned as Boston's pitching coach in 1995 and 1996, and came back as bullpen coach in 2006. He currently serves as one of the team's professional scouts and their Special Assignment Pitching Evaluator.

MOST OBSCURE RED SOX PLAYER TO WEAR #49—Mike Hartley was a right-hander who showed some promise as a Dodger. He went 6–3 in his second year with a 2.95 ERA, making the only six starts of his career and collecting his lone hit as a big leaguer (.043 career average). He put up a very respectable total of 17–11 and a 3.50 ERA over four seasons in Los Angeles and then Philly. He was 1–2 for the Twins in 1993, and then spent 1994 with the Chiba Lotte Marines in Japan. The Red Sox signed him in mid-April 1995 before the players' strike was resolved. He opened the season with Boston and in five games over 17 days threw seven innings and gave up seven earned runs: four of Chicago's 17 runs in one game and three of New York's 12 runs in another. He pitched 26 games with Pawtucket, was released in early August, latched on with the Orioles, and threw seven more innings (this time only giving up one run). Baltimore cut him loose after the season, but after several years away from the game he reappeared in the independent Golden League as a Mesa Miner at age 43 in 2005, pitching for his 20th—and final—professional team.

Robins Crack Open Sox Numbers

And here we were all this time telling you the Red Sox first wore uniforms numbers in 1931. True, the first sighting of numbers on a Boston uniform came that spring with a pair of exhibitions between the Sox and Boston Braves; and then the digits were worn for the first time in a major league game at Yankee Stadium on April 14, 1931. But the Red Sox had been spied in numbers 14 years earlier.

The two-time defending world champion Red Sox departed their 1917 spring training encampment at Hot Springs, Arkansas, for Memphis, Tennessee, where they were to play a series of exhibition games with the Brooklyn Robins (so dubbed for manager Wilbert Robinson). Brooklyn owner Charles Ebbets suggested that the players on the tour be numbered, so that fans unfamiliar with the players could tell who was who. The Red Sox donned red and white sleeves with bands bearing a number. The Robins had blue and white sleeves. Numbers were printed on scorecards, yet none survive to tell us who might have worn what number. The practice of wearing numbers in the regular season had been tried by the Cleveland Indians in 1916 (other numbering experiments had existed in the 19th century as well). The practice of numbering players, however, would not catch hold until 1929, when both the Indians and Yankees played the first major league game with two teams wearing uniform numbers.

#50–59: Looking Cool in the Fifties

#50

Player	Year
Andy Merchant	1975–76
Mike O'Berry	1979
Rich Gedman	1980
Dave Schmidt	1981
Dave Sax	1986
Tom Bolton	1987–92
Ken Ryan	1992–95
Jamie Moyer	1996
Mark Brandenburg	1996–97
Lou Merloni	1998
Chad Fonville	1999
Pete Schourek	2000–01
Ralph Treuel	2001 (coach)
Benny Agbayani	2002
Mike Timlin	2003–08
Aaron Bates	2009
Dusty Brown	2009
Ron Johnson	2010–11
Justin Thomas	2012 (started season at #78, but changed by mid-April)
Mauro Gomez	2012 (debuting May 13)
Quinton Berry	2013
Mookie Betts	2014–15

Number of times this number was issued: 22
Longest tenure by any given player: 6 seasons, Mike Timlin (394 games) and Tom Bolton (128 games)

#51

Player	Year
Bob Guindon	1964
Butch Hobson	1975
Reid Nichols	1980–84
Rey Quinones	1986
Josias Manzanillo	1991
Luis Ortiz	1993–94
Brian Looney	1995
Willie McGee	1995
Heathcliff Slocumb	1996–97
Keith Johns	1998
Pete Schourek	1998
Tommy Harper (coach)	2000–02
Kevin Tolar	2003
Byung-Hyun Kim	2003–04
Cla Meredith	2005

There have been 132 men assigned a double-digit number starting with 5. Relatively few—only 11—of the 132 were coaches, a lot less than the 19 coaches who wore #32 alone. The rest were players, and 90 of those 121 had it for just one year or less; 34 only donned it for part of the season.

The first was **Bobby Guindon**, who wore #51 in 1964. He was a Brookline boy, signed at age 17 by the Red Sox in June 1961. His active stay in the majors lasted nine days late in '64, from a pinch-running debut (he stayed camped on first) on September 19 through September 27, when he collected his only major league hit (a double). The first baseman struck out in four of his eight at-bats, including the last out of what turned out to be his final game. Guindon spent six more years in the minors, even using his strong left arm to win 10 games for Pittsfield (Class AA). He wasn't joined by another 50s player until 1972 when **Bob Veale** drew a double-five (#55). Many more would follow.

#50

Mike Timlin was one of just six Red Sox to see action in both the 2004 and 2007 World Series, adding those rings to the ones he'd won with the Blue Jays

Mike Barnett	2005 (assistant coach)
Julian Tavarez	2006–08
Charlie Zink	2008
Gil Velazquez	2008–09
Enrique Gonzalez	2009
Daniel Bard	2010–11

Number of times this number was issued: 21
Longest tenure by any given player: 5 seasons, Reid Nichols

#52

Player	Year
Jody Reed	1987
Mike Boddicker	1988–90
Vaughn Eshelman	1995–97
Donnie Sadler	1998
John Cumberland	1999–2001 (coach)
James Lofton	2001
Freddy Sanchez	2002
Bruce Chen	2003
Jamie Brown	2004
Wade Miller	2005
Kyle Snyder	2006
John Farrell	2007–10 (coach)
Bobby Jenks	2011
Chris Carpenter	2012
Joel Hanrahan	2013
Yoenis Cespedes	2014
Eduardo Rodriguez	2015

Number of times this number was issued: 18
Longest tenure by any given player: 4 seasons John Farrell (coach)

#53

Player	Year
Sammy Stewart	1986
Steve Curry	1988
Tim Van Egmond	1994–95
Kerry Lacy	1996–97
Tomokazu Ohka	1999–2000
Angel Santos	2001
Josh Hancock	2002
Andy Abad	2003
Phil Seibel	2004
Terry Adams	2004
Chad Bradford	2005
Ralph Treuel	2006 (coach)
Brendan Donnelly	2007
David Aardsma	2008

in 1992 and 1993. The right-handed reliever stabilized the Boston bullpen beginning with his first season with the ballclub in 2003. He appeared in eight postseason games that fall and allowed just one hit; he pitched in a club-record 28 postseason games for the Sox.

The other #50 who wore the jersey for six seasons was **Tom Bolton**, a left-handed reliever his first three years and then a starter (still left-handed) the next three. His best year was 1990: 10–5 with a 3.38 ERA and—back in the bullpen—three scoreless innings in that year's ALCS. Honolulu native **Benny Abgayani** gets a mention not because he did anything spectacular in Boston but because of the nickname that matched his state of birth and was the reason he wore #50: "Hawaii Five-0"— the TV police drama (1968–1980) of the same name had a killer surfer theme song. Though he had some memorable moments as a Met, Benny's biggest game with Boston was his first, when his three RBIs off Roy Halladay helped beat Toronto, 7–2. He was a Red Sox player for a month, September 2002, his last in the majors.

Ken Ryan looked like he might be a star for the Red Sox. A native of Pawtucket, he finished 26 games in '93, but only had one save; his record was 7–2, and he had a 3.60 ERA, which he lowered by more than a run

Fernando Cabrera	2009–10
Rich Hill	2010–12
John Farrell	2013–15 (manager)

Number of times this number was issued: 17
Longest tenure by any given player: 3 seasons, John Farrell

#54

Player	Year
Roger LaFrancois	1982
Mike Rochford	1988–90
Jeff Plympton	1991
Keith Shepherd	1995
Joe Hudson	1995–97
Mandy Romero	1998
Morgan Burkhart	2000–01
Euclides Rojas	2003–04 (coach)
John Halama	2005
Geremi Gonzalez	2005
David Riske	2006
Craig Breslow	2006
Chris Carter	2008–09
Dustin Richardson	2009
Darnell McDonald	2010–11
Pedro Beato	2012–13
Edward Mujic	2014–15
Carl Willis	2015 (pitching coach, from May 10)

Number of times this number was issued: 17
Longest tenure by any given player: 3 seasons, Mike Rochford and Joe Hudson

#55

Player	Year
Bob Veale	1972–74
LaSchelle Tarver	1986
Randy Kutcher	1988
Joe Hesketh	1990–94
Jeff Suppan	1995–97
Brian Shouse	1998
Carlos Reyes	1998
Rich Croushore	2000
Todd Erdos	2001
Ramiro Mendoza	2003
Lenny DiNardo	2004–06
Jeff Bailey	2007–09
Ryan Kalish	2010, 2012
Joey Gathright	2011
Chris Capuano	2014
Christian Vazquez	2014 (debut July 9)
Brian Butterfield	2015 (coach)

Number of times this number was issued: 17
Longest tenure by any given player: 5 seasons, Joe Hesketh

the following year. Again he closed 26 games, but this time Ryan recorded 13 saves. In January 1996, he was a key component of a trade with the Phillies for Heathcliff Slocumb (#51).

#51

Heathcliff Slocumb of 1996 epitomized the term graceful transition. He more or less matched the All-Star season he'd enjoyed with the Phillies in '95, with a 3.02 ERA and 31 saves. He struggled badly in 1997, though, putting on almost two batters (1.971) every inning. With an ERA that had ballooned to 5.76, accompanied by a record of 0–5, GM Dan Duquette must have been astounded when he found a taker—and traded him to Seattle for two players who would become mainstays with the Red Sox for years to come: Jason Varitek and Derek Lowe. Many count this as the best trade the Red Sox ever made.

A notable trade that wasn't made was in 1990, when **Willie McGee** was hitting .335 for the Cardinals. Asked about trading for McGee to help the Red Sox down the stretch, GM Lou Gorman famously said, "What would we do with Willie McGee?" He wound up in Oakland instead, and the A's swept the Sox in the ALCS (admittedly, without much help from McGee). Might that year's NL batting champion have helped the Red Sox? Maybe, maybe not, but the Sox did sign him as a free agent in June 1995 and he hit .285.

The #51 with the most tenure was **Reid Nichols**. A speedy outfielder, the two seasons when he got the most playing time he hit .302 and .285, but Nichols dropped off sharply when the Red Sox added Tony Armas in 1984. Will we ever see **Charlie Zink** again? The knuckleballer appeared in just one game, a start on August 12, 2008. He was well-set for a win, since the Sox had scored 10 times in the first inning and held a 12–2 lead after four, but he couldn't close out the top of the fifth to qualify for a win and was charged with eight runs. The Sox held on to beat the Rangers, 19–17.

#52

The number of weeks in a year, the number of cards in a deck, this number is as useful as its top practitioner, **Mike Boddicker**. It was a good deal when the Red Sox got the right-hander from Baltimore for Brady Anderson and Curt Schilling on July 29, 1988, though the passage of time has created some skeptics. Here's the facts. First, the Sox got Schilling back when it counted. Second, Boddicker helped Boston twice secure postseason berths (he was 7–3, 2.86, and 17–8, 3.36, in 1988 and 1990, respectively). Though Oakland overwhelmed the Red Sox each time in the ALCS,

#56

Player	Year
Zach Crouch	1988
Scott Taylor	1992–93
Jeff Pierce	1995
Alex Delgado	1996
Darren Bragg	1996–98
Tim Harikkala	1999
Steve Lomasney	1999
Israel Alcantara	2000 01
Chris Haney	2002
Jimmy Anderson	2004
Craig Hansen	2005–06, 2008
Ramon Ramirez	2009–10
Yamaico Navarro	2010
Trever Miller	2011
Ivan De Jesus Jr.	2012
Franklin Morales	2013
Joe Kelly	2014

Number of times this number was issued: 17
Longest tenure by any given player: 3 seasons, Darren Bragg and Craig Hansen

#57

Player	Year
Nate Minchey	1993–94
Brian Bark	1995
Ken Grundt	1996
Rudy Pemberton	1996
Ron Mahay	1997–98
Juan Pena	1999
Rod Beck	1999
Calvin Pickering	2001
Jason Shiell	2003
Joe Nelson	2004
Scott Cassidy	2005
Manny Delcarmen	2005–06
Gary Tuck	2007–12 (coach)
Victor Rodriguez	2013–15 (coach)

Number of times this number was issued: 14
Longest tenure by any given player: 6 seasons, Gary Tuck (coach)

#58

Player	Year
Jeff McNeely	1993
Nate Minchey	1996
Bill Moloney	1997–2000 (coach)
Hector Carrasco	2000

Nellie Norman	2001 (coach)
Luis Aguayo	2002 (coach)
Bryant Nelson	2002
Hector Almonte	2003
Sandy Martinez	2004
Jonathan Papelbon	2005–11
Jose Iglesias	2012
Dana Levangie	2013–15 (coach)

Number of times this number was issued: 12
Longest tenure by any given player: 7 seasons, Jonathan Papelbon

#59

Player	Year
Daryl Irvine	1990–92
Brent Knackert	1996
Pat Mahomes	1996–97
Ken Grundt	1997
Brian Barkley	1998
Tim Young	2000
Casey Fossum	2001
Luis Aguayo	2002 (coach)
Matt White	2003
Todd Jones	2003
Blaine Neal	2005
Abe Alvarez	2004–06
Mike Burns	2006
Chris Smith	2008
Dusty Brown	2009
Robert Manuel	2010
Dennys Reyes	2011
Clayton Mortensen	2012
Tommy Layne	2014–15

Number of times this number was issued: 19
Longest tenure by any given player: 3 seasons, Daryl Irvine and Abe Alvarez

Boddicker had a complete-game loss in '90—more innings than Roger Clemens had in his two starts total.

A lefty who started like a house afire was Rule V pickup **Vaughn Eshelman**. He tossed 18 shutout innings to start his career in 1995, winning three games. Eshelman then cooled off and saw his ERA climb for eight games in a row, up to 6.43 (he eventually lowered it to 4.85). In three seasons, he was 6–3, 6–3, and 3–3.

Probably the most important coach numbered in the 50s is **John Farrell.** A pitching coach is a club's most vital assistant, especially nowadays with the mixing and matching of pitchers on a nightly basis, the dreaded pitch count, and trying to keep pitchers both busy and rested. In Farrell's first season with the Sox in 2007—and his first year as a major league pitching coach—Boston had the lowest ERA in the league and won the World Series. Works here.

#53

Some tragedy has haunted this number. **Josh Hancock** was killed in a car crash in St. Louis in April 2007. He'd been 0–1 with the Red Sox in 2002, appearing in just three games, then traded to the Phillies for Jeremy Giambi. Stan Grossfeld broke the sad story of **Sammy Stewart** in the October 25, 2006, *Boston Globe*. A right-handed reliever, Stewart was 4–1 for the 1986 Red Sox in 27 appearances, one of his 10 seasons in major league ball. His last year in ball was 1987; his police record began to build in 1989, accumulating 26 arrests and serving six prison sentences for a variety of offenses.

Though far from tragic, it was unfortunate the careers of some of the others #53s didn't work out in Boston. **Tomokazu Ohka** had three losing seasons with the Sox and pitched better after a trade to Montreal for Ugueth Urbina, a tragic figure himself (see Chapter #41). Reliever **Terry Adams**, who had never appeared in the postseason in a career that began in 1995, was picked up from Toronto in late July 2004. He went 2–0 for the Sox, but his 6.00 Boston ERA kept him off the postseason roster.

#54

Tragedy, in the form of a bolt of lightning, struck former Red Sox reliever **Geremi Gonzalez** on March 25, 2008. He was peacefully positioned on a pier at the Venezuelan beach town of Punta Palma, when the fatal bolt shot from the sky. Gonzalez, just 33 at the time of his death, pitched for five teams and appeared for the 2005 Red Sox in the ALDS. Suspicion of foul play led to his body being exhumed because jewelry he was wearing when he was killed turned up at auction.

Undrafted out of college, the chunky **Morgan Burkhart** (5 feet, 11 inches, 225 pounds) won the MVP award three times for the Richmond Roosters in the independent Frontier League. It took a .404 average and 36 homers in an 80-game season to catch the attention of major

2015 Opening Day Lineup	
#50 Mookie Betts	CF
#15 Dustin Pedroia	2B
#34 David Ortiz	DH
#13 Hanley Ramirez	LF
#48 Pablo Sandoval	3B
#18 Shane Victorino	RF
#2 Xander Bogaerts	SS
#10 Ryan Hanigan	C
#11 Clay Buckholz	P
#Total: 201	

Then in 2015, manager **John Farrell** went in for hernia surgery and learned that he also had Stage 1 Non-Hodgkin's lymphoma and had to leave the team for cancer treatment as of August 11. Bench coach Torey Lovullo was interim manager in his absence, which lasted through the end of the season.

league scouts. The Red Sox purchased his contract in October 1998. He was called up to Boston in June 2000 and each of his first four games was a multi-hit game. This version of "Morgan Magic" soon cooled off, but the switch-hitting DH still finished the season with a respectable .288 average and a stellar .422 OBP. It wasn't anything he was able to replicate in the majors, though he did hit 26 homers in 2005 in Saltillo, Mexico.

Mike Rochford was a 1982 first-round pick from Methuen, Massachusetts. Three years in a row he tried to earn a win, but all three times he fell short. His only start ended in his only major league decision—a loss. **Joe Hudson** also pitched over three straight seasons, but he earned a win. It took him 47 games to get it, and then he added five more in a 6–7 career (4.82 ERA). He even threw a scoreless ninth in Game Three of the 1995 ALDS.

#55

A Pirate for 11 seasons before being demoted to the minors, **Bob Veale** was purchased by the Red Sox in early September 1972—the year the Sox finished just a half-game out of first place. The 6-foot, 6-inch lefty's 116–91 pitching record and stellar 3.06 ERA with Pittsburgh made the Red Sox take a gamble on the aging southpaw. It worked. He was 2–0 with the Sox in September of '72, throwing eight innings in six relief appearances, allowing just two hits and no runs. What more could you ask of a pitcher than a 0.00 ERA? Veale appeared in 32 games in '73, closing 24, and saving 11 with a 3.47 ERA. He only threw 13 innings in 1974, spent a stint at Pawtucket, and was released after the season.

After seven serviceable seasons with the Expos (including a stellar 1988 campaign), southpaw starter-turned-reliever **Joe Hesketh** was placed on waivers at the end of April 1990. The Braves claimed him, only to release him three months later. The Sox snapped him up as a free agent; his 0–4 record masking a pretty good 3.51 ERA. Given 17 starts in 1991, Hesketh relieved in 22 more games for a 12–4 record that was second on the club in wins to Cy Young winner Roger Clemens—and Joe's .750 winning percentage topped The Rocket. Hesketh never came close to that win total or a 3.29 ERA in his final three seasons.

Taking on Hesketh's number was **Jeff Suppan** in 1995. He won once that year and the next, and went 7–3 in '97—despite a 5.69 ERA. Left unprotected by Boston, the Arizona Diamondbacks took him in that November's expansion draft. Six years later, at the 2003 trading deadline, Suppan returned (wearing #35) in a trade from the Pirates. He was released after posting an ERA (5.57) that was as bad as it had been six years before. He turned up as a Cardinal facing the Sox in the 2004 World Series. He'd had a career-best 16–9 season and won a game in each of the prior two postseason series, but he lost Game Three of the Series to the Sox, memorably committing a horrendous baserunning gaffe.

There was also a might-have-been. Left-handed pitcher Fabio Castro was brought up from Pawtucket, and installed in the Boston bullpen for one day (April 27, 2010), wearing #55, but he wasn't called on and was then sent back down and Alan Embree brought up. He wasn't used, either.

#56

Unfortunately, the Red Sox gave up too quickly on Jamie Moyer (a too-brief #50), and swapped him to Seattle for outfielder **Darren Bragg** in mid-1996. The 5-foot, 9-inch Bragg requested #56, says Sox clubbie Joe Cochran, because he was a fan of New York Giants linebacker Lawrence Taylor, an NFL Hall of Famer. Bragg ended up getting more work than originally anticipated, accumulating 1,315 plate appearances through 1998 (hitting .264) and turning in some good play in the field before being released.

Izzy Alcantara may have gotten a bum rap. After eight years in the minors, mostly for the Expos, he signed three years in a row with the Red Sox as a free agent. He got into 21 games in 2000, batting .289 with some power (.578 slugging). Unfortunately, he misplayed a couple of easy balls in the outfield, ran into some outs on the basepaths, and was—in Leigh Grossman's words—"widely accused by Boston media outlets of not hustling or caring about the game." That's a damnable offense in a baseball town. The biggest headlines came in the minors during 2000 for karate-kicking the Scranton catcher in the mask after a tight pitch and then rushing the mound. Though he was leading the International League in both homers and batting average at the time, all anyone ever remembers is the mid-game martial arts.

Drafted as a closer out of St. John's, **Craig Hansen** enjoyed a rapid rise to the big leagues, turning up in September 2005 some 76 days after signing with a grand total of just 25 1/3 innings of pro ball. Over three seasons, the Sox inserted him into 74 games. Despite Hansen's great promise, his overall ERA was 6.15. After being traded to the Pirates in the Manny Ramirez/Jason Bay three-team, six-player trade, Hansen's ERA with Pittsburgh exceeded 6.00, too. The Sox had much better luck with ex-Royal **Ramon Ramirez**. Acquired for Coco Crisp, he went 7–4 in 70 games with a 2.84 ERA in 2009. Crisp, paid 13 times more than Ramirez, played just 49 games in the Royals outfield before undergoing shoulder surgery.

#57

A tall Texan who's found a home in Japan is **Nate Minchey**, a 6–foot-8 right-hander drafted by the Expos but who debuted with a complete-game 11–1 win for the Red Sox in September 1993. It was mostly down-hill from there. Four more outings left him with an ERA of 3.55, and then a 1994 ERA of 8.61 in 23 midseason innings. After some good work at Pawtucket, he was given another couple of starts in 1996—and #58—but he couldn't make it in Boston. Seven seasons pitching with the Hiroshima Toyo Carp and the Chiba Lotte Marines led to a job scouting Japan for the Indians organization.

Juan Pena almost defined "flash in a pan." In May 1999, the 21-year-old won his first two games, striking out 15 batters. A sore right shoulder shelved him for the season and another look in spring training resulted in surgery. He never made it back, making only a few brief appearances in independent ball and Mexican League action in 2004 and 2005. A player who might have become a trivia footnote is **Calvin Pickering**, an on-again, off-again big leaguer who looked to have finished his career Ted Williams-style with a home run in his last at-bat in the majors. It was a pinch-hit three-run homer in the top of the seventh against his first team, the Orioles, on October 5, 2001. He didn't play the next year, presumably basking on the beaches in his native Virgin Islands. But he made it off the beach all the way back to the majors in 2004. He played parts of two years with the Royals, but in what we'll declare his final at-bat, on April 21, 2005, he whiffed.

#58

The dramatic opening notes of Dropkick Murphys' "Shipping Up to Boston" always foreshadow the arrival of closer **Jonathan Papelbon** (pictured) from the Fenway bullpen. Originally envisioned as a starting pitcher, the fiery competitor came to revel in his warrior role as closer. Papelbon entered 2009 needing just 20 more saves to break Bob Stanley's team saves record of 132; he reached that on the first of July. He finished with 38 saves for the year and finished his time with the Sox with 219 in six full seasons—he had none as a rookie in 2005. Papelbon had never allowed a postseason run in 17 career appearances before getting tagged by the Angels in the 2009 ALDS.

Fascinated as we are with members of the 2004 Sox who didn't play much, let's consider **Sandy Martinez**. The veteran catcher was one of three Martinezes on the team—the other two being pitchers: his cousin Anastacio and an unrelated one named Pedro. Despite the possibility of a Martinez/Martinez battery, the Martinez cousins' tenures didn't match up. And Sandy never caught Pedro, either.

Jeff McNeely seemed like a capable utility outfielder during the 1993 season, when he batted .297 in 44 plate appearances (and stole six bases without

Jonathan Papelbon

ever being caught). He may have been hitting over his head; the next year, he batted a meager .231 in a full season with Pawtucket and was traded in December (with Nate Minchey) for Luis Alicea.

#59

The first Red Sox player to wear #59—and still the only Red Sox player whose last name starts with the letter "I"—was right-hander **Daryl Irvine**. A first-round pick in 1985, he had 41 opportunities to show his wares in Boston spread over parts of 1990, 1991, and 1992. Irvine's intolerable 6.11 ERA in '92 got him traded from a last-place team to a three-time division winner in Pittsburgh—the Pirates haven't won since. Coincidence? **Abe Alvarez**'s 11.32 ERA in four games over three years earned led to no more callups and his eventual change from the International League to the independent Atlantic League in 2008.

Todd Jones was a 10-year veteran closer when he signed in Boston as a free agent in mid-2003. Now a columnist for *The Sporting News*, in his 16 seasons in the majors he pitched in 982 games, starting one, and racking up 319 saves. He was nothing special for the Sox: 2–1, with a 5.25 earned run average. He had no saves for the '03 Sox, but Jones still got 135 more in his career of eight teams and nine lives.

Dusty Brown caught six games for the Red Sox in 2009—and even pitched once, allowing a run in a Blue Jays blowout—but in his first three trips to the plate all he had was a walk and two hard-hit outs. His last at-bat came with two outs in the home eighth in the penultimate game of the season. He launched a home run off Mike Gossling for his first major league hit in an 11–6 win over Cleveland.

MOST OBSCURE RED SOX PLAYER TO WEAR A NUMBER IN THE 50s—There are sooooo many candidates that in this case the obscure overwhelm the ordinary. We're going with just one player for the 50s. But first there was a runoff election to find the most significant obscure player in an oxymoron category:

#50: Andy Merchant—A coulda-been backup to Pudge Fisk, he started once in 1975 and then "I just went home and watched old Carlton on TV like everybody else."

#51: **Keith Johns** (1998)—A 1.000 OBP, .000 BA. Nuf ced.

#52: Jamie Brown (2004)—Eleven days, four games, 5.87 ERA, one ring.

#53: Phil Seibel—Another guy with a ring who didn't do a thing. He pitched twice in 2004 and was released before the '04 postseason.

#55: LaSchelle Tarver—The coolest name on this list, he batted .120 for the '86 Sox, but he did score the winning run in walkoff fashion on September 3.

#56: Steve Lomasney—In the catcher's only game he was one of 27 Sox players used in the season finale after the '99 club had clinched the wild card. Lomansey fanned twice on 3–2 pitches. "It wasn't like I got up there and struck out on three pitches," he told us. "I fouled off a couple of balls."

#57: Brian Bark—He faced eight batters, allowed two singles, and had a 0.00 ERA, but there were no more appearances in major league baseball for Bark. Rough!

#58: Hector Almonte—This righty pitched for three teams but threw just seven times for Boston with an 8.22 ERA and one loss.

#59: Ken Grundt—Versatile, he could have been the nominee from #57 as well. His ERA at that number was 27.00 in '96 and 9.00 at #59 the next year. All in all, 10.80 in 3 1/3 innings made for a brief Boston stay.

And the winner is . . .

#54: Roger LaFrancois—The last Red Sox to hit .400 for a full season. You'd think he'd be lionized forever like Ted Williams, but alas, LaFrancois did it in just 10 at-bats. Still, to be mentioned in the same breath as Teddy Ballgame means a lot—and it was the reason he wore #54. "Ted Williams was one of my childhood idols," he told us. "His number was already retired. I wanted number 54. It was the closest thing. Five plus four equals nine." As third-string catcher behind Gary Allenson and Rich Gedman in 1982, LaFrancois didn't miss a game all year. Unfortunately, he only played in eight of them. As the final day of the season rolled around, October 3, LaFrancois had only recorded five at-bats: with a double and a single he was batting .400. When manager Ralph Houk gave him the chance to start the season's last game in New York, LaFrancois faced a dilemma: Should he sit it out and preserve his average? "There was a lot of pressure on me that last day, but I didn't want to sit on my average. I decided to play." LaFrancois hit a solid single up the middle early in the game before seeing his average sink to .333 as the game went into extra innings. He was 3-for-9 on the year, and in his major league career. In the top of the 11th, he jumped on a two-strike breaking ball from Rudy May and bounced it over the pitcher's head for an infield hit. Three batters later, he scored what proved to be the winning run on a Rick Miller single. After suiting up for 162 games with the 1982 Red Sox, he never played again in the majors, retiring at an even .400. Like his idol, LaFrancois made the right choice not to sit.

Exclusive Club No More

It was 1986 when things really started getting out of hand. No, we're not talking about on-field decisions or curses or anything like that; 1986 is when the explosion of the 50s began.

The Red Sox begrudgingly handed out high numbers, and they didn't issue any number as high as #50 between 1944 and 1963. Through the 1985 season, only once did the Red Sox issue as many as three numbers at #50 or beyond. That was in 1975—their last pennant-winning year before '86. Catcher Andy Merchant made his major league debut on the last day of the '75 season, wearing #50 against Cleveland after the Sox had wrapped up the division. Callup Butch Hobson, #51, got his first start in that season finale against the Indians. He'd been with the club all month watching the Red Sox wrap up the AL East (he entered an earlier game as a pinch runner). Hobson moved on to #4 the next year and into the starting lineup. Eddie Popowski, the other member of the 50-plus trio in '75, swapped #54 for #36 the next year. Merchant wore #50 for two games in '76 and never played in the majors again.

The 50-plus club grew to four for the first time in '86: Dave Sax at #50, Rey Quinones #51, Sammy Stewart #53, and LaSchelle Tarver, who wore #55 until he was replaced on the roster by the infamous Calvin Schiraldi. From that point on, there were high numbers all over. The 50-plusers reached double digits in another Sox postseason year: 1995. It reached 14 for the first time in 1996 (not such a wonderful season) and hit 14 again in 2004 (absolutely wonderful). Boston touched 15 50-plusers in 2005, when they took the wild card. That year the most famous member of the 50-plus club made his debut: #58, Jonathan Papelbon. Twenty Sox players had #50 or higher in 2006; they topped that with 21 in 2009. In 2014, there were 25—if you count the two coaches who each had the number for one day (and 23, if you don't count either).

Bat rack at Fenway, 2011.

#60–88: Another Stratosphere

As we are now well into the second century of Red Sox baseball, we can expect to see a higher number of Sox players wearing higher numbers. Although there are still relatively few retired numbers at Fenway, there are also some that remain unofficially retired, #21 and #45, for example. Recent years, though, have seen players wearing #5 and #25, numbers that might have lain dormant had some things worked out otherwise. The perceived favored status of lower numbers that was common in earlier times no longer appears prevalent. Younger players seem to enjoy wearing some of the higher numbers, going where no man has gone before . . . unless that man was the bullpen catcher. The 70s and 90s are both largely untapped frontiers ripe for future development. They're not just for spring training anymore.

The first thing that strikes us is how some of the higher number players have gone on to success with other teams (and lower numbers). **Hanley Ramirez**, the first Sox player to wear #60, was the key figure for the Marlins in the November 2005 trade for Josh Beckett and Mike Lowell (four other players were also involved). His Red Sox record was almost amusing—two games, two at-bats, two

#64

Dustin Pedroia	2006
Michael Bowden	2008–11
Will Middlebrooks	2012
Jean Machi	2015

#65

Carlos Valdez	1998
Ino Guerrero	2003–08 (batting practice pitcher–coach)
Jose De La Torre	2013
Jonathan Aro	2015

#66

Joe Cascarella	1935
Johnny Pesky	1992, 1995–96 (coach)
Daniel Nava	2012
Drake Britton	2013
Noe Ramirez	2015

#67

Eddie Riley	2001 (coach)
Anastacio Martinez	2004
David Page	2006–09 (strength coach)
Che-Hsuan Lin	2012 (from August)
Brandon Workman	2013–14

#68

Devern Hansack	2006
George Kottaras	2008
Josh Reddick	2009
Dusty Brown	2010
Robert Coello	2010
Jose Iglesias	2011 (May 8 only, then switched to #76)
Randy Niemann	2012 (coach)
Alex Hassan	2014
Matt Barnes	2014

#70

Kyle Weiland	2011
Ryan Kalish	2012 (June 17 game only)
Garin Cecchini	2014

#71

| Nate Spears | 2011–12 |
| Edwin Escobar | 2014 |

#72

| Xander Bogaerts | 2013 |
| Carlos Rivero | 2014 |

strikeouts—but he put up impressive numbers in four minor league seasons for the Sox: .297 average with 129 extra-base hits and 99 steals. He was 2006 National League Rookie of the Year, edging out Washington's Ryan Zimmerman. Ramirez had 200 hits his second year, led the majors in runs scored in '08, and won a batting title in '09. It was one of those trades that left both teams pleased—the Sox, don't forget, did get a world championship out of it.

Unlike Ramirez, **David Murphy** (also #60) was someone who didn't seem likely to find a ready place on the team. A first-round draft pick in 2003, Murphy was an outfielder who hit just .250 in his first 24 at-bats with Boston, but the tall Texan seemed useful trade bait for the Sox to secure the reliever they sought for the 2007 stretch drive. At the July 31 trading deadline, Murphy, pitcher Kason Gabbard, and minor leaguer Engel Beltre went to Texas for **Eric Gagne** (assigned #83) and some cash (not that the Red Sox really were hard-up for money). The Sox won the '07 World Series, but it certainly wasn't because of Gagne. Monsieur Gagne was an ace closer, a three-time All-Star in his Dodgers days, and the Cy Young Award winner in 2003—thanks to his 55-for-55 save season (part of a record 84 straight saves from 2002–04). Former BoSox owner Joseph Lannin, he of the back-to-back World Series wins (1915–16) was—like

#73

Bryce Brentz	2014

#76

Jose Iglesias	2011 (beginning May 9)
Jonathan Diaz	2013

#77

Josh Bard	2006
Rob Leary	2010–11
Pedro Ciriaco	2012
Tim Hyers	2014 (interim hitting coach, following Greg Colbrunn's sub-arachnoid hemorrhage)
Billy McMillon	2014 (coach for a day, in September—the day before Kevin Boles)
Kevin Boles	2014 (coach for a day, in September—the day after Billy McMillon)
Bob Kipper	2015

Note: McMillon, who had managed Portland, and Boles, who had managed Pawtucket, were both invited to suit up with the team as a major-leaguer for one day each.

#78

Justin Thomas	2012

#81

Lou Lucier	1943

#82

Johnny Lazor	1943

#83

Eric Gagne	2007

#84

J. T. Snow	2006

#85

Don Kalkstein	2006–08 (psychology coach)
Che-Hsuan Lin	2012
Ino Guerrero	2013 (coach)

Gagne—a native of Quebec, but Gagne was the first Québécois to play for the team (he spoke only French before going to junior college in Oklahoma). Gagne appeared in 20 games for Boston and finished 11 of them. His saves? Zero. He put almost two men on base per inning, giving up 14 earned runs in 18 2/3 innings for a 6.75 ERA. Worse than the statistics showed, fans feared him coming in from the pen lest he throw gasoline on the fire . . . as he did when he turned the 11th inning of ALCS Game Two into a seven-alarm (run) blaze.

Gagne would have worn #38, but Curt Schilling had it so he flipped the digits and went with #83. Someone beat Gagne to the highest uniform number worn by a Red Sox player. **J. T. Snow**, a 14-year veteran, took #84 in 2006 in honor of his father, 1965–75 Los Angeles Rams wide receiver Jack Snow, who died in January that year. "I know it's not a typical baseball number," said J. T. "It's to honor him, because I wouldn't be sitting here without his support and upbringing. . . . He knew I was going to sign with the Red Sox, and he knew I was going to wear his number. I think he felt good about it." Snow's stay with Boston was a brief one, hitting .205 in 44 at-bats.

Something had to be in the water back in 1943. That year saw **Lou Lucier** wear #81 and **Johnny Lazor** don #82. It wasn't as if the team was overrun with prospects

#86

Brian Abraham	2013–14
Adrian Lorenzo	2015 (coach)

#87

Mike Brenly	2015 (bullpen catcher)

#88

Jason Larocque	2005–07 (bullpen catcher)
Alex "Mani" Martinez	2007–09 (bullpen catcher)

#91

Alfredo Aceves	2011–12

#94

Dalier Hinojosa	2015

#97

Wally the Green Monster 1991 (mascot)
NOT OFFICIAL NUMBER
Number of times any number 60 and above was issued: 94
Longest tenure by any given player: 8 seasons, coach Dana Levangie (#60) and 3 seasons, Bronson Arroyo (#61)

during spring training. Because of a common effort to cut down on unnecessary travel during World War II, the Sox trained at Tufts College in Medford, Massachusetts, and had fewer players in camp than usual. In a December 2001 interview, we asked Lazor why he'd worn #82. He said he didn't know; he thought he'd worn #29. Lou Lucier was still a spry 91 as we wrote *Red Sox by the Numbers*, so we asked him. He didn't know why, either; he just figured the club hadn't thought he was going to make it, so they gave him a high number. Asked at what point during 1943 he'd switched to #15, he didn't recall having switched—he always thought of himself as #81. Lucier appeared in 16 games in 1943, then three more in '44. His Red Sox ERA was 3.97 in 79 1/3 innings. Lazor played for four years in the Boston outfield (he caught one game), batting .263 in 431 at-bats. His last game was the season finale in 1946, but he did not

Wally the Green Monster

appear in the '46 World Series.

More recently, Jamaican-born **Justin Masterson** wore #63 for the Sox in 2008 and 2009, putting together a 9–8 record and 3.97 ERA in 67 appearances, plus a 1–0, 1.59, mark in five ALCS games in '08. He was one of the keys to the Victor Martinez deal and immediately joined Cleveland's rotation, though going from contender to surrender was reflected in his 1–7, 4.55, mark with the Tribe. Taking Masterson's number was **Junichi Tazawa**. The 23-year-old Yokohama native asked out of Japanese baseball before he was even in it (Tazawa contacted each club in his native land, asking he not to be draft-

Clay Buchholz

ed so he could play in the States). After signing with the Red Sox, he debuted in the 14th inning on August 7, 2009, taking the loss when Alex Rodriguez homered in the 15th. He went 2–2 in his starts, but two batterings by the White Sox bloated his ERA to 7.46.

The best known Sox in the sixes is musical impresario **Bronson Arroyo**. With his high-straight-leg kick and flowing blond locks, Arroyo brought panache to #61 and a 24–19 record to the 2004–05 rotation. Perhaps his most famous moment came in relief of Curt Schilling when the ball was swatted out of his glove in Game Six of the '04 ALCS. The umpires huddled and called bad sport Alex Rodriguez out—the second ump reversal that rightfully went Boston's way in "The Bloody Sock Game." If there ever was a "Curse," it ended there. Arroyo, stolen from the Pirates off waivers in '03, was swiped by Cincinnati in the lamentable Wily Mo Pena deal in March 2006. Arroyo led the NL in starts and innings and was an All-Star that year.

New #61 **Clay Buchholz** did better with the ladies than with AL hitters in 2008—dating a *Penthouse* Pet of the Year and one of *People* magazine's "100 Most Beautiful People." In November 2009, he married Briefcase Model #26 (yes, they had numbers, too) from the television show *Deal or No Deal*, Lindsay Clubine. The two had been introduced by none other than Donald Trump (and we'd gotten this far without dipping into the gossipy, tabloid world, but hey, this is the 60s). Whatever the trick, something else clicked in 2009 for Buchholz; his record improved from 2–9 to 7–4 and his ERA dropped from 6.75 to 4.21, finally showing some payoff from the tantalizing promise of tossing a no-hitter in just his second major league start in 2007.

A pair of unrelated Bards found their way on this list: catcher **Josh Bard** (#77), the only member of the Red Sox to ever wear a number in the 70s, and pitcher **Daniel Bard** (#60), who broke in during the 2009 season (and saw his younger brother, Luke, drafted by the Red Sox in the same year—though the younger righty opted for Georgia Tech and grabbed Yellow Jacket #38). Daniel, a 2005 first-rounder out of UNC, appeared in 49 games as a rookie in '09, putting together a 2–2 record, 3.95 ERA, and notching a 101-mph JUGS gun reading in a game against Oakland. Josh came over from Cleveland in the 2006 Coco Crisp deal and was unable to handle Tim Wakefield's knuckleball (10 passed balls in 53 innings). That earned him a ticket to San Diego—Cla Meredith went along for the ride—and set up the dramatic return of Wake's "personal catcher" Doug Mirabelli. Three years later, the Padres released Josh Bard and the Sox signed him again in 2009, but they too released him during spring training. He caught on with the Nationals, taking #7. Washington Nationals media relations man Mike Gazda served as spokesman regarding the catcher's choice of #77 with Boston: "His number of preference is 7, but that was taken so he wore 77." A simple explanation, but about that #44 he wore with the Indians . . .

And if it all gets too much to take, talk it out with someone who understands and can help. The Red Sox employed a psychology coach, **Don Kalkstein**, for three years. They won a World Series in that span, so maybe there's some residual effect. Despite being incredibly fortunate and immensely compensated to play major league baseball, there's unrelenting travel, constant stress to perform or be shoved aside, unblinking media attention, and, let's face it, the Red Sox mean more to more people per capita than perhaps any team in the game. And never mind what happens when the Yankees come to town or the postseason approaches. It can wear a person down. Maybe that's one of the reasons why this book lists so many players who lasted a year, a week, a day in the major leagues. Just a thought.

Though Dr. Kalkstein no longer appears in uniform, we do have a question for him: "Doctor, how did #85 make you feel?"

MOST OBSCURE RED SOX PLAYER TO WEAR #60 AND HIGHER—It's too close to call between **Carlos Valdez** and **Marino Santana.** Both came from the Dominican, threw right-handed, arrived in Boston from other organizations, played one year apart, and wore numbers in the 60s. Valdez (#65) was a little shorter, a little older, and a lot more successful in Boston than Santana. Purchased from the Giants, Valdez was called up to Boston in September 1998 and was unscored upon as the wild card Sox prepped for the postseason. He notched the win in relief in the final game of the year in what became the final game of his major league career. The end also came for Santana in a Red Sox uniform. Santana, who'd appeared briefly for the '98 Tigers, got through his first two Sox relief appearances unscathed in July 1999. He faced his old team at Tiger Stadium with the Sox down 7–0; Santana surrendered another touchdown. He converted his 0.00 ERA to 15.75 and threw his last pitch in the majors.

And now, ladies and gentleman, the Red Sox uniform with a decimal point. If uniform numbers ever get scarce in Boston, this is one solution, but for now the number belongs to Usain Bolt, who held both the Olympic and world records for the 100 meters at 9.69 seconds. The Jamaican sprinter threw out the ceremonial first pitch at Fenway Park on April 25, 2009, caught by Kingston, Jamaica, native Justin Masterson. Less than four months later, Bolt improved his record time to 9.58. It's not just ballplayers who change numbers.

Higher Numbers Add Up

On August 2, 2012, the Red Sox set a major-league record, thanks to a Will, a Pedro, and a couple of Ryans.The bottom four hitters in Boston's batting order that night were:

Ryan Lavarnway—uniform #60
Will Middlebrooks—64
Ryan Kalish—55
Pedro Ciriaco—77

The total of 256 did indeed set a new big-league record.

A Japanese ballplayer with the Hanshin Tigers wearing uniform #107, before an exhibition against the Red Sox at the Toyko Dome, March 2008.

The Unresolved

Though we've been as thorough as possible to nail down each uniform number in Red Sox history, a few bleeders got through. Hey, even the 2004 and '07 Sox nearly lost in the ALCS yet swept their other two October series.

While these unresolved issues all come from before the expansion era (pre-1961), we're hopeful that all of these numbers will one day be pinned down—but we suspect that we will never reach full resolution on all of them. We've tried the best we can, even contacting next of kin when possible. Mel Almada died in his native Mexico in 1988, but we were able to locate his son, Eduardo. He has a photograph of his father showing Almada wearing #21 in 1933. We could independently confirm him wearing the same number in 1935, but we're not 100 percent sure about 1934. Hence, that entry on the list.

We spent a lot of time scrolling through microfilm looking for photographs in newspapers of the day, sports-page cartoons, and mentions of uniform numbers (which were extremely rare). The cartoons provided the most evidence of all.

The most careful of all the list-keepers in terms of insisting on documentation is Mark Stang, co-author—with Linda Harkness—of *Baseball by the Numbers* (Scarecrow Press, 1996). Unless he's seen the number in print, in a scorecard for instance, he doesn't record the connection between number and player. As Mark explains, "The *only* source I used for my listings is the regular season game-issued scorecard. No pre- or postseason listings, no media guides, no Red and Green Books, no photos, no cartoons, etc."

That Andy Spognardi's grandson wrote to Bill Walsh that his ancestor had worn #2 didn't satisfy Stang's threshold. When we began work on *Red Sox by the Numbers*, the list below was Stang's list of unresolved numbers, to which we've added annotations. Others who've extensively researched the subject are also noted, including author Jack Looney, (*Now Batting, Number . . .*), Bill Walsh (whose list is used by baseball-almanac.com), and journalist Bill Ballou, who maintains the extensive list of Red Sox numbers compiled by the late Ben Ells.

1932

Spognardi, Andy (IF): Andy's son, also named Andy, directed us to a Bob Coyne sports-page cartoon in the *Boston Post*, Saturday, September 24, 1932, which shows Spognardi wearing #2.

1933

Almada, Mel (OF): Mel's son Eduardo reports a 1933 photograph in his possession of Almada with Babe Ruth, showing Mel wearing #21. That was good enough for us.

Fullerton, Curt (P): After a seven-year absence, Fullerton returned to the major leagues but only appeared in six games. We were unable to find any mention of a uniform number in the Boston papers of the day, but we've listed him at #14 because both Bill Ballou and Jack Looney did.

1934

Almada, Mel (OF): Eddie Almada did not have definitive proof regarding his father in 1934.

Graham, Skinny (OF): See comments below.

Hockette, George (P): He wore #28 in 1935. Maybe he did in 1934, too, but we haven't been able to prove it. He debuted on September 17, but both Doc Legett and coach Bibb Falk are said to have also worn #28. Legett's listed in '34 with #24. It would appear he started with #28, but switched to #24.

Merena, Spike (P): His debut was one day before Hockette's and Bill Ballou's list says he wore #30. There's no conflict, but we couldn't find any confirmation of Merena or Hockette in the Boston papers.

Niemiec, Al (P): Niemiec's debut came two days after Hockette's. Bill Ballou says he wore #29, and there's no conflict but it's another number we can't confirm.

1935

Kroner, John (IF): Kroner wore #26 in 1936, but did he wear #29 in his September 29, 1935, debut? We couldn't confirm Bill Ballou's listing. Looney lists his number as unknown.

1936

Dahlgren, Babe (1B): Babe's grandson Matt wrote a whole book on his famous forefather, but even he has not been able to document a number for 1936. Ben Ells's list doesn't include him, but Bill Ballou has him wearing #16 as does Looney. Both Mike Meola and Stew Bowers are listed wearing #16, too, though the timing of their comings and going appear to make that a possibility.

Gaffke, Fabian (OF): Fabe's daughter Judy Magerowski was unable to determine the number he wore in 1936.

Olson, Ted (P): Everyone seems to agree he wore #28 in 1937. Ballou has him wearing #28 in 1936 as well. Looney has him wearing #23 in 1936, the same number worn that year by Bowers and George Dickey. Olson debuted on June 21. Bowers was in five games, in April, May, and August. Dickey was called up at the end of May.

Poindexter, Jennings (P): Both Ballou and Looney have him wearing #20. The original Ells list did not. We couldn't confirm it one way or another.

1938

Lefebvre, Lefty (P): Bill Nowlin interviewed the late Lefty a couple of times, but unfortunately never asked him if he could pin down his number.

1942

Gilbert, Andy (IF): Gilbert debuted on September 14 and appeared in six games. He wore #42 in 1946, but did he wear it in 1942? There's a good chance of it. Ells agrees, but Looney says he wore #2. Both numbers were available.

1951

Guerra, Mike (C): Ells has him in a #8 jersey. So does Looney (perhaps because Ells did), but Stang isn't fully satisfied yet. Tom Wright and Aaron Robinson both wore #8 that year, Ells admits. Guerra had been traded to the Senators on May 7. Robinson arrived on waivers on August 6. Tom Wright got off to a difficult start and spent most of the year in Louisville, but was there an overlap between Guerra and Wright? Both played on April 21; who wore what number? Possibly Wright wore #28 until Guerra left, then switched to #8.

1952

Bolling, Milt (IF): Jeremiah Woolsey, writing Ted Lepcio's biography for SABR, asked Milt, who recalled his number for 1953 and onward but not what he'd worn in 1952.

Maxwell, Charley (OF): Did he revert to #37 in 1952, the same number he'd worn in 1950? Ballou has George Schmees, Paul Lehner, and Faye Throneberry all wearing #37, too. That's a lot of 37s in one year.

1954

Morton, Guy (C): Ells says he wore #39 in 1954. So does Looney. Moose Morton only played in one major league game, on September 17, though he was up with Boston for more than three weeks. No one else had #39.

1956

Mauch, Gene (2B): We've got the future manager wearing #24 in both 1956 and 1957 per Ballou and Looney, but he's not in #24 on the original Ben Ells list.

Minarcin, Rudy (P): We've got Minarcin wearing #29 in both 1956 and 1957, per Ballou, Looney, and the original Ells list.

1959

Gile, Don (C): Don wrote us, "I was #35 in 1959 and then #38 from 1960–62. In spring training in 1960, I wore # 36, but when I got to Boston I was changed to #38. Why? I have no idea." Unfortunately, he mentions Bill Walsh's list, leading to some skepticism that there's some circular citation going on here. Gile's memory of the 1960 preseason, however, was clear, convincing to us that he had a good memory for such things.

Lepcio, Ted (2B): Tom Harkins talked with Ted, who says he wore #5 for his first three years and #12 after. When incoming manager Pinky Higgins took his #5, Ted came into the clubhouse and didn't see his uniform. He thought he'd been traded.

Moford, Herb (P): We have him with #42, but without definitive scorecard evidence. Herb only appeared in four games, making it difficult to pin down.

Back to the issue of Skinny Graham in 1934 . . . he was only with the Red Sox from September 14 to September 30 that year. We looked up stories in the *Post*, *Herald*, and *Globe*. There was no reference to Graham's uniform number, though on the same library visit we did find a 1933 cartoon showing Fatty Fothergill wearing #13 so we could confirm that one.

It doesn't look like Skinny could have been wearing #14, though, since Joe Mulligan had it (starting June 28 right through September 30). We went through all the box scores for those final 16 days, and based on who was playing and what numbers they wore, the only numbers 1–30 not accounted for are these four:

#13: Perhaps Graham's number; perhaps not.

#17: Worn by Herb Pennock. The future Hall of Famer's last career game was August 27, 1934, so the number was seemingly available; his SABR bio implies he did not accompany the team from that point on.

#19: Had been worn by Fritz Ostermueller, but he was injured on September 12 and didn't pitch from that point onward.

#25: Joe Judge had worn it (his last game was May 12, so the number was available).

This assumes that it's correct that George Hockette wore #28, Al Niemiec wore #29, and Spike Merena wore #30. Complicating matters, there is still uncertainty as to what number Mel Almada wore. He's listed as #21, but so was Lyn Lary. (Muller's last game was May 13, 1934, and Lary arrived on May 15 in trade for Muller.) Both Lary and Almada played in some of those September games, and it's unlikely they both wore #21!

There's just one more problem—1935. Graham is listed as wearing #14 in 1935, but so is Ostermueller. Graham played in eight games, the last one being September 25. Ostermueller played in 22 games (19 starts), his last start coming on September 22. They seem to have been playing at the same time—suggesting that perhaps Graham might have even worn #13 in 1935.

We asked Skinny's son, Patriots wide receiver Art Graham, but he didn't know and none of the newspaper clippings he has shed any light.

We've done all the checking we could, short of hopping into a time machine—and if such a contraption did exist, would you really want to use it to see a fourth-place club?

The Phantom

While there are several unconfirmed numbers of men who actually played for the Red Sox, there's also the case of Al Olsen. At one point the pitcher was listed as having batted in a game for the 1943 Red Sox, reportedly May 16. With manpower at a premium during World War II, the Red Sox had taken a look at the southpaw, not yet 22 and coming off an 18–16 record for his native San Diego in the Pacific Coast League. Olsen had worn uniform #14 during spring training, but the most likely scenario is that the pinch hitter was Johnny Lazor. Lazor wore #14 for most of 1943, and he was often used by the Sox for pinch-hitting duties.

Cliff Kachline, historian of the Hall of Fame from 1969 to 1982, pointed out that scorecards were often not kept up to date as to uniform numbers and that some of the spring training names and numbers would often include incorrect attributions. Kachline located a scorecard from the week before the phantom at-bat, when the Red Sox had played in Washington on the same road trip. Olsen was listed as #14 despite the evidence that he was indeed with the San Diego ballclub. Ira Berkow of the *New York Times* called Lazor to ask him in 1990, but it was "so many darn years ago" that his memory was far from certain. At this distance, it seems a safe enough guess that the "phantom" player was Johnny Lazor. Al Olsen has been expunged from American League records.

RED SOX ALPHABETICAL ROSTER (1931–2015)

#	NAME	YEAR
	A	
53	Dave Aardsma	2008
45	Don Aase	1977
53	Andy Abad	2003
86	Brian Abraham	2013 (coach)
91	Alfredo Aceves	2011–13
14	Jerry Adair	1967–68
53	Terry Adams	2004
50	Benny Agbayani	2002
6	Harry Agganis	1954–55
58	Luis Aguayo	2002 (coach)
59	Luis Aguayo	2002 (coach)
38	Rick Aguilera	1995
32	Matt Albers	2011–
56	Israel Alcantara	2000–01
15	Dale Alexander	1932–33
29	Manny Alexander	2000
10	Luis Alicea	1995
16	Luis Alicea	2007–08 (coach)
39	Gary Allenson	1979–84
32	Gary Allenson	1992–94 (coach)
21	Mel Almada	1933, 1935 (his number in 1934 is not confirmed)
1	Mel Almada	1936–37
58	Hector Almonte	2003
41	Luis Alvarado	1968
12	Luis Alvarado	1969–70
1	Luis Alvarado	1970
59	Abe Alvarez	2004–06
42	Larry Andersen	1990

#	NAME	YEAR
48	Larry Andersen	1990
5	Brady Anderson	1988
32	Brian Anderson	2009
46	Jimmy Anderson	2004
44	Lars Anderson	2010
62	Lars Anderson	2011
35	Ernie Andres	1946
11	Kim Andrew	1975
25	Ivy Andrews	1932
16	Ivy Andrews	1933
39	Mike Andrews	1966
2	Mike Andrews	1967–70
2	Shane Andrews	2002
11	Luis Aparicio	1971–73
45	Luis Aponte	1980–83
21	Pete Appleton	1932 (see also Pete Jablonowski)
53	David Aardsma	2008
20	Tony Armas	1983–86
65	Jonathan Aro	2015
19	Rolando Arrojo	2000
46	Rolando Arrojo	2000
44	Rolando Arrojo	2001–02
61	Bronson Arroyo	2003–05
23	Billy Ashley	1998
7	Ken Aspromonte	1957–58
39	Pedro Astacio	2004
48	Scott Atchison	2010–11
12	Jim Atkins	1950
25	Jim Atkins	1952

#	NAME	YEAR
13	Elden Auker	1939
27	Tex Aulds	1947
33	Steve Avery	1997–98
12	Bobby Avila	1959
3	Mike Aviles	2011
11	Ramon Aviles	1977
1	Joe Azcue	1969

	B	
35	Burke Badenhop	2014
17	Jim Bagby	1938–40, 1946
10	Carlos Baerga	2002
30	Bob Bailey	1977–78
43	Buddy Bailey	2000 (coach)
43	Cory Bailey	1993–94
55	Jeff Bailey	2007–09
15	Al Baker	1938
30	Del Baker	1945–48 (coach)
41	Del Baker	1953–54 (coach)
32	Del Baker	1955–60 (coach); 1960 (manager)
29	Floyd Baker	1953
12	Floyd Baker	1954
41	Jack Baker	1976–77
5	Rocco Baldelli	2009
29	Scott Bankhead	1993–94
18	Willie Banks	2001
17	Willie Banks	2002
60	Daniel Bard	2009
51	Daniel Bard	2010
77	Josh Bard	2006
57	Brian Bark	1995
59	Brian Barkley	1998
42	Babe Barna	1943

#	NAME	YEAR
68	Matt Barnes	2014
51	Mike Barnett	2005–09 (assistant coach)
46	Steve Barr	1974–75
17	Frank Barrett	1944–45
17	Marty Barrett	1982–90
33	Tommy Barrett	1992
9	Charlie Berry	1931–32
50	Quintin Berry	2013
50	Aaron Bates	2009
5	Matt Batts	1947
14	Matt Batts	1948–51
40	Frank Baumann	1955–56
15	Frank Baumann	1957–59
44	Jason Bay	2008–09
25	Don Baylor	1986–87
54	Pedro Beato	2012
57	Rod Beck	1999
47	Rod Beck	1999–2001
19	Josh Beckett	2006–10
23	Erik Bedard	2011
43	Stan Belinda	1995–96
39	Gary Bell	1967–68
29	Juan Bell	1995
12	Mark Bellhorn	2004–05
29	Adrian Beltre	2010
10	Esteban Beltre	1996
20	Juan Beniquez	1971–72, 1974–75
28	Mike Benjamin	1997–98
28	Dennis Bennett	1965–67
27	Al Benton	1952
38	Todd Benzinger	1987–88
33	Dick Berardino	1989–91 (coach)

#	NAME	YEAR
36	Lou Berberet	1958
19	Moe Berg	1935
22	Moe Berg	1936–39 (player); 1940–41 (coach)
6	Boze Berger	1939
26	Sean Berry	2000
6	Damon Berryhill	1994
50	Mookie Betts	2014
8	Hal Bevan	1952
43	Arnie Beyeler	2013 (coach)
16	Jeff Bianchi	2015
19	Dante Bichette	2000–01
28	Jack Billingham	1980
42	Doug Bird	1983
1	Max Bishop	1934–35
39	Tim Blackwell	1974–75
47	Greg Blosser	1993–94
52	Mike Boddicker	1988–90
31	Larry Boerner	1932
72	Xander Bogaerts	2013
2	Xander Bogaerts	2013
10	Tim Bogar	2009–10 (coach)
17	Tim Bogar	2011–12 (coach)
26	Wade Boggs	1982–92
77	Kevin Boles	2014 (coach for a day, up from Pawtucket for one day in September—the day after Billy McMillon from Portland)
16	Bob Bolin	1970
26	Bob Bolin	1971–73
18	Milt Bolling	1952
2	Milt Bolling	1953–57

#	NAME	YEAR
50	Tom Bolton	1987–92
30	Boof Bonser	2010
39	Ray Boone	1960
47	Toby Borland	1997
21	Tom Borland	1960
19	Tom Borland	1961
4	Lou Boudreau	1951–52 (player); 1952–54 (manager)
64	Michael Bowden	2008–11
29	Sam Bowen	1977–78, 1980
23	Stew Bowers	1935
16	Stew Bowers	1936
32	Stew Bowers	1937
28	Joe Bowman	1944–45
28	Ted Bowsfield	1958–59
29	Ted Bowsfield	1960
23	Dennis Boyd	1982–89
53	Chad Bradford	2005
44	Jackie Bradley Jr.	2013
25	Jackie Bradley Jr.	2013 (September)
56	Darren Bragg	1996–98
50	Mark Brandenburg	1996–97
27	Darrell Brandon	1966–68
87	Mike Brenly	2015 (bullpen catcher)
73	Bryce Brentz	2014
54	Craig Breslow	2006
32	Craig Breslow	2012
1	Ed Bressoud	1962–65
36	Ken Brett	1967
15	Ken Brett	1969
42	Ken Brett	1969
18	Ken Brett	1970–71

#	NAME	YEAR
23	Tom Brewer	1954–61
26	Ralph Brickner	1952
39	Ralph Brickner	1952
27	Jim Brillheart	1931
66	Drake Britton	2013
24	Dick Brodowski	1952
27	Dick Brodowski	1952
42	Dick Brodowski	1955
11	Rico Brogna	2000
3	Jack Brohamer	1978–80
17	Adrian Brown	2003
39	Corey Brown	2014
59	Dusty Brown	2009
50	Dusty Brown	2009
68	Dusty Brown	2010
52	Jamie Brown	2004
38	Kevin Brown	2002
26	Lloyd Brown	1933
25	Mace Brown	1942–43, 1946
33	Mace Brown	1965 (coach)
27	Mike Brown	1982–86
27	Skinny Brown	1953–55
10	Mike Brumley	1991–92
23	Tom Brunansky	1990–92, 1994
31	Don Bryant	1974–75 (coach)
33	Don Bryant	1976 (coach)
24	Jim Bucher	1944
5	Jim Bucher	1945
61	Clay Buchholz	2007–09
11	Clay Buchholz	2010
16	Bill Buckner	1984
6	Bill Buckner	1985–87
22	Bill Buckner	1990

#	NAME	YEAR
24	Don Buddin	1956, 1958–59
1	Don Buddin	1960–61
2	Damon Buford	1998–99
33	Kirk Bullinger	1999
37	Al Bumbry	1988–93 (coach)
3	Bob Burda	1972
16	Tom Burgmeier	1978–82
19	John Burkett	2002–03
54	Morgan Burkhart	2000–01
12	Ellis Burks	1987–92
25	Ellis Burks	2004
7	Rick Burleson	1974–80 (player); 1992–93 (coach)
31	Jack Burns	1955–59 (coach)
59	Mike Burns	2006
43	Jim Burton	1975, 1977
30	Bill Burwell	1944 (coach)
7	Jim Busby	1959–60
28	Bill Butland	1940, 1946
24	Bill Butland	1942
27	Bill Butland	1947
61	Dan Butler	2014
13	Brian Butterfield	coach (2013–14)
55	Brian Butterfield	coach (2015)
15	Bud Byerly	1958
30	Jim Byrd	1993
36	Paul Byrd	2008, 2009

C

#	NAME	YEAR
53	Fernando Cabrera	2009–10
36	Orlando Cabrera	2004
44	Orlando Cabrera	2004
23	Ivan Calderon	1993
20	Earl Caldwell	1948

#	NAME	YEAR
23	Mike Cameron	2010–11
28	Dolf Camilli	1945
34	Doug Camilli	1970–73 (coach)
22	Bill Campbell	1977–81
37	Paul Campbell	1941
15	Paul Campbell	1942
46	Paul Campbell	1946
33	Jose Canseco	1995–96
55	Chris Capuano	2014
1	Bernie Carbo	1974–78
14	Tom Carey	1939–42, 1946
35	Dave Carlucci	1996 (coach)
37	Mike Carp	2013
52	Chris Carpenter	2012
58	Hector Carrasco	2000
54	Chris Carter	2008–09
19	Jerry Casale	1958–60
66	Joe Cascarella	1935
19	Joe Cascarella	1936
22	Sean Casey	2008
36	Kevin Cash	2007–08
30	Kevin Cash	2008
36	Kevin Cash	2010
57	Scott Cassidy	2005
43	Carlos Castillo	2001
37	Frank Castillo	2001–02, 2004
38	Rusney Castillo	2014
5	Danny Cater	1972–74
70	Garin Cecchini	2014
29	Garin Cecchini	2015
31	Rex Cecil	1944–45
25	Orlando Cepeda	1973
6	Rick Cerone	1988–89

#	NAME	YEAR
51	Yoenis Cespedes	2014
26	Bob Chakales	1957
40	Bob Chakales	1957
26	Wes Chamberlain	1994
32	Wes Chamberlain	1995
1	Ben Chapman	1937
9	Ben Chapman	1938
15	Pete Charton	1964
10	Ken Chase	1942–43
40	Robinson Checo	1997–98
52	Bruce Chen	2003
28	Nels Chittum	1959–60
61	Cho Jin Ho	1998–99
20	Joe Christopher	1966
35	Lloyd Christopher	1945
77	Pedro Ciriaco	2012
23	Pedro Ciriaco	2013
15	Galen Cisco	1961–62
39	Galen Cisco	1967
40	Galen Cisco	1967
2	Bill Cissell	1934
25	Jack Clark	1991–92
18	Otie Clark	1945
23	Phil Clark	1996
22	Tony Clark	2002
11	Royce Clayton	2007
25	Mark Clear	1981–85
21	Roger Clemens	1984–96
30	Matt Clement	2005–06
42	Lance Clemons	1974
33	Reggie Cleveland	1974
26	Reggie Cleveland	1974–78
26	Tex Clevenger	1954

#	NAME	YEAR
4	Lu Clinton	1960
19	Lu Clinton	1961
24	Lu Clinton	1961–62
6	Lu Clinton	1962–64
40	Tony Cloninger	2002–03 (coach)
68	Robert Coello	2010
28	Greg Colbrunn	2013 (coach)
2	Alex Cole	1996
30	Dave Coleman	1977
44	Michael Coleman	1997
40	Michael Coleman	1999
16	Lou Collier	2003
32	Shano Collins	1931 (coach)
31	Shano Collins	1932 (manager)
40	Bartolo Colon	2008
32	Earle Combs	1948–51 (coach)
41	Earle Combs	1952 (coach)
32	Merrill Combs	1947
24	Merrill Combs	1949–50
36	David Cone	2001
4	Billy Conigliaro	1969
1	Billy Conigliaro	1969
40	Billy Conigliaro	1970–71
25	Tony Conigliaro	1964–67, 1969–70, 1975
18	Gene Conley	1961–63
29	Ed Connolly Jr.	1964
11	Ed Connolly Sr.	1931
10	Ed Connolly Sr.	1932
23	Bill Conroy	1942–44
8	Billy Consolo	1953–54
11	Billy Consolo	1955
7	Billy Consolo	1956–57

#	NAME	YEAR
1	Billy Consolo	1957–59
35	Aaron Cook	2012
46	Ryan Cook	2015
7	Dusty Cooke	1933
6	Dusty Cooke	1934
9	Dusty Cooke	1935–36
17	Cecil Cooper	1971–76
15	Cecil Cooper	1976
45	Scott Cooper	1990–92
34	Scott Cooper	1993–94
12	Wil Cordero	1996–97
23	Alex Cora	2005–06
13	Alex Cora	2006–08
48	Vic Correll	1972
63	Bryan Corey	2006
41	Bryan Corey	2007
30	Bryan Corey	2008
34	Rheal Cormier	1995
37	Rheal Cormier	1999–2000
41	Jim Corsi	1997–99
2	Marlan Coughtry	1960
18	Ted Cox	1977
5	Allen Craig	2014
8	Doc Cramer	1935–40
13	Carl Crawford	2011–12
63	Paxton Crawford	2000–01
28	Steve Crawford	1980–82, 1984–87
8	Pat Creeden	1931
31	Cesar Crespo	2004
10	Coco Crisp	2006–08
42	Coco Crisp	2007, 2008 (Jackie Robinson tribute)

#	NAME	YEAR
4	Joe Cronin	1935, 1937–45 (player–manager); 1946–47 (manager)
6	Joe Cronin	1936 (player–manager)
56	Zach Crouch	1988
55	Rich Croushore	2000
32	Jose Cruz Jr.	2005
39	Mike Cubbage	2002–03 (coach)
22	Mike Cubbage	2003 (wore Ron Jackson's shirt for portion of one game)
27	Leon Culberson	1943
11	Leon Culberson	1944–47
21	Ray Culp	1968–73
41	John Cumberland	1995 (coach)
52	John Cumberland	1999–2001 (coach)
29	Midre Cummings	1998
18	Midre Cummings	2000
53	Steve Curry	1988
44	John Curtis	1970
22	John Curtis	1971–73
30	Kiki Cuyler	1949 (coach)
15	Milt Cuyler	1996
D		
8	Babe Dahlgren	1935
16	Babe Dahlgren	1936
24	Pete Daley	1955
8	Pete Daley	1956–59
16	Dom Dallessandro	1937
30	Tom Daly	1935–43 (coach)
32	Tom Daly	1945–46 (coach)
18	Johnny Damon	2002–05
42	Bobby Darwin	1976–77

#	NAME	YEAR
44	Danny Darwin	1991–94
23	Brian Daubach	1999–2002, 2004
25	Red Daughters	1936
21	Red Daughters	1937
44	Chili Davis	2015 (coach)
10	Andre Dawson	1993–94
29	Cot Deal	1947
28	Cot Deal	1948
31	Alejandro DeAza	2015
23	Rob Deer	1993
56	Ivan De Jesus Jr.	2012
62	Rubby De la Rosa	2013–14
65	Jose De la Torre	2013
57	Manny Delcarmen	2005–06
17	Manny Delcarmen	2007–10
56	Alex Delgado	1996
29	Ike Delock	1952–53
12	Ike Delock	1953
15	Ike Delock	1953
14	Ike Delock	1955–63
4	Don Demeter	1966–67
46	Ryan Dempster	2013
31	Brian Denman	1982
17	Sam Dente	1947
35	Sam Dente	1947
23	Mike Derrick	1970
23	Gene Desautels	1937
2	Gene Desautels	1938–40
34	Mel Deutsch	1946
39	Bo Diaz	1977
76	Jonathan Diaz	2013
46	Juan Diaz	2002
28	George Dickey	1935

#	NAME	YEAR
23	George Dickey	1936
19	Emerson Dickman	1936
16	Emerson Dickman	1936, 1938–41
48	Bob Didier	1974
49	Steve Dillard	1975
3	Steve Dillard	1976–77
7	Dom DiMaggio	1940–42, 1946–53
55	Lenny DiNardo	2004–06
39	Bob DiPietro	1951
17	Joe Dobson	1941–43
19	Joe Dobson	1943
15	Joe Dobson	1946–50, 1954
27	Pat Dodson	1986–88
9	Bobby Doerr	1937
1	Bobby Doerr	1938–44, 1946–51
31	Bobby Doerr	1967–69 (coach)
45	John Doherty	1996
39	Andy Dominique	2004
53	Brendan Donnelly	2007
6	Chris Donnels	1995
25	Pete Donohue	1932
40	John Dopson	1989–93
20	Harry Dorish	1947–48
28	Harry Dorish	1949
35	Harry Dorish	1949
16	Harry Dorish	1956
34	Harry Dorish	1963 (coach)
44	Jim Dorsey	1984–85
61	Felix Doubront	2010–12
22	Felix Doubront	2013
48	Rick Down	2001 (coach)
24	Danny Doyle	1943
15	Denny Doyle	1975

#	NAME	YEAR
5	Denny Doyle	1975–77
41	Dick Drago	1974–75, 1978–80
29	Clem Dreisewerd	1944
32	Clem Dreisewerd	1945
23	Clem Dreisewerd	1946
7	J. D. Drew	2007–10
7	Stephen Drew	2013
3	Walt Dropo	1949–52
17	Frank Duffy	1978–79
31	Hugh Duffy	1939 (coach)
14	Bob Duliba	1965
25	Ed Durham	1931
20	Ed Durham	1932
1	Jim Dwyer	1979–80

E

#	NAME	YEAR
21	Arnold Earley	1960–65
7	Mike Easler	1984–85
45	Mike Easler	1993–94 (coach)
43	Dennis Eckersley	1978–84, 1998
41	Sammy Ellis	1996 (coach)
46	Jacoby Ellsbury	2007–09
2	Jacoby Ellsbury	2010
36	Dick Ellsworth	1968–69
28	Steve Ellsworth	1988
43	Alan Embree	2002–05
55	Todd Erdos	2001
7	Nick Esasky	1989
71	Edwin Escobar	2014
52	Vaughn Eshelman	1995–97
2	Al Evans	1951
25	Bill Evans	1951
40	Dwight Evans	1972–73
24	Dwight Evans	1973–90

#	NAME	YEAR
25	Dwight Evans	2002 (coach)
2	Carl Everett	2000–01
31	Hoot Evers	1952–54
	F	
28	Bibb Falk	1934 (coach)
20	Carmen Fanzone	1970
41	Steve Farr	1993
31	Jeff Fassero	2000
22	Doc Farrell	1935
52	John Farrell	2007–10 (coach)
53	John Farrell	2013 (manager)
9	Rick Ferrell	1933
7	Rick Ferrell	1934–35
2	Rick Ferrell	1936–37
12	Wes Ferrell	1934–37
33	Dave Ferriss	1945–50, 1955–59 (coach)
44	Joel Finch	1979
23	Tommy Fine	1947
26	Lou Finney	1939
25	Lou Finney	1940
8	Lou Finney	1941–42, 1945
16	Lou Finney	1944
46	Gar Finnvold	1994
3	Mike Fiore	1970–71
34	Bill Fischer	1985–91 (coach)
38	Hank Fischer	1966–67
21	Hank Fischer	1967
40	Carlton Fisk	1969
27	Carlton Fisk	1971–80
15	John Flaherty	1992–93
16	Al Flair	1941
28	Bill Fleming	1940

#	NAME	YEAR
23	Bill Fleming	1941
5	Scott Fletcher	1993–94
39	Bryce Florie	1999–2001
36	Ben Flowers	1951
25	Ben Flowers	1953
12	Cliff Floyd	2002
50	Chad Fonville	1999
20	Mike Fornieles	1957–63
48	Tony Fossas	1991–94
59	Casey Fossum	2001
15	Casey Fossum	2002
23	Casey Fossum	2003
13	Bob Fothergill	1933
29	Keith Foulke	2004–06
44	Chad Fox	2003
43	Matt Fox	2010
12	Pete Fox	1941–45
3	Jimmie Foxx	1936–42
1	Joe Foy	1966–68
47	Terry Francona	2004–10 (manager)
28	Hersh Freeman	1952
23	Hersh Freeman	1953
25	Hersh Freeman	1955
6	Bernie Friberg	1933
22	Owen Friend	1955
35	Todd Frohwirth	1994
3	Jeff Frye	1996–97, 1999–2000
14	Curt Fullerton	1933
	G	
61	Kason Gabbard	2006–07
6	Gary Gaetti	2000
25	Fabian Gaffke	1938
19	Fabian Gaffke	1937

#	NAME	YEAR
26	Fabian Gaffke	1939
1	Phil Gagliano	1971–72
83	Eric Gagne	2007
30	Rich Gale	1984
35	Rich Gale	1992–93 (coach)
11	Denny Galehouse	1939
12	Denny Galehouse	1940
25	Denny Galehouse	1947–49
44	Bob Gallagher	1972
1	Ed Gallagher	1932
61	Mike Gambino	2002 (coach)
27	Bob Garbark	1945
34	Rich Garces	1996–2002
5	Nomar Garciaparra	1996–2004
47	Mike Gardiner	1991–92
10	Billy Gardner	1962
24	Billy Gardner	1962
15	Billy Gardner	1963
31	Billy Gardner	1965–66
44	Wes Gardner	1986–90
39	Mike Garman	1969, 1971–73
15	Ford Garrison	1943
19	Milt Gaston	1931
20	Milt Gaston	1931
23	Joey Gathright	2009
55	Joey Gathright	2011
50	Rich Gedman	1980
10	Rich Gedman	1981–90
37	Gary Geiger	1959–60
7	Gary Geiger	1960–62
3	Gary Geiger	1963–65
15	Charlie Gelbert	1940
14	Dick Gernert	1952

#	NAME	YEAR
3	Dick Gernert	1953–54
41	Dick Gernert	1955
25	Dick Gernert	1956–59
25	Jeremy Giambi	2003
35	Russ Gibson	1967–69
42	Andy Gilbert	1942, 1946
35	Don Gile	1959
38	Don Gile	1960–62
28	Bernard Gilkey	2000
21	Bob Gillespie	1950
24	Joe Ginsberg	1961
26	Joe Glenn	1940
48	Chuck Goggin	1974
5	Jonny Gomes	2013
61	Wayne Gomes	2002
50	Mauro Gomez	2012
19	Joe Gonzales	1937
35	Joe Gonzales	1937
28	Adrian Gonzalez	2011–12
11	Alex Gonzalez	2006
13	Alex Gonzalez	2009
3	Alex Gonzalez	2009
51	Enrique Gonzalez	2009
32	Geremi Gonzalez	2005
54	Geremi Gonzalez	2005
8	Johnny Gooch	1933
28	Billy Goodman	1947
10	Billy Goodman	1948–57
36	Tom Gordon	1996–99
25	Jim Gosger	1963
4	Jim Gosger	1965–66
10	Tony Graffanino	2005
12	Lee Graham	1983

#	NAME	YEAR
14	Skinny Graham	1934–35
24	Dave Gray	1964
38	Jeff Gray	1990–91
15	Craig Grebeck	2001
7	Lennie Green	1965–66
22	Nick Green	2009
12	Pumpsie Green	1959–62
39	Mike Greenwell	1985–96
35	Goose Gregson	2003 (coach)
2	Doug Griffin	1971–77
37	Guido Grilli	1966
15	Marv Grissom	1953
27	Kip Gross	1999
10	Lefty Grove	1934–41
57	Ken Grundt	1996
59	Ken Grundt	1997
39	Creighton Gubanich	1999
8	Mike Guerra	1951
65	Ino Guerrero	2003–12 (batting practice pitcher–coach)
85	Ino Guerrero	2013 (coach)
41	Mario Guerrero	1973
18	Mario Guerrero	1973–74
51	Bob Guindon	1964
24	Randy Gumpert	1952
28	Eric Gunderson	1995–96
40	Mark Guthrie	1999
41	Jackie Gutierrez	1983–85
16	Ricky Gutierrez	2004
10	Don Gutteridge	1946–47

	H	
33	Harvey Haddix	1971 (coach)

#	NAME	YEAR
54	John Halama	2005
22	DeMarlo Hale	2011 (coach)
35	DeMarlo Hale	2006–10 (coach)
42	DeMarlo Hale	2007, 2008 (coach; Jackie Robinson tribute)
6	Odell Hale	1941
22	Bill Hall	2010
32	Chris Hammond	1997
38	Garry Hancock	1978
37	Garry Hancock	1980–82
53	Josh Hancock	2002
56	Chris Haney	2002
10	Ryan Hanigan	2015
52	Joel Hanrahan	2013
68	Devern Hansack	2006
46	Devern Hansack	2007
43	Devern Hansack	2007–08
56	Craig Hansen	2005–06, 2008
40	Erik Hanson	1995
16	Carroll Hardy	1960–62
56	Tim Harikkala	1999
4	Tommy Harper	1972–74
32	Tommy Harper	1980–84 (coach)
51	Tommy Harper	2000–02 (coach)
10	Billy Harrell	1961
40	Ken Harrelson	1967–69
11	Bill Harris	1938
27	Bucky Harris	1934 (manager)
42	Greg Harris	1989
27	Greg Harris	1989–94
20	Mickey Harris	1940
19	Mickey Harris	1941, 1946–49

#	NAME	YEAR
23	Reggie Harris	1996
2	Willie Harris	2006
39	Jack Harshman	1959
23	Chuck Hartenstein	1970
49	Mike Hartley	1995
43	Chad Harville	2005
37	Bill Haselman	1995–97 (player); 2005 (coach)
44	Bill Haselman	2003 (player); 2004 (coach)
32	Bill Haselman	2005 (coach)
29	Herb Hash	1940
24	Herb Hash	1941
68	Alex Hassan	2014
31	Andy Hassler	1978–79
22	Billy Hatcher	1992–94
39	Fred Hatfield	1950
27	Fred Hatfield	1951
1	Fred Hatfield	1952
30	Scott Halleberg	1995
47	Scott Hatteberg	1996
10	Scott Hatteberg	1997–2001
1	Grady Hatton	1954–56
21	Clem Hausmann	1944–45
25	Frankie Hayes	1947
32	Richie Hebner	1989–91 (coach)
29	Danny Heep	1989–90
20	Bob Heffner	1963–65
37	Randy Heflin	1945
19	Randy Heflin	1945
26	Randy Heflin	1946
12	Bob Heise	1975–76

#	NAME	YEAR
49	Tommy Helms	1977
12	Tommy Helms	1977
38	Heath Hembree	2014 (prior to September 17)
37	Heath Hembree	2014–15 (as of September 17, 2014)
40	Dave Henderson	1986
42	Dave Henderson	1987
35	Rickey Henderson	2002
26	Bill Henry	1952
28	Bill Henry	1953–54
29	Bill Henry	1954–55
27	Butch Henry	1997–98
21	Jim Henry	1936–37
35	Billy Herman	1960–64 (coach); 1964–66 (manager)
31	Dustin Hermanson	2002
32	Jeremy Hermida	2010
29	Ramon Hernandez	1977
10	Jonathan Herrera	2014
24	Tom Herrin	1954
55	Joe Hesketh	1990–94
31	Eric Hetzel	1989–90
19	Joe Heving	1938–40
5	Pinky Higgins	1937–38 (player); 1955–62 (manager)
36	Pinky Higgins	1946
53	Rich Hill	2010–11
62	Rich Hill	2015
29	Shea Hillenbrand	2001–03
17	Dave Hillman	1960–61
9	Gordie Hinkle	1934
94	Dalier Hinojosa	2015

#	NAME	YEAR
24	Paul Hinrichs	1951
12	Eric Hinske	2006–07
24	Harley Hisner	1951
11	Billy Hitchcock	1948–49
51	Butch Hobson	1975
4	Butch Hobson	1976–80
17	Butch Hobson	1992–94 (manager)
28	George Hockette	1934–35
5	Johnny Hodapp	1933
2	Mel Hoderlein	1951
28	Mel Hoderlein	1951
39	Billy Hoeft	1959
18	Glenn Hoffman	1980–87
14	Ken Holcombe	1953
27	Dave Hollins	1995
23	Billy Holm	1945
26	Brock Holt	2013
43	Mike Holtz	2006
30	Sam Horn	1987–89
30	Tony Horton	1964–65
11	Tony Horton	1966–67
46	Dwayne Hosey	1995–96
35	Ralph Houk	1981–84 (manager)
29	Tom House	1976–77
17	Wayne Housie	1991
31	Chris Howard	1994
18	Elston Howard	1967–68
46	Bob Howry	2002–03
31	Peter Hoy	1992
33	Walt Hriniak	1977–88 (coach)
40	Ken Huckaby	2006
54	Joe Hudson	1995–97
20	Sid Hudson	1952–54

#	NAME	YEAR
38	Terry Hughes	1974
15	Tex Hughson	1941
29	Tex Hughson	1941
21	Tex Hughson	1942–43, 1946–49
27	Tex Hughson	1944
33	Rudy Hulswitt	1931 (coach)
32	Rudy Hulswitt	1932 (coach)
31	Rudy Hulswitt	1933 (coach)
19	Bill Humphrey	1938
38	Buddy Hunter	1971, 1973
3	Buddy Hunter	1973
5	Buddy Hunter	1975
28	Tom Hurd	1954, 1956
47	Bruce Hurst	1980–88
44	Butch Huskey	1999
77	Tim Hyers	2014 (interim hitting coach) following Greg Colbrunn's subarachnoid hemorrhage
37	Adam Hyzdu	2004
25	Adam Hyzdu	2005
I		
68	Jose Iglesias	2011 (May 8 only)
76	Jose Iglesias	2011 (beginning May 9)
58	Jose Iglesias	2012
10	Jose Iglesias	2013
59	Daryl Irvine	1990–92
J		
21	Pete Jablonowski	1932 (changed name to Pete Appleton in 1933)
32	Al Jackson	1977–79 (coach)

#	NAME	YEAR
36	Conor Jackson	2011
2	Damian Jackson	2003
5	Ron Jackson	1960
22	Ron D. Jackson	2003–05 (coach)
15	Ron D. Jackson	2006 (coach)
22	Chris James	1995
39	Kevin Jarvis	2006
17	Ray Jarvis	1969–70
26	Ray Jarvis	1970
48	Dave Jauss	1997–98 (coach)
43	Dave Jauss	1999 (coach)
38	Dave Jauss	2001 (coach)
18	Reggie Jefferson	1995–99
31	Ferguson Jenkins	1976–77
52	Bobby Jenks	2011
30	Jackie Jensen	1954
4	Jackie Jensen	1955–59, 1961
28	Marcus Jensen	2001
16	Luis Jimenez	2015
51	Keith Johns	1998
8	Bob Johnson	1944–45
61	Brian Johnson	2015
33	Darrell Johnson	1968–69 (coach)
22	Darrell Johnson	1974–76 (manager)
15	Deron Johnson	1975
30	Deron Johnson	1974, 1976
20	Earl Johnson	1940–41
12	Earl Johnson	1946–50
18	Hank Johnson	1933
16	Hank Johnson	1934–35
18	Jason Johnson	2006
48	John Henry Johnson	1983–84
7	Kelly Johnson	2014

#	NAME	YEAR
50	Ron Johnson	2010 (coach)
18	Roy Johnson	1932
3	Roy Johnson	1933, 1935
4	Roy Johnson	1934
17	Tim Johnson	1995–96 (coach)
16	Vic Johnson	1944
34	Vic Johnson	1945
45	Joel Johnston	1995
9	Smead Jolley	1932
4	Smead Jolley	1933
36	Bobby M. Jones	2004
39	Dalton Jones	1964–65
3	Dalton Jones	1966–69
62	Hunter Jones	2009
3	Jake Jones	1947–48
35	Lynn Jones	2004–05 (coach)
46	Rick Jones	1976
59	Todd Jones	2003
20	Eddie Joost	1955
24	Duane Josephson	1971–72
34	Oscar Judd	1941
29	Oscar Judd	1942–45
23	Joe Judge	1933
25	Joe Judge	1934
22	Ed Jurak	1982–85
16	Bill Jurges	1959–60 (manager)
K		
55	Ryan Kalish	2010, 2012
70	Ryan Kalish	2012 (June 17 game only)
85	Don Kalkstein	2006–08 (psychology coach)
29	Gabe Kapler	2003

#	NAME	YEAR
19	Gabe Kapler	2004
44	Gabe Kapler	2005–06
19	Andy Karl	1943
24	Andy Karl	1943
2	Eddie Kasko	1966
30	Eddie Kasko	1970–73 (manager)
1	George Kell	1952–54
8	Red Kellett	1934
56	Joe Kelly	2014
4	Ken Keltner	1950
24	Russ Kemmerer	1954
40	Russ Kemmerer	1955
28	Russ Kemmerer	1957
18	Fred Kendall	1978
18	Bill Kennedy	1953
12	John Kennedy	1970–74
44	Kevin Kennedy	1995–96 (manager)
20	Marty Keough	1956
41	Marty Keough	1957
2	Marty Keough	1958–60
16	Joe Kerrigan	1997–2001 (coach)
19	Dana Kiecker	1990–91
32	Bobby Kielty	2007
25	Leo Kiely	1951
27	Leo Kiely	1951
19	Leo Kiely	1954–56
17	Leo Kiely	1958–59
51	Byung–Hyun Kim	2003–04
31	Wendell Kim	1997 (coach)
12	Wendell Kim	1998–2000 (coach)
62	Sun–Woo Kim	2001
47	Sun–Woo Kim	2002
16	Ellis Kinder	1948–55

#	NAME	YEAR
16	Bob Kipper	2002
77	Bob Kipper	2015 (interim bullpen coach, from August 17)
29	Bruce Kison	1985
35	Billy Klaus	1955–58
28	Bob Kline	1931
24	Bob Kline	1932–33
26	Ron Kline	1969
37	Bob Klinger	1946–47
59	Brent Knackert	1996
42	Hal Kolstad	1962
28	Hal Kolstad	1962–63
17	Cal Koonce	1970–71
44	Andy Kosco	1972
11	Casey Kotchman	2009
11	Mark Kotsay	2008
68	George Kottaras	2008
16	George Kottaras	2009
18	Jack Kramer	1948–49
18	Lew Krausse	1972
21	Rick Kreuger	1975–77
29	John Kroner	1935
26	John Kroner	1936
55	Randy Kutcher	1988
5	Randy Kutcher	1989–90
L		
36	Rene Lachemann	1985–86 (coach)
40	John Lackey	2010
53	Kerry Lacy	1996–97
1	Ty LaForest	1945
54	Roger LaFrancois	1982
15	Joe Lahoud	1968

#	NAME	YEAR
24	Joe Lahoud	1968
14	Joe Lahoud	1969–71
7	Eddie Lake	1943–45
33	Al Lakeman	1963–64 (coach)
34	Al Lakeman	1967–69 (coach)
36	Jack Lamabe	1963–65
31	Gene Lamont	2001 (coach)
15	Dennis Lamp	1988–91
10	Rick Lancellotti	1990
29	Bill Landis	1967–69
15	Jim Landis	1967
4	Carney Lansford	1981–82
3	Mike Lansing	2000–01
23	Adam LaRoche	2009
88	Jason LaRocque	2005–07 (Bullpen coach)
26	John LaRose	1978
21	Lyn Lary	1934
60	Ryan Lavarnway	2011–12
20	Ryan Lavarnway	2013
59	Tommy Layne	2014
82	Johnny Lazor	1943
14	Johnny Lazor	1943–45
29	Johnny Lazor	1946
77	Rob Leary	2010 (coach)
37	Bill Lee	1969–78
40	Sang–Hoon Lee	2000
15	Lefty Lefebvre	1938–39
21	Lou Legett	1933
28	Lou Legett	1934
24	Lou Legett	1934–35
25	Regis Leheny	1932
37	Paul Lehner	1952

#	NAME	YEAR
22	John Leister	1987
38	John Leister	1990
15	Mark Lemke	1998
31	Don Lenhardt	1952
32	Don Lenhardt	1954
31	Don Lenhardt	1970–73 (coach)
3	Sandy Leon	2015
12	Ted Lepcio	1952, 1955–59
5	Ted Lepcio	1953–54
30	Curtis Leskanic	2004
62	Jon Lester	2006
31	Jon Lester	2007–10
60	Dana LeVangie	1997–2004 (coach)
58	Dana LeVangie	2013 (coach)
20	Darren Lewis	1998–2001
31	Jim Leyritz	1998
29	John Lickert	1981
23	Brent Lillibridge	2012
28	Derek Lilliquist	1995
85	Che–Hsuan Lin	2012 (first time)
67	Che–Hsuan Lin	2012 (from August)
6	Johnny Lipon	1952–53
24	Hod Lisenbee	1931
22	Hod Lisenbee	1932
35	Grady Little	1997–99 (coach)
3	Grady Little	2002–03 (manager)
34	Dick Littlefield	1950
28	Greg Litton	1994
18	Don Lock	1969
38	Skip Lockwood	1980
52	James Lofton	2001
48	Tim Lollar	1985–86
56	Steve Lomasney	1999

#	NAME	YEAR
16	Jim Lonborg	1965–71
22	James Loney	2012
51	Brian Looney	1995
32	Felipe Lopez	2010
48	Javier Lopez	2006–09
23	Javy Lopez	2006
18	Javy Lopez	2006 (did not appear in a game with this number)
86	Adrian Lorenzo	2015 (coach)
3	Mark Loretta	2006
17	Torey Lovullo	2013–14 (coach)
43	Derek Lowe	1997
32	Derek Lowe	1998–2004
25	Mike Lowell	2006–10
12	Jed Lowrie	2008–10
16	Johnny Lucas	1931–32
15	Lou Lucier	1943
81	Lou Lucier	1943
24	Lou Lucier	1944
23	Julio Lugo	2007–09
32	Tony Lupien	1940
16	Tony Lupien	1942
3	Tony Lupien	1943
15	Sparky Lyle	1967
28	Sparky Lyle	1967–71
19	Fred Lynn	1974–80
38	Brandon Lyon	2003
12	Steve Lyons	1985–86
7	Steve Lyons	1991
19	Steve Lyons	1992
30	Steve Lyons	1993

M

#	NAME	YEAR
15	Mike MacFarlane	1895
21	Danny MacFayden	1931
18	Danny MacFayden	1932
40	Alejandro Machado	2005
64	Jean Machi	2015
15	Shane Mack	1997
24	Shane Mack	1997
47	Billy MacLeod	1962
31	Keith MacWhorter	1980
19	Mike Maddux	1995–96
29	Dave Magadan	2007–08, 2009 (coach)
28	Dave Magadan	2009–10 (coach)
33	Sal Maglie	1960–62, 1966–67 (coach)
36	Pete Magrini	1966
46	Ron Mahay	1995
57	Ron Mahay	1997–98
59	Pat Mahomes	1996–97
1	Jim Mahoney	1959
46	Mark Malaska	2004
38	Jose Malave	1996–97
39	Jerry Mallett	1959
32	Harry Malmberg	1963–64 (coach)
43	Frank Malzone	1955
11	Frank Malzone	1956–65
31	Matt Mantei	2005
12	Felix Mantilla	1963–65
48	Jeff Manto	1996
2	Jeff Manto	1996
59	Robert Manuel	2010
7	Heinie Manush	1936
51	Josias Manzanillo	1991
26	Phil Marchildon	1950

#	NAME	YEAR
12	Johnny Marcum	1938
11	Johnny Marcum	1936–37
21	Juan Marichal	1974
7	Ollie Marquardt	1931
16	Deven Marrero	2015
7	Bill Marshall	1931
22	Mike Marshall	1990–91
34	Babe Martin	1948–49
88	Alex "Mani" Martinez	2007–10 (bullpen catcher)
67	Anastacio Martinez	2004
45	Pedro Martinez	1998–2004
48	Ramon Martinez	1999–2000
58	Sandy Martinez	2004
41	Victor Martinez	2009–10
37	John Marzano	1987
20	John Marzano	1988–92
63	Justin Masterson	2008–09
20	Walt Masterson	1949–52
3	Tom Matchick	1970
18	Daisuke Matsuzaka	2007–10
24	Gene Mauch	1956–57
37	Charley Maxwell	1950, 1952
26	Charley Maxwell	1951
35	Charley Maxwell	1954
33	Eddie Mayo	1951 (coach)
3	Dick McAuliffe	1974–75
42	Tom McBride	1943
25	Tom McBride	1944–45
18	Tom McBride	1946–47
35	Windy McCall	1948–49
–	Joe McCarthy	1948–50 (manager; wore no number)

#	NAME	YEAR
43	Tommy McCarthy	1985
10	David McCarty	2003–05
33	Tim McCarver	1974–75
22	Bob McClure	2012 (coach)
36	Mickey McDermott	1948–49
19	Mickey McDermott	1949–53
46	Allen McDill	2001
54	Darnell McDonald	2010
26	Jim McDonald	1950
10	John McDonald	2013
38	Ed McGah	1946
2	Ed McGah	1947
27	Ed McGah	1947
51	Willie McGee	1995
36	Lynn McGlothen	1972–73
20	Archie McKain	1937
14	Archie McKain	1938
40	Bill McKechnie	1952–53 (coach)
45	Walt McKeel	1996–97
36	John McLaren	1991 (coach)
30	Jud McLaughlin	1931
16	Jud McLaughlin	1932
44	Don McMahon	1966–67
28	Marty McManus	1932
3	Marty McManus	1932
2	Marty McManus	1933 (manager)
77	Billy McMillon	2014 (coach for a day, up from Portland in September)
4	Eric McNair	1936
6	Eric McNair	1937–38
1	John McNamara	1985–88 (manager)
2	John McNamara	1988 (manager)

#	NAME	YEAR
16	Gordon McNaughton	1932
58	Jeff McNeely	1993
32	Jerry McNertney	1988 (coach)
27	Bill McWilliams	1931
4	Roman Mejias	1963–64
37	Mark Melancon	2012
14	Sam Mele	1947
4	Sam Mele	1948–49
31	Sam Mele	1954
7	Sam Mele	1955
19	Jose Melendez	1993–94
5	Oscar Melillo	1935
24	Oscar Melillo	1935–37
42	Oscar Melillo	1952–53 (coach)
3	Bob Melvin	1993
55	Ramiro Mendoza	2003
26	Ramiro Mendoza	2003–04
3	Mike Meola	1933
23	Mike Meola	1933
16	Mike Meola	1936
26	Orlando Merced	1998
50	Andy Merchant	1975–76
41	Kent Mercker	1999
51	Cla Meredith	2005
40	Cla Meredith	2005
30	Spike Merena	1934
50	Lou Merloni	1998
26	Lou Merloni	1999–2002
13	Lou Merloni	2003
12	Jack Merson	1953
2	George Metkovich	1943–46
20	Russ Meyer	1957
27	John Michaels	1932

#	NAME	YEAR
64	Will Middlebrooks	2012
16	Will Middlebrooks	2013
27	Dick Midkiff	1938
13	Doug Mientkiewicz	2004
2	Dee Miles	1943
20	Wade Miley	2015
15	Kevin Millar	2003–05
30	Andrew Miller	2011
25	Bing Miller	1935
27	Bing Miller	1936
27	Bing Miller	1937 (coach)
36	Corky Miller	2006
5	Otis Miller	1931
8	Otis Miller	1932
35	Rick Miller	1971
16	Rick Miller	1972–77
3	Rick Miller	1981–85
52	Wade Miller	2005
58	Trever Miller	2011
7	Buster Mills	1937
40	Buster Mills	1954 (coach)
2	Brad Mills	2004–05, 2007 (coach)
31	Brad Mills	2006 (coach)
36	Dick Mills	1970
29	Rudy Minarcin	1956–57
57	Nate Minchey	1993–94
58	Nate Minchey	1996
28	Doug Mirabelli	2001–07
38	Charlie Mitchell	1984–85
30	Keith Mitchell	1998
24	Kevin Mitchell	1996
42	Herb Moford	1959

#	NAME	YEAR
18	Dustan Mohr	2006
44	Gustavo Molina	2010
58	Bill Moloney	1997–2000 (coach)
27	Bill Monbouquette	1958–65
39	Bob Montgomery	1970
10	Bob Montgomery	1971–79
37	Jackie Moore	1968 (coach)
31	Wilcy Moore	1931
19	Wilcy Moore	1932
46	Franklin Morales	2011–12
56	Franklin Morales	2013
23	Dave Morehead	1963–66
17	Dave Morehead	1967
37	Dave Morehead	1968
29	Roger Moret	1970–75
23	Roger Moret	1975 (wore number for one game)
3	Eddie Morgan	1934
35	Joe Morgan	1985–88 (coach); 1988–91 (manager)
23	Ed Morris	1931
59	Clayton Mortensen	2012
39	Guy Morton	1954
43	Kevin Morton	1991
41	Jerry Moses	1965
10	Jerry Moses	1968–70
24	Wally Moses	1946–48
44	Brandon Moss	2007–08
14	Les Moss	1951
50	Jamie Moyer	1996
11	Bill Mueller	2003–05
25	Gordy Mueller	1950

#	NAME	YEAR
36	Billy Muffett	1960–62
54	Edward Mujica	2014
26	Greg Mulleavy	1933
21	Freddie Muller	1934
14	Joe Mulligan	1934
60	David Murphy	2006
44	David Murphy	2007
38	Johnny Murphy	1947
47	Rob Murphy	1989–90
47	Tom Murphy	1976–77
29	Walter Murphy	1931
45	Matt Murray	1995
43	Tony Muser	1969
28	Alex Mustaikis	1940
36	Mike Myers	2004–05
	N	
49	Chris Nabholz	1994
11	Tim Naehring	1990–97
15	Mike Nagy	1969–72
12	Mike Napoli	2013
41	Jerry Narron	2003 (coach)
60	Daniel Nava	2010–11
66	Daniel Nava	2012
29	Daniel Nava	2013
56	Yamaico Navarro	2010
60	Yamaico Navarro	2011
59	Blaine Neal	2005
58	Bryant Nelson	2002
57	Joe Nelson	2004
46	Joe Nelson	2010
28	Don Newhauser	1972–74
5	Jeff Newman	1983–84

#	NAME	YEAR
12	Bobo Newsom	1937
28	Dick Newsome	1941–43
26	Skeeter Newsome	1941–44
6	Skeeter Newsome	1945
11	Gus Niarhos	1952–53
31	Chet Nichols	1960–63
51	Reid Nichols	1980–84
13	Reid Nichols	1985
68	Randy Niemann	2012 (coach)
29	Al Niemiec	1934
47	Juan Nieves	2013 (coach)
49	Al Nipper	1983–87
47	Al Nipper	1995–96 (coach)
41	Al Nipper	2006 (coach)
15	Merlin Nippert	1962
19	Merlin Nippert	1962
2	Otis Nixon	1994
22	Russ Nixon	1960–62
5	Russ Nixon	1963–65
15	Russ Nixon	1968
7	Trot Nixon	1996, 1998–2006
21	Willard Nixon	1950–54, 1957–58
15	Willard Nixon	1955–56
58	Nellie Norman	2001 (coach)
11	Hideo Nomo	2001
24	Leo Nonnenkamp	1938–40
60	Matt Noone	2007–09 (batting practice pitcher–coach)
29	Jon Nunally	1999

0

#	NAME	YEAR
50	Mike O'Berry	1979
19	Syd O'Brien	1969

#	NAME	YEAR
23	Tom O'Brien	1949–50
36	Alex Ochoa	2012 (coach)
30	Jose Offerman	1999–2002
41	Alexi Ogando	2015
4	Ben Oglivie	1971
14	Ben Oglivie	1972–73
53	Tomokazu Ohka	1999–2000
18	Tomokazu Ohka	2001
28	Bob Ojeda	1980
19	Bob Ojeda	1981–85
37	Hideki Okajima	2007–10
33	Len Okrie	1952
34	Len Okrie	1952
32	Len Okrie	1961–62 (coach)
34	Len Okrie	1965–66 (coach)
25	Troy O'Leary	1995–2001
19	John Olerud	2005
16	Dave Oliver	1995–96 (coach)
36	Darren Oliver	2002
22	Gene Oliver	1968
39	Joe Oliver	2001
14	Tom Oliver	1931–32
12	Tom Oliver	1933
28	Karl Olson	1951
34	Karl Olson	1953–54
21	Karl Olson	1955
10	Marv Olson	1931
5	Marv Olson	1932
14	Marv Olson	1933
28	Ted Olson	1936–37
12	Ted Olson	1938
15	Emmett O'Neill	1943–45

#	NAME	YEAR
30	Steve O'Neill	1950 (coach); 1950–51 (manager)
26	Jack Onslow	1934 (coach)
41	Steve Ontiveros	2000
34	David Ortiz	2003–10
42	David Ortiz	2007, 2008, 2009 (Jackie Robinson tribute)
51	Luis Ortiz	1993–94
19	Dan Osinski	1966
37	Dan Osinski	1967
19	Fritz Ostermueller	1934
24	Fritz Ostermueller	1935
14	Fritz Ostermueller	1935–37
21	Fritz Ostermueller	1938–40
27	Johnny Ostrowski	1948
6	Marv Owen	1940
11	Mickey Owen	1954
30	Mickey Owen	1955–56 (coach)
5	Spike Owen	1986
12	Spike Owen	1986
7	Spike Owen	1987–88
60	Henry Owens	2015

P

#	NAME	YEAR
44	Vicente Padilla	2012
67	David Page	2006–10 (strength coach)
22	Jim Pagliaroni	1955
29	Jim Pagliaroni	1960–62
20	Mike Palm	1948
42	Jim Pankovits	1990
34	Al Papai	1950
58	Jonathan Papelbon	2005–10
12	Stan Papi	1979–80

#	NAME	YEAR
17	Mel Parnell	1947–56
25	Larry Parrish	1988
6	Roy Partee	1943–44
16	Roy Partee	1946–47
26	Stan Partenheimer	1944
3	Eric Patterson	2010
11	Hank Patterson	1932
33	Marty Pattin	1972–73
60	David Pauley	2006
62	David Pauley	2008
19	Don Pavletich	1970–71
48	Mike Paxton	1977
44	Jay Payton	2005
23	Johnny Peacock	1937–40, 1944
11	Johnny Peacock	1941–43
9	Johnny Peacock	1944 (wore number for one game)
44	Jake Peavy	2013
64	Dustin Pedroia	2006
15	Dustin Pedroia	2007–10
39	Carlos Peguero	2015
39	Eddie Pellagrini	1946–47
57	Rudy Pemberton	1996
44	Rudy Pemberton	1997
26	Alejandro Pena	1995
37	Carlos Pena	2006
38	Jesus Pena	2000
57	Juan Pena	1999
6	Tony Pena	1990–93
22	Wily Mo Pena	2006–07
17	Herb Pennock	1934
31	Herb Pennock	1936–38 (coach)
31	Brad Pennington	1996

#	NAME	YEAR
36	Brad Penny	2009
5	Tony Perez	1980–82
46	Matt Perisho	2005
31	Robert Person	2003
6	Johnny Pesky	1942, 1946–52 (player); 1981–84, 2002, 2004 (coach)
22	Johnny Pesky	1963–64 (manager)
35	Johnny Pesky	1975–80 (coach); 1980 (manager)
13	Roberto Petagine	2005
43	Gary Peters	1970–72
38	Rico Petrocelli	1963, 1965
6	Rico Petrocelli	1966–76
46	Dan Petry	1991
19	Dave Philley	1962
27	Ed Phillips	1970
35	Hipolito Pichardo	2000–01
57	Calvin Pickering	2001
1	Urbane Pickering	1931
34	Urbane Pickering	1931
8	Urbane Pickering	1931
7	Urbane Pickering	1932
56	Jeff Pierce	1995
24	Jimmy Piersall	1950
2	Jimmy Piersall	1952
37	Jimmy Piersall	1953–58
40	A.J. Pierzynski	2014
36	Joel Pineiro	2007
11	George Pipgras	1933
14	George Pipgras	1934
18	George Pipgras	1935
45	Greg Pirkl	1996

#	NAME	YEAR
24	Juan Pizarro	1968–69
7	Phil Plantier	1990
29	Phil Plantier	1991–92
1	Herb Plews	1959
54	Jeff Plympton	1991
34	Johnny Podres	1980 (coach)
26	Scott Podsednik	2012
20	Jennings Poindexter	1936
45	Dick Pole	1973–76
38	Dick Pole	1998 (coach)
19	Nick Polly	1945
32	Ed Popowski	1967–74 (coach); 1969 (manager)
36	Ed Popowski	1975–76 (coach)
17	Tom Poquette	1979, 1981
22	Rick Porcello	2015
23	Dick Porter	1934
16	Bob Porterfield	1956
20	Bob Porterfield	1956
19	Bob Porterfield	1957–58
31	Mark Portugal	1999
24	Nelson Potter	1941
17	Ken Poulsen	1967
48	Arquimidez Pozo	1996
29	Arquimidez Pozo	1997
49	Joe Price	1989
2	Curtis Pride	1997
11	Curtis Pride	2000
41	Bill Pulsipher	2001
46	Bill Pulsipher	2001
5	Nick Punto	2012
2	Frankie Pytlak	1941

#	NAME	YEAR
24	Frankie Pytlak	1945–46
Q		
49	Paul Quantrill	1992–94
26	Frank Quinn	1949–50
51	Rey Quinones	1986
18	Carlos Quintana	1988–91, 1993
62	Guillermo Quiroz	2012
R		
17	Dick Radatz	1962–66
15	Dave Rader	1980
42	Chuck Rainey	1979–82
60	Hanley Ramirez	2005
13	Hanley Ramirez	2015
24	Manny Ramirez	2001–08
66	Noe Ramirez	2015
56	Ramon Ramirez	2009–10
5	Anthony Ranaudo	2014
28	Pat Rapp	1999
41	Jeff Reardon	1990–92
68	Josh Reddick	2009
46	Josh Reddick	2010
39	Josh Reddick	2010
16	Josh Reddick	2011
28	Johnny Reder	1932
45	Jerry Reed	1990
52	Jody Reed	1987
3	Jody Reed	1988–92
3	Pokey Reese	2004
2	Bobby Reeves	1931
37	Mike Remlinger	2005
49	Win Remmerswaal	1979–80
2	Jerry Remy	1978–84
25	Steve Renko	1979–80

#	NAME	YEAR
30	Bill Renna	1958–59
3	Edgar Renteria	2005
16	Edgar Renteria	2005
28	Rip Repulski	1960–61
55	Carlos Reyes	1998
59	Dennys Reyes	2011
5	Carl Reynolds	1934
6	Carl Reynolds	1935
29	Tuffy Rhodes	1995
19	Gordon Rhodes	1932
17	Gordon Rhodes	1933
11	Gordon Rhodes	1934–35
6	Hal Rhyne	1931
4	Hal Rhyne	1932
14	Jim Rice	1974–89 (player); 1995–2000 (coach)
15	Woody Rich	1939–41
54	Dustin Richardson	2009
62	Dustin Richardson	2010
20	Jeff Richardson	1993
34	Al Richter	1951
35	Al Richter	1953
12	Ernie Riles	1993
67	Eddie Riley	2001 (coach)
28	Allen Ripley	1979
18	Walt Ripley	1935
54	David Riske	2006
19	Jay Ritchie	1964–65
2	Luis Rivera	1989–93
72	Carlos Rivero	2014
33	Mike Roarke	1994 (coach)
31	Dave Roberts	2004
7	Ryan Roberts	2014

#	NAME	YEAR
13	Billy Jo Robidoux	1990
8	Aaron Robinson	1951
24	Aaron Robinson	1951
28	Aaron Robinson	1951
11	Floyd Robinson	1968
28	Jack Robinson	1949
54	Mike Rochford	1988–90
3	Carlos Rodriguez	1994–95
52	Eduardo Rodriguez	2015
30	Frankie Rodriguez	1995
7	Steve Rodriguez	1995
31	Tony Rodriguez	1996
57	Victor Rodriguez	2013 (coach)
15	Lee Rogers	1938
18	Garry Roggenburk	1966
26	Garry Roggenburk	1968
17	Garry Roggenburk	1968
37	Garry Roggenburk	1969
15	Billy Rohr	1967
54	Euclides Rojas	2003–04 (coach)
7	Ed Romero	1986
11	Ed Romero	1987–89
32	J. C. Romero	2007
54	Mandy Romero	1998
13	Niuman Romero	2010
16	Kevin Romine	1985–91
24	Vicente Romo	1969–70
11	Buddy Rosar	1950–51
19	Brian Rose	1997–2000
7	Cody Ross	2012
28	David Ross	2008
3	David Ross	2013
28	Robbie Ross Jr.	2015

#	NAME	YEAR
3	Jack Rothrock	1931
12	Jack Rothrock	1932
18	Rich Rowland	1994
12	Rich Rowland	1995
27	Stan Royer	1994
43	Jerry Royster	2012 (coach)
26	Joe Rudi	1981
10	Muddy Ruel	1931
3	Pete Runnels	1958–62
32	Pete Runnels	1965–66 (coach); 1966 (manager)
30	Ryan Rupe	2003
22	Jack Russell	1931
21	Jack Russell	1932
17	Jack Russell	1936
25	Jeff Russell	1993–94
5	Rip Russell	1945–47
30	Jeff Rutledge	2015
50	Ken Ryan	1992–95
40	Mike Ryan	1964–65
22	Mike Ryan	1966–67
25	Mike Ryba	1941
20	Mike Ryba	1942–46
16	Gene Rye	1931
S		
17	Bret Saberhagen	1997–1999, 2001
52	Donnie Sadler	1998
15	Donnie Sadler	1999–2000
21	Bob Sadowski	1966
8	Ed Sadowski	1960
24	Takashi Saito	2009
39	Jarrod Saltalamacchia	2010

#	NAME	YEAR
43	Joe Sambito	1986–87
13	Angel Sanchez	2010
52	Freddy Sanchez	2002
26	Freddy Sanchez	2003
13	Rey Sanchez	2002
29	Ken Sanders	1966
48	Pablo Sandoval	2015
62	Marino Santana	1999
30	Jose Santiago	1966–69
36	Jose Santiago	1970
53	Angel Santos	2001
1	Tom Satriano	1969
4	Tom Satriano	1969–70
48	Scott Sauerbeck	2003
47	Scott Sauerbeck	2003
16	Dave Sax	1985
50	Dave Sax	1986
12	Dave Sax	1987
17	Bill Sayles	1939
18	Ray Scarborough	1951–52
12	Russ Scarritt	1932
26	Al Schacht	1935 (coach)
32	Al Schacht	1936 (coach)
18	Charley Schanz	1950
39	Bob Scherbarth	1950
2	Chuck Schilling	1961–65
38	Curt Schilling	2004–07
40	Calvin Schiraldi	1986
31	Calvin Schiraldi	1986–87
4	Bill Schlesinger	1965
37	George Schmees	1952
50	Dave Schmidt	1981
21	Johnny Schmitz	1956

#	NAME	YEAR
60	Scott Schoenweis	2010
11	Dick Schofield	1969–70
51	Pete Schourek	1998
50	Pete Schourek	2000–01
31	Paul Schreiber	1946–51 (coach)
45	Paul Schreiber	1952–54 (coach)
34	Paul Schreiber	1955–58 (coach)
29	Al Schroll	1958
30	Al Schroll	1959
29	Johnny Schulte	1949–50 (coach)
37	Don Schwall	1961–62
5	George Scott	1966–71, 1979
15	George Scott	1977–78
39	George Scott	1966 (first eight games of season)
10	Marco Scutaro	2011
16	Marco Scutaro	2010
17	Rudy Seanez	2003
37	Rudy Seanez	2006
41	Tom Seaver	1986
10	Bob Seeds	1933
23	Bob Seeds	1934
36	Diego Segui	1974
28	Diego Segui	1975
29	Bill Selby	1996
36	Aaron Sele	1993–95
26	Aaron Sele	1996–97
27	Jeff Sellers	1985
19	Jeff Sellers	1986–88
47	Travis Shaw	2015
9	Merv Shea	1933
18	Andy Sheets	2000
53	Phil Seibel	2004

#	NAME	YEAR
29	Danny Sheaffer	1987
30	Ryan Shealy	2010
40	Rollie Sheldon	1966
31	Frank Shellenback	1940–44 (coach)
54	Keith Shepherd	1995
48	Kelly Shoppach	2005
23	Neill Sheridan	1948
26	Neill Sheridan	1948
57	Jason Shiell	2003
29	Strick Shofner	1947
15	Bill Short	1966
55	Brian Shouse	1998
2	Terry Shumpert	1995
4	Norm Siebern	1967–68
27	Sonny Siebert	1969
42	Sonny Siebert	1970–73
8	Al Simmons	1943
39	Dave Sisler	1956–59
38	Grady Sizemore	2014
11	Ted Sizemore	1979–80
49	Craig Skok	1973
36	Rac Slider	1987–90 (coach)
51	Heathcliff Slocumb	1996–97
28	Al Smith	1964
39	Bob Smith	1955
59	Chris Smith	2008
41	Dan Smith	2000
18	Eddie Smith	1947
14	George Smith	1966
9	John Smith	1931
48	Lee Smith	1988–90
49	Pete Smith	1962–63
41	Reggie Smith	1966

#	NAME	YEAR
7	Reggie Smith	1967–73
28	Riverboat Smith	1958
48	Zane Smith	1995
41	Mike Smithson	1988–89
29	John Smoltz	2009
26	Chris Snopek	1998
84	J. T. Snow	2006
23	Brandon Snyder	2013
37	Earl Snyder	2004
52	Kyle Snyder	2006
39	Kyle Snyder	2007–08
22	Moose Solters	1934
5	Moose Solters	1935
14	Bill Spanswick	1964
71	Nate Spears	2011
24	Stan Spence	1940
21	Stan Spence	1941
2	Stan Spence	1948–49
2	Andy Spognardi	1932
22	Andy Spognardi	1932
44	Ed Sprague	2000
36	Jack Spring	1957
47	Bobby Sprowl	1978
35	Matt Stairs	1995
39	Tracy Stallard	1960–62
37	Lee Stange	1966
20	Lee Stange	1967–70
35	Lee Stange	1972–74 (coach)
34	Lee Stange	1981–84 (coach)
26	Rob Stanifer	2000
46	Bob Stanley	1977–89
22	Mike Stanley	1996

#	NAME	YEAR
20	Mike Stanley	1997 (player); 2002 (coach)
24	Mike Stanley	1998–2000
32	Mike Stanton	1995–96
37	Mike Stanton	2005
26	Dave Stapleton	1980
11	Dave Stapleton	1980–86
23	Herm Starrette	1995, 1997 (coach)
40	Herm Starrette	1996 (coach)
1	Ben Steiner	1945
44	Ben Steiner	1946
16	Red Steiner	1945
37	Mike Stenhouse	1986
38	Gene Stephens	1952, 1955–58
36	Gene Stephens	1953
10	Gene Stephens	1959–60
5	Vern Stephens	1948–52
29	Jerry Stephenson	1963
18	Jerry Stephenson	1965–67
38	Jerry Stephenson	1967–68
39	Adam Stern	2005–06
53	Sammy Stewart	1986
47	Zach Stewart	2012
42	Dick Stigman	1966
42	Chuck Stobbs	1947
22	Chuck Stobbs	1948–51
28	Dean Stone	1957
19	Jeff Stone	1989
28	Jeff Stone	1990
16	Howie Storie	1931
19	Howie Storie	1931
11	Howie Storie	1932
26	Lou Stringer	1948

#	NAME	YEAR
27	Lou Stringer	1948–50
7	Dick Stuart	1963–64
23	George Stumpf	1931
17	George Stumpf	1932
25	George Stumpf	1933
15	Tom Sturdivant	1960
12	Chris Stynes	2001
21	Jim Suchecki	1950
37	Jim Suchecki	1950
18	Frank Sullivan	1953–60
44	Haywood Sullivan	1955
30	Haywood Sullivan	1960
16	Haywood Sullivan	1957, 1959
15	Marc Sullivan	1982, 1984–87
55	Jeff Suppan	1995–97
35	Jeff Suppan	2003
37	Jeff Suppan	2003
36	George Susce	1950 (coach)
29	George Susce	1951 (coach)
43	George Susce	1952–54 (coach)
41	George D. Susce	1955
27	George D. Susce	1955–58
44	Drew Sutton	2011
41	Dale Sveum	2004–05 (coach)
1	Bill Sweeney	1931
12	Ryan Sweeney	2012
23	Blake Swihart	2015
37	Greg Swindell	1998
T		
26	Jim Tabor	1938
5	Jim Tabor	1939–44
40	Frank Tanana	1981
12	Jose Tartabull	1966–68

#	NAME	YEAR
55	LaSchelle Tarver	1986
10	Willie Tasby	1960
8	Bennie Tate	1932
48	Jim Tatum	1996
25	Ken Tatum	1971
41	Ken Tatum	1971
19	Ken Tatum	1972–73
30	Jesus Tavarez	1997
51	Julian Tavarez	2006–08
35	Harry Taylor	1950–51
12	Harry Taylor	1951
23	Harry Taylor	1952
56	Scott Taylor	1992–93
63	Junichi Tazawa	2009, 2011, 2012
36	Junichi Tazawa	2013
8	Birdie Tebbetts	1947–50
27	Yank Terry	1940
18	Yank Terry	1942–45
24	George Thomas	1966–67
22	George Thomas	1968–71 (player-coach for part of 1970)
78	Justin Thomas	2012
50	Justin Thomas	2012 (started the year as 78, but soon changed to 50)
6	Lee Thomas	1964–65
32	Tommy Thomas	1937
25	Bobby Thomson	1960
38	Matt Thornton	2013
2	Faye Throneberry	1952
37	Faye Throneberry	1952
26	Faye Throneberry	1956–57
3	Joe Thurston	2008

#	NAME	YEAR
23	Luis Tiant	1971–78
30	Bob Tillman	1962
10	Bob Tillman	1963–67
50	Mike Timlin	2003–08
38	Lee Tinsley	1994–95
26	Lee Tinsley	1995
10	Lee Tinsley	1996
47	Lee Tinsley	1996
3	John Tobin	1945
51	Kevin Tolar	2003
30	Andy Tomberlin	1994
32	Tony Torchia	1985 (coach)
21	Mike Torrez	1978–82
40	Billy Traber	2009
42	John Trautwein	1988
50	Ralph Treuel	2001
53	Ralph Treuel	2006 (coach)
44	Joe Trimble	1955
15	Ricky Trlicek	1994
43	Ricky Trlicek	1997
25	Dizzy Trout	1952
45	Mike Trujillo	1985–86
57	Gary Tuck	2007–10 (coach)
30	John Tudor	1979–83
29	Bob Turley	1963
34	Bob Turley	1964 (coach)
U		
19	Koji Uehara	2013
41	Ugueth Urbina	2001–02
38	Tom Umphlett	1953
V		
65	Carlos Valdez	1998
12	Julio Valdez	1980–83

#	NAME	YEAR
40	Sergio Valdez	1994
23	Danny Valencia	2012
13	John Valentin	1992–2001
25	Bobby Valentine	2012 (manager)
23	Dave Valle	1994
46	Jermaine Van Buren	2006
17	Al Van Camp	1931
1	Al Van Camp	1932
53	Tim VanEgmond	1994–95
30	Jonathan Van Every	2008–09
60	Jonathan Van Every	2008
44	Jonathan Van Every	2010
47	Jason Varitek	1997–99
33	Jason Varitek	1999–2010
46	Anthony Varvaro	2015
42	Mo Vaughn	1991–98
55	Christian Vazquez	2014 (debuting July 9)
23	Ramon Vazquez	2005
55	Bob Veale	1972–74
51	Gil Velazquez	2008–09
31	Dario Veras	1998
38	Wilton Veras	1999–2000
6	Mickey Vernon	1956–57
18	Shane Victorino	2013
60	Brayan Villarreal	2013
16	Frank Viola	1992–94
23	Clyde Vollmer	1950–51
30	Clyde Vollmer	1952–53
7	Joe Vosmik	1938–39
W		
12	Jake Wade	1939
13	Billy Wagner	2009

#	NAME	YEAR
11	Charlie Wagner	1938
25	Charlie Wagner	1939
27	Charlie Wagner	1940–42, 1946
33	Charlie Wagner	1970 (coach)
41	Gary Wagner	1969
35	Gary Wagner	1970
19	Hal Wagner	1944
8	Hal Wagner	1946–47
49	Tim Wakefield	1995–2010
15	Rube Walberg	1934–37
3	Chico Walker	1980
1	Chico Walker	1981–84
12	Todd Walker	2003
26	Murray Wall	1957–59
37	Dave Wallace	2003 (coach)
35	Dave Wallace	2003 (coach)
17	Dave Wallace	2004–06 (coach)
6	Bucky Walters	1933
8	Bucky Walters	1934
26	Fred Walters	1945
4	Rabbit Warstler	1931
2	Rabbit Warstler	1932
1	Rabbit Warstler	1933
46	John Wasdin	1997–2000
19	Gary Waslewski	1967–68
12	John Wathan	1994 (coach)
5	Bob Watson	1979
12	Johnny Watwood	1932
25	Monte Weaver	1939
15	Earl Webb	1931–32
38	Lenny Webster	1999
31	Ray Webster	1960
22	Eric Wedge	1991, 1994

#	NAME	YEAR
36	Eric Wedge	1992
7	Jemile Weeks	2014
30	Jemile Weeks	2015
26	Bob Weiland	1932
19	Bob Weiland	1933
12	Bob Weiland	1934
70	Kyle Weiland	2011
6	Johnny Welch	1932
20	Johnny Welch	1933
18	Johnny Welch	1934
17	Johnny Welch	1935–36
3	David Wells	2005
16	David Wells	2005–06
24	Fred Wenz	1968
26	Fred Wenz	1969
22	Billy Werber	1933
20	Billy Werber	1934
2	Billy Werber	1935–36
5	Billy Werber	1936
28	Bill Werle	1953
14	Bill Werle	1954
6	Vic Wertz	1959–61
39	David West	1998
32	Dan Wheeler	2011–
20	Frank White	1994–96 (coach)
38	Sammy White	1951
22	Sammy White	1952–54, 1956–59
8	Sammy White	1955
27	Mark Whiten	1995
59	Matt White	2003
22	Ernie Whitt	1976
32	Al Widmar	1947
15	Bill Wight	1951–52

#	NAME	YEAR
33	Del Wilber	1952–54
20	Dallas Williams	2003 (coach)
20	Dana Williams	1989
19	Dana Williams	1989
27	Dib Williams	1935
16	Dick Williams	1963–64
23	Dick Williams	1967–69 (manager)
22	Jimy Williams	1997–2001 (manager)
43	Randy Williams	2011
25	Stan Williams	1972
32	Stan Williams	1975–76 (coach)
9	Ted Williams	1939–42, 1946–60
36	Scott Williamson	2003
48	Scott Williamson	2003–04
54	Carl Willis	2015 (pitching coach, from May 10)
38	Jim Willoughby	1975–77
30	Maury Wills	1996 (coach)
28	Ted Wills	1959
25	Ted Wills	1960–62
63	Alex Wilson	2013
30	Alex Wilson	2014
32	Archie Wilson	1952
15	Duane Wilson	1958
26	Earl Wilson	1959–60, 1962–66
16	Jack Wilson	1935
20	Jack Wilson	1935
18	Jack Wilson	1936–41
16	Jim Wilson	1945
10	Jim Wilson	1946
5	Herm Winningham	1992
18	Tom Winsett	1931
12	Tom Winsett	1931

#	NAME	YEAR
11	Tom Winsett	1933
40	Rick Wise	1974–77
35	Johnnie Wittig	1949
29	Bob Wolcott	1999
20	Larry Wolfe	1979–80
17	Joe Wood	1944
32	Ken Wood	1952
33	Ken Wood	1952
28	Wilbur Wood	1961
41	Wilbur Wood	1962
19	Wilbur Wood	1963–64
22	Larry Woodall	1942–47 (coach)
29	Larry Woodall	1948 (coach)
10	Pinky Woods	1943–45
47	Steve Woodard	2003
3	Chris Woodward	2009
30	Chris Woodward	2009
42	Rob Woodward	1985–86
45	Rob Woodward	1987–88
10	Shawn Wooten	2005
67	Brandon Workman	2013
39	Al Worthington	1960
45	Jim Wright	1978–79
35	Steven Wright	2013
23	Tom Wright	1948
28	Tom Wright	1949–51
8	Tom Wright	1951
26	John Wyatt	1966–68
Y		
8	Carl Yastrzemski	1961–83
3	Rudy York	1946–47
34	Rudy York	1959–62 (coach); 1959 (manager)

#	NAME	YEAR
36	Eddie Yost	1977–84 (coach)
20	Kevin Youkilis	2004–10
30	Matt Young	1991–92
28	Tim Young	2000
59	Tim Young	2000
Z		
2	Al Zarilla	1949–50
32	Al Zarilla	1952–53
35	Norm Zauchin	1951
3	Norm Zauchin	1955–57
34	Don Zimmer	1974–76, 1992 (coach); 1976–80 (manager)
21	Don Zimmer	1976 (coach; number worn during A's–Sox series)
23	Don Zimmer	1980 (manager)
51	Charlie Zink	2005
26	Bill Zuber	1946–47
16	Bob Zupcic	1991
28	Bob Zupcic	1992–94

ACKNOWLEDGMENTS

In the course of creating this book, we were able to speak individually with each member of the Boston Red Sox regarding their number choices (or lack of), and to find out exactly how the numbers are distributed. (It's not by Ouija board.) In September, we made a pre-dawn laundry run with the Red Sox duds and met the nice people who wash the uniforms, patch the rips and tears, and get new jerseys ready so the latest Sox acquisitions can play later in the day. We were able to get photos of the numbers up close, whether it's Opening Day standing for the Anthem or standing next to Arthur Giddon, the world's oldest batboy back on the job after 85 years off. The Red Sox generously also allowed us to borrow some great shots of numbers. We did a lot of digging to find Topps baseball cards of your favorite—and sometimes forgotten—Sox of the past, present, and future. Thanks to Topps—notably Clay Luraschi—for permission to use the cards in this book.

Thanks . . . .

First of all to the numerologists for helping greatly in the task of straightening out who really did wear which number, and when: Bill Ballou, Joe Kuras, Jack Looney, Mark Stang, and Bill Walsh. They're the number consultant's dream team.

An inspirational article was "The Evocative Power of Mere Cloth Numerals" by David Nevard, with Larry McCray, which appeared in the Buffalo Head Society's journal and is available at: http://webpages .charter.net/joekuras/numbers.htm.

The following additional people helped us in one way or another, and their assistance is much appreciated:

Edward Almada, Scott Billington, Dick Bresciani, Steve Buckley, Joe Cochran, Jon Deeble, Neil DeTeso, Valentina Federico, Pam Ganley, Matt Gazda, Jon Goode, Henry Mahegan, Brad Hainje, Sean Holtz, Masa Hoshino, Joanne Hulbert, Edward "Pookie" Jackson, Tom Keegan, Jason Latimer, David Laurila, Alan Levy, Paul Lukas, Frank Marshall, Tom McLaughlin, Larry McCray, Sarah McKenna, Mark Mueller, Peter Nash, David Nevard, Todd Radom, Tim Samway, Aaron Schmidt, Anna Shaheen, Jon Shestakofsky, Pete Van Wieren, David Vincent, Jim Walsh, Tim Wiles, and Jeremiah Woolsey.

And let's hear it for the 2009 Red Sox and some of the 2015 team for sharing their thoughts with us on the subject.

Players:

Brian Anderson, Jeff Bailey, Rocco Baldelli, Daniel Bard, Aaron Bates, Jason Bay, Josh Beckett, Mookie Betts, Xander Bogaerts, Michael Bowden, Jackie Bradley Jr., Dusty Brown, Clay Buchholz, Paul Byrd, Fernando Cabrera, Chris Carter, Manny Delcarmen, J.D. Drew, Jacoby Ellsbury, Joey Gathright, Alex Gonzalez, Enrique Gonzalez, Nick Green, Bock Holt, Hunter Jones, Casey Kotchman, Mark Kotsay, George Kottaras, Adam LaRoche, Jon Lester, Javier Lopez, Mike Lowell, Jed Lowrie, Julio Lugo, Victor Martinez, Justin Masterson, Daisuke Matsuzaka, Hideki Okajima, David Ortiz, Jonathan Papelbon, Dustin Pedroia, Brad Penny, Hanley Ramirez, Ramon Ramirez, Josh Reddick, Dustin Richardson, Takashi Saito, Travis Shaw, John Smoltz, Blake Swihart, Junichi Tazawa, Billy Traber, Jonathan Van Every, Jason Varitek, Christian Vasquez, Gil Velasquez, Billy Wagner, Tim Wakefield, Chris Woodward, and Kevin Youklis.

Coaching Staff:

Tim Bogar, John Farrell, Terry Francona, Ino Guerrero, Dave Magadan, Brad Mills, Mani Martinez, David Page, and Gary Tuck

Past Red Sox players gracious with their time:

Mike Andrews, Milt Bolling, Sean Casey, Pete Charton, Roger Clemens, Dennis Eckersley, Boo Ferriss, Don Gile, Pumpsie Green, Tommy Harper, Roger LaFrancois, Lou Merloni, Gene Michael, Reid Nichols, Johnny Pesky, Brandon Puffer, Jim Rice, and Frank Sullivan.

Jon Springer trailblazed the idea of a team history told through uniform numbers with his venerable site, metsbythenumbers.com (also mbtn.net), and the book that came out of it, *Mets by the Numbers* (with Matthew Silverman). That site in turn led to Kasey Ignarski's Cubs site (cubsbythenumbers.com) and the book that followed, *Cubs by the Numbers*, with Al Yellon, Ignarski, and Silverman. If there are queries or corrections for *Red Sox by the Numbers*, please forward them to bnowlin@rounder.com.

Lastly, kudos to Mark Weinstein at Skyhorse Publishing, who recognized the appeal of this concept for team-oriented books. You can't tell the numbers without a book.

ABOUT THE AUTHORS

Bill Nowlin was born in Boston and still lives fairly near Fenway, in Cambridge. He is the author or editor of 50 or so baseball books, most of them Red Sox-related. He is also co–founder of America's premier roots music label, Rounder Records. In 2004, Nowlin was elected Vice President of the Society for American Baseball Research (SABR) and remains in that position.

Matthew Silverman is co-author of *Mets by the Numbers* (with Jon Springer) and *Shea Goodbye* (with Keith Hernandez), and author of *Mets Essential* and *100 Things Mets Fans Should Know and Do Before They Die*. He edited *The Ultimate Red Sox Companion* and *Ted Williams: My Life in Pictures*. He served as associate publisher at Total Sports Publishing, editing *Total Baseball Total Football*, and *Baseball: The Biographical Encyclopedia*. A former resident of Charlemont, Massachusetts, he lives in High Falls, New York.

Photo Credits

Photos courtesy of Bill Nowlin:
Pg. vi–vii (Red Sox Team), 7 (Edward "Pookie" Jackson), 48, (Section 1), 54 (Ted Williams Number), 55 (Ted Williams Number), 81 (Valentina Federico), 87 (Dustin Pedroia), 92 (Fenway Park), 103 (Daisuke Matsuzaka), 190 (Arthur Giddon), 202 (Bullpen Door), 211 (David Ortiz), 229 (Hideki Okajima), 250 (Red Sox Jerseys), 276 (Retired Numbers), 277 (Retired Numbers), 292 (Gyllenhaal and Bauman), 314 (Bat Rack at Fenway), 318 (Wally the Green Monster), 321 (Usain Bolt), 322 (Japanese Ballplayer)

Photos courtesy of the Boston Public Library, Leslie Jones Collection:
Pg. 22 (Jimmie Foxx), 37 (Johnny Pesky), 44 (Dom DiMaggio)

Photos courtesy of AP Images:
Pg. 49 (Carl Yastrzemski), pg. 53 (Ted Williams), 162 (Carlton Fisk), 275 (David Ortiz and Pedro Martinez)

Photo courtesy of the Boston Red Sox:
Pg. 56 (Helen Robinson)

Photos courtesy of Dan Carubia:
Pg. 205 (Jason Varitek), 212 (David Ortiz)

Photos courtesy of Keith Allison via Wikicommons:
Pg. 117 (Kevin Youkilis), 156 (Wade Boggs), 192 (Jon Lester), 269 (Jason Bay), 287 (Terry Francona), 310 (Jonathan Papelbon), 319 (Clay Buchholz)

Photo courtesy of Waldo Jaquity via WikiCommons:
Pg. 298 (Tim Wakefield)

Photos from the Public Domain via WikiCommons:
Pg. 31 (Nomar Garciaparra), 112 (Josh Beckett), 204 (Jason Varitek), 282 (Jacoby Ellsbury)